AF594847

LUCA MASSIMO BARBERO

osvaldo LICINI

Marsilio | PEGGY GUGGENHEIM COLLECTION

Let Sheer Folly Sweep Me Away

OSVALDO LICINI

Peggy Guggenheim Collection, Venice
September 22, 2018
January 14, 2019

curated by
Luca Massimo Barbero

with the support of

INSTITUTIONAL PATRONS
EFG
Lavazza

GUGGENHEIM INTRAPRESÆ
Aermec
Allegrini
Apice
Arclinea
Arper
Davide Groppi
Distilleria Nardini
Florim
Foodies Bros
Gruppo Campari
Hangar Design Group
Istituto Europeo di Design
Mapei
MST-Gruppo Maccaferri
Orsoni
René Caovilla
Rubelli
Safilo Group
Swatch

The Peggy Guggenheim Collection is pleased to present a retrospective exhibition of the painter Osvaldo Licini on the sixtieth anniversary of his death. Though not represented in the Peggy Guggenheim Collection, Licini, who hailed from the Italian region of the Marches, is a major figure in the development of Italian art in the first half of the twentieth century. In 1958 he received the Grand Prize for Painting at the twenty-ninth Venice Biennale for his lyrical paintings composed of colors and signs that convey expressions of energy, poetry, and magic.

We extend our sincere thanks to all those who were involved in the realization of the exhibition, and our gratitude goes to all the lenders who are listed elsewhere in the catalogue. We are especially grateful to Silvia Poli Licini and Lorenzo Licini, the daughter-in-law and the grandson of the artist, who have enthusiastically supported the exhibition. Special thanks are also due to Stefano Papetti, Director of the Museum of Contemporary Art Osvaldo Licini, Ascoli Piceno, and to Daniela Simoni, Director of Centro Studi Osvaldo Licini, Monte Vidon Corrado.

We are grateful to Luca Massimo Barbero, Associate Curator, for the thesis of the exhibition and for bringing this significant artist to Venice, as well as for the illuminating catalogue.

We are pleased to acknowledge the support of the Peggy Guggenheim Collection exhibitions provided by its Institutional Patrons, Lavazza and EFG, and by the Guggenheim Intrapresæ, whose assistance allows the museum to develop its long-term exhibition program, as well as the Peggy Guggenheim Collection Advisory Board. We are grateful that the Fondazione Araldi Guinetti underwrites the educational activities of the museum, and as always, we are most appreciative of the museum staff for their tireless efforts.

We hope that visitors will delight in encountering this unique artist whose distinctive approach to painting, literature, and nature enchants the eye and spirit.

RICHARD ARMSTRONG, Director, Solomon R. Guggenheim Museum and Foundation
KAROLE P. B. VAIL, Director, Peggy Guggenheim Collection

In order to curate an exhibition on Osvaldo Licini one has to create a path among works of art that have been held in the most important and refined Italian art collections for years and compose a constellation within a larger, international panorama of twentieth-century art. I am extremely appreciative to everyone who has participated in this journey as we celebrate one of the most significant and elusive European painters of the last century.

Organized by the Peggy Guggenheim Collection, the exhibition brings together a hundred works that represent the various aspects of this journey. After decades Licini's paintings are together again, not so much in the celebration of the death of the artist, but rather on the occasion of the sixtieth anniversary of the Grand Prize for Painting at the twenty-ninth Venice Biennale, when the art world saw, at last, in an enlightened moment, the art of this extraordinary artist and his search for broader limits and horizons.

My deepest gratitude goes to Silvia and Lorenzo Licini, who with their generous support, assiduous presence, and commitment have made this extraordinary retrospective possible.

I would like to thank Stefano Papetti, Director of the Galleria d'Arte Contemporanea Osvaldo Licini, Ascoli Piceno; Daniela Simoni, Director of the Centro Studi Osvaldo Licini, Monte Vidon Corrado; Assunta Porciani, Manager of the Archivio Biblioteca Quadriennale, Roma; and the Archivio Giuseppe Marchiori, Lendinara.

I also extend my thanks to Lorenzo Balbi, Artistic Director of the Istituzione Bologna Musei, Museo Morandi, Bologna; Gabriella Belli, Director of the Fondazione Musei Civici di Venezia; Elisabetta Barisoni, Manager of the Galleria Internazionale d'Arte Moderna, Ca' Pesaro, Venice; Rosaria del Balzo Ruiti, President of the Fondazione Carima, Museo Palazzo Ricci, Macerata; Giuliano Gori, Director of the Collezione Gori – Fattoria di Celle, Santomato, Pistoia; Paolo Laurini, President of the Fondazione Lucio Fontana, Milan; Gianfranco Maraniello, Director of the Museo di Arte Moderna e Contemporanea di Trento e Rovereto; Giorgio Marconi, Director of the Fondazione Marconi Arte Moderna e Contemporanea; Alessandro Mazzucco, President of the Fondazione Cariverona, Collezioni, Verona; Anna Maria Montaldo, Director of the Area Polo Arte Moderna e Contemporanea del Museo del Novecento, Milan; Riccardo Passoni, Director of the Galleria Civica d'Arte Moderna e Contemporanea, Turin; Silvia Penna, Manager of the Musei Civici Fiorentini, Florence; Sergio Risaliti, Director of the Museo del Novecento di Firenze; Gloria Piaggio, Comune di Genova, Direzione Beni Culturali del Museo d'Arte Contemporanea Villa Croce; and Silvia Piccinini, Senior Coordinator of the Collezione Maramotti, Reggio Emilia.

I am grateful to Francesca Ghiringhelli and Enrica Colombo Ghiringhelli of Galleria Il Milione, Milan, and Giulio Tega, Director of the Galleria Tega, Milan. I would also like to thank Matteo Lorenzelli, Director of Lorenzelli Arte, Milan; the Lorenzelli family; and in particular Bruno Lorenzelli for his continued commitment to Osvaldo Licini, whom he has exhibited since the 1960s.

My sincere and profound thanks to Francesca Palma and Claudio Fonti, Fermo; Paola Giovanardi and the Augusto and Francesca Giovanardi Collection, Bologna; Luisa Cristiana Curti, Venice; and Sergio Casoli, Milan. I remain deeply grateful, as always, to the private collectors who prefer to remain anonymous. Special thanks to Mariolina Bassetti of Christie's and Claudia Dvek of Sotheby's, once again invaluable supporters of my projects.

I would like to recognize with heartfelt gratitude the entire staff of the Peggy Guggenheim Collection for their professional dedication during these years and for their support of this important retrospective dedicated to Licini. Special thanks goes to Laura Corazzol for the coordination and organization of my exhibitions and Giovanni Casini for his precise and enthusiastic curatorial assistance during the preparation of the exhibition.

Finally, I extend my appreciation to Sileno Salvagnini, Federica Pirani, and Chiara Mari for their valuable contribution to the catalogue, a superb editorial project made possible thanks to the entire staff of Marsilio Editori, Venice. Thanks to Fabrizio Galatea who, with Zenit Arti Audiovisive, explores my exhibitions through videos.

LUCA MASSIMO BARBERO

Photo Credits
pp. 33, 44, 49, 167 photo Domenico Oddi; pp. 52, 180 photo Serge Domingie, Florence; p. 53 © 2018 Archivio Fotografico – Fondazione Musei Civici di Venezia; p. 54 photo Sergio Buono; pp. 54, 83 photo Luca Carrà; p. 55 Fototeca Musei Civici Fiorentini; pp. 62, 63 photo Sergio Martucci; p. 77 photo François Fernandez; pp. 81, 97, 120, 158, 161 photo Alvise Aspesi; pp. 85, 93 Museo d'Arte Contemporanea di Villa Croce, Genoa; p. 87 MART – Archivio Fotografico e Mediateca; pp. 88, 89, 171 © Comune di Milano – all rights reserved © Mondadori PortfolioElecta/Luca Carrà; pp. 90, 100, 106 © Fondazione Lucio Fontana; p. 103 Studio Gonella, 2009; pp. 108, 113, 127, 156 photo Andrea Lazzari; p. 131 © Christie's Images / Bridgeman Images; pp. 133, 141, 144 © foto studiobruno; p. 150 photo Carlo Chiavacci, Pistoia; p. 163 Studio Gonella, 2008; p. 185 photo Carlo Fei, Florence; p. 197 Archivio Biblioteca Quadriennale di Roma; p. 199 photo C. H. Ford, courtesy Centro Studi Osvaldo Licini, Monte Vidon Corrado; pp. 200, 206 Galleria d'arte contemporanea Osvaldo Licini, Ascoli Piceno, Archivio iconografico del Comune, Ascoli Piceno; p. 209 Museo Civico del Risorgimento, Bologna; pp. 210, 219, 220, 222, 223, 224, 225, 236 Archivio Storico delle Arti Contemporanee, La Biennale, Venice; p. 215 Centro Studi Osvaldo Licini, Monte Vidon Corrado; p. 218 Fondazione Solomon R. Guggenheim, photo Archivio Cameraphoto Epoche, Donazione, Cassa di Risparmio di Venezia, 2005; p. 229 Biblioteca Comunale Ariostea, Ferrara; p. 234 photo B. Degenhart, courtesy Lorenzo Licini.

cover
REBEL ANGEL AND MOON
(ANGELO RIBELLE E LUNA), 1947
(*detail*, pp. 168–69)

pp. 13–14
REBEL ANGEL (ANGELO RIBELLE), 1952
pencil on paper
23.5 × 33 cm
Private collection

pp. 234–35
REBEL ANGEL WITH HEART
(ANGELO RIBELLE CON CUORE), 1951
pencil on paper
24 × 33.5 cm
Private collection

editing
Tas Skorupa, Berlin

translations
Jeffrey Jennings–Language Consulting, Milan; Sylvia Notini

first edition: September 2018
ISBN 978-88-317-4382-2

www.marsilioeditori.it

CONTENTS

OSVALDO LICINI

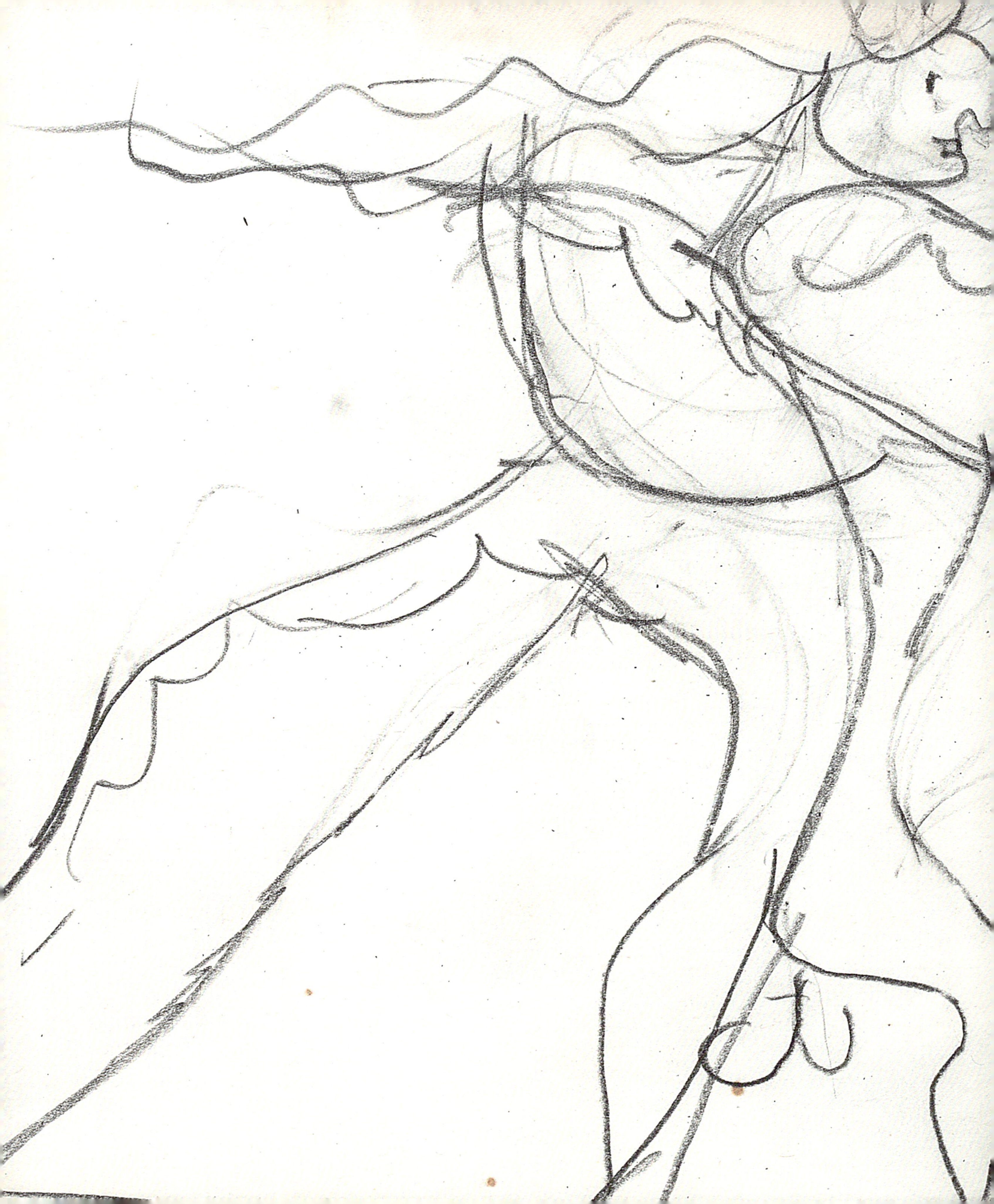

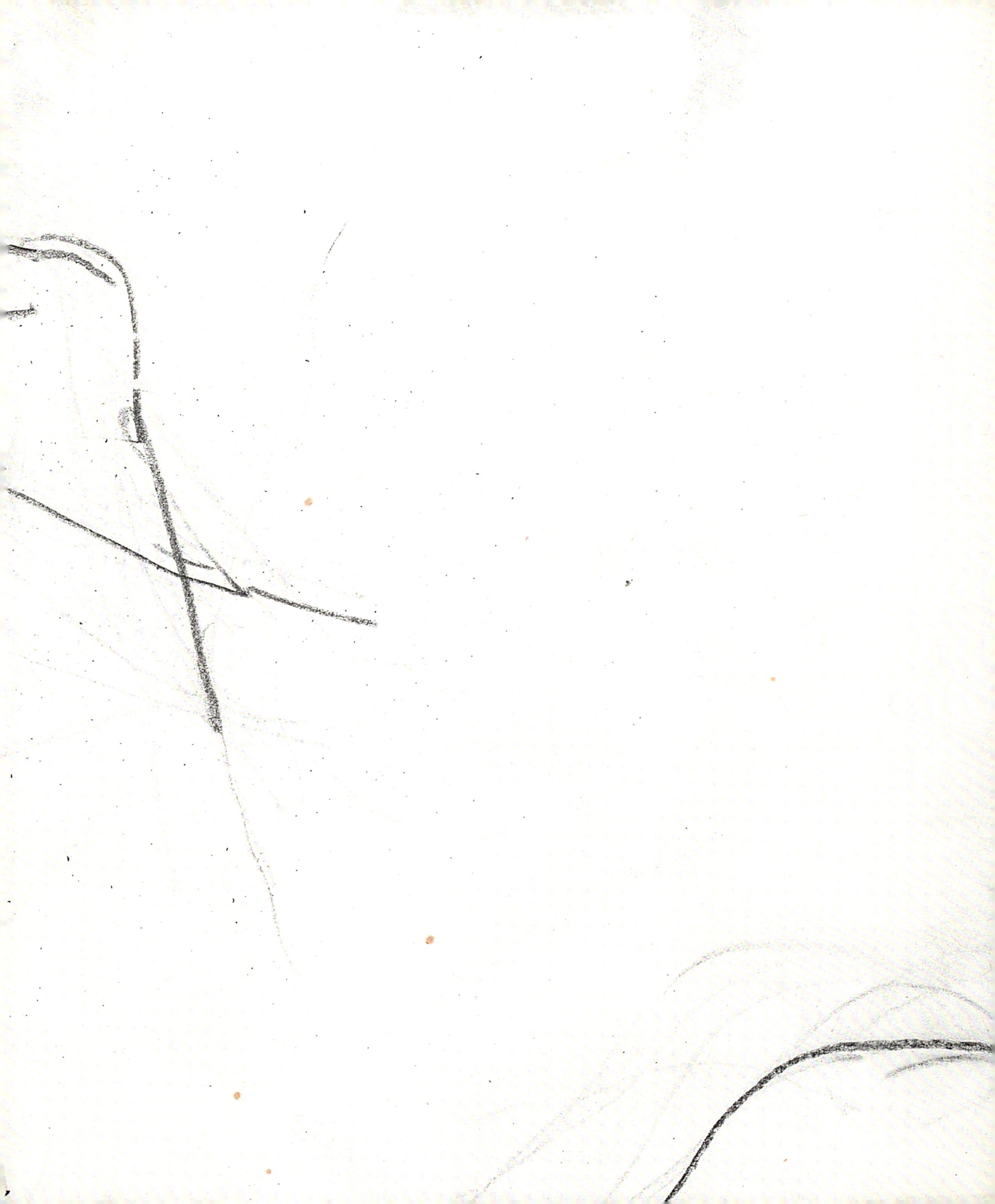

LET SHEER FOLLY SWEEP ME AWAY

LUCA MASSIMO BARBERO

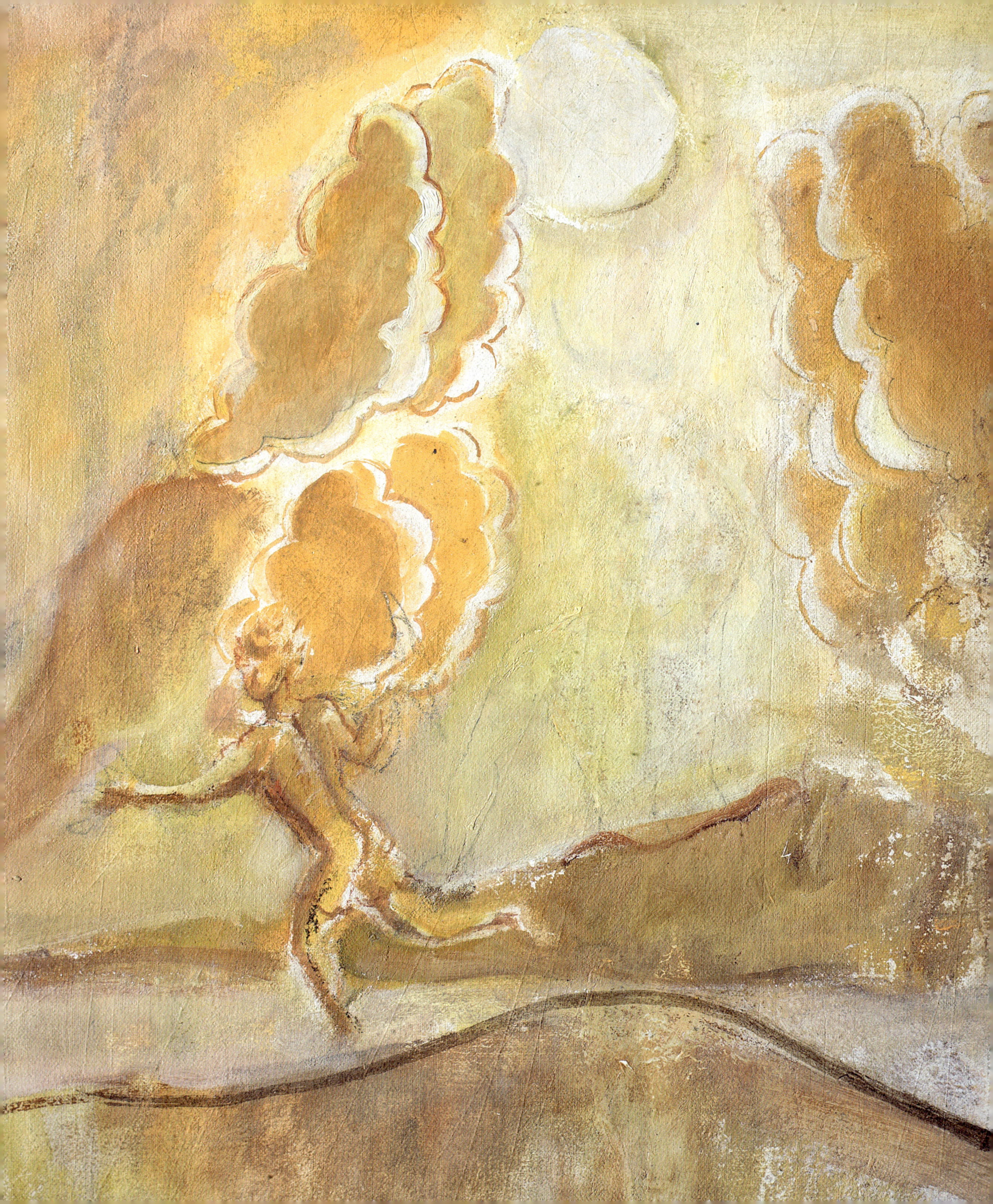

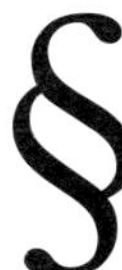

BEGINNINGS: THE "CRUCIAL" BOLOGNA OF THE 1910S AND THE FIRST PARISIAN SOJOURN

He who seeks certainty rarely finds it | I have often searched but to no avail
a certainty where I could throw | all the strength of my distant | miraculous life perhaps dreamed
perhaps spent a bit too much | with heart in hand | with heart and thought in hand
the soul a bit too beautiful | that I still search for | without ever tiring | hoping beyond hope
to find it one day

OSVALDO LICINI[1]

On the evening of March 20, 1914, Osvaldo Licini, together with friends and art school companions Mario Bacchelli (brother of the writer Riccardo), Giorgio Morandi, Severo Pozzati (who would later take the *nom d'art* Sepo), and Giacomo Vespignani, inaugurated an exhibition in a room of the Hotel Baglioni in central Bologna, subsequently identified as a "crucial" event in the artistic life of the city. The first to recognize its importance was Carlo Ludovico Ragghianti, who in his 1969 essay "Bologna cruciale 1914" chose this exhibition as the starting point for a reconstruction of the Bolognese art scene of the 1910s, reading it as a critical geographical and chronological junction.[2] Through the musician Francesco Balilla Pratella, a friend of Vespignani, it is likely that Filippo Tommaso Marinetti, Carlo Carrà, Umberto Boccioni, and Luigi Russolo visited the exhibition. Consequently the event was absorbed into the narrative of Futurist proselytism. While the relationship of the newcomers with the exponents of the movement is well documented,[3] the press of the time actually referred to them as "secessionists," pointing to an attitude of rebellion and a desire for renewal that were not entirely identifiable with the

ARCHANGEL (ARCANGELO)
1919
oil on canvas
44 × 51 cm
Galleria d'Arte Contemporanea Osvaldo Licini, Ascoli Piceno
detail

movement.[4] The young artists saw Futurism, and Marinetti in particular, as an unavoidable benchmark of contemporaneity, but their adhesion was largely theoretical, and only partially influenced their artistic investigation. The term *secession*, in its broader meaning, is perhaps the most accurate for understanding the shared ferment of dissent that involved numerous groups of artists at the time, sparking in some the hope of a possible coordinated effort to consolidate a "young movement" that would rejuvenate the Italian cultural milieu, as Gino Rossi proposed, for example, in 1912.[5] Not finding stimuli in the teachings of the academy, bound as it was to a figurative culture of the nineteenth century, nor in the more institutional cultural context in which often magniloquent and regressive regional schools still prevailed, Licini and his associates found that necessary impetus toward modernity in Futurism.

One of the rare paintings ascribable to this early period, and one of the few works we know to have been exhibited at the Hotel Baglioni is the *Self-Portrait* (*Autoritratto*) of 1913 (p. 23), which the artist later gave his friend Morandi. Described at the time as "satanic"[6] for the intensity and power of the gaze, so piercing as to seem almost satirical, the image reflects Licini's youthful exuberance and restlessness, which find a literary counterpoint in the coeval *Racconti di Bruto* (Tales of Brutus), written in Monte Vidon Corrado in the summer of that same year. If these irreverent stories, "saturated with an extremely brutal cynicism,"[7] can be placed alongside the biting prose of Ardengo Soffici and the asyntactic poetry of Aldo Palazzeschi, the self-portrait is far from the dynamism of Futurist painting proper, built as it is on an expressionism of the mark and an almost Nordic palette, which in the portrait of Giacomo Vespignani (1913), also exhibited at the Bologna show, emphasize the young artist's state of intoxication even more dramatically.

While the scarcity of works from this period makes it difficult to identify specific models, our understanding of Licini's beginnings is certainly buttressed by the contacts we know he had with the art scene in Florence, where he occasionally went to visit relatives, eventually deciding to move there in 1914 to complete his studies. His interest in the art and writings of Soffici, mentioned on numerous occasions, can be tied to the critical stance toward official culture and, more generally, toward the bourgeois conformism against which the Tuscan painter inveighed in the articles he published during those years, first in Prezzolini's magazine *La Voce*—his invective against the "regrettable" exhibitions of the Venice Biennale is particularly memorable[8]—and later in the pages of *Lacerba*, founded in 1913 with Giovanni Papini. It was in the latter that Licini hoped to publish his *Racconti di Bruto*, relying on the mediation of Balilla Pratella, to whom he wrote in September of the same year.[9] Soffici, on the other hand, was a pivotal figure in keeping Licini up to date on French art: from Paul Cézanne, whom both Licini and Morandi were looking at in these years, to Cubism, to Henri Rousseau, an interesting counterpoint in the progressive emergence of a prim-

DANCERS
(BALLERINE)
1917
oil on canvas
59.5 × 45.5 cm
Private collection
detail

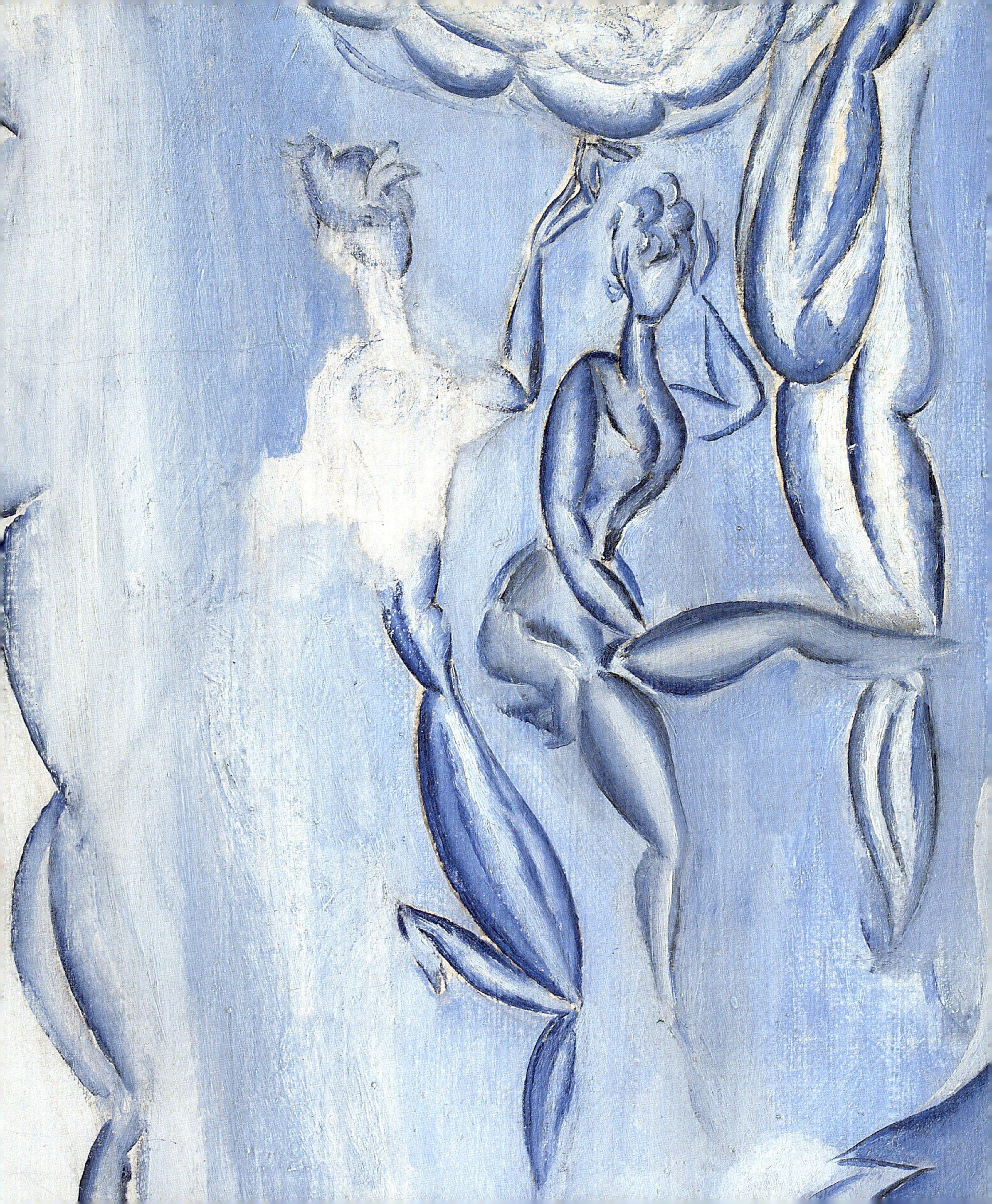

itive thread in his work, with anti-classical, even infantile features.[10] In Italy Licini had access to some of the innovations underway beyond the Alps, but it was his stay in Paris in 1917 that opened the way to new stimuli and a rapid evolution of his pictorial language.

After being drafted and wounded in the leg at the front, in early 1917 he was granted a furlough that allowed him to join his mother and sister in the French capital to convalesce. This is the period of the so-called *War Episodes* (*Episodi di guerra*), as Licini himself referred to the works produced between 1915 and 1920, almost all of which have been destroyed. The present exhibition proposes a comparison between Licini's *Dancers* (*Ballerine*) of 1917 (p. 27) and Morandi's *Bathers* (*Bagnanti*) of 1915 (p. 26), in which critics have identified a reference to Cézanne, perhaps mediated by the example of Soffici (*Bathers*, 1911). We can also add to the equation André Derain, whose *Bathers* of 1908 was published in *Emporium* in 1913, in an article by Ugo Nebbia titled "Sul movimento pittorico contemporaneo." The work was reproduced in juxtaposition with a work by Marie Laurencin, in whose atypical Cubism we cannot but see a certain affinity with the elongated and synthetic forms of Licini's dancers. The various possible references are in any case taken up by Licini in terms of line, a sort of primacy of the painterly sign that synthetically embodies the volume, the composition, and the focalization of the pictorial structure. If the palette of Morandi's *Bathers* constructs the forms in terms of Cézanne, Licini's *Dancers* is wholly antinaturalistic and seems to open up a different dimension.

The works of 1917 are often compared to Pablo Picasso's theatrical pieces, like the sets and costumes for *Parade*, a ballet by Léonide Massine with music by Erik Satie on a poetic text by Jean Cocteau. Licini saw the premiere performed in 1917 by Diaghilev's Ballets Russes at the Théâtre du Châtelet in Paris. More than to Picasso, however, the figures of the soldiers, the hunter, and the dancers seem indebted to a Futurist vision of reconstruction, somewhere between Giacomo Balla and Fortunato Depero, filtered through a personal narrative and a composition synthetically abstracted from naturalism. In *Italian Soldiers* (*Soldati italiani*) of 1917 (p. 25), the landscape composition—the mountains, the sun, the flying figure, and the extraterrestrial aspect of the soldiers, who paradoxically seem more connected to their own shadows than to the ground on which they stand—becomes at once symbolic. The work is constructed around a series of planes where everything is upended and abstracted. Similarly, the *Dancers* are not Futurist-inspired in their movement, but in their mechanical stiffness, like puppets.

Hunter (*Cacciatore*) of 1917 (p. 29) could be described as symbolically primitive. It is built, like *Italian Soldiers*, on a two-dimensional perspectival spyglass structure defined by a sequence of trees that guides the eye toward the line of the high horizon of the mountains and sun. It is precisely in these elements that we witness the birth of Licini's symbolism, which came to full maturity in the paintings of the *Archangel Gabriel* (*Arcangelo Gabriele*) (p. 30). Masterpieces created outside the currents of contemporary Italian painting—one thinks of the crystalline metaphysical period of Morandi, of the Masaccio-influenced primitivism of Carrà, and the different declensions of the so-called "return to order"—they are centered on the theme of the landscape, which is yet further simplified. Reduced to just a few lines, it is infused with unreal color in tones of pink and yellow-ocher that bestow a distinctive luminosity to the paintings, almost theatrical in the dramatic backlighting of the clouds. Nature becomes the site of the apparition of the archangel, the central poetic and visual *topos* of Licini's oeuvre. Painted at the end of the 1910s,[11] these two works are later revisited, as we see in the profile of the man with his back to us on the right side of the *Archangel* (*Arcangelo*) (1919, pp. 32–33), drawn with a dark and heavy line, similar to that of the figures of the 1940s.

This reworking his own paintings, almost as if they had never been finished, reveals a conception of each individual painting as an ongoing quest, an unresolved thought, a continuous excavation that undermines the traditional problems of dating. Zeno Birolli wisely reflected on the temporal dimension of Licini's works, defining it as "apparent":

> for Licini, the work is exempt from temporal duration and exists in a transitive, ideal dimension, such that the painting can reveal itself in different and subsequent moments of execution and reading. He suspends the procedure and reasserts the unitary character of its ethical tension, which then must be verified in a more direct reason of language and image construction.[12]

Temporal jumps and rebounds constitute an exploration that cannot be pigeonholed by stylistic labels, characterized by a poetic and linguistic originality rooted in an inexhaustible and never complacent exploration of painting. ▸

1. Osvaldo Licini, undated poem, in Licini, *Errante, erotico, eretico. Gli scritti letterari e tutte le lettere*, ed. Gino Baratta, Francesco Bartoli, and Zeno Birolli (Milan: Feltrinelli, 1974), 85.
2. Carlo Ludovico Ragghianti, "Bologna cruciale 1914," in *Critica d'arte* XVI (XXXIV), n.s., fasc. 106–07 (October–November 1969): 3–142, then published as a monograph in 1982.
3. See Mattia Patti, "Verso la modernità. Licini, Morandi e la mostra all'Hotel Baglioni," in *Licini Morandi divergenze parallele*, exh. cat., Fermo, Palazzo dei Priori, and Monte Vidon Corrado, Centro Studi Osvaldo Licini, June 25–September 25, 2011, curated by Marilena Pasquali and Daniela Simoni (Pistoia: Gli Ori, 2011), 73–87; Marilena Pasquali, "L'interesse per il Futurismo," in *Licini Morandi*, 203–05.
4. See, for example, Ask [Ascanio Forti], "La mostra dei 'secessionisti' al Baglioni," *Il Resto del Carlino*, March 22, 1914, also in *Licini Morandi*, 214–15.
5. Letter from Gino Rossi to Nino Barbantini of 1912, cited in Guido Perocco, *Artisti del primo Novecento italiano* (Turin: Bolaffi, 1965), 135. In these years there were various groups of young "secessionist" artists cropping up in Italy with the intention of opposing official academic art, like the Ca' Pesaro, of which Gino Rossi was a member, and Secessione group in Rome.
6. Ask, "La mostra dei 'secessionisti'."
7. Letter from Osvaldo Licini to Balilla Pratella of September 17, 1913, in Licini, *Errante, erotico, eretico*, 103.
8. See, for example, Ardengo Soffici, "L'Esposizione di Venezia," *La Voce* 46 (October 28, 1909).
9. Letter from Osvaldo Licini to Balilla Pratella of September 17, 1913.
10. In addition to publishing several articles on the subject, in 1910 Soffici organized the *Prima mostra italiana dell'impressionismo francese* at the Lyceum in Florence.
11. Mattia Patti has proposed a later date on the basis of infrared reflectography analysis: Mattia Patti, *Tracce disperse e segni nuovi. Osvaldo Licini attraverso la riflettografia infrarossa* (Pisa: Scuola Normale Superiore, 2006), 9–19 and the plates on 97–98.
12. Zeno Birolli, "Storia e temporalità circolare," in Licini, *Errante, erotico, eretico*, 14.

SELF-PORTRAIT
(AUTORITRATTO)
1913
oil on cardboard
37 × 29 cm
Lorenzo Licini Collection

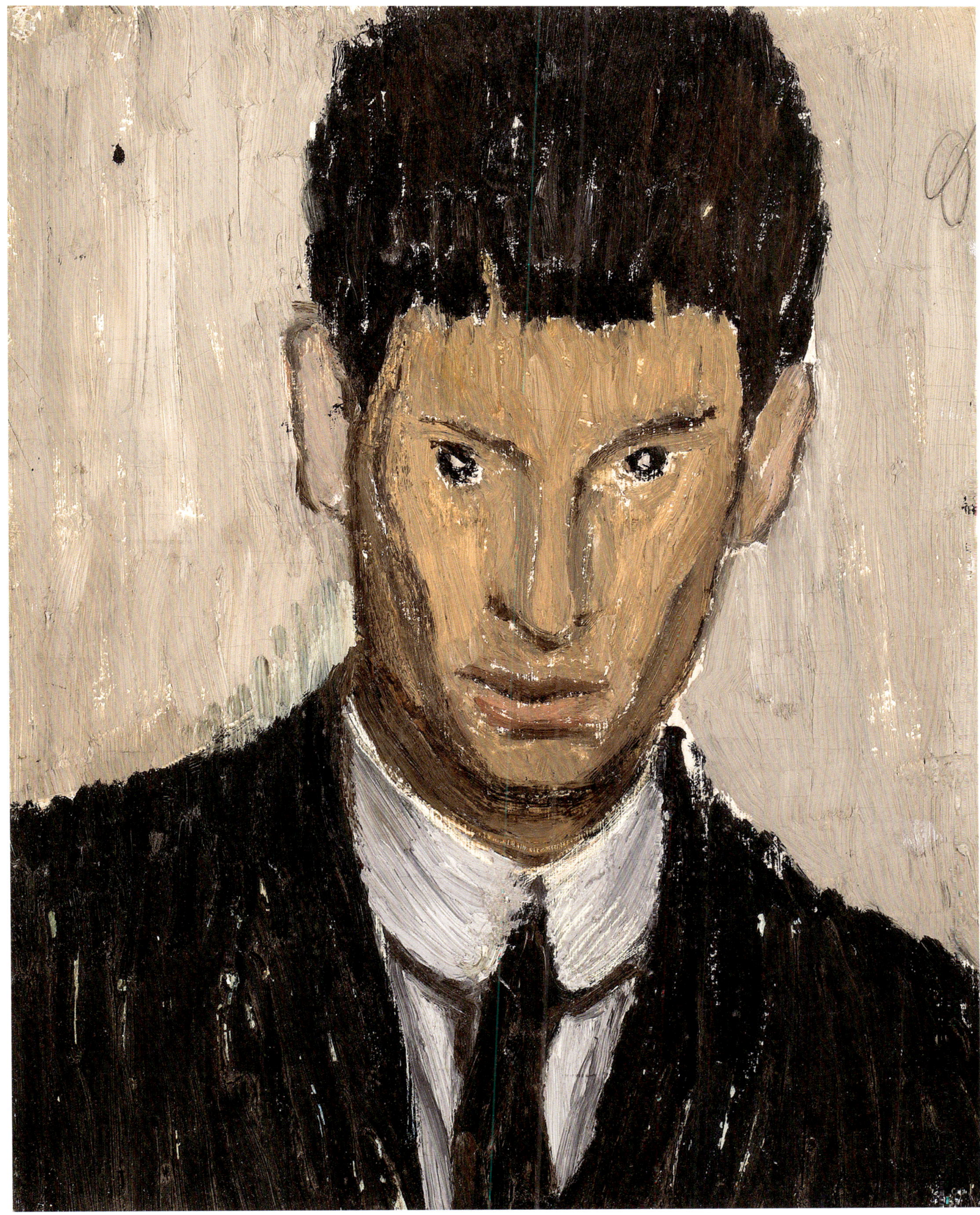

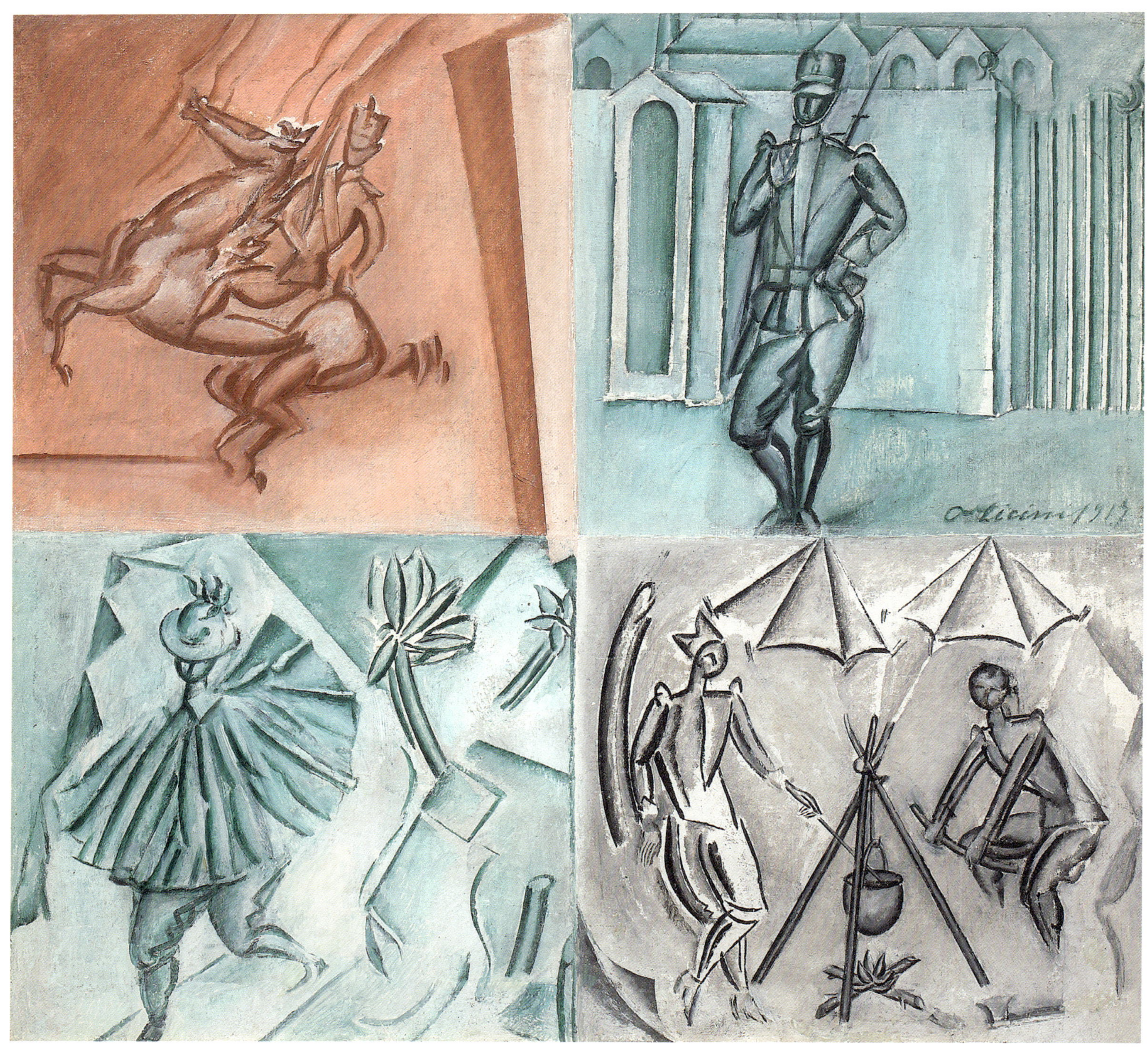

ITALIAN SOLDIERS (WAR MEMORIES)
(SOLDATI ITALIANI [RICORDI DI GUERRA])
1917
oil on canvas
60 × 63.5 cm
Private collection

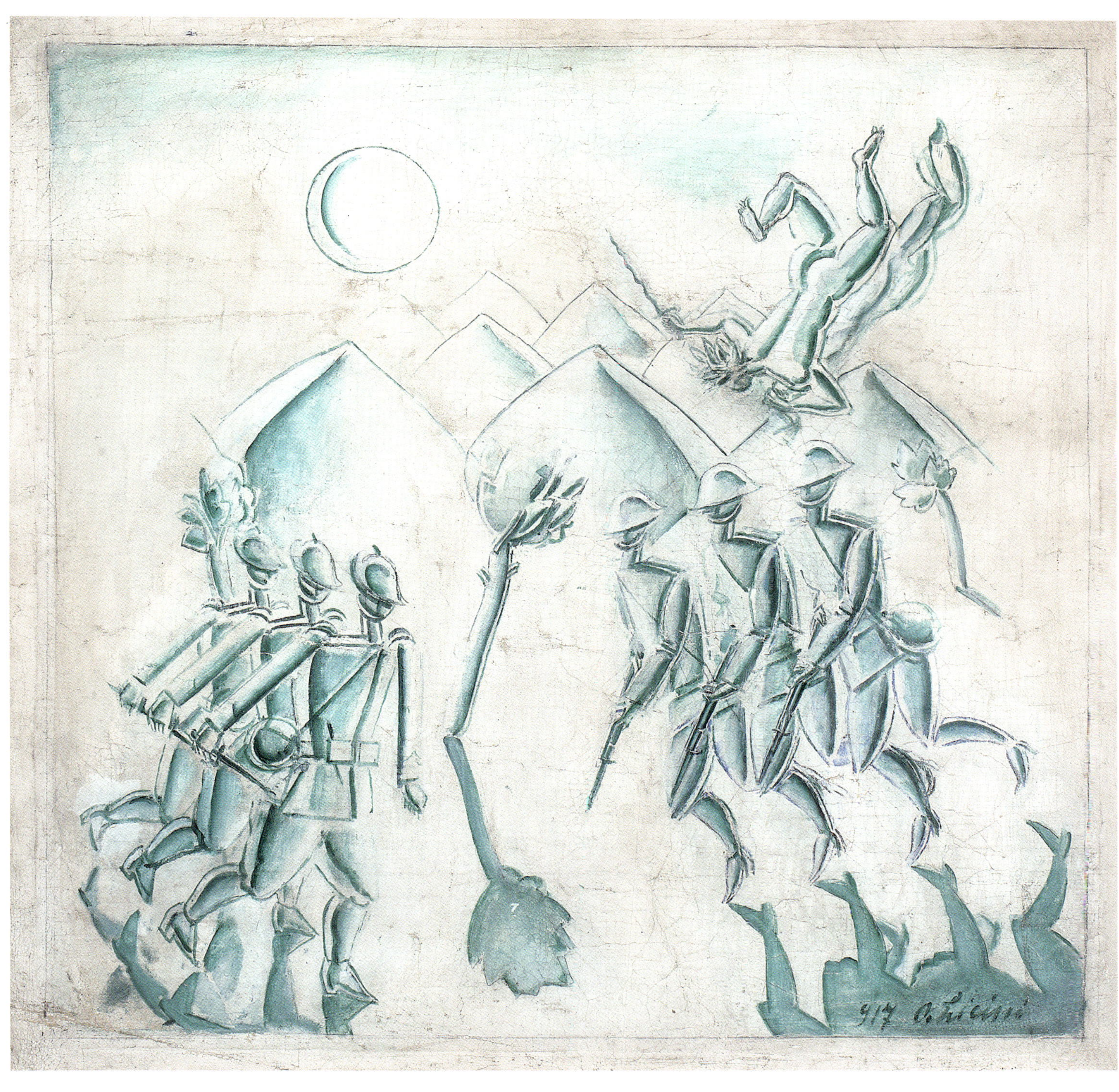

ITALIAN SOLDIERS
(SOLDATI ITALIANI)
1917
oil on canvas
60 × 60 cm
Private collection

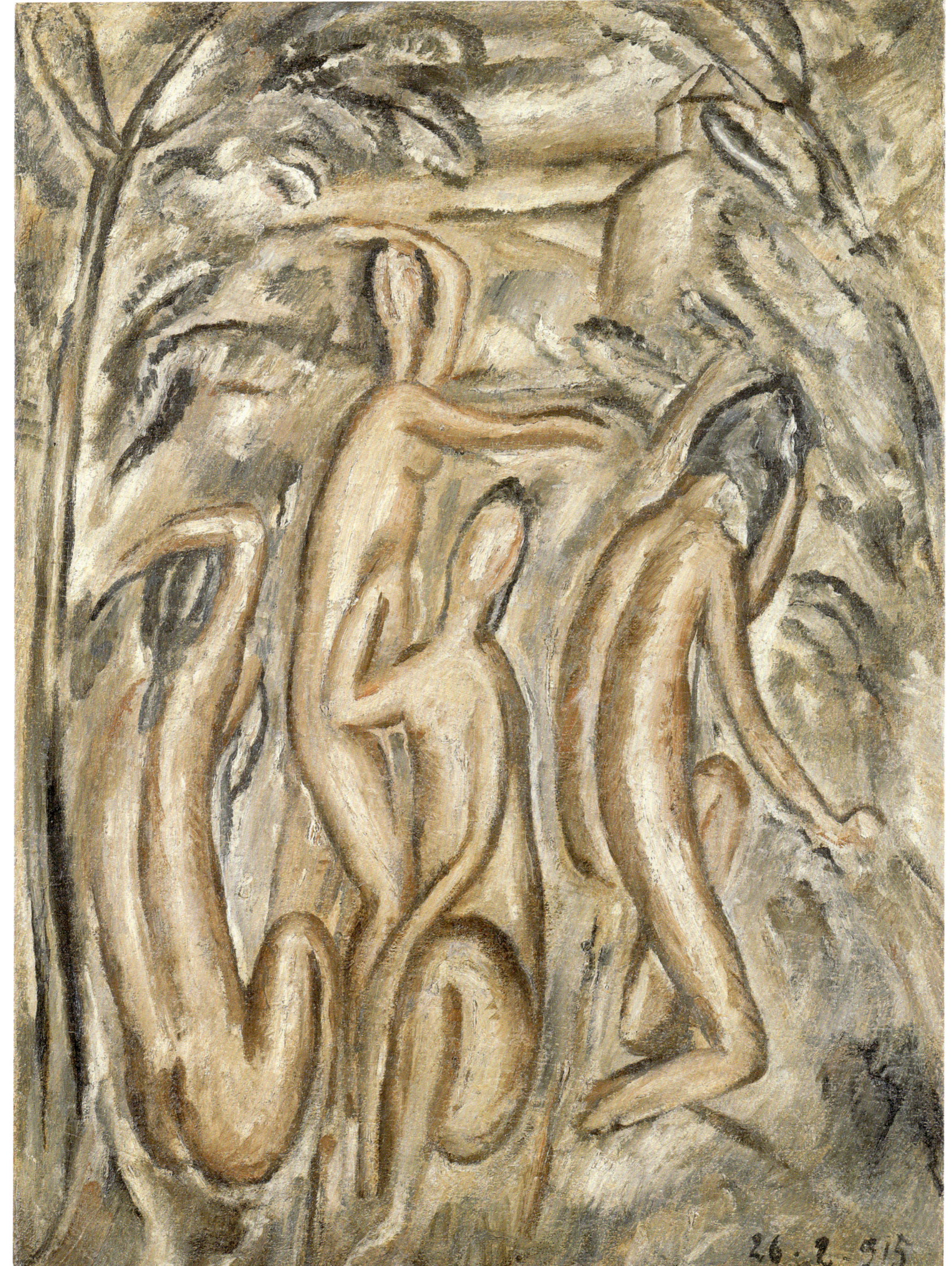

Giorgio Morandi
BATHERS
(BAGNANTI)
1915
oil on canvas
76 × 54 cm
Collection of Fondazione Cariverona, Verona

DANCERS
(BALLERINE)
1917
oil on canvas
59.5 × 45.5 cm
Private collection

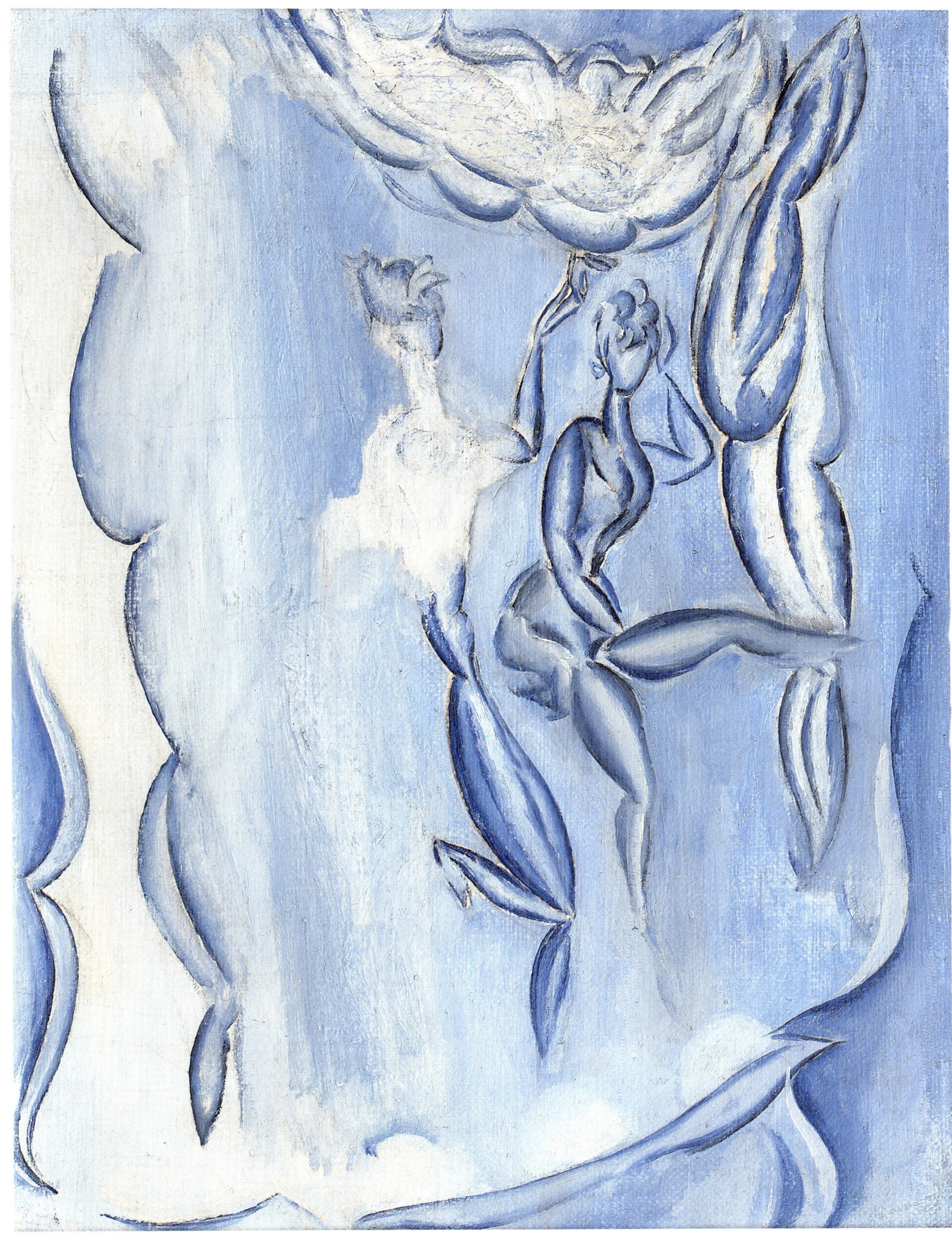

HUNTER
(CACCIATORE)
1917
oil on canvas
63 × 55.5 cm
Private collection

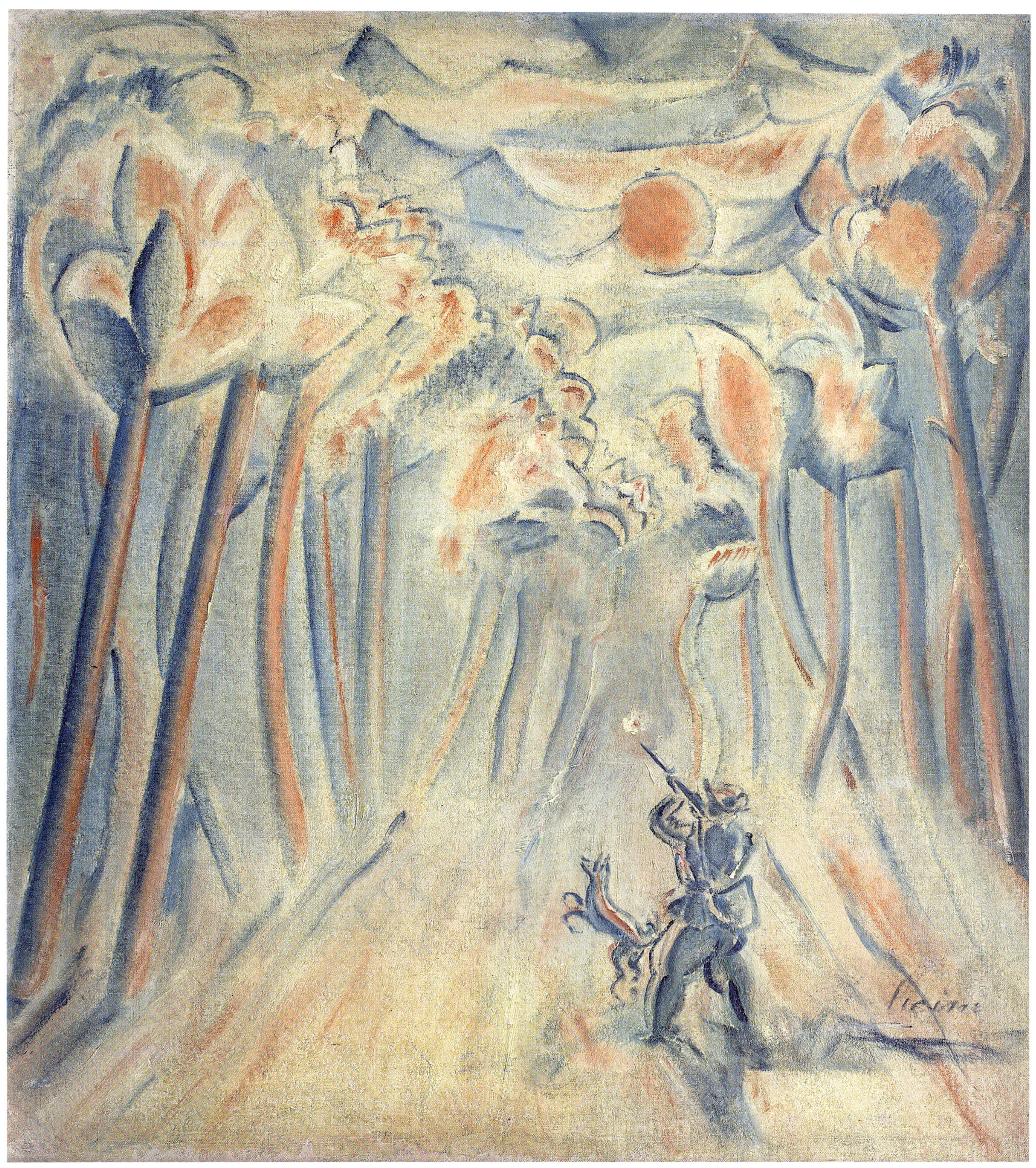

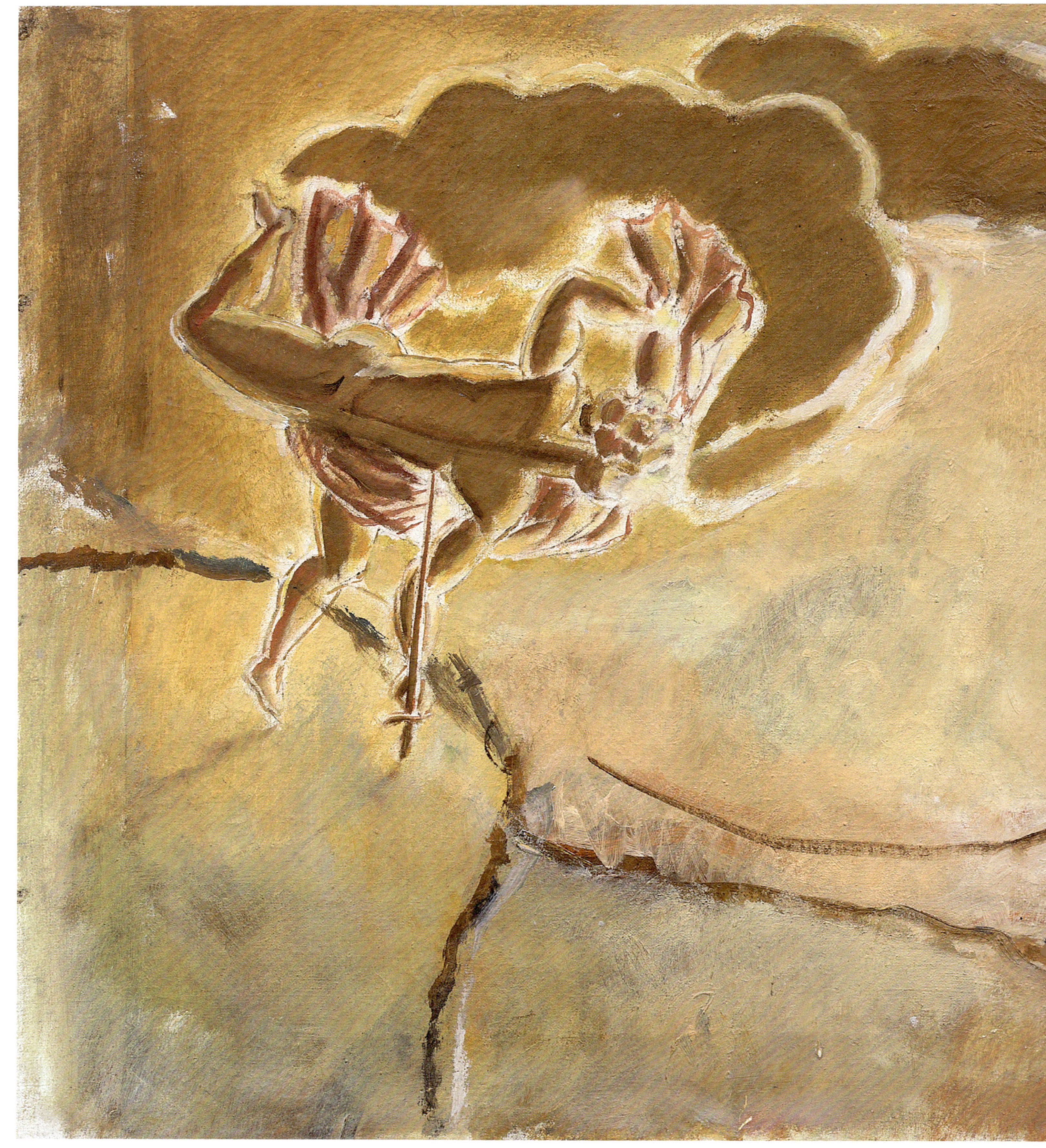

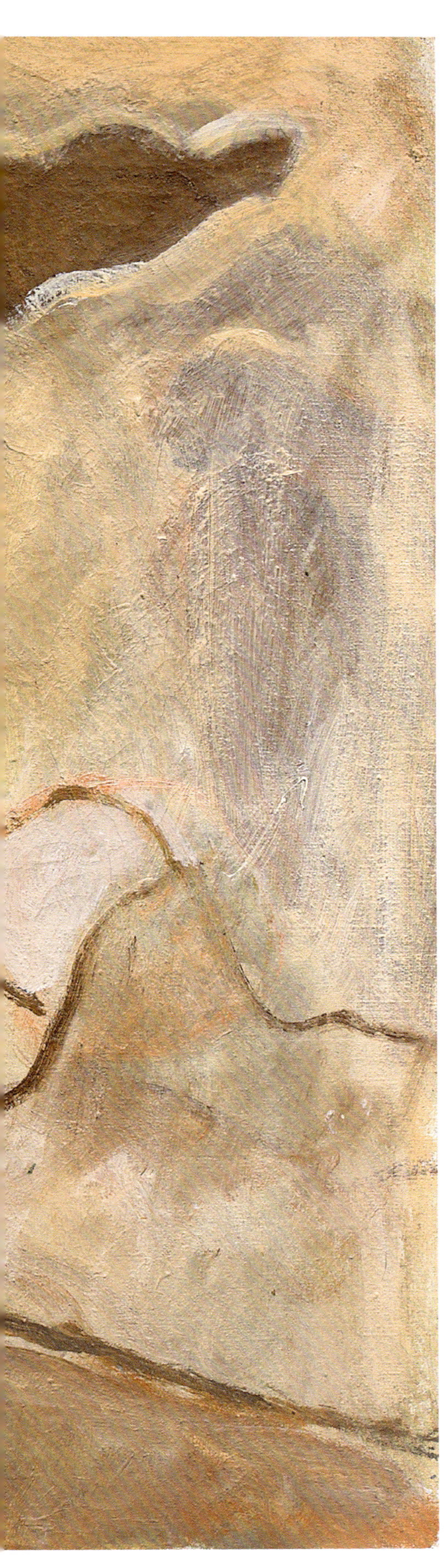

ARCHANGEL GABRIEL
(ARCANGELO GABRIELE)
1919 (with subsequent modifications)
oil on canvas
37.5 × 45.5 cm
Private collection

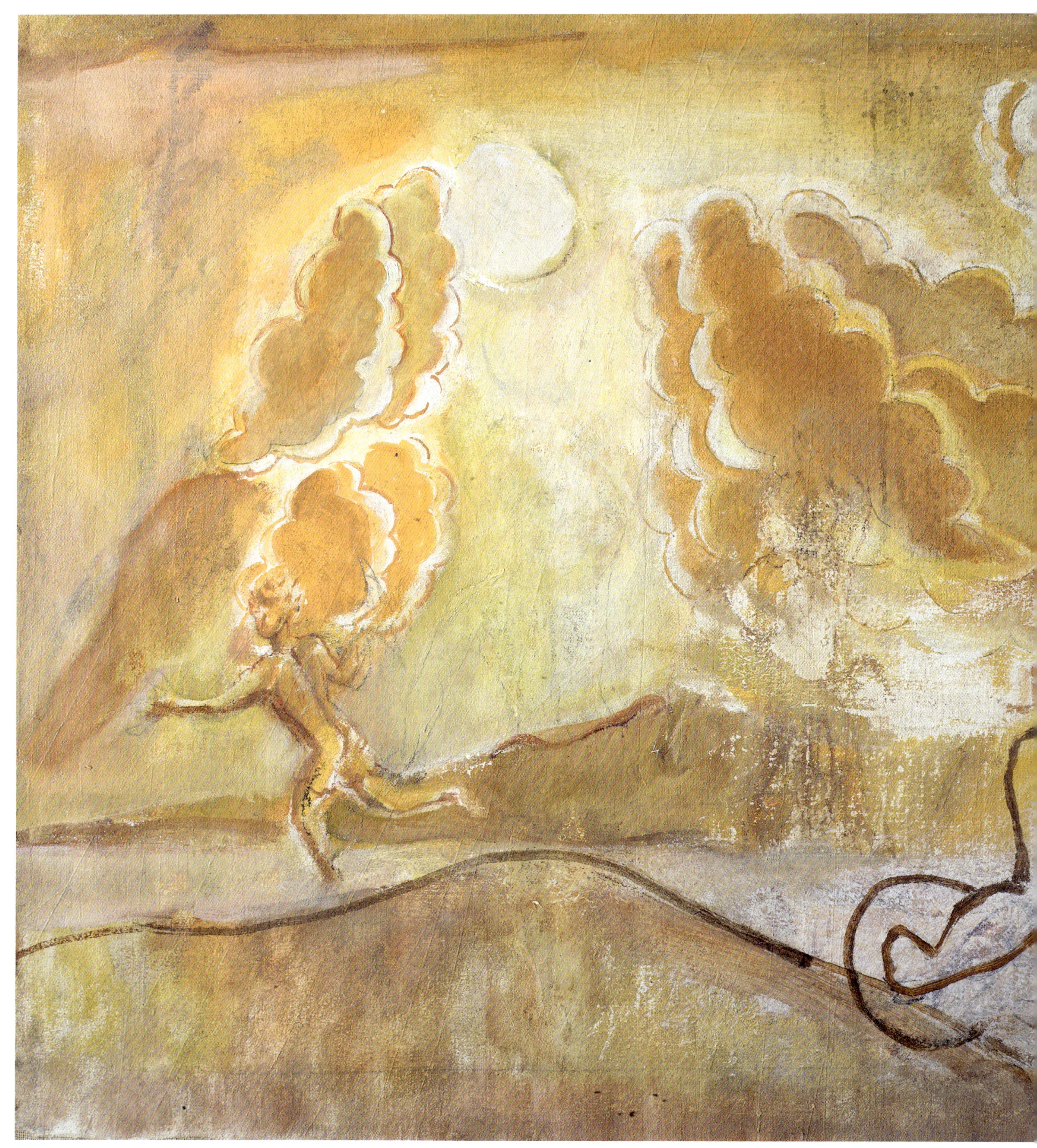

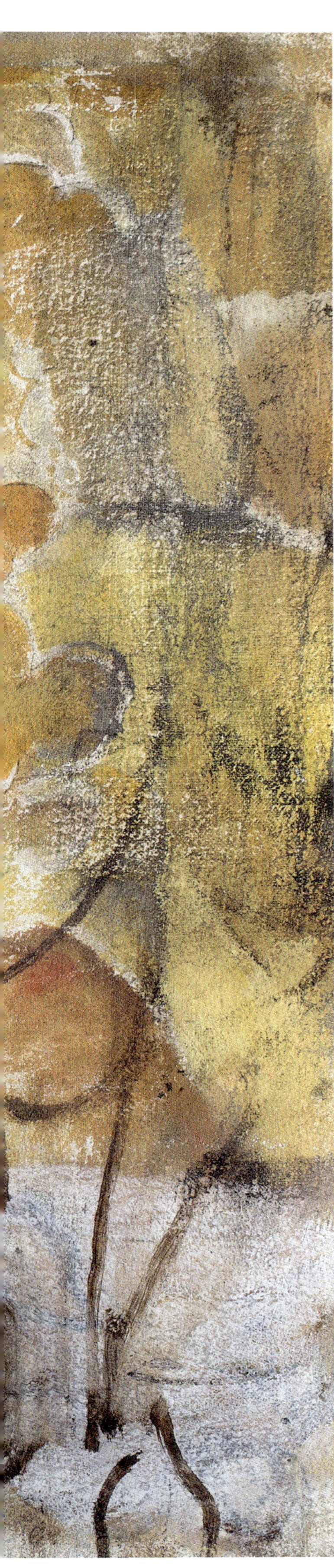

ARCHANGEL
(ARCANGELO)
1919
oil on canvas
44 × 51 cm
Galleria d'Arte Contemporanea
Osvaldo Licini, Ascoli Piceno

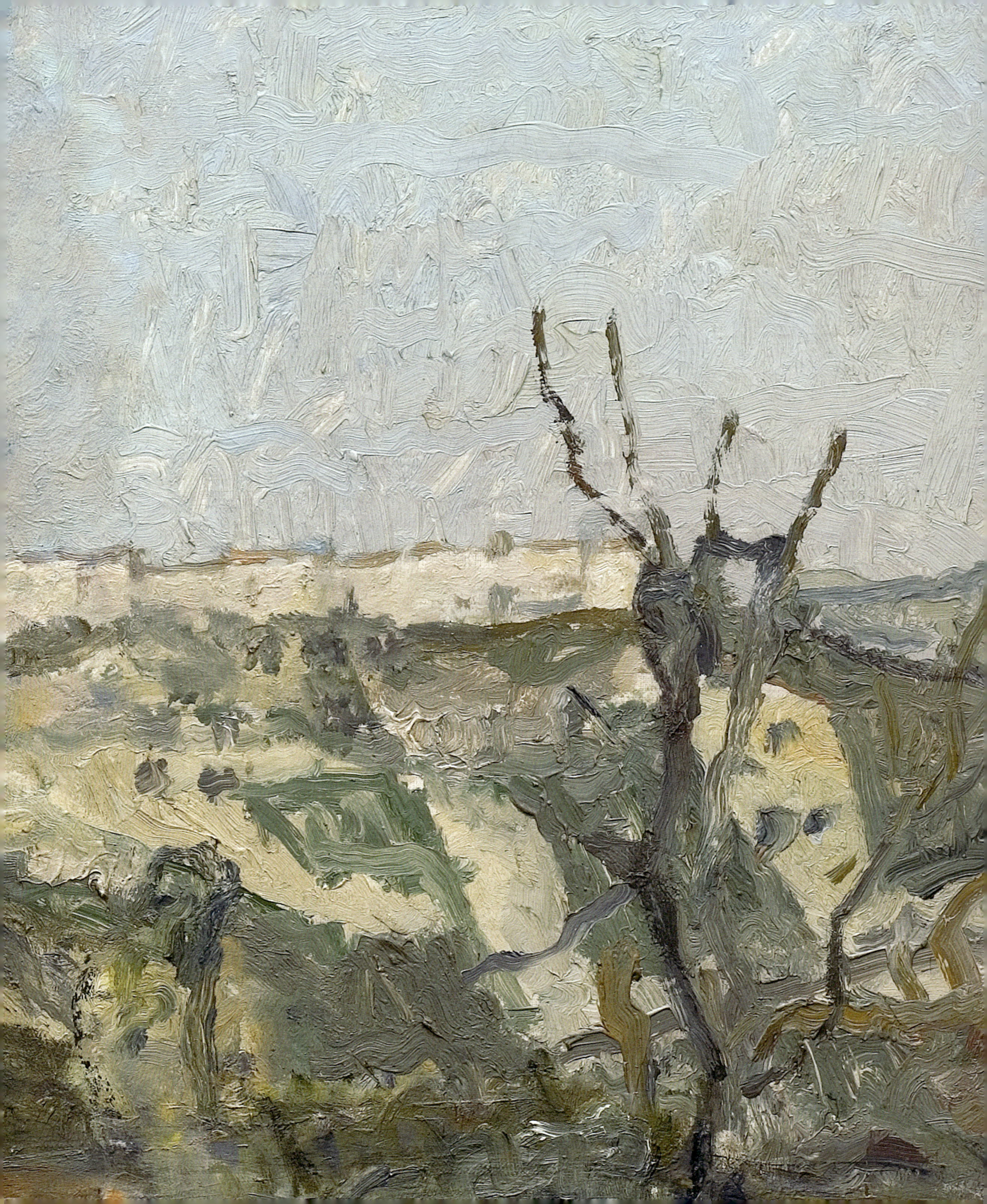

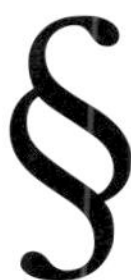

THE 1920S: THE NUDE AND THE LANDSCAPE

From 1921 onward, Licini stayed for long periods in Paris, where he frequented the lively artistic and literary milieu of Montparnasse, associating with the likes of Pablo Picasso, Jean Cocteau, Blaise Cendrars, and Moïse Kisling and starting to exhibit his work rather often, thanks to the encouragement of the painter Mario Tozzi, his companion back at the art academy:

> In Paris I soon ran into Licini, whom I had met along with Morandi in Bologna ... and we would meet every day at a cafe in Montparnasse .... I had left Licini a Futurist in Bologna, and here I found him a Post-Impressionist: Matisse + Dufy + Friesz in the landscapes and flowers; a bit à la Modigliani in the figures ....[13]

After abandoning the almost mechanical synthesis of the *War Episodes*, the artist approached the "return to figuration" that characterized the widespread climate of return to order in personal terms. Meeting Amedeo Modigliani and discovering his work in 1917, recounted by Licini in a memoir written in 1934, exposed him to a way of painting that feels close to his own:

> I was struck and won over almost instantly by the powerful and mysterious charm of those half-lengths of ecstatic women, bound to their dreams, emerging from simple yet deep backgrounds, with a rich, incandescent, unexpected palette. The organic lines of certain figures blossomed from the colorful impasto, plunging back into the flesh to create the impression of powerful relief, obtained effortlessly and without the use of shadows, with the simple game of linear emergence, which alone gave a sense of all four dimensions.[14]

LANDSCAPE, FALERONE (PAESAGGIO FALERONE)
1925
oil on canvas
54.5 × 81 cm
Gori Collection, Fattoria di Celle, Pistoia
detail

This reflection on the line that blossoms and plunges into the paint is particularly indicative of the direction Licini was taking at that moment. If we compare Licini's *Portrait of Nella* (*Ritratto di Nella*) (1926, p. 41) or the *Young Shepherd* (*Pastorello*) paintings (1925, pp. 46, 47) with the robust and defined volumes of the artist of the Novecento Italiano group (Licini participated in their exhibitions thanks to Tozzi), we recognize, in the words of Elena Pontiggia, "an already potentially antivolumetric dimension, a linearity that drains the masses from within rather than enclosing them in compact forms."[15]

Licini's nudes of this period seem to assimilate the principles of his landscapes, in the emphatic horizontality of the figures defined by lines that become space. It is here that Licini takes an unexpected detour: instead of striving for plastic regularity, he uses the nude as a pictorial gymnasium, a place to wrestle with painting and interrogate his own artistic process. The works of the 1920s are emblematic of those he had destroyed from the period of "realism?"—as he wrote in response to a questionnaire in 1929[16]—which covered the entire decade and prefigured his exploration of abstraction. It is no accident that, in describing his art, he added a dubious question mark.

Decisive in this regard is the *Portrait of Nanny* (*Ritratto di Nanny*) of 1926 (p. 49), a masterpiece that clearly shows the main feature of Licini's painting: the balance between brushstroke and material. Nanny Hellström, a young Swedish painter he met in Paris in 1925 and married in Monte Vidon Corrado at the end of the following year, is depicted in reductive terms, far removed from the forms of analytical or illustrative realism. Perhaps it is not by chance that the portrait was exhibited alongside his abstract works at the 1958 Biennale, as if to underline the "unitary character" of his vision. Nanny is captured in an intimate moment of everyday life, her face resting on the back of her hand as if absorbed in thought. The brushwork is not fully defined, but bare and expressively inaccurate in filling the contours. The contemporaneous landscapes of the Marches show a similar application of color. Unlike Morandi and Carrà, who treat buildings and nature as geometric and compact forms, Licini seems to transcribe them metaphorically, starting from direct observation of the "real" and then simplifying and abstracting.

Settling permanently in Monte Vidon Corrado in 1926, Licini resumed his bond with his native land, which became his preferred subject matter. *Landscape of the Marches (The Trough)* (*Paesaggio marchigiano [Il trogolo]*) of 1928 (p. 61) is emblematic of the complexity of painting the landscape, the struggle of the artist to get it right that shines through in the "revisitations" of 1942, and of the fascination for the primordial character of nature in the Marches, with which he establishes a profound intimacy.[17]

For Licini, the landscape corresponds to the horizon and is related once again to the idea of transcending reality, of using painting as a window into the supernatural. These cropped landscape, these "screens" are designed to focus on the infinite: the front and back of a mountain, the front and back of the hills. The portions of sky, rendered with dense brushstrokes of blue-gray paint, increasingly expand, while the construction of "backdrops," in the form of a hill or a house or a field, block the view and thus open up to a dimension of incommensurability. This is best seen in *Landscape with Man (Montefalcone)* (*Paesaggio con l'uomo [Montefalcone]*) (1926, pp. 58–59), but above all in *Imaginary Landscape (Billy Goat)* (*Paesaggio fantastico [Il capro]*) (1927, p. 63). *Billy Goat* is the synthesis of two great themes: the perspective of the observer—the painter who is out of sight, behind the viewer—and the real, though imaginary world of the protagonist—in this case the goat, who looks toward the horizon. Licini builds the landscape like the optical chamber of a thought, of a gaze into the here and into the beyond. In the end, his painting shows us planes that are also obstacles, making the yearning for the infinite even stronger.

These works are a meditation on the idea of time and on the meaning of the ineffable nature of perfection, charged with a thrilling melancholy. In this sense, Licini's painting recalls the poetry of Giacomo Leopardi. Melancholy—the impossibility of defining a perfect painting—does not cause him to quit trying, but to wrestle to define spaces of color and to then correct them in other dimensions.[18] The reference to Leopardi, which underlies many of his works, is explicitly addressed in a series of drawings dedicated to the poet dating from the mid-1940s, whose subject draws attention to the poetic meaning, thus obscuring the exceptional pictorial quality of the work to which these drawings are connected.

Imaginary Landscape (Billy Goat) is also emblematic of Licini's personality and his isolation in the hills of Monte Vidon Corrado. This was at times misunderstood and portrayed as a romantic legend, but Licini did not distance himself from the reality of his own time. He was very present and attentive to contemporary culture, informed and up to date, thanks in part to the absence of financial worries in his life. His isolation thus resulted in the privilege to reflect and examine the present. It marked his stance as an outsider, and his scathing judgment of the Novecento Italiano he had exhibited but never aligned himself with (he described one such show as an assembly "of innocuous and disparate trends").[19] The Novecento project felt immediately restrictive to him, as he shared neither its critical premises nor the desire to represent an exclusively Italian notion of art, as he explained in 1937, in a text that effectively captures his vision and the "nature" of his pictorial discourse:

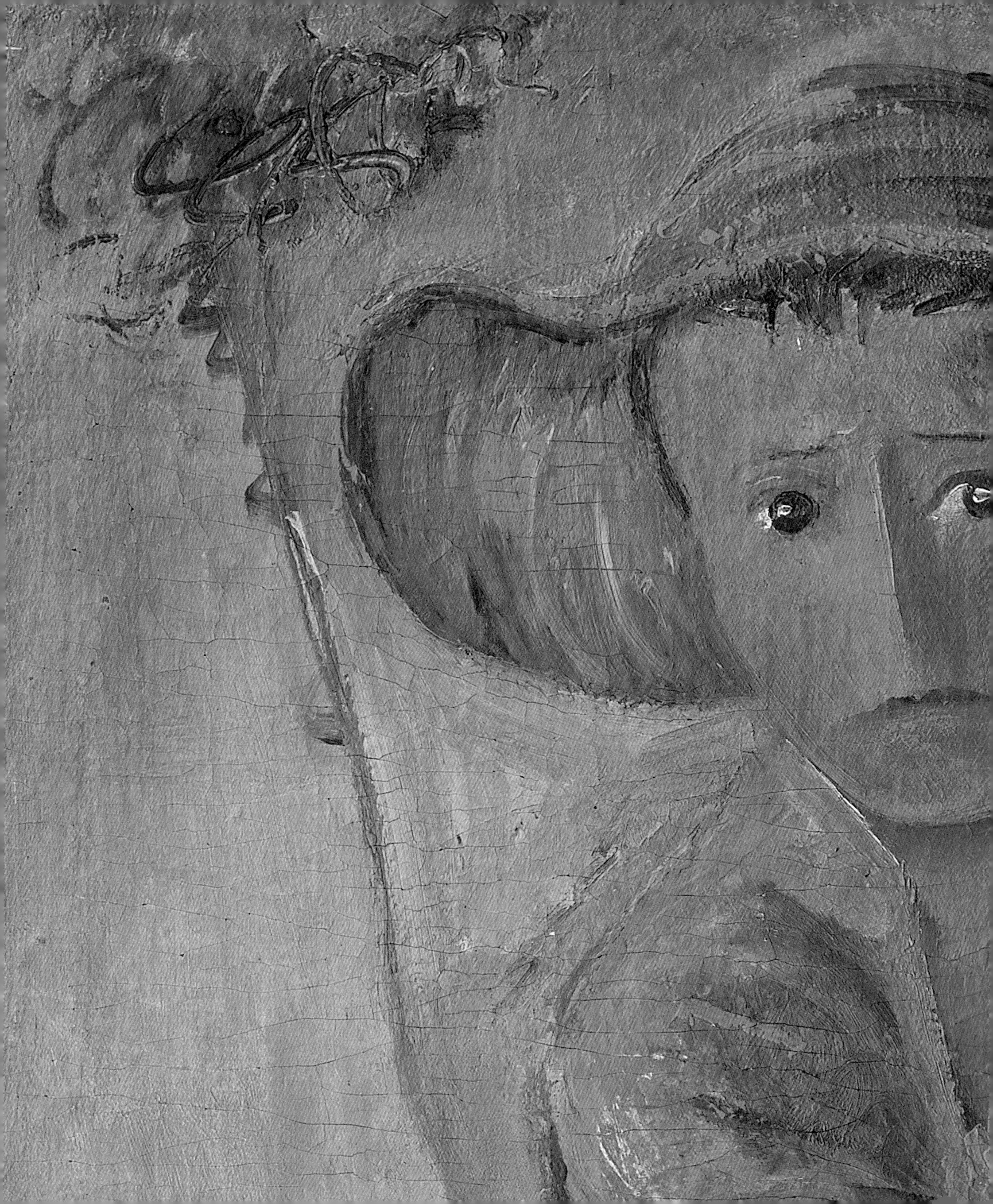

The Scorpion believed he was the most beautiful of all creatures and wanted to proclaim the female Scorpion Queen and venerate her. But Man said he was the most beautiful and proclaimed himself King of the world. Then came Ojetti, Waldemar George, and all the Maraini of the earth, and man was again crowned king of the world. Time after time, man was the microcosm of the universe, man was the yardstick, the measure of all things; everything was in everything, and using the yardstick extracted from the bowels of man, one could obtain the key to the cosmos. Older than the hills, these words had to be used to extract the spider from the hole: Art. And they were spoken for the salvation of Mediterranean Art .... The optimistic thesis of the Man King can be countered with that of the Man Worm who slithers across the earth, incapable of deciphering the mystery or of taming any force of nature. Taking the proportional average, it turns out that man is a hyena with a propensity for poetry.[20]

Licini is strongly critical of the classicist wave washing over Europe between the two wars, berating in no uncertain terms some of greatest supporters and theorists, from Antonio Maraini, director the Venice Biennale, to Ugo Ojetti, who in 1924 had written "placing man back at the center of the world, reestablishing the human body as the measure of the world, this is the primary duty of modern art,"[21] to Waldemar George, founder of a "neo-humanist" movement in Paris and one of the promoters of the so-called Italiens de Paris and of a number of traveling shows of the Novecento group. The simply drawn characters that populate his landscapes and the figure of the goat fully reflect his not anthropocentric, personal vision of the world, interconnected in a profound dialogue between humans, animals, nature, and the cosmos, and infused by an idea of metamorphosis that comports a dimension of instability and mutability, far from the solid immobility of the figures and landscapes appreciated in contemporary criticism. ▸

YOUNG SHEPHERD
(PASTORELLO)
1925
oil on canvas
64 × 54 cm
Private collection
detail

13. Mario Tozzi, cited in Marilena Pasquali, *Catalogo ragionato generale dei dipinti di Mario Tozzi* (Milan: Giorgio Mondadori, 1988), 74.
14. Osvaldo Licini, "Ricordo di Modigliani," *L'Orto* IV, no. 1 (January–February 1934), also in Licini, *Errante, erotico, eretico*, 91–92.
15. Elena Pontiggia, "Filosofia di Licini," in *Osvaldo Licini. Tra le Marche e l'Europa*, curated by Elena Pontiggia and Enrica Torelli Landini, exh. cat., Ascoli Piceno, Galleria Civica d'Arte Moderna e Contemporanea "Osvaldo Licini," April 18–November 4, 2008 (Cinisello Balsamo: Silvana Editoriale, 2008), 17.
16. Osvaldo Licini, response to the *Questionario Scheiwiller*, 1929, in Licini, *Errante, erotico, eretico*, 98.
17. See also Fabrizio D'Amico, "Rifacimenti, revisioni, ritorni. L'incontentabile percorso di Licini," in *Osvaldo Licini. Capolavori*, exh. cat. Turin, Galleria Civica d'Arte Moderna e Contemporanea, October 24, 2010–January 30, 2011, curated by D. Eccher (Milan: Electa, 2010), 120–43.
18. On the relationship with Leopardi, see: Stefano Papetti, "'Recanati e Monte Vidon Corrado sono forse la stessa cosa?'. Giacomo Leopardi e Osvaldo Licini, due intellettuali marchigiani 'Erranti, erotici, eretici,'" in *Osvaldo Licini. Tra le Marche e l'Europa*, 55–58.
19. Osvaldo Licini, response to the *Questionario Scheiwiller*, 1929, in Licini, *Errante, erotico, eretico*, 98.
20. Osvaldo Licini, "Natura di un discorso," *Corriere Padano* (October 9, 1937), also in Licini, *Errante, erotico, eretico*, 101.
21. Ugo Ojetti, preface to *Esposizione di venti artisti italiani*, exh. cat., Milan, Galleria Pesaro, December 1924–January 1925 (Milan [1924]).

PORTRAIT OF NELLA
(RITRATTO DI NELLA)
1926 (with subsequent modifications)
oil on canvas
80 × 64.5 cm
Private collection

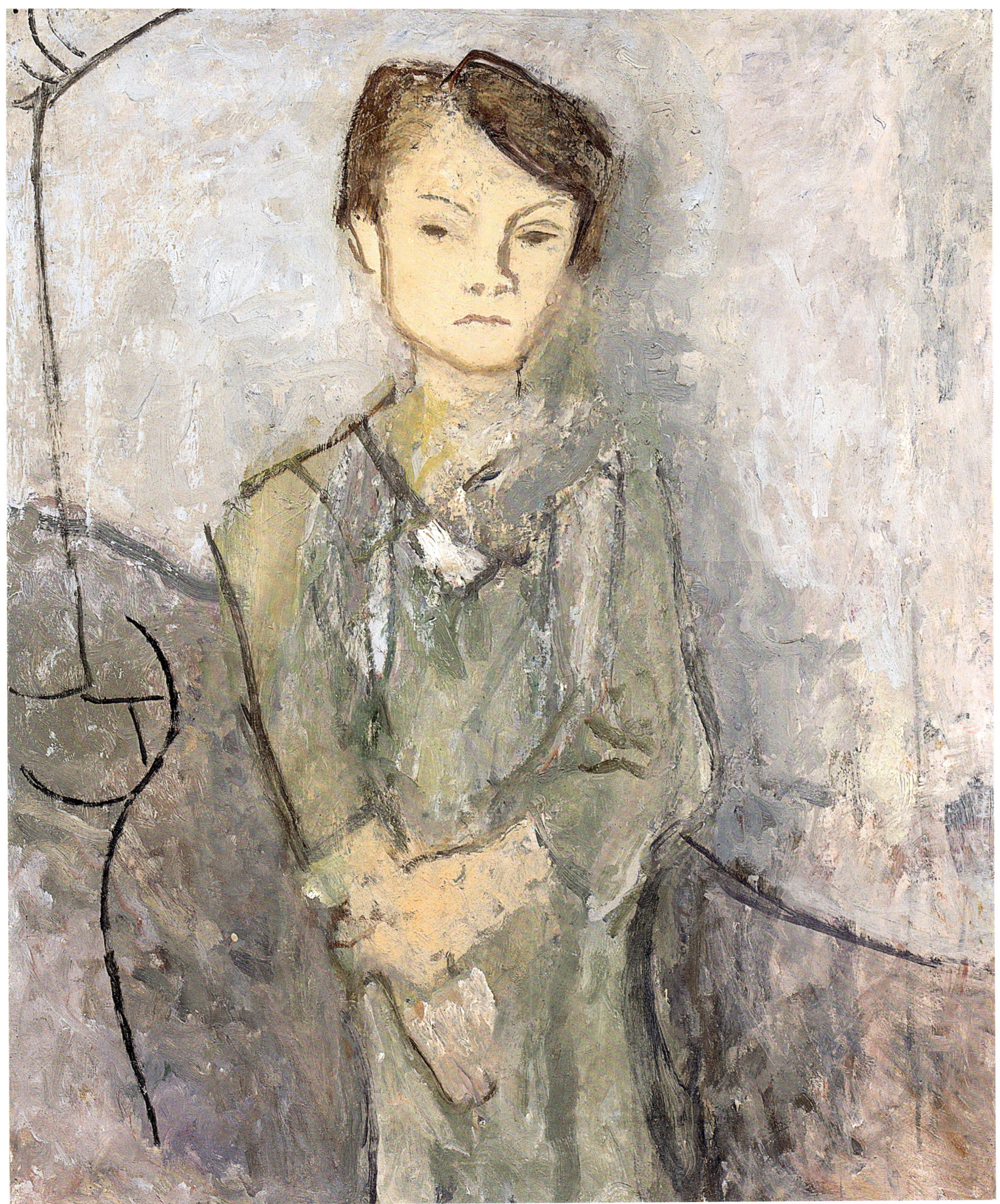

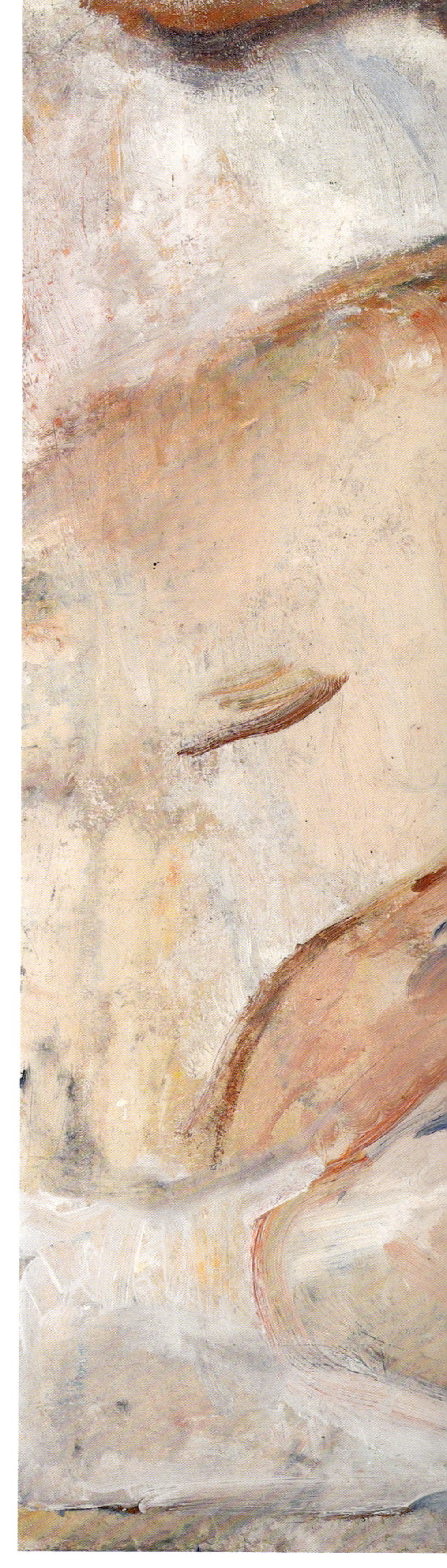

PORTRAIT OF NANNY
(RITRATTO DI NANNY)
1925
oil on canvas
47 × 56 cm
Private collection,
Casa Museo Osvaldo Licini

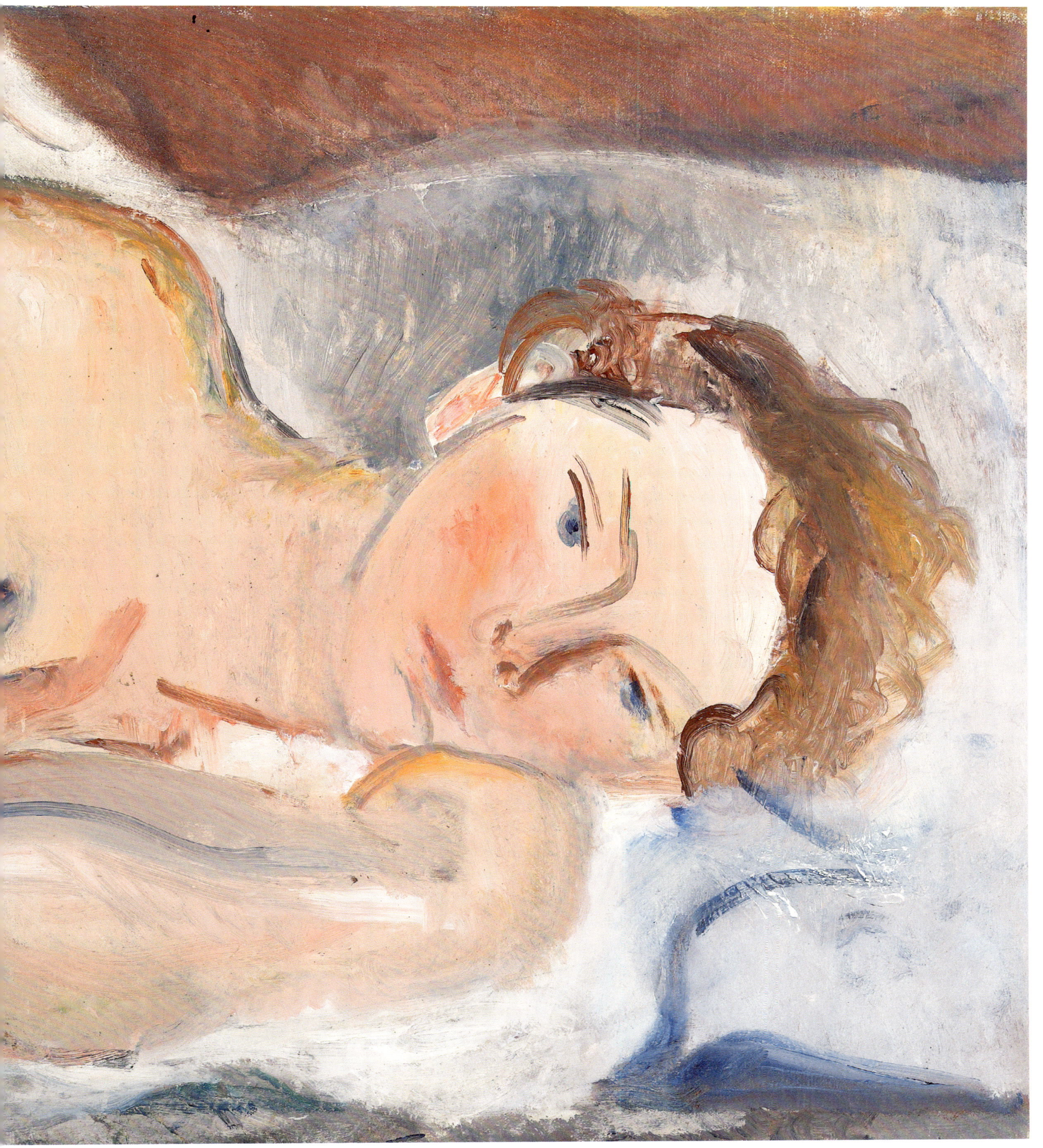

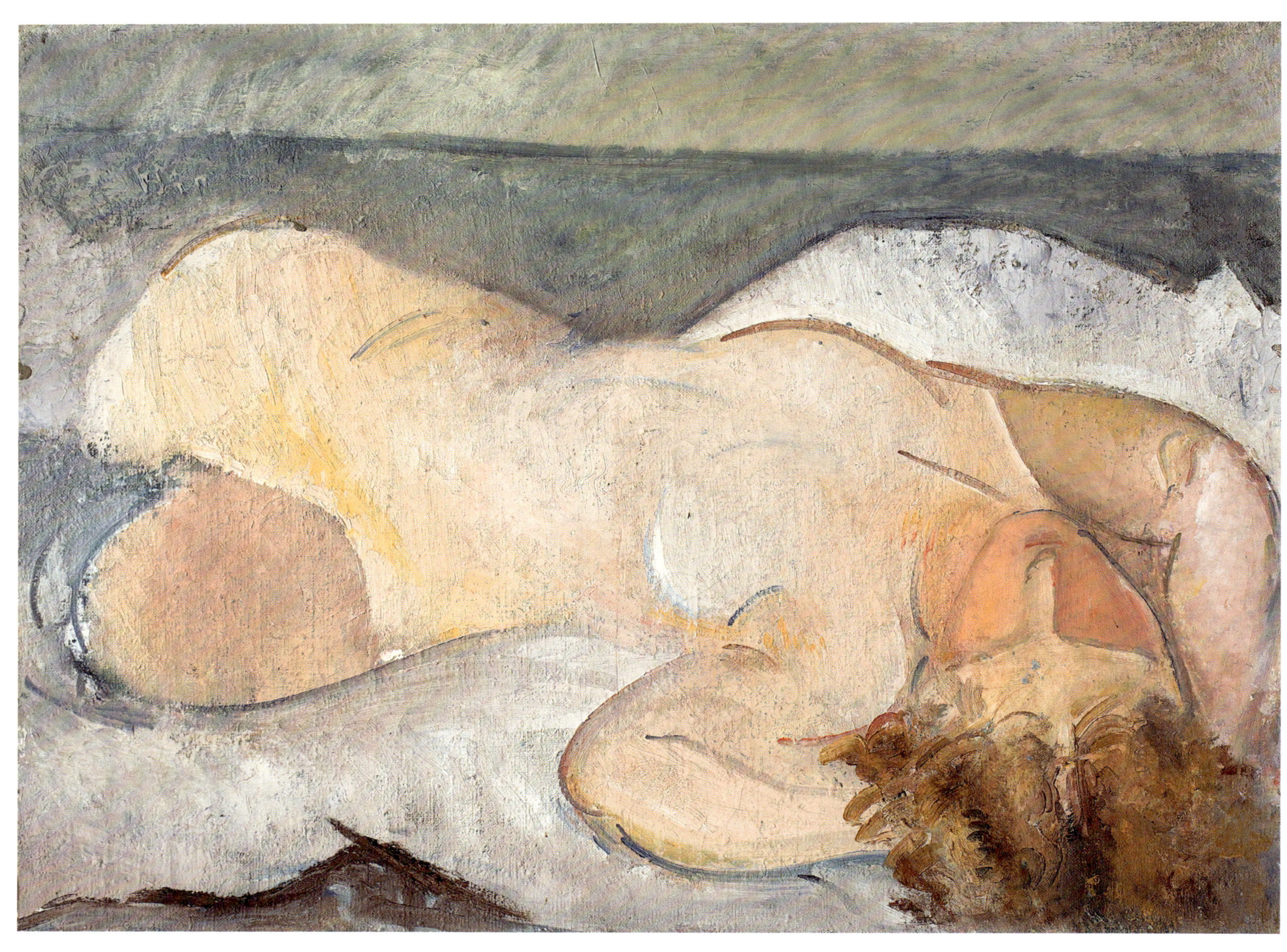

NUDE
(IL NUDO)
1925
oil on canvas
60 × 81 cm
Galleria d'Arte Contemporanea
Osvaldo Licini, Ascoli Piceno

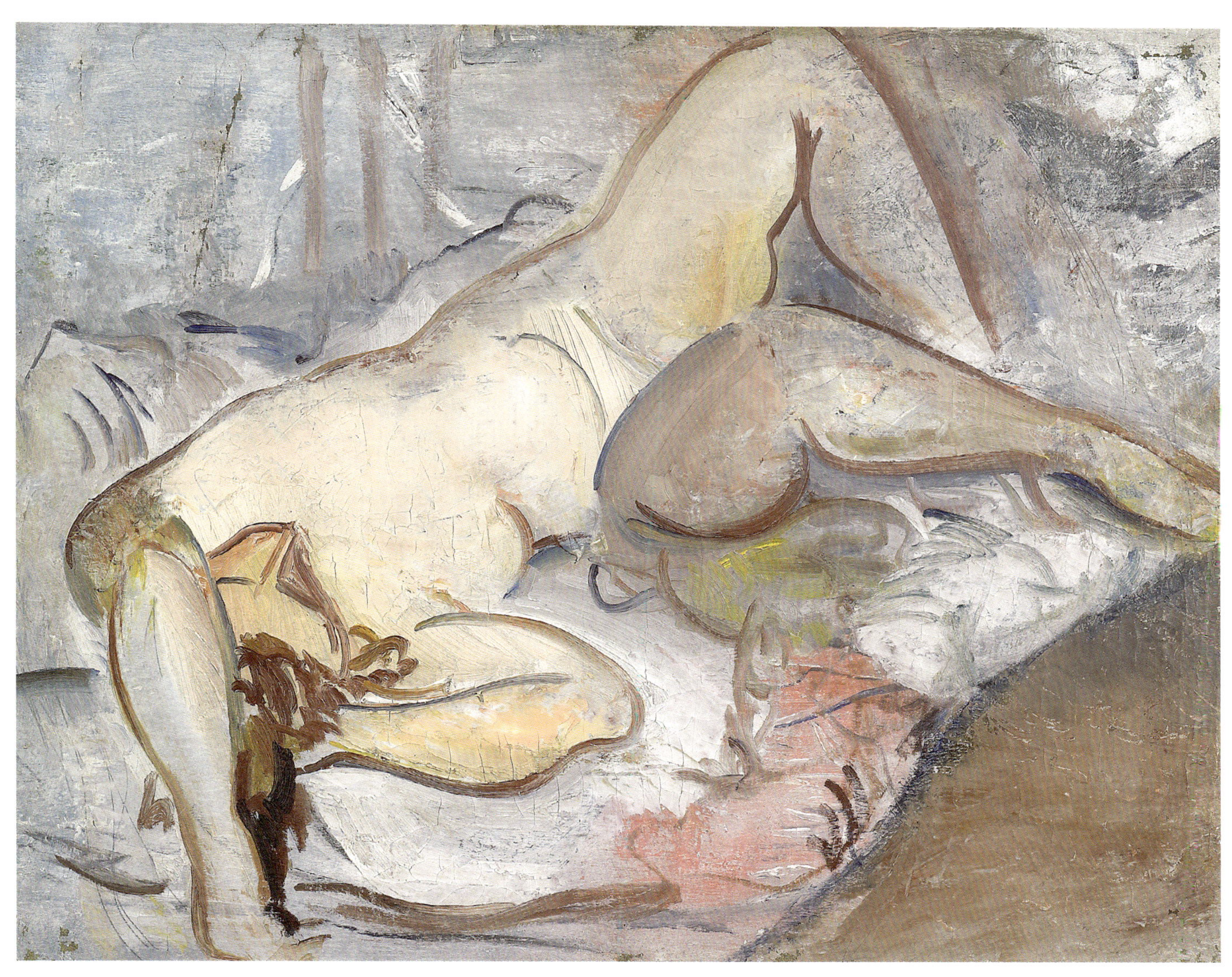

NUDE
(NUDO)
1926
oil on canvas
66 × 82 cm
Private collection

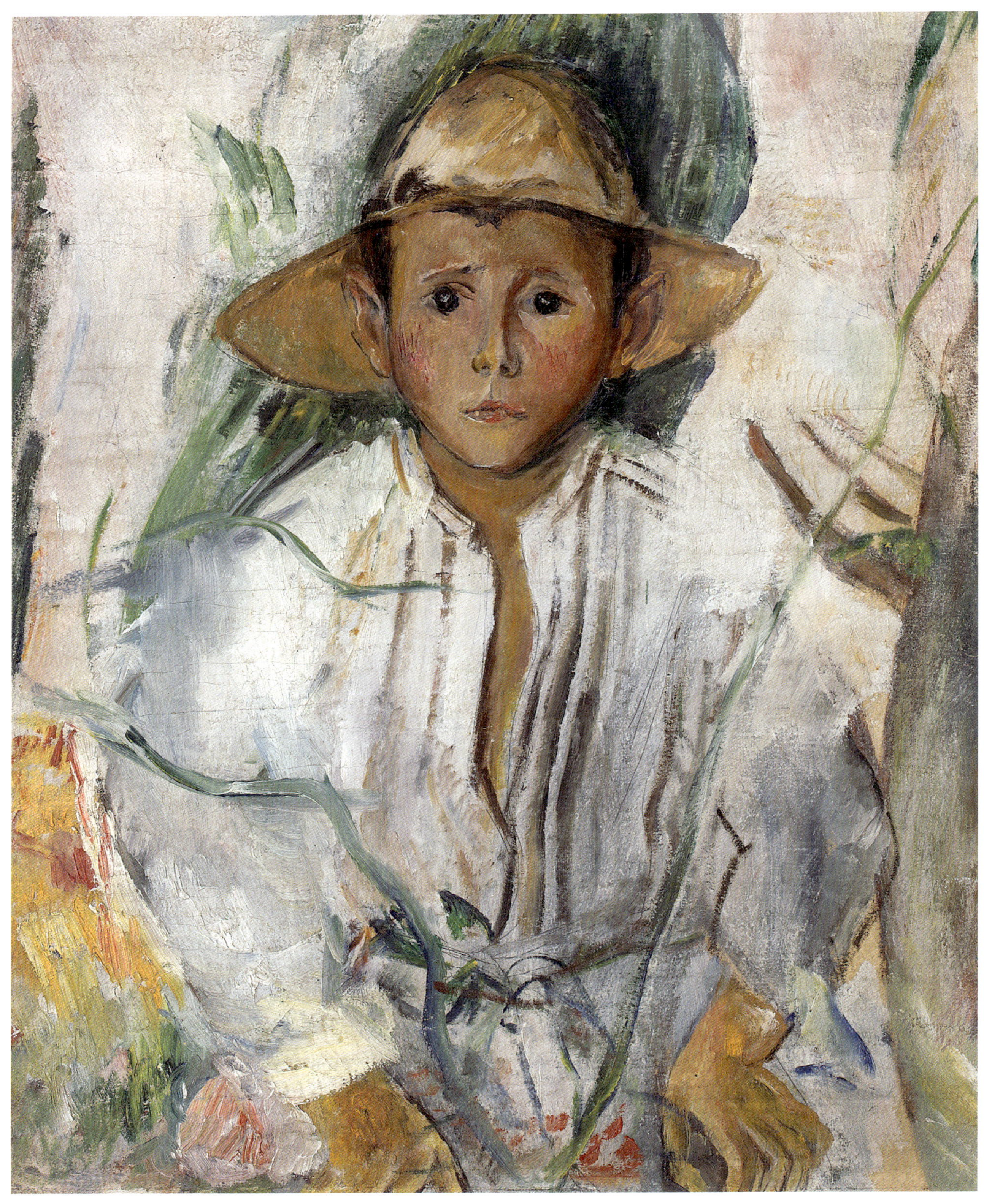

YOUNG SHEPHERD
(PASTORELLO)
1925
oil on canvas
62 × 50 cm
Private collection

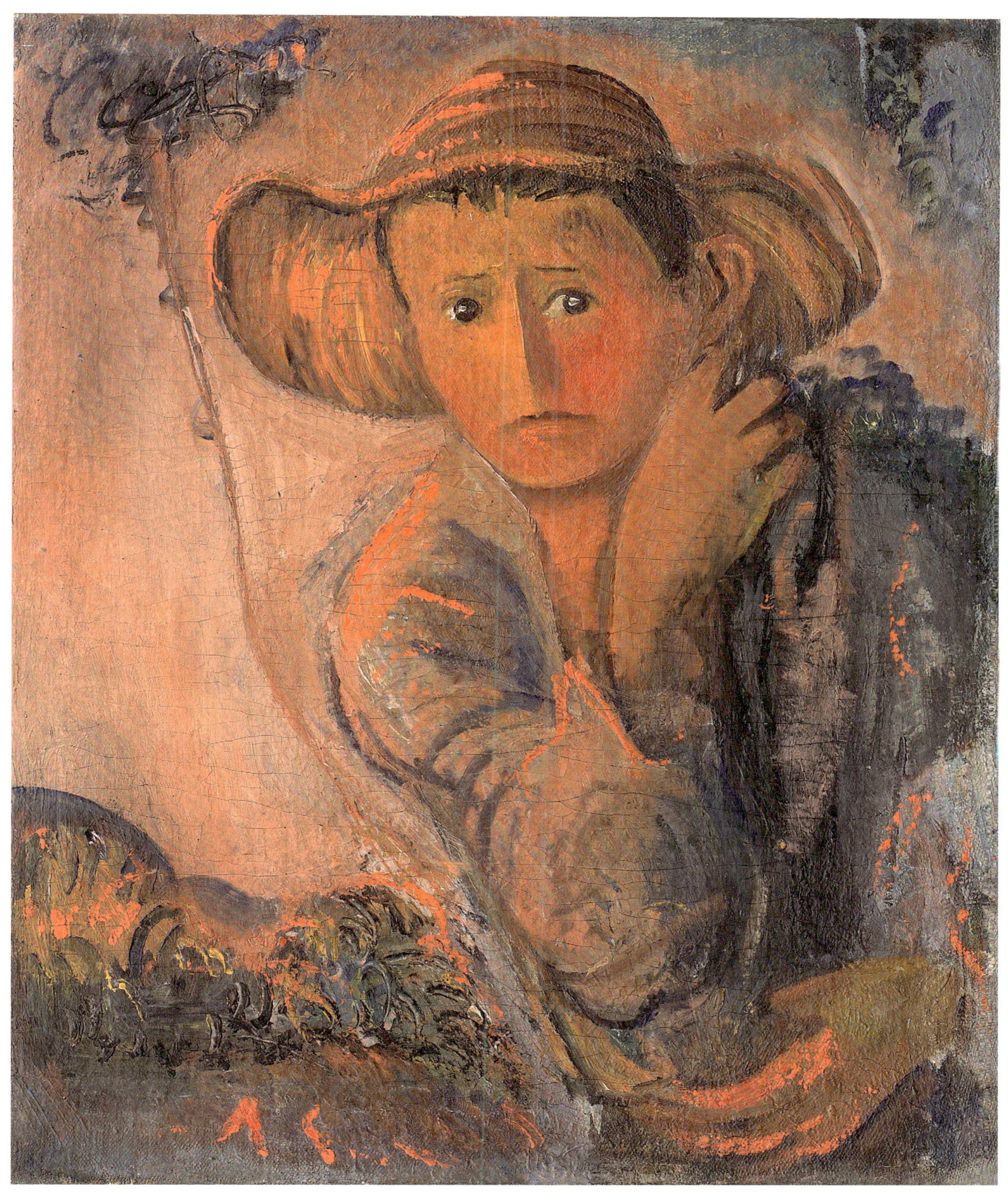

YOUNG SHEPHERD
(PASTORELLO)
1925
oil on canvas
64 × 54 cm
Private collection

PORTRAIT OF NANNY
(RITRATTO DI NANNY)
1926
oil on canvas
62.5 × 75.5 cm
Galleria d'Arte Contemporanea
Osvaldo Licini, Ascoli Piceno

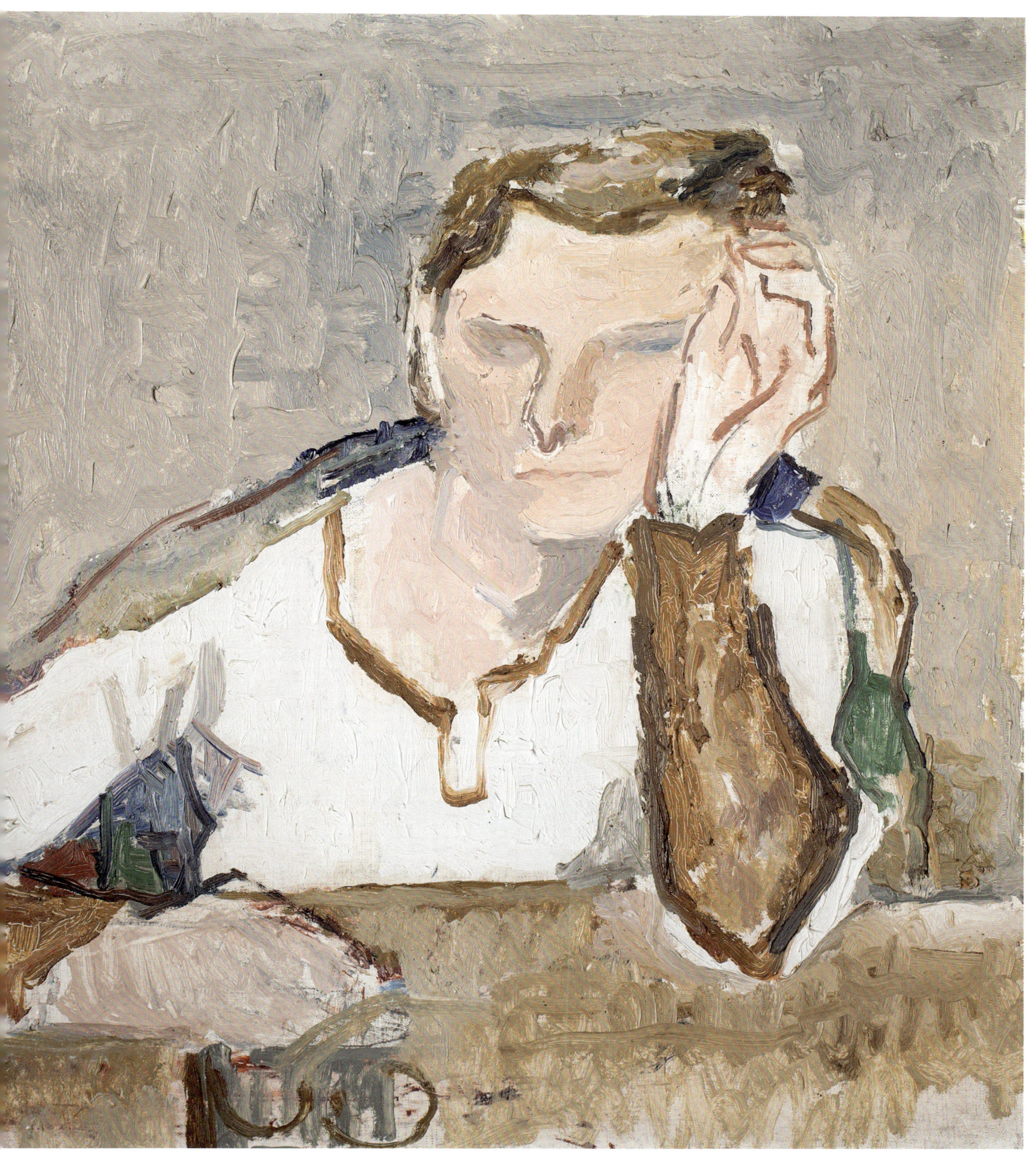

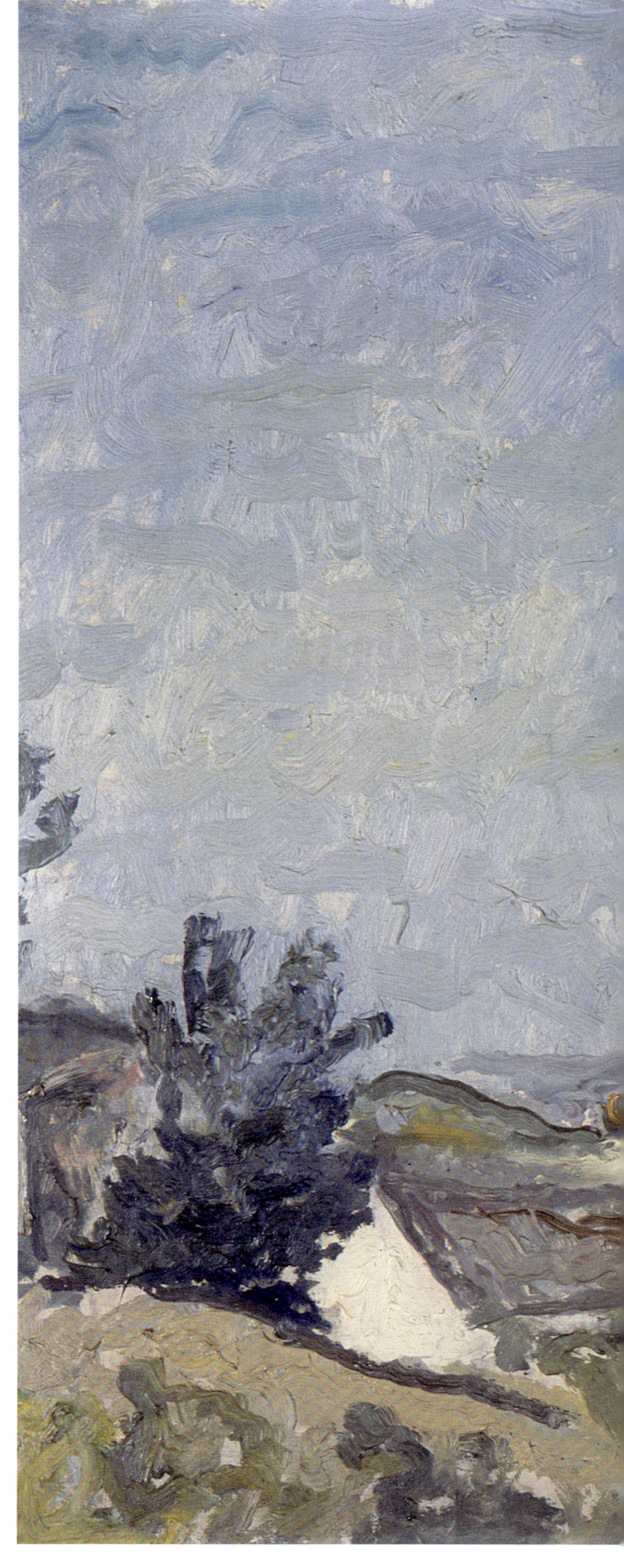

LANDSCAPE
(PAESAGGIO)
1925–29
oil on canvas
61 × 83 cm
Private collection

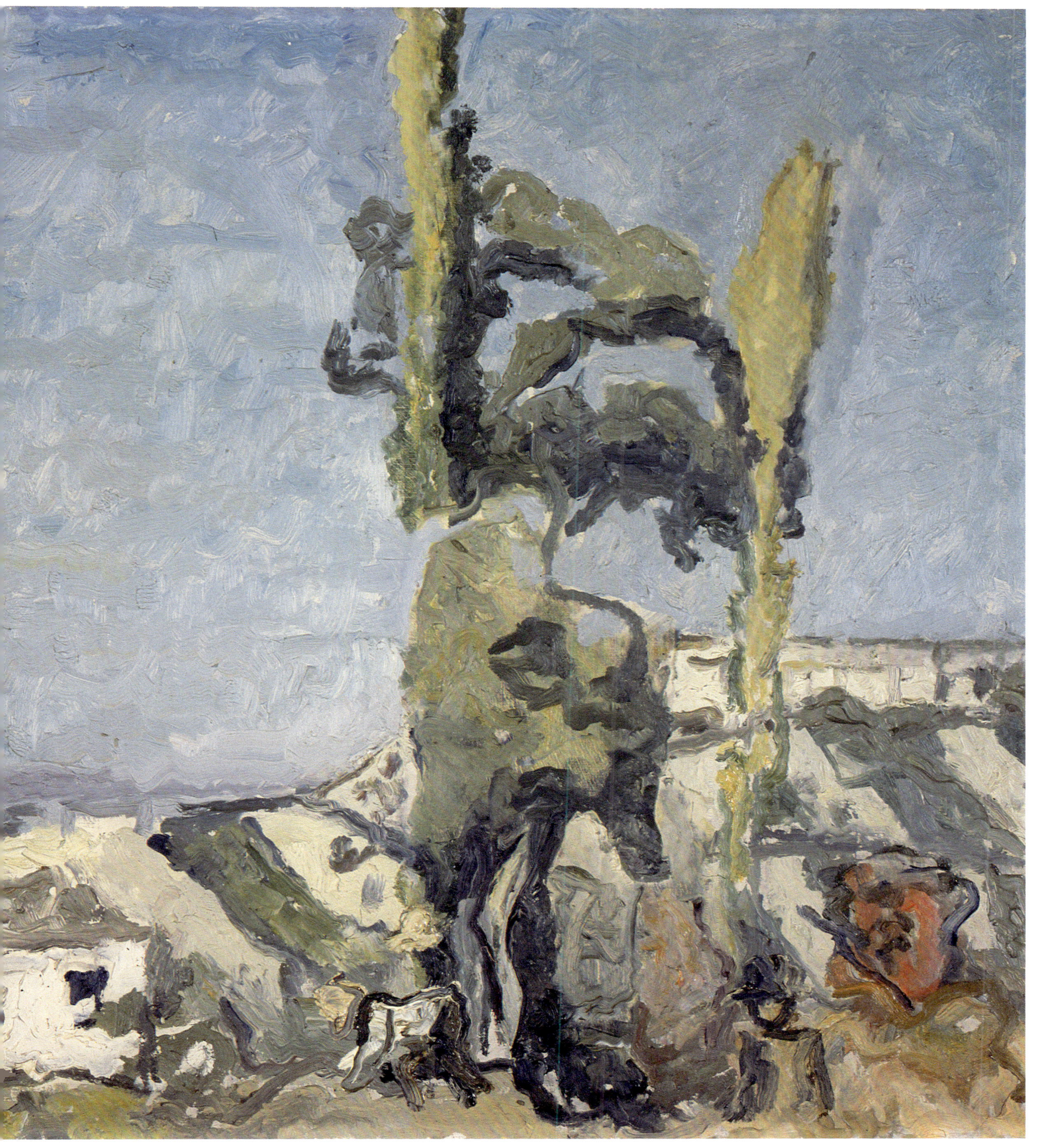

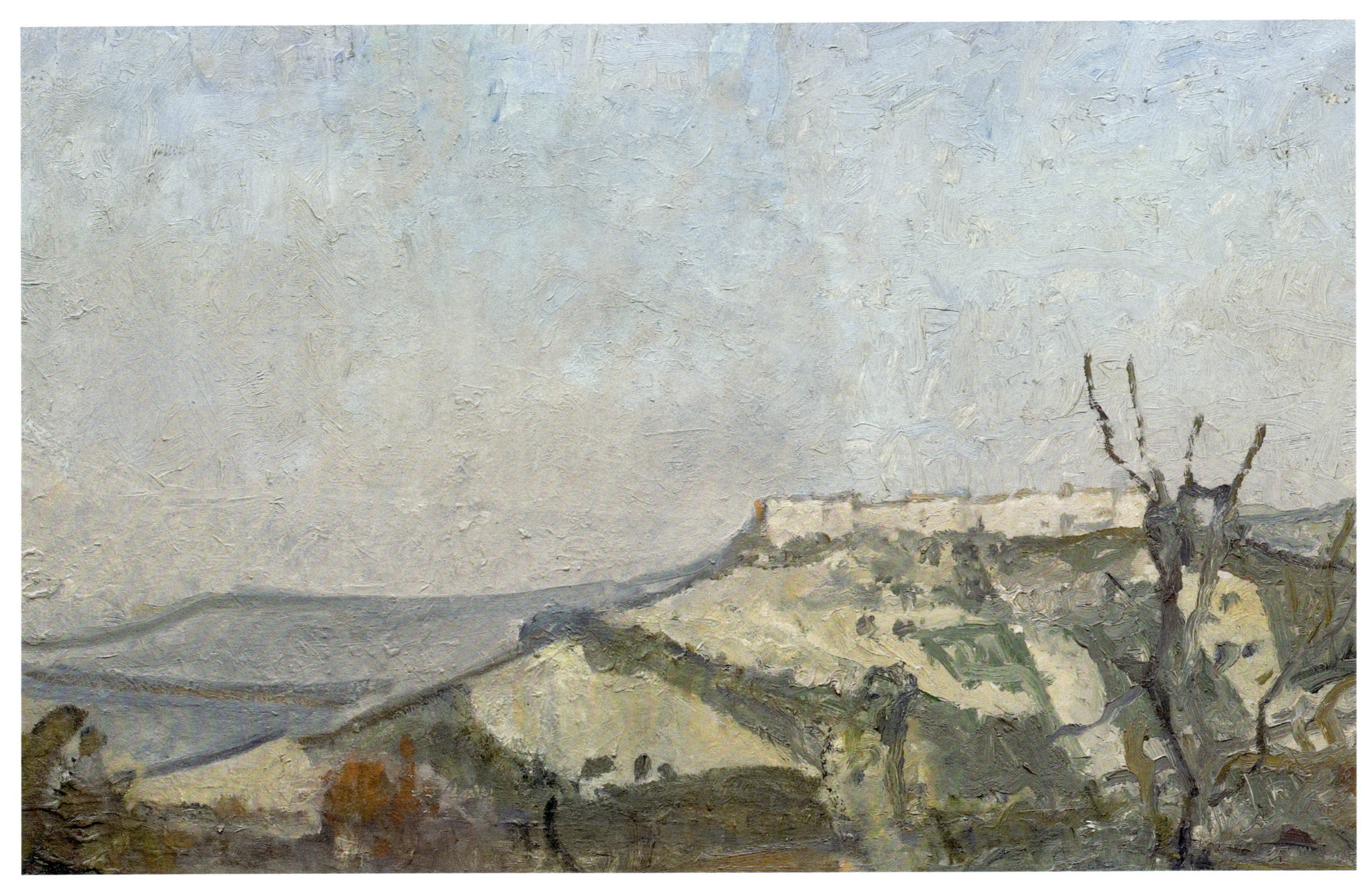

LANDSCAPE, FALERONE
(PAESAGGIO FALERONE)
1925
oil on canvas
54.5 × 81 cm
Gori Collection,
Fattoria di Celle, Pistoia

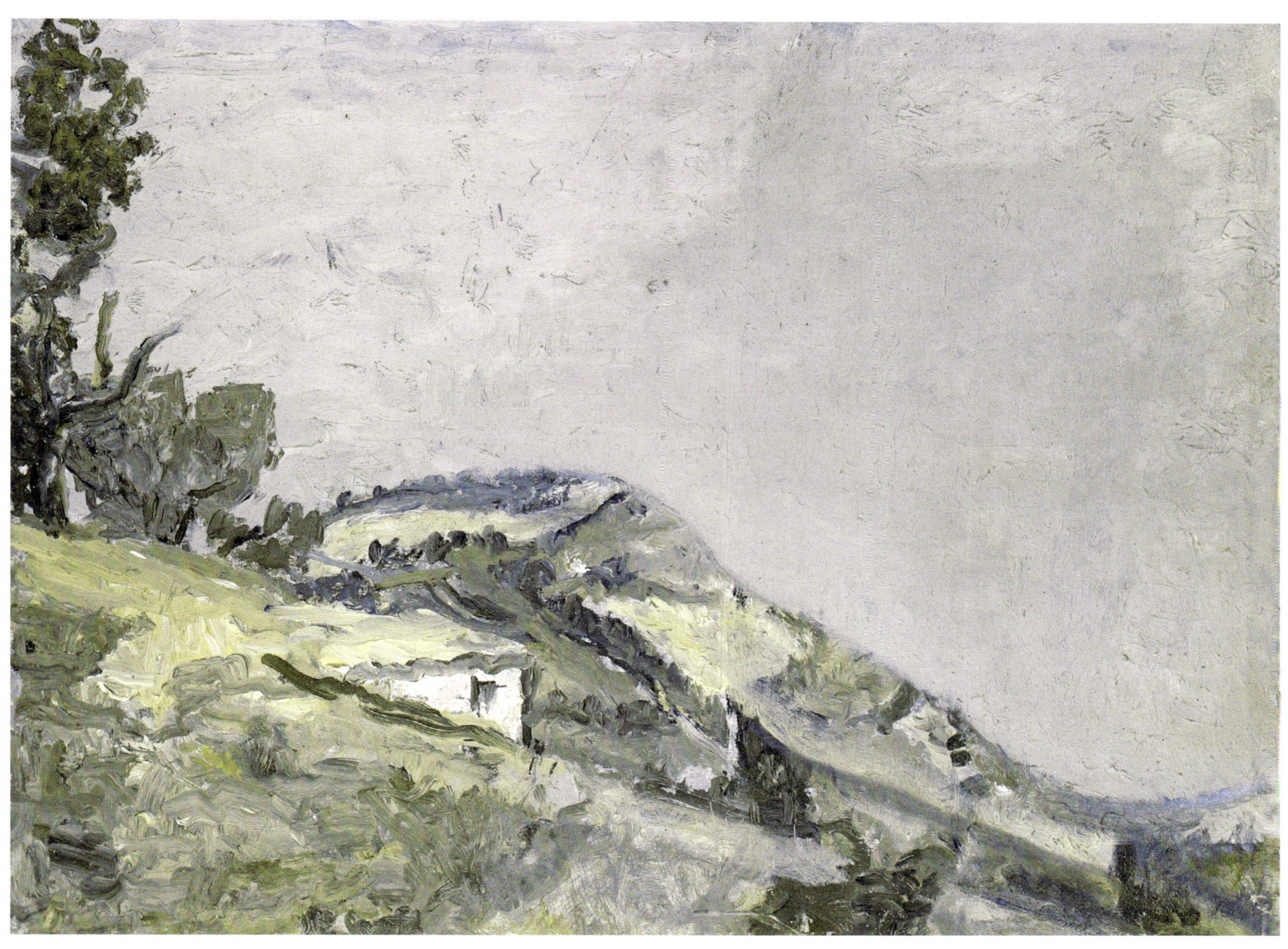

LANDSCAPE OF THE MARCHES
(PAESAGGIO MARCHIGIANO)
1926
oil on canvas
50.5 × 65.5 cm
Fondazione Musei Civici di Venezia,
Galleria Internazionale d'Arte Moderna,
Ca' Pesaro, Venice (inv. 2219)

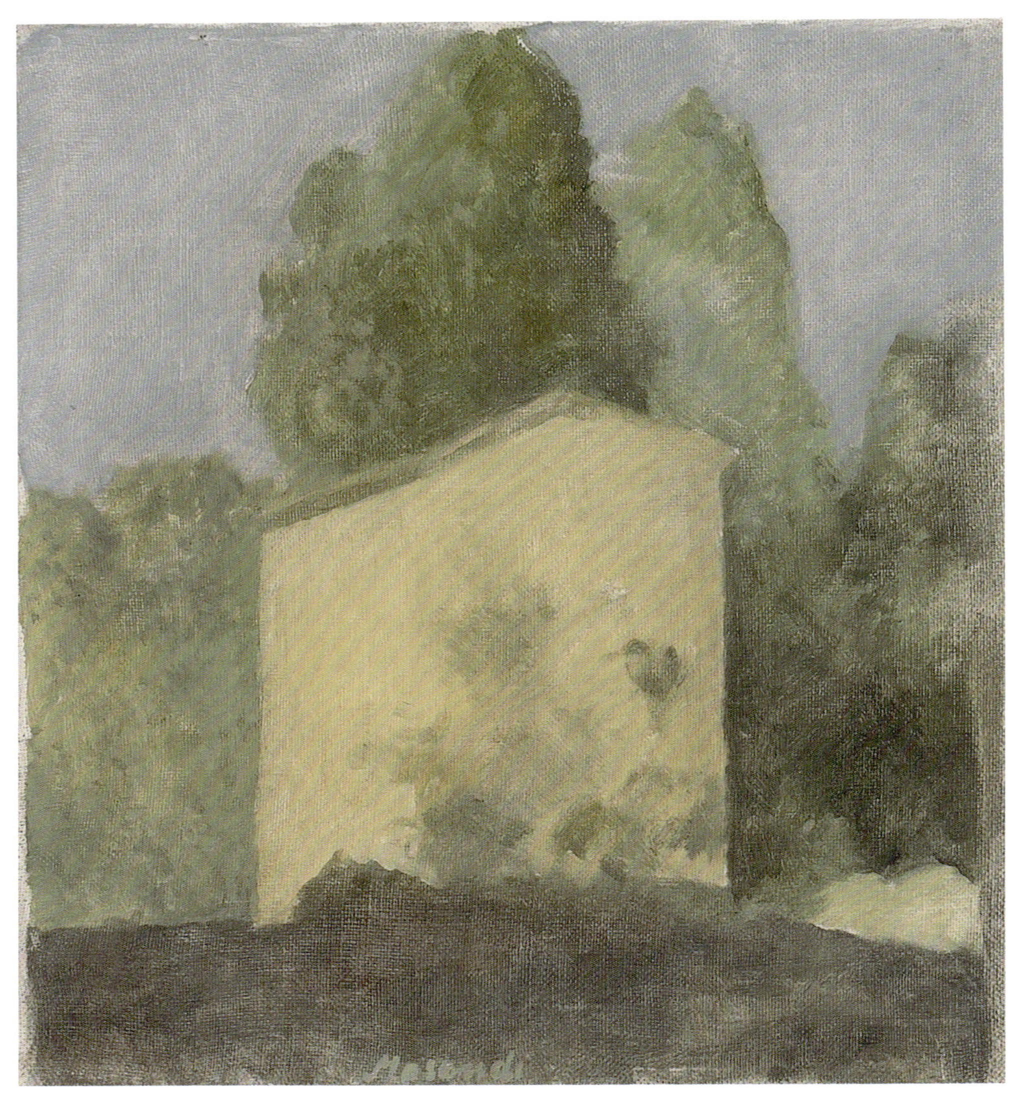

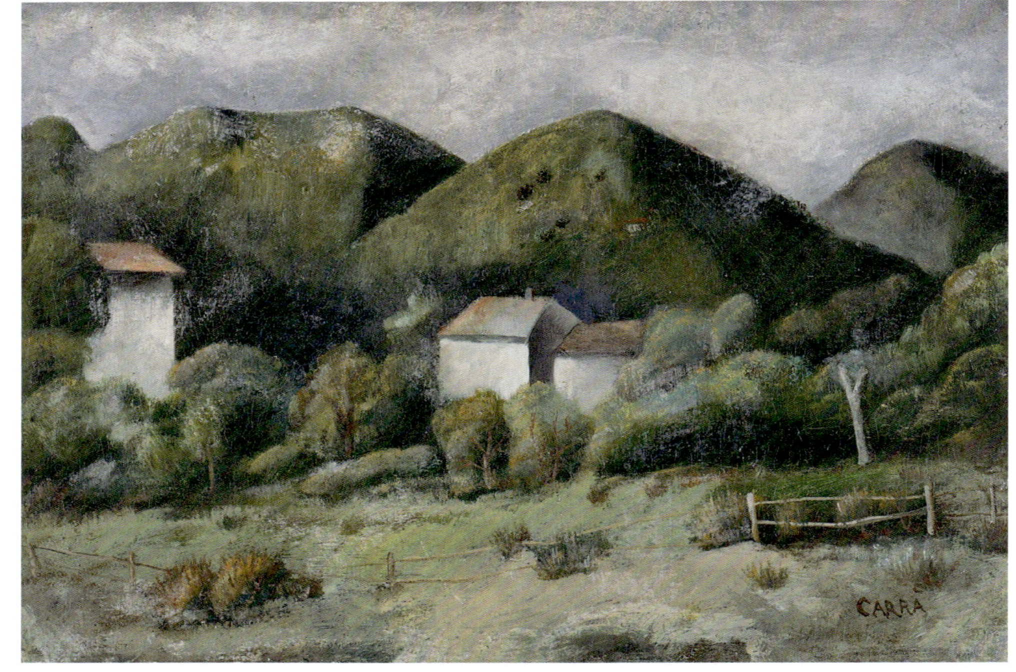

Giorgio Morandi
LANDSCAPE
(PAESAGGIO)
1921
oil on canvas
33 × 29 cm
Istituzione Bologna Musei,
Museo Morandi v.66

Carlo Carrà
LANDSCAPE OF VALSESIA
(HOUSES ON THE PLAIN)
(PAESAGGIO DI VALSESIA
[CASINE NEL PIANO])
1924
oil on lined cardboard
31 × 44 cm
Private collection, Milan

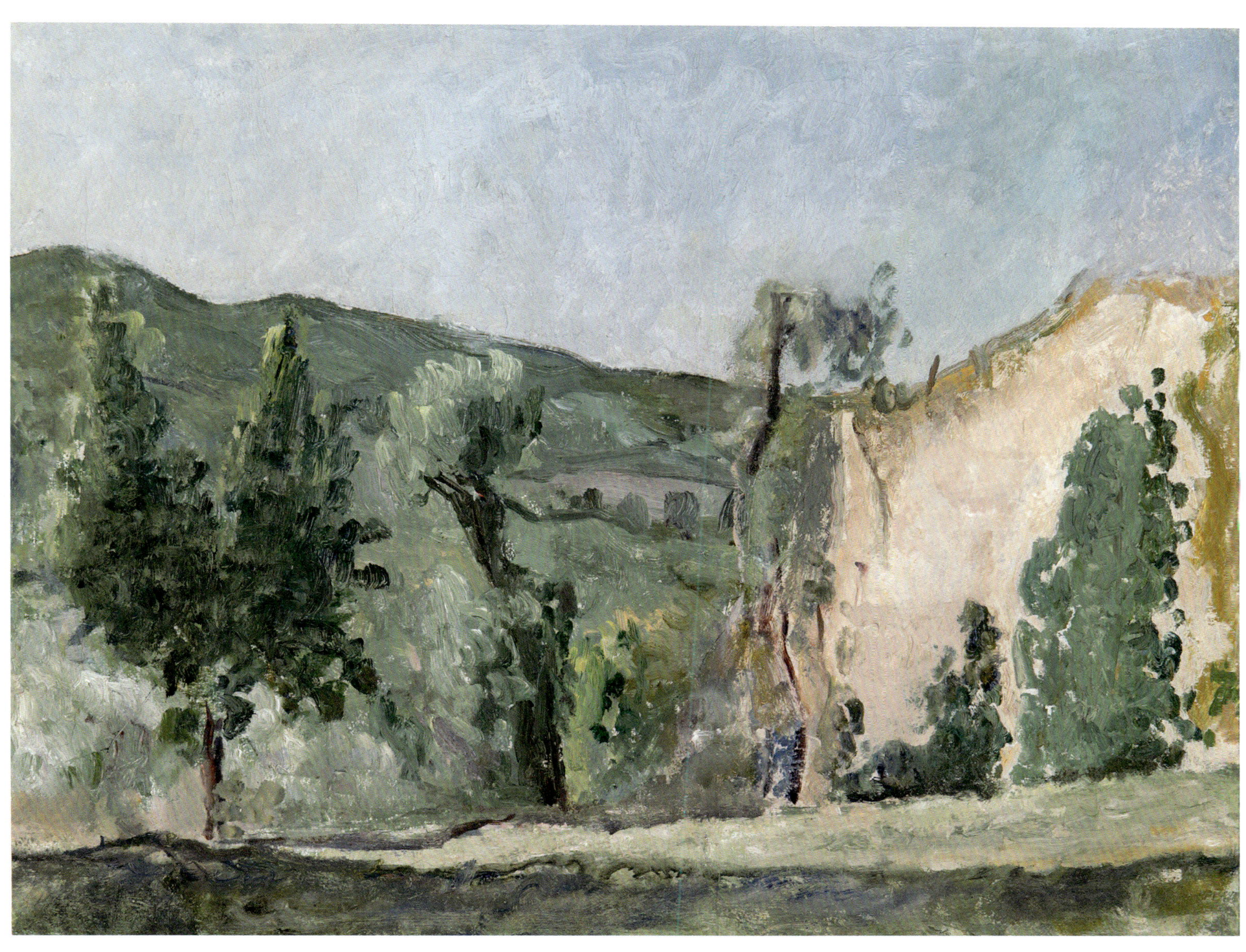

LANDSCAPE
(PAESAGGIO)
1928
oil on canvas
50 × 65 cm
Musei Civici Fiorentini –
Collezione del Novecento, Florence

LANDSCAPE NO. 2
(PAESAGGIO N. 2)
1926
oil on canvas
44.5 × 64 cm
Fondazione Carima –
Museo Palazzo Ricci, Macerata

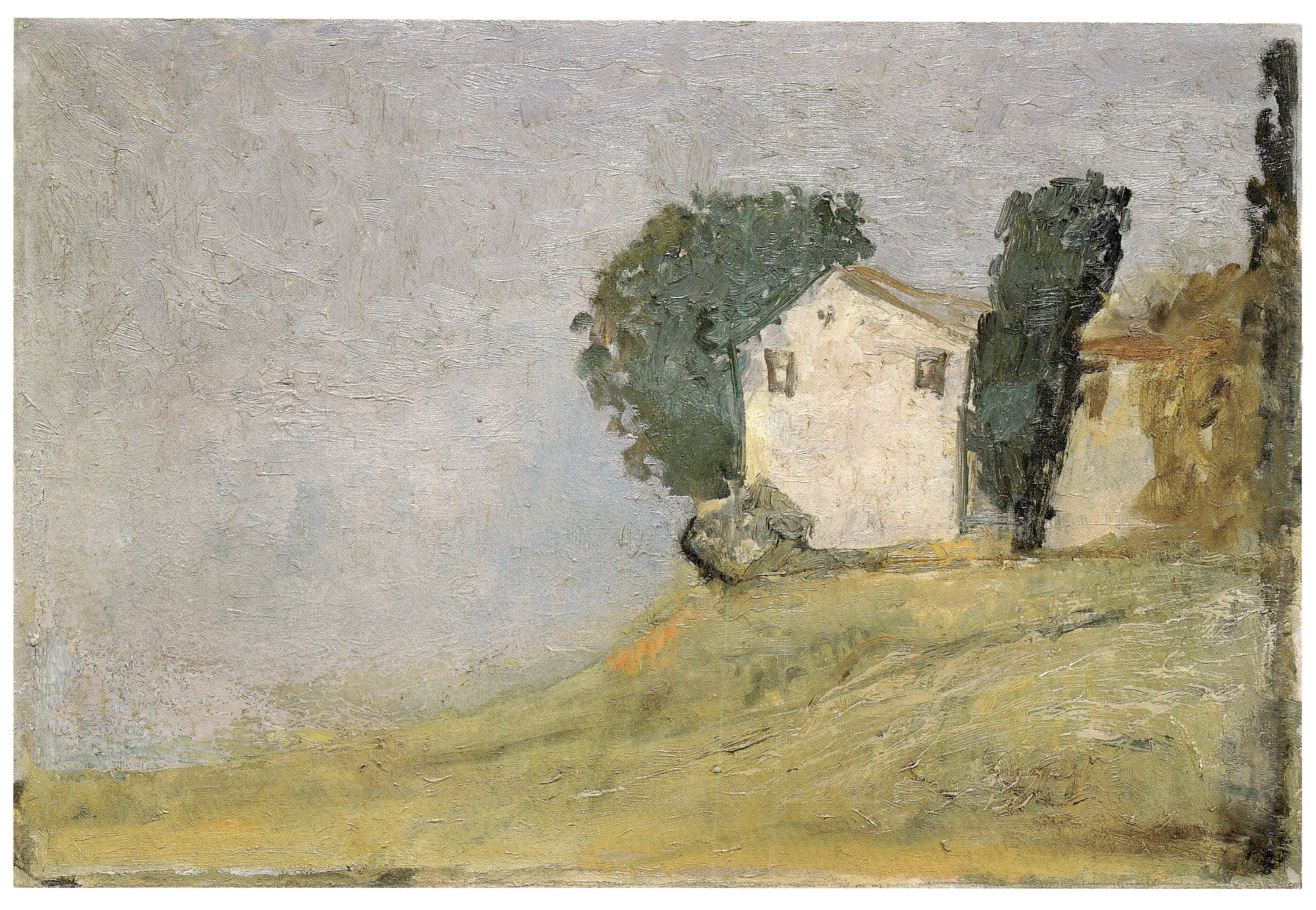

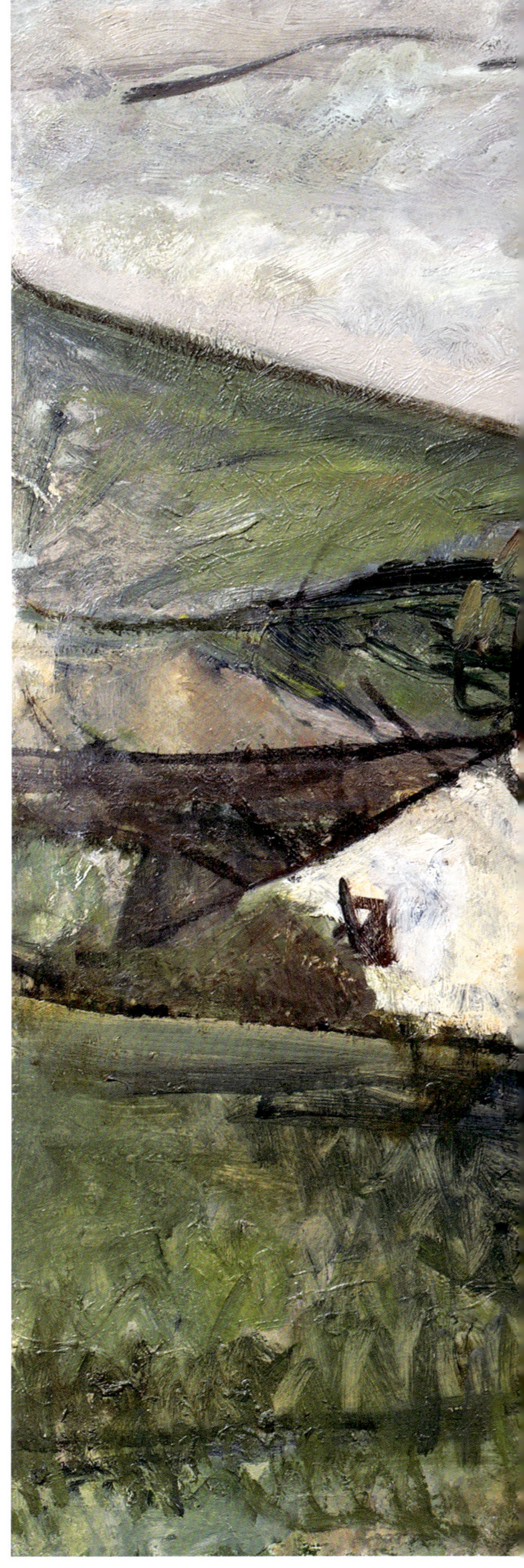

LANDSCAPE WITH MAN (MONTEFALCONE)
(PAESAGGIO CON L'UOMO [MONTEFALCONE])
1926
oil on canvas
65.5 × 81 cm
Lorenzo Licini collection

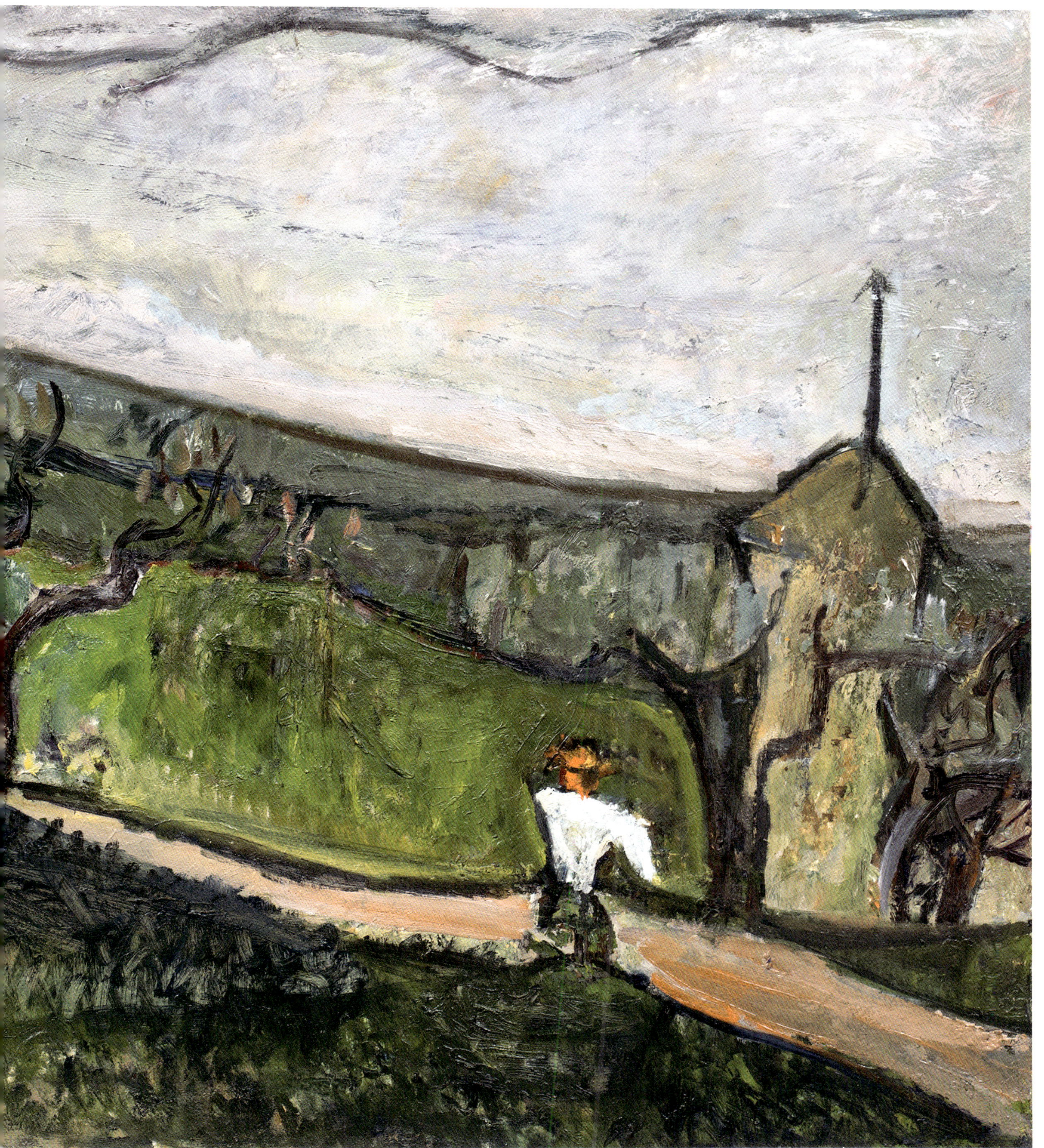

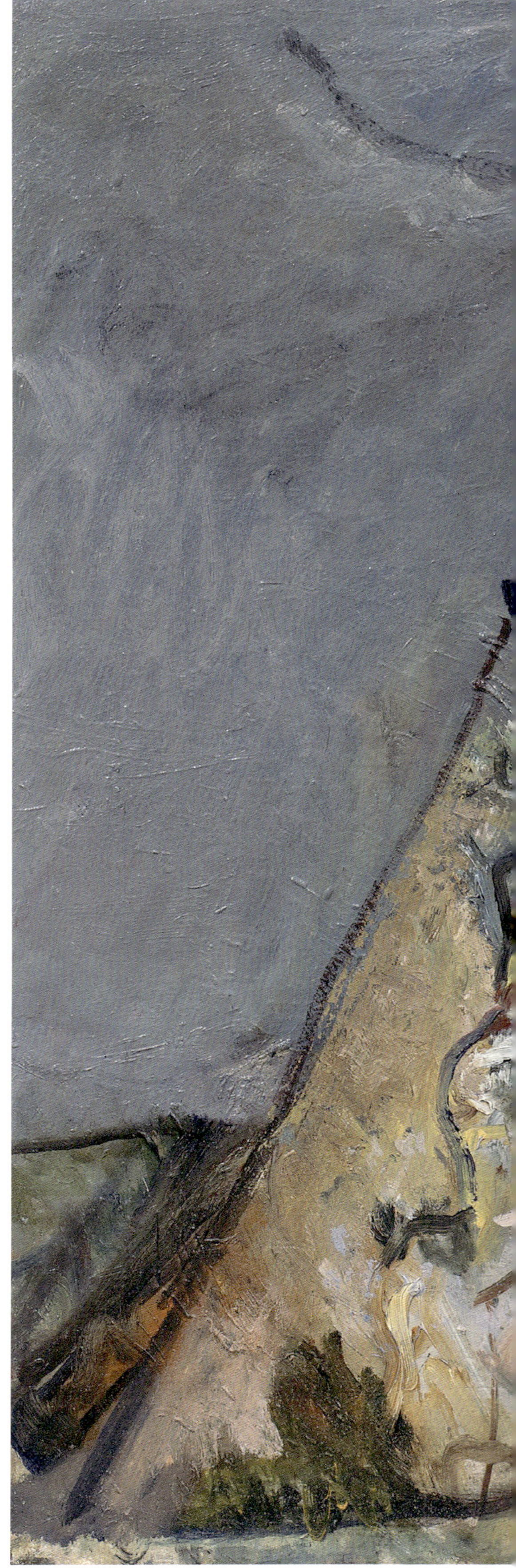

landscape of the marches (the trough)
(paesaggio marchigiano [il trogolo])
1928 (reworked in 1942)
oil on canvas
64 × 80.5 cm
Silvia Poli Licini collection

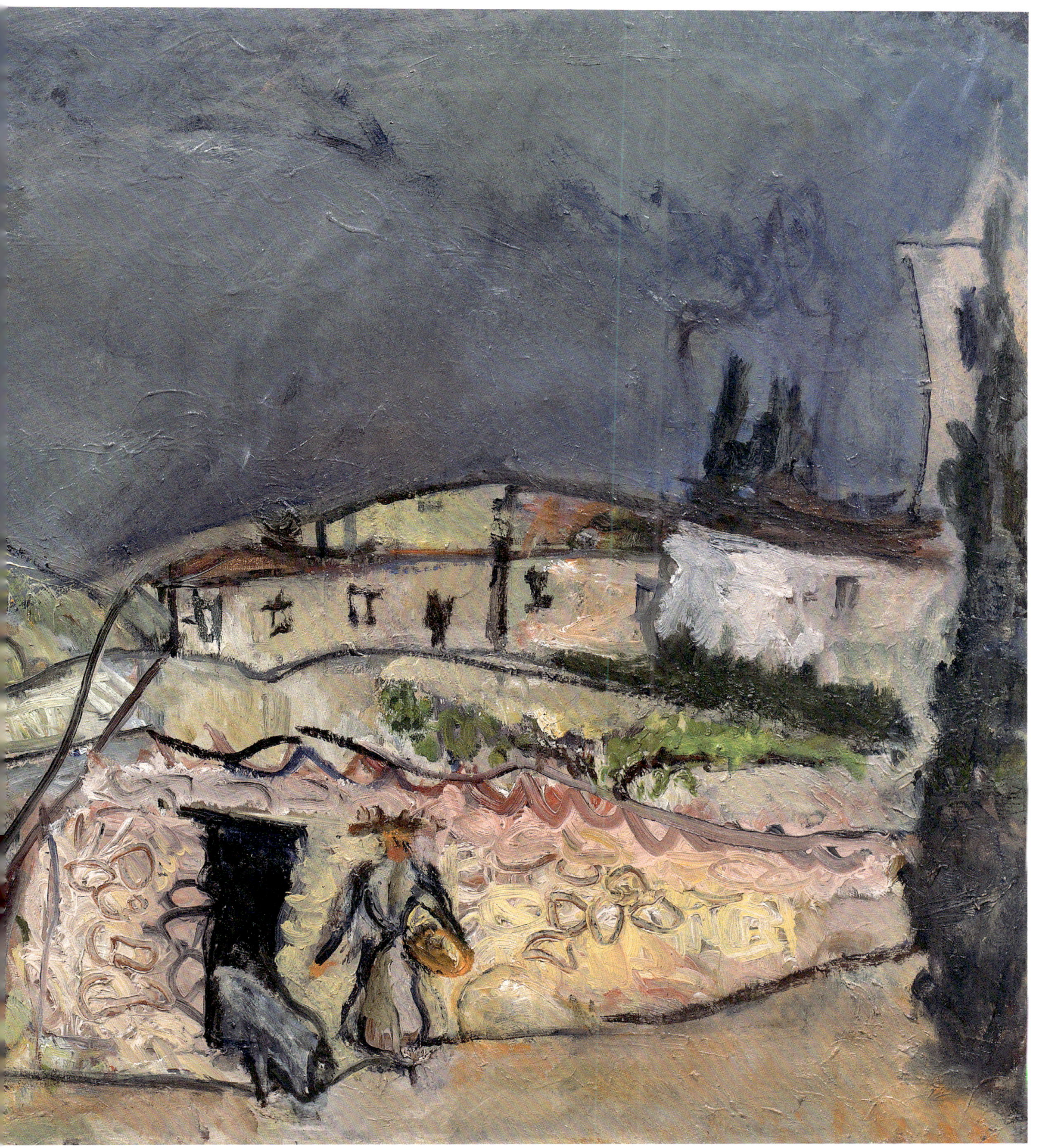

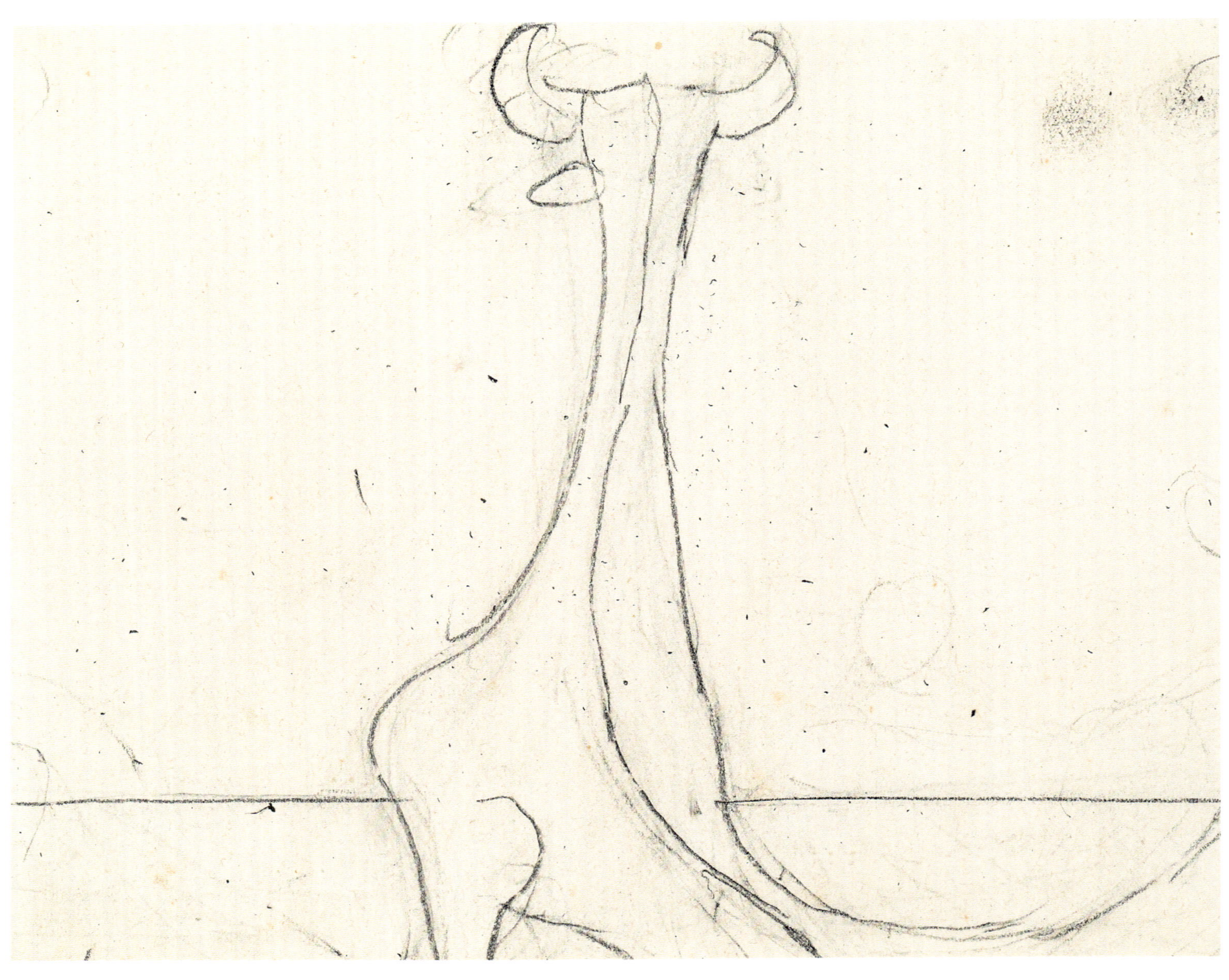

STUDY FOR IMAGINARY LANDSCAPE (BILLY GOAT)
(STUDIO PER PAESAGGIO FANTASTICO [IL CAPRO])
1927
pencil on paper
19.5 × 24.5 cm
Private collection

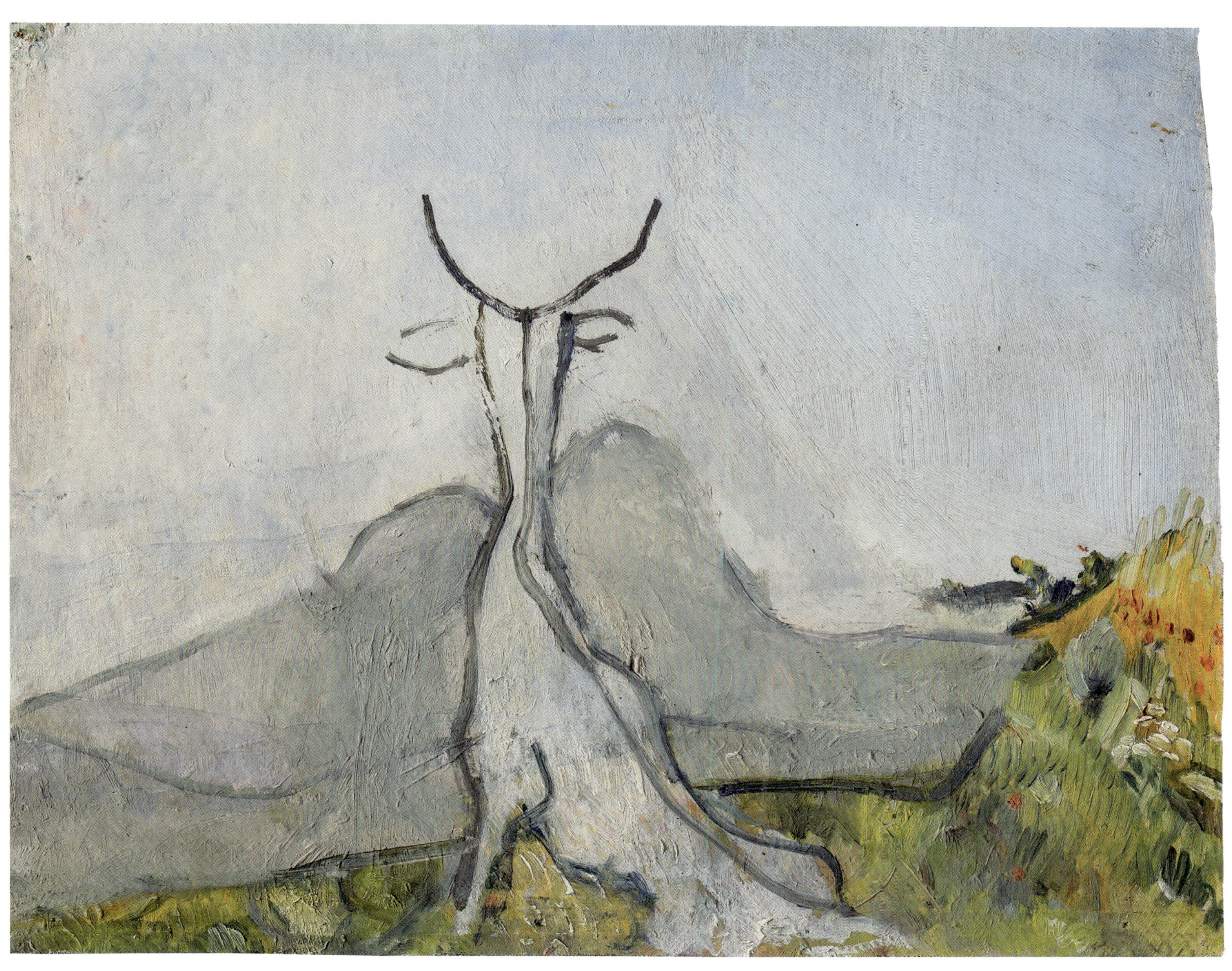

IMAGINARY LANDSCAPE (BILLY GOAT)
(PAESAGGIO FANTASTICO [IL CAPRO])
1927
oil on canvas
33 × 42 cm
Private collection

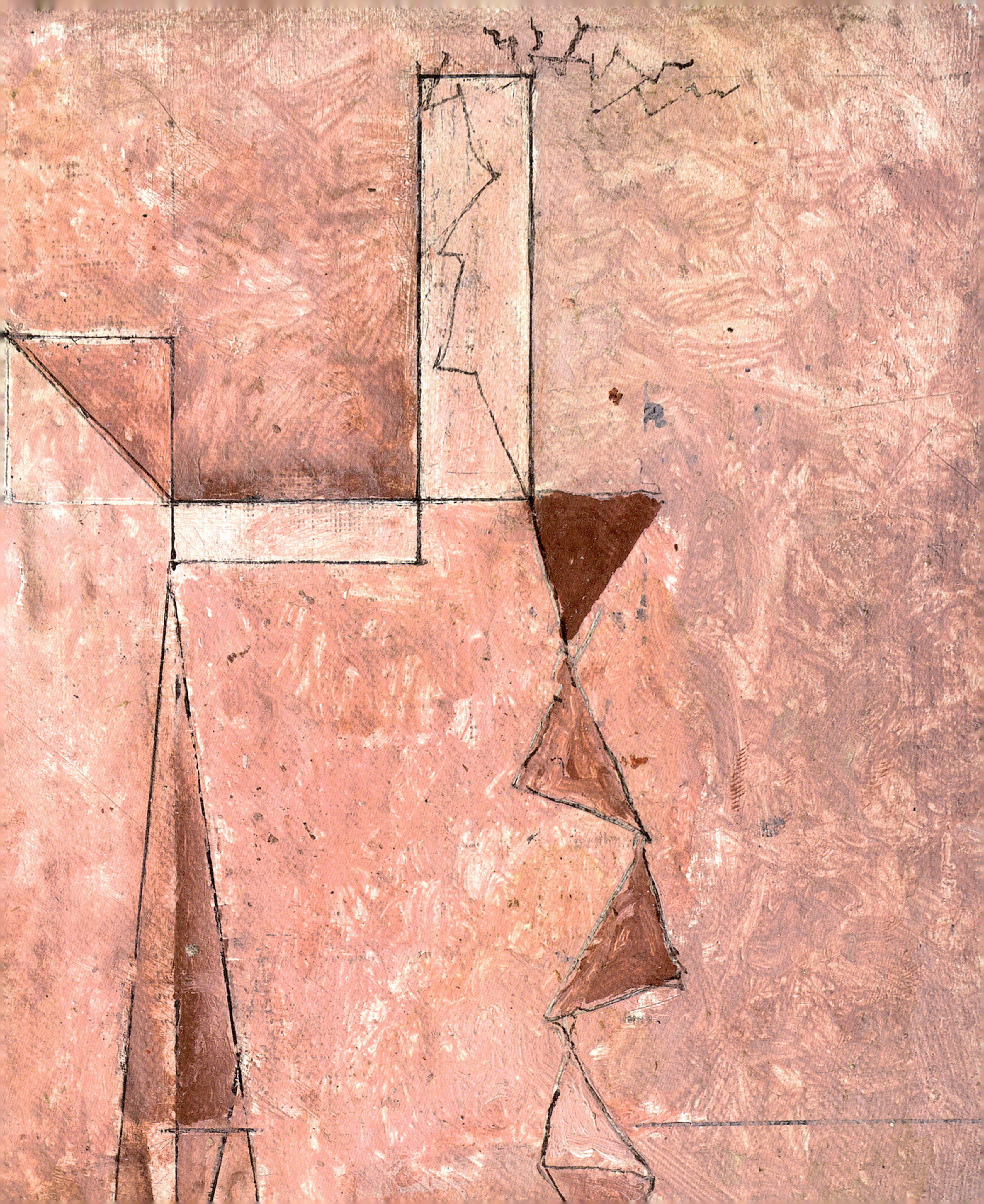

§

EXPLORING ABSTRACTION

> Until four years ago I did all I could to make good paintings by working from life. Then I began to have doubts. Doubt is not a weakness, but an act of strength, like forging, as Descartes said. And I came to the realization that I was making, like many others, outdated art, out of time and contrary to its own true nature, which is not imitation. Painting is the art of colors and forms, freely conceived, and it is also an act of will and of creation, and contrary to architecture, it is an irrational art, predominated by imagination and fantasy, which is to say, poetry. So, I took two hundred good canvases that I had painted from life and I brought them up to the attic. And four years ago, I began inventing my own paintings.[22]

In this 1935 text, written on the occasion of his first solo exhibition in Italy, held at the Galleria del Milione in Milan, Licini identifies the beginning of the decade as the transition point from paintings made "from life" to abstract compositions, unbound by figurative references. The text had a long incubation, as evidenced by the description of the landscapes of the 1920s. It conveys neither a reduction of the representational to abstract form nor a purely geometric composition. On December 1, 1932, Licini wrote to the publisher Giovanni Scheiwiller:

> You are certainly unaware that for the past two years I have been making completely abstract paintings, which I have never exhibited. Almost all of these latest paintings are in Paris, as I brought only a dozen very small works (ca. 30 × 20 cm) in a surrealist style of my own.[23]

VARIABLE
(L'INCOSTANTE)
1932
oil on canvas
mounted on board
24.5 × 18.3 cm
Galleria Tega,
Milan
detail

Toward the end of 1931, returning from a trip to Sweden, Licini stopped in Paris, where interest in abstraction had been revived by the emergence of several new groups and affiliated magazines: Art Concret, promoted by Theo van Doesburg, and Cercle et Carré, mainly associated with Michel Seuphor, were already active in 1930, and in the following year the international association Abstraction-Création was founded. Licini would join the association in 1935 and appear in the fourth issue of the eponymous magazine together with Lucio Fontana, Virginio Ghiringhelli, Fausto Melotti, Mauro Reggiani, and Luigi Veronesi. As Luciano Caramel pointed out: "The evolution of Licini's abstraction within an international milieu … is proof not only of his diversity [but] also of his chronological priority with respect to the other currents of Italian abstraction."[24] With the exception of the atypical Fontana, and of the investigations by Prampolini and Munari, Italian abstraction commenced in 1934, the year of the *Prima mostra di arte astratta* by Oreste Bogliardi, Ghiringhelli, and Reggiani at the Galleria del Milione in Milan. The gallery was the driving force of Italian Rationalism and abstraction, and Licini had taken an interest in its activity in 1932.[25] His involvement with the latest developments in international abstraction ran concurrently with his rediscovery of an "elementarism," Birolli pointed out, that constituted a "renewed moment of 'revelation'":

> Licini does not reduce the world to just any image, he searches for platonic archetypal ideals in a sort of limbo, in an Elysian field, in his own *Memories of the Afterlife*; for this reason, he sets about his work as an abstract artist by starting from primordial forms and corrupting them with foreign organic bodies (*Nocturne* [*Notturno*],1932), or an absolute chromatic-emotional factor (*Rhythm* [*Ritmo*], 1932).[26]

Licini's quest was first identified by Birolli, but it has been examined further in more recent studies, namely by Stefano Bracalente, who documented the references and readings that clarify the artist's interests between 1929 and 1932, the generative phase of his abstraction.[27] Along with reflecting anew on Cubism, which, as the artist writes to Giuseppe Marchiori in 1933, "will fatefully lead to abstract painting," Licini turns an attentive eye to the theme of the "primitive," which the Cubists were among the first to address. He explores it in the pages of the magazine *Cahiers d'art*, to which he subscribes in 1929, sharing its condemnation of the mechanization of society, which led to a departure from spiritual values and the depths of interior life. And it is precisely in this rediscovery of an authentic, primordial dimension that he cultivates an important dialogue in the years to come with the philosopher and historian of religion Franco Ciliberti, as we shall see.

The first opportunity to exhibit the results of his new abstract course was at the second Rome Quadriennale in 1935, where he showed three works, *Castle in the Air* (*Castello in aria*) (1933–36, pp. 94–95), *Stratosphere* (*Stratosfera*) (1933), and *Precarious Balance* (*Il bilico*) (1934), in room nine with a grouping, albeit unofficial, of abstract painters, including Bogliardi, Ghiringhelli, Cristoforo De Amicis, Alberto Magnelli, and Atanasio Soldati. It is interesting to read an excerpt of the review written on that occasion by the critic Marchiori, who had been very close to Licini since 1932, becoming one of his greatest interpreters and supporters. Marchiori argues that Italian abstraction finds its precedents not only in Cubism, but in Vasily Kandinsky, who had exhibited for the first time in Italy at the Milione in 1934:[28]

> Traces of his influence can be found in *Castle in the Air* by Osvaldo Licini, an artist for many years in flight from reality through a surrealism still not entirely left behind, as is evident in *Stratosphere*, an allusive and symbolic painting far removed from abstract absolutism. A first taste of his march toward purification is *Precarious Balance*, an inverted triangle suspended in white space on the vertex of another gray triangle, which rises from the base of the painting like an assertion of unshakeable certainty. This geometry will not convince the observer accustomed to positivist experiences: "How can a triangle remain suspended like this?" Licini, a solitary sage of the mountains and, like all hermits devoted to contemplation, also a poet, will answer: "By miracle!" An irrefutable logic, because creations of this kind obey laws other than those of gravity. Licini is still too restless to ascend to the Olympian serenity of the abstract skies of sublime platonic speculations.... Hermits have a calm appearance that can be misleading: Licini is an artist who carries a load of explosives in his body.[29]

Marchiori's opinion is significant not only because it highlights the anything but "platonic" temperament of Licini's abstraction, but also because of his astute description of the artist's character and his often-mystic isolation. Already from the title, *Castle in the Air* becomes representative of both Licini's lyrical soul—his constant openness to an aerial, immaterial, and unearthly dimension of flight—and his peculiar abstract language—far from mathematical investigations of space and flowing instead from the rhythms and "arabesques" of line and sign. Licini tellingly defines this painting as "irrational," fundamentally built on imbalances, on analogies, on the subtle dialogue of colors, as we see in *Rhythm* (*Ritmo*) of 1933 (p. 93), incunabulum of a theme subsequently taken up and developed in *Castle in the Air*.

In the first half of the 1930s drawing returns to the fore. Drawing is a leitmotif of Licini's art, with its compositional value as a generator of space, but also in its "infantile," "originary," and "primitive" dimension. In *Pink Kite* (*Aquilone rosa*) (1935, p. 101) the delicate and evocative color scheme, the linearity of the human figure, and the landscape reduced to a few sparse marks (the kite-sun, the horizon line that echoes the mountains and hills of the works from the 1920s) seem to approach the graphic language of Paul Klee.[30] This is also true in the distribution of triangles in *Variable* (*L'incostante*) (1932, p. 77). A "variable" cypher characterizes a work Licini exhibited at the Milione, *Capriccio No. 2* (*Capriccio n. 2*) of 1932 (p. 83), where it delineates an open form, almost a *V*, a spatial architecture that we encounter in later works, like *The Millionaire* (*Il milionario*) and *Memories of the Afterlife* (*Memorie d'oltretomba*) (both 1938, pp. 127, 112–13). A geometric, triangular motif that creates outward directional lines lies instead at the center of other, apparently more rational works. *Abstract Lines on a White Background* (*Fili astratti su fondo bianco*) of 1930 (p. 73) and *Precarious Balance* (*Il bilico*) of 1932 (p. 75)[31] recall the forms in *pointe sur pointe* equilibrium of the Swiss artist Sophie Taeuber-Arp, one of the key figures of the Cercle et Carré and Abstraction-Création groups. However, the personal, authorial aspect of these works is detached from any influence, whether French or German: these diminutive paintings are incunabula, foundational even in their dimensions, and reflect the intimacy of his underlying quest.

In Licini's work we never find a purely monochromatic field of color, a contour simply filled with paint, but invariably a dynamic dialogue between sign, drawing, and material. Perhaps the most emblematic examples of this are *Abstract Outlines on a Red Background (Scherzo)* (*Schemi astratti su fondo rosso [Scherzo]*) (1932, p. 85), characterized by a sense of extreme synthesis, and *Dragon* (*Drago*) (1933, p. 91), which is born of the encounter between the rhythmic play of the triangles on the left and the free line drawing on the right. The title of the latter suggests a recognizable image and carries with it a series of historical references, from Paolo Uccello to Vittore Carpaccio and Cosmè Tura, however charged with irony.

Moreover, in Licini's abstractions a crepuscular mood emerges—as in *Nocturne* (*Notturno*) (1932–33, pp. 80–81), *Memories of the Afterlife*, and *Bird 2* (*Uccello 2*) (ca. 1936, pp. 102–03)—or a cloudy, dreamlike atmosphere—as in *Capriccio No. 2*. This alchemical aspect, this profundity, leads us to a surrealist realm. What Licini calls "a surrealist style all my own" is not the Surrealism of André Breton, but that of the nineteenth-century French poets to whom Breton's movement was also looking: from Comte de Lautréamont to Charles Baudelaire to the *poètes maudits*. Elsewhere, when he is irreverent, Licini's humor is akin to Guillaume Apollinaire's, and when he is heretical, his blasphemy recalls Alfred Jarry.

Licini is like a receptive antenna, capable of detecting international signals ahead of his peers, then reconfiguring them in the extraordinary creative workshop of his mind, from which arises his highly personal grammar of signs. One must not forget that abstract art was at the time considered avant-garde, opposed to the realism dictated by the regime. Licini looked to abstraction from an almost intimist point of view to protest the "hyperreality" that was gaining the upper hand in Italy, in a much bolder and resistant way than other forms of geometric ornamentation.

What emerges is the ineffable discourse of Licini's abstract sign: in this exhibition it enters into a dialogue with the contemporary and equally radical investigations of Fontana and Melotti. Like Licini, the two artists participated in the Milione show of 1935: Fontana with his extraordinary abstract sculptures and metal and scratched concrete; Melotti with works in which "geometry [is the] foundation of the harmony of the sculptural counterpoint."[32] Later that year, in March, the three artists participated in the *Prima Mostra Collettiva d'Arte Astratta Italiana*, organized in Turin and accompanied by a declaration from the exhibitors, where geometry is defined as "the key to modernity": "With its inflexible and infinite laws, it excludes any arbitrary flights of creative imagination."[33] The declaration showed some affinity with Melotti's aesthetic, but was very far from the intrinsic freedom from rules and canons and the anticlassicism that characterized both Licini's and Fontana's poetics, though in different ways. As Enrico Crispolti pointed out, writing about the Milione, "only Licini" and Fontana:

> ultimately brought a very astute and in-depth criticism, in the imaginative sense, of the rigor of the 'concrete' approach prevalent in the rest of the group (more or less rigorous constructions of geometric forms and fields of pure color). However, Licini always tended toward the ideal imaginary sphere, while Fontana favored an imaginative pragmatism that dealt directly with matter, light and space, clearly understood as physical."[34]

Licini's alterity with respect to the theoretical positions of the group emerges clearly in his "Lettera aperta al Milione," published as a self-presentation of his solo exhibition, in which he declared "we will demonstrate that geometry can become feeling," and above all in his text "Natura di un discorso" of 1937, in which he expounded his conception of art:

> Art is mysterious to us and cannot be defined. We also confess that beauty will always escape our calculations, and it is good that this be so. Like all things of nature, enigmatic, deceitful, beautiful but fraudulent. What is important is that the lie is clever.... Enemies of every formula, we refuse to give an exact definition of Abstraction.... We are abstract artists by the psychological law of compensation, that is, by reaction to the excessive naturalism and materialism of the nineteenth century.... We would be architects, but not being able to stand a cone or a pyramid upside down, to suspend a sphere or build castles in the air, ours will be the art of painting. We take this opportunity to remind that painting is the art of colors and marks. Gestures express strength, will, ideas. Colors express magic. We said marks, not dreams.[35]

The "fraudulent" beauty described by Licini is reflected in the "deceitful," ironic, and playful geometry of *Tasting* (*Assaggiare*) (1934–36, pp. 96–97) and *Biting* (*Addentare*) (1935–36, pp. 98–99), whose abstract forms recall the image of a mouth, a subject addressed in the same years with words (*Mouth* [*Bocca*], 1934, p. 121). And it is precisely the irony, the instability, the "precarious balance" between the abstraction and the lyrical and imaginative attachment to the forms of the world, often evoked in the titles, that marks Licini's distance from Carlo Belli, the theorist of the group. Belli had published with the Galleria del Milione in 1935 the essay "Kn," the "bible of abstract art." To Belli's proclamation of art as "universality," unbound from the human sphere and from any state of mind, Licini responded with the idea that geometry can become feeling and be fully rooted in humanity. To Belli's hypothesis of works with no titles nor authors, thus only identified by sequential acronyms (k, k1, k2, and so on), he responded with titles that are rich with meaning, active on the level of analogy, and at times agents of a dislocation between reality and unreality. In the same way, Licini's declaration of an impossible architectural stability of pictorial signifiers, free from the force of gravity, puts him in a position of difference with respect to the notion of a collaboration between the arts that are guided by architecture, as sustained by Rationalist architects and by Belli himself. As such, Licini's *Archipaintings* (*Archipitture*) are in the end "anti-architectures": "what is the purpose of a painting if not to … cheer up a wall," he wrote in 1935.[36] His geometry acquires an almost heraldic purity, though with a slight imbalance based on lines of force as origins of asymmetries and rhythms that are emphasized by the alternation of colors. ▸

22. Osvaldo Licini, "Lettera aperta al Milione," *Bollettino della Galleria del Milione*, no. 39 (April 19–May 1, 1935), also in Licini, *Errante, erotico, eretico*, 99.
23. Lettera from Osvaldo Licini to Giovanni Scheiwiller of December 1, 1932, in Licini, *Errante, erotico, eretico*, 135.
24. Luciano Caramel, "L'astrattismo anomalo degli anni trenta dell'anomalo Osvaldo Licini," in *Osvaldo Licini. Capolavori*, 28–73.
25. See the letters of Osvaldo Licini to Acruto Vitali of April 4 and November 22, 1932, in Licini, *Errante, erotico, eretico*, 128–29.
26. Birolli, *Storia e temporalità*, 15.
27. Stefano Bracalente, "5R=(2+3) →∞ … Solo una simbologia pitagorica. Le lettere e i numeri enigmatici di Osvaldo Licini," in *Annali della Facoltà di Lettere e Filosofia*, Università di Macerata, XXXVII, 2004, 7–42.
28. The solo show, which opened in May, presented watercolors and drawings from 1924 to 1933. See *Bollettino della Galleria del Milione*, no. 27 (1934).
29. Giuseppe Marchiori, "Arte e fantasia, gli astratti alla II Quadriennale," *Corriere Padano*, March 20, 1935.
30. The 1954 monograph of the Swiss artist by Will Grohmann was preserved in Licini's library, but his knowledge of Klee's work through travel and assiduous reading of international magazines certainly dates back many years prior. Klee showed two works in the German pavilion at the 1928 Venice Biennale, which Licini intended to visit, as he wrote in May to his friend Acruto whom he invited to join him (letter to Acruto of May 26, 1928, in Licini, *Errante, erotico, eretico*, 123).
31. As is known, in most cases Licini's works present problems of dating, due to the absence of documentary sources and because they were often repeatedly reworked over time.
32. Fausto Melotti, introduction for the solo exhibition at the Galleria del Milione, 1935.
33. Introductory manifesto of the participating artists, published in the brochure/catalogue of the *Prima Mostra Collettiva d'Arte Astratta Italiana*: *Bogliardi, De Amicis, D'Errico, Fontana, Ghiringhelli, Licini, Melotti, Reggiani, Soldati, Veronesi,* Studio di Casorati e Paolucci, Turin, Via Barolo 2, March 1935.
34. Enrico Crispolti, "L'avventura creativa di Fontana nell'arte del XX secolo," in Crispolti, *Lucio Fontana. Catalogo ragionato di sculture, dipinti, ambientazioni* (Milan: Skira, 2006), vol.1, 50.
35. Osvaldo Licini, "Natura di un discorso," *Corriere Padano*, October 9, 1937; also in Licini, *Errante, erotico, eretico*, 102.
36. Osvaldo Licini, "Lettera aperta al Milione," *Bollettino della Galleria del Milione*, no. 39 (April 19–May 1, 1935); also in Licini, *Errante, erotico, eretico*, 99.

ABSTRACT LINES ON A WHITE BACKGROUND
(FILI ASTRATTI SU FONDO BIANCO)
1930
oil on board
26.5 × 20.5 cm
Private collection

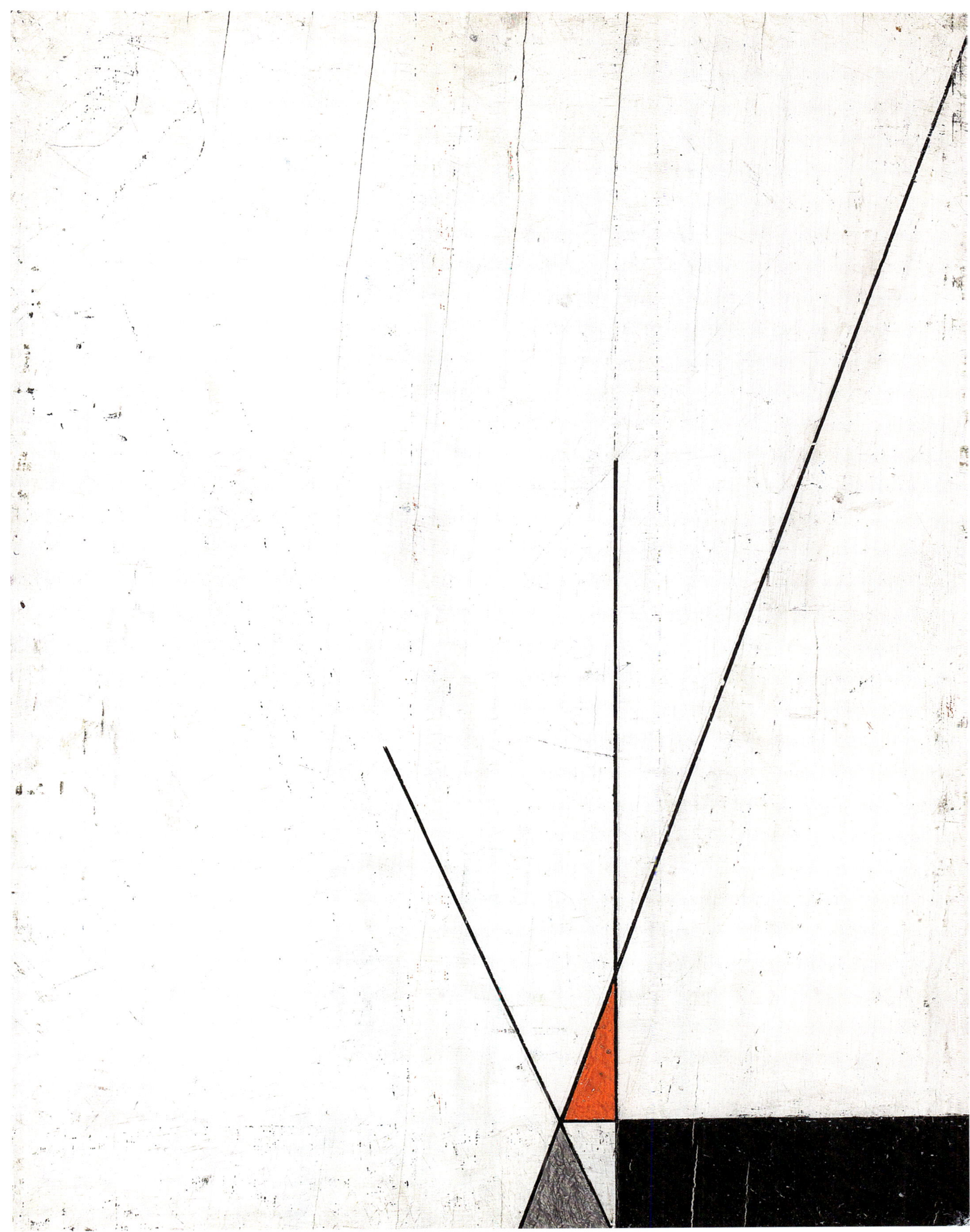

PRECARIOUS BALANCE
(IL BILICO)
1932
oil on canvas
90.5 × 67 cm
Private collection

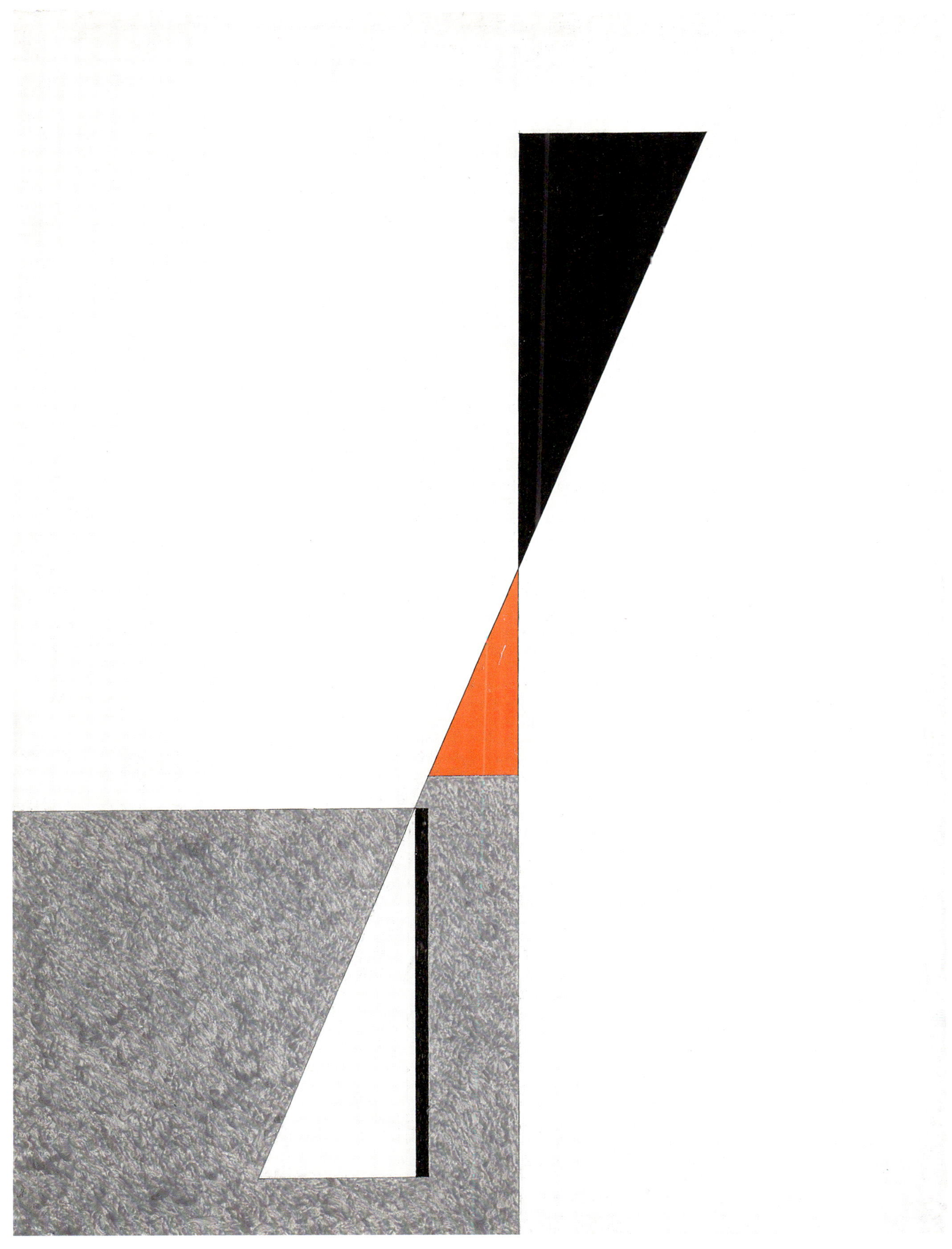

VARIABLE
(L'INCOSTANTE)
1932
oil on canvas mounted on board
24.5 × 18.3 cm
Galleria Tega, Milan

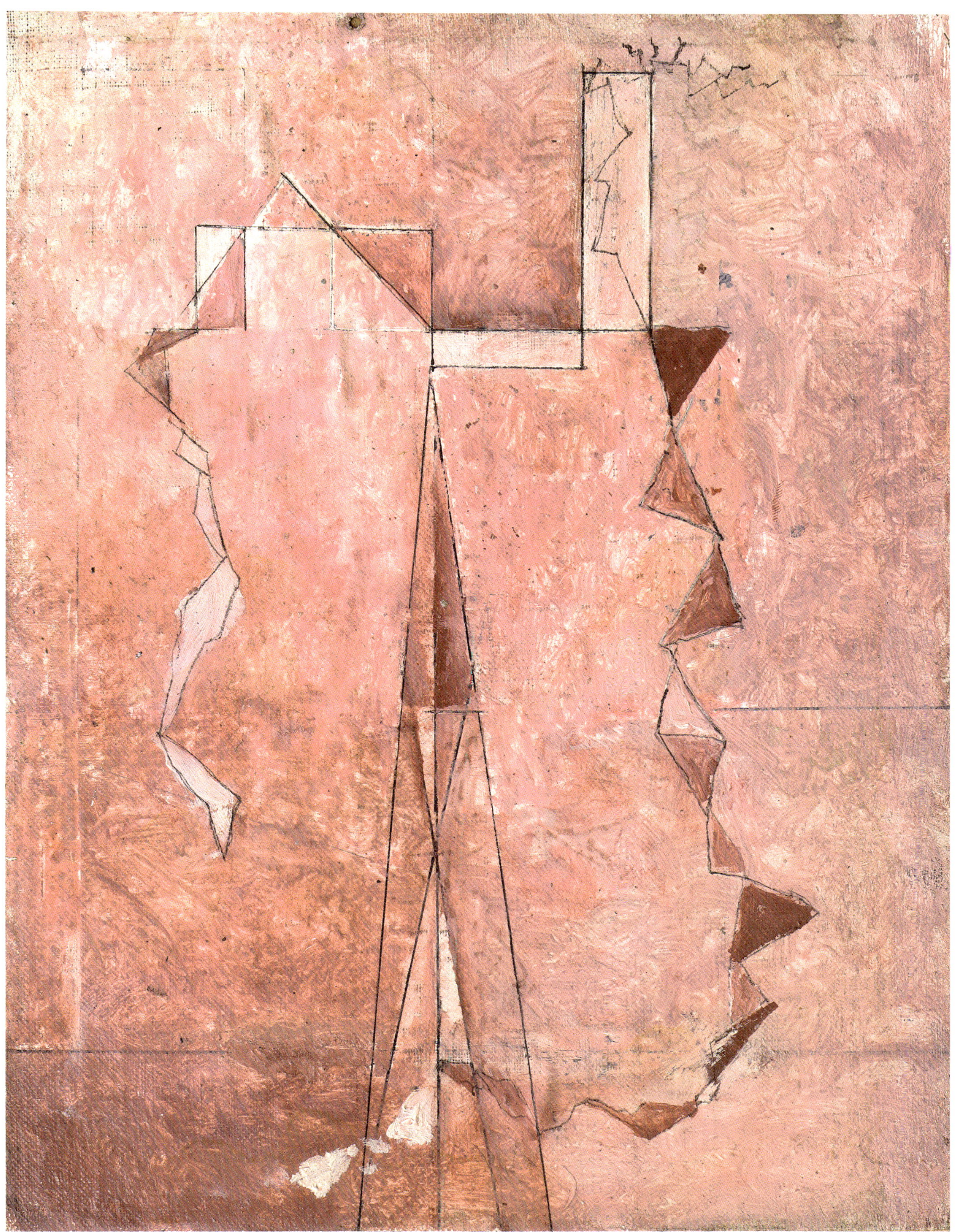

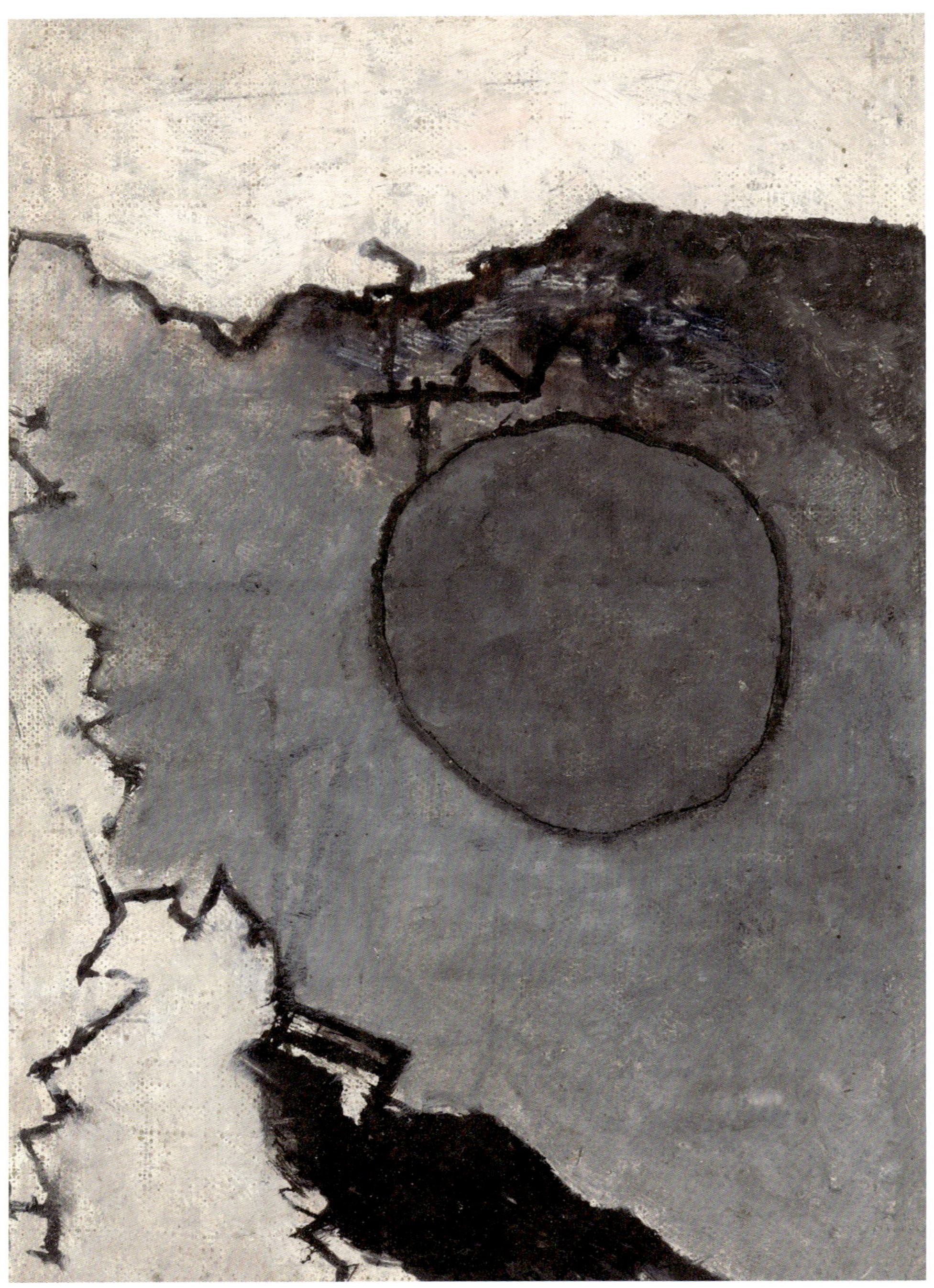

COMPOSITION: TWILIGHT
(COMPOSIZIONE: CREPUSCOLO)
1932
oil on canvas
19.7 × 27.2 cm
Private collection

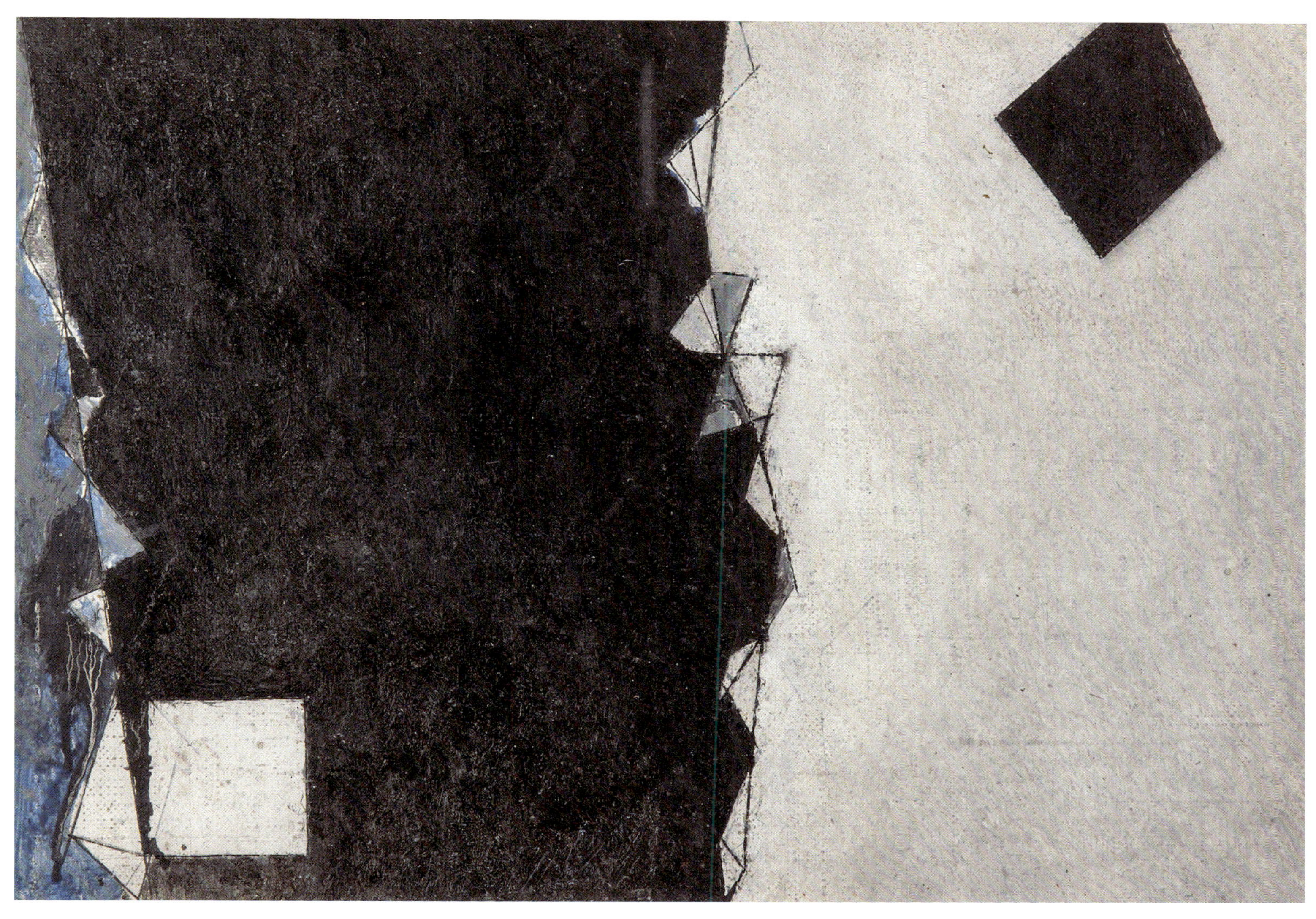

COMPOSITION NO. 10
(COMPOSIZIONE N. 10)
1933
oil on canvas
19.2 × 27 cm
Private collection

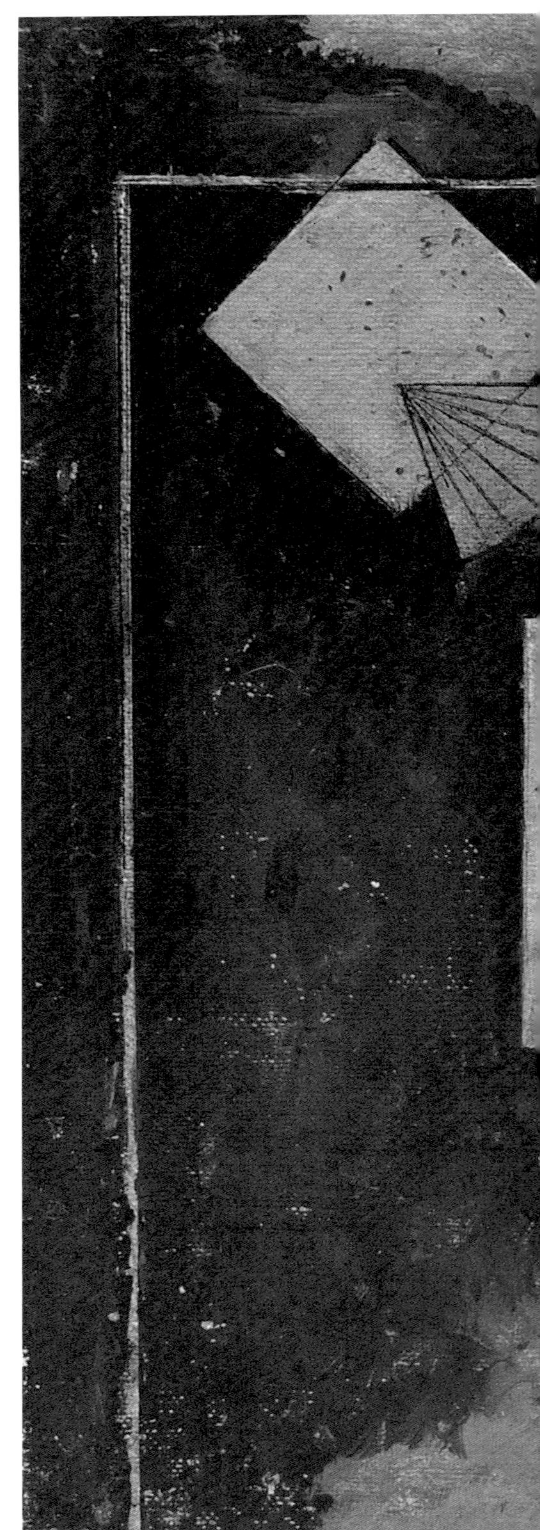

NOCTURNE
(NOTTURNO)
1932–33
oil on canvas
20.1 × 28.1 cm
Augusto and Francesca
Giovanardi Collection

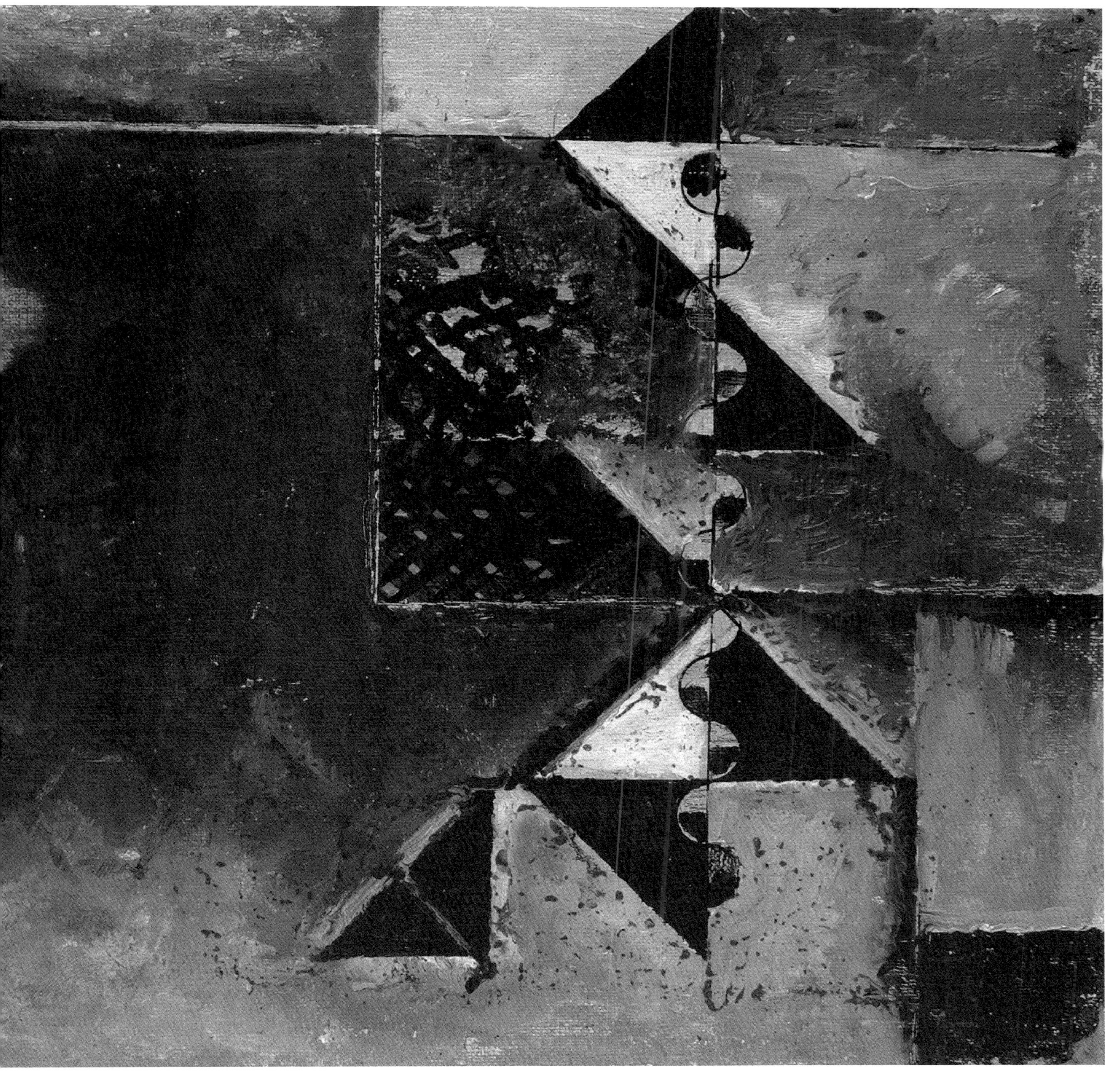

CAPRICCIO NO. 2
(CAPRICCIO N. 2)
1932
oil on canvas
28 × 21.6 cm
Private collection, Milan

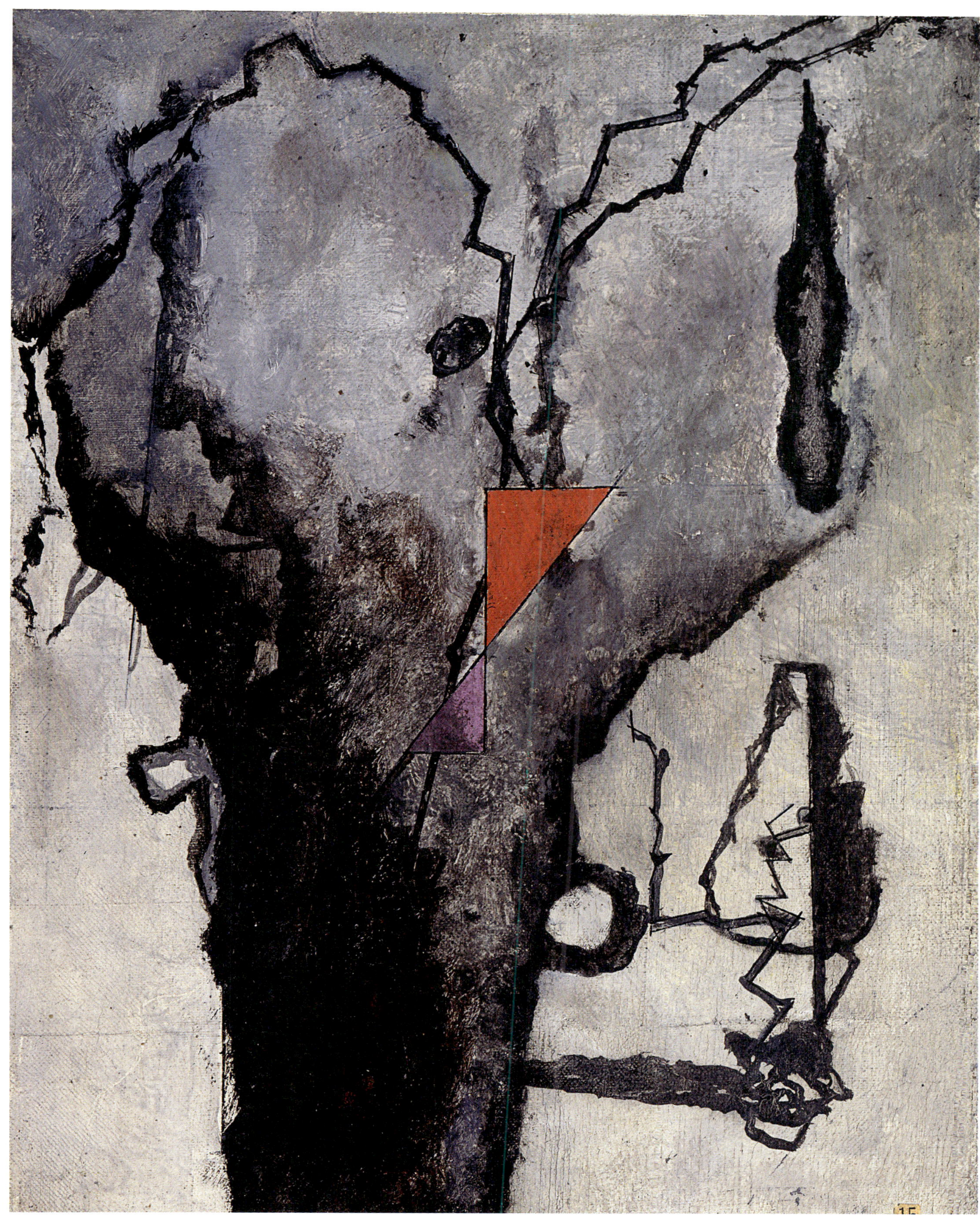

ABSTRACT OUTLINES ON A RED BACKGROUND (SCHERZO)
(SCHEMI ASTRATTI SU FONDO ROSSO [SCHERZO])
1932
oil on lined canvas
18.5 × 26 cm
Collection of the Museo d'Arte Contemporanea
di Villa Croce, Genoa

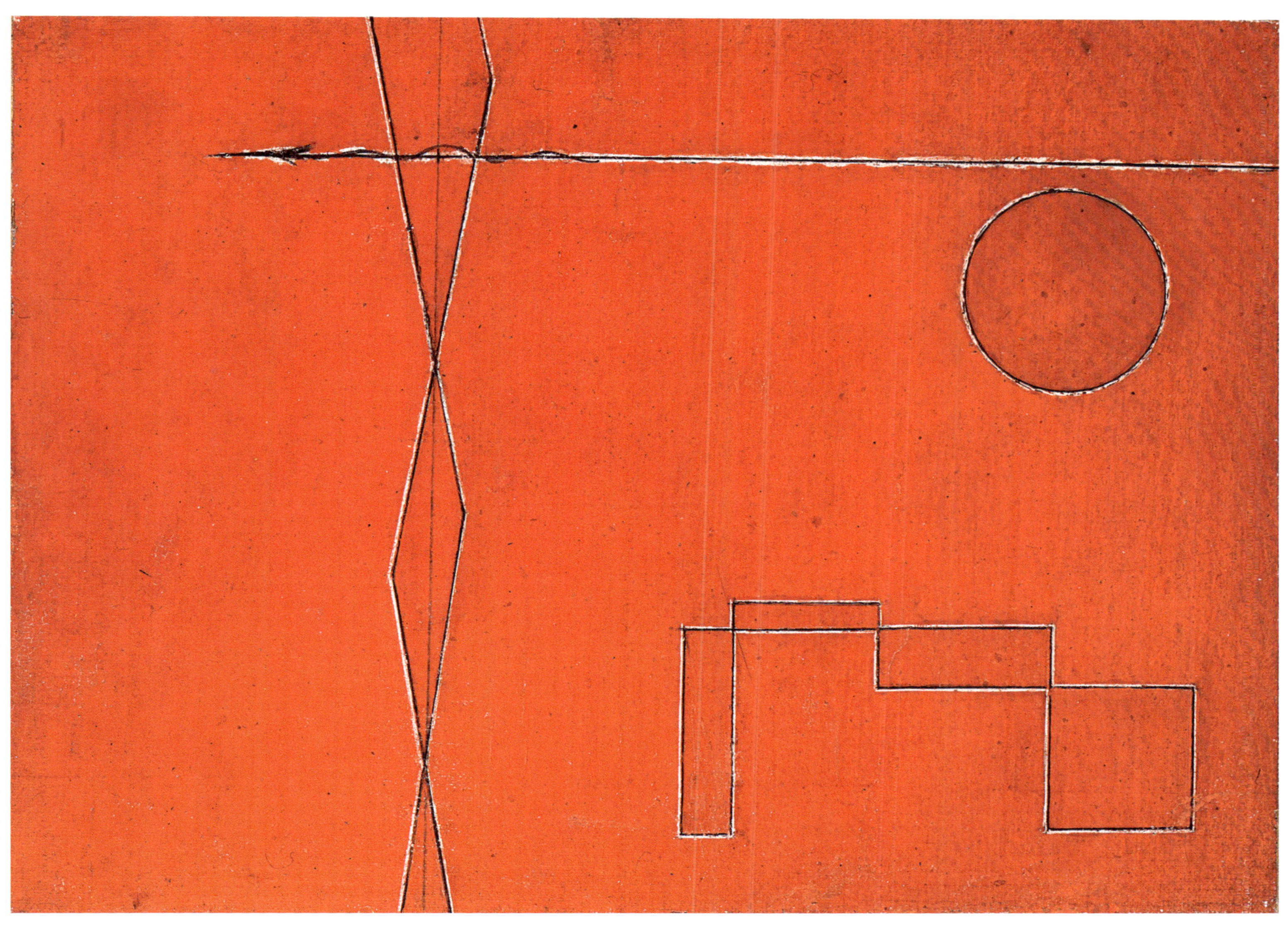

COMPOSITION
(COMPOSIZIONE)
1933
oil on canvas
64 × 48 cm
MART, Museo di arte moderna
e contemporanea di Trento e Rovereto
Provincia autonoma di Trento –
Soprintendenza per i beni culturali

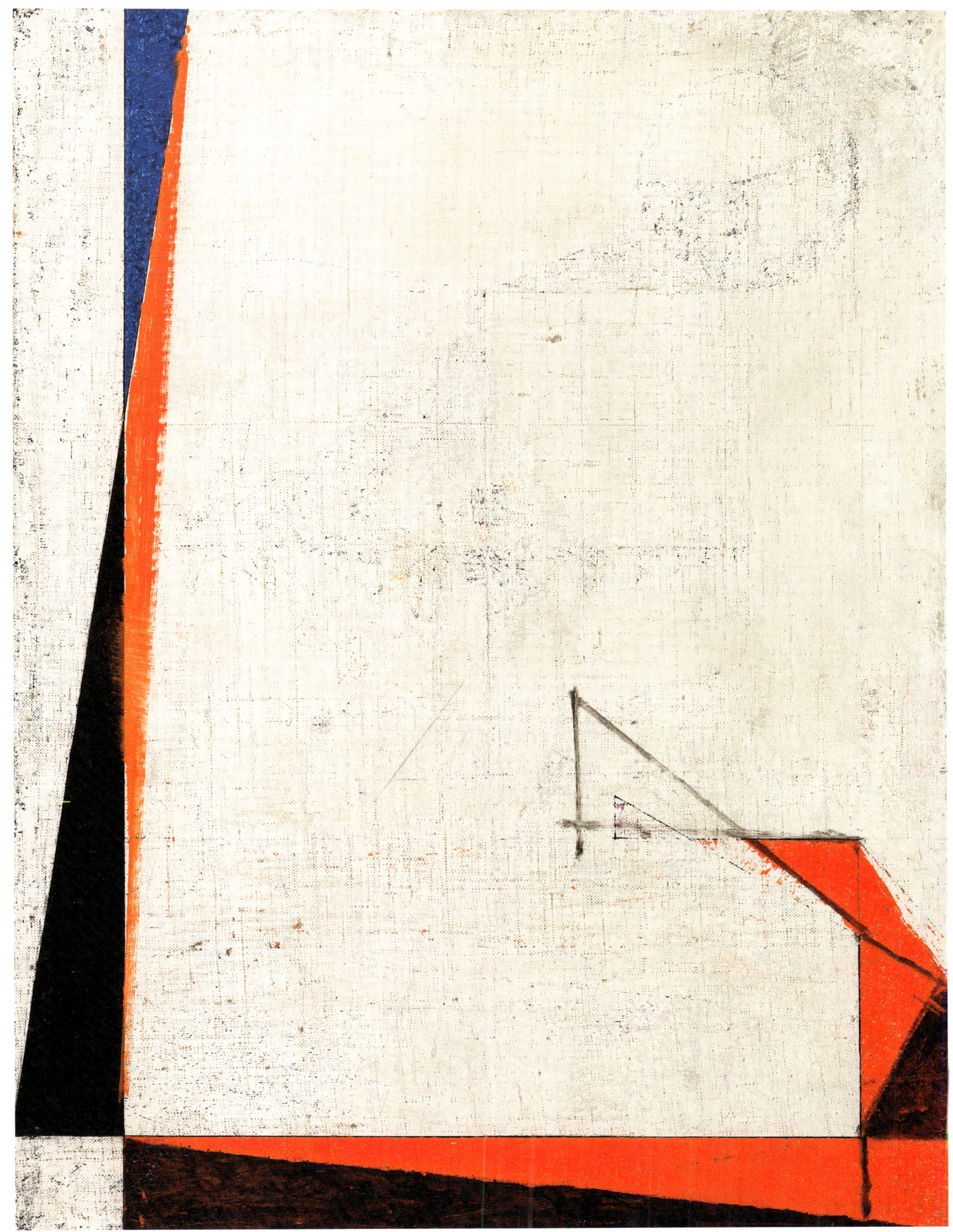

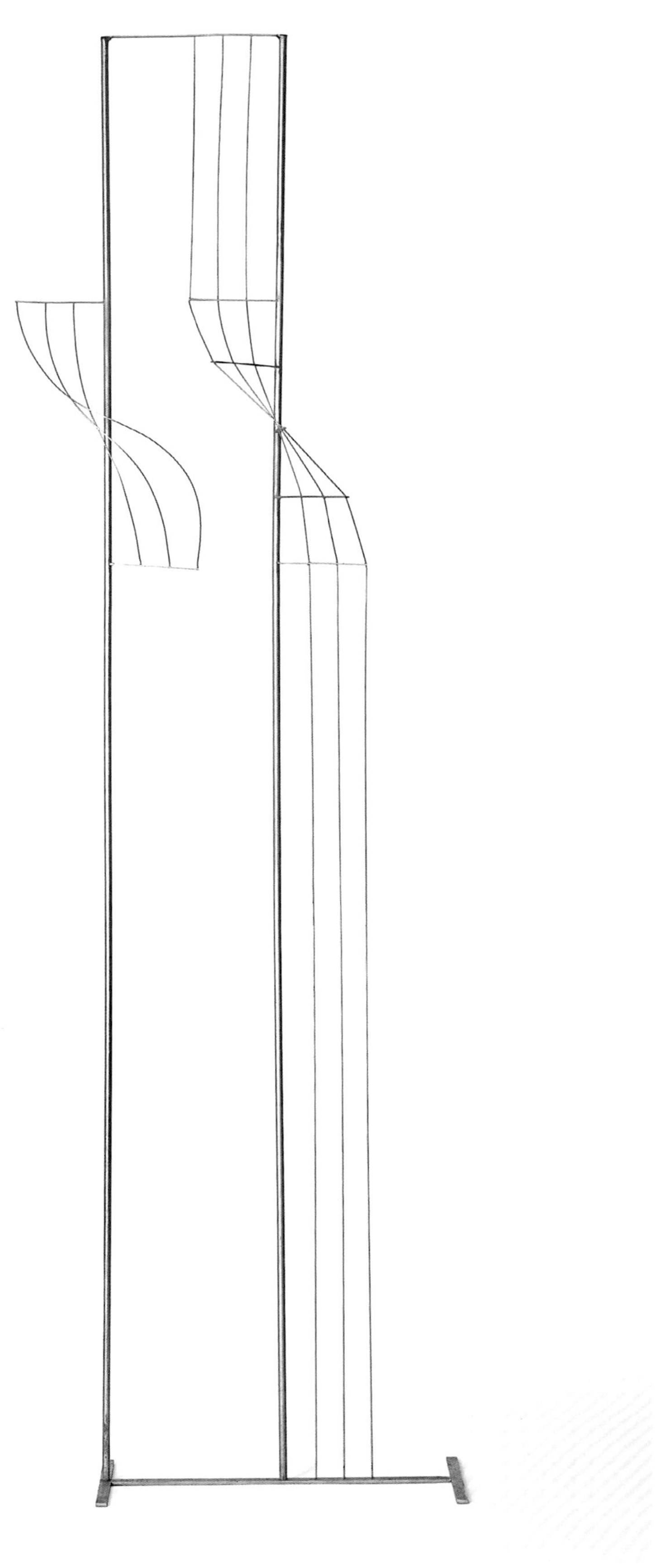

Fausto Melotti
SCULPTURE NO. 17
(SCULTURA N. 17)
1935 (reconstruction, 1968)
stainless steel
196.8 × 59.3 × 24 cm
Museo del Novecento, Milan

OBELISK
(OBELISCO)
1932
oil on canvas
32 × 27 cm
Museo del Novecento, Milan

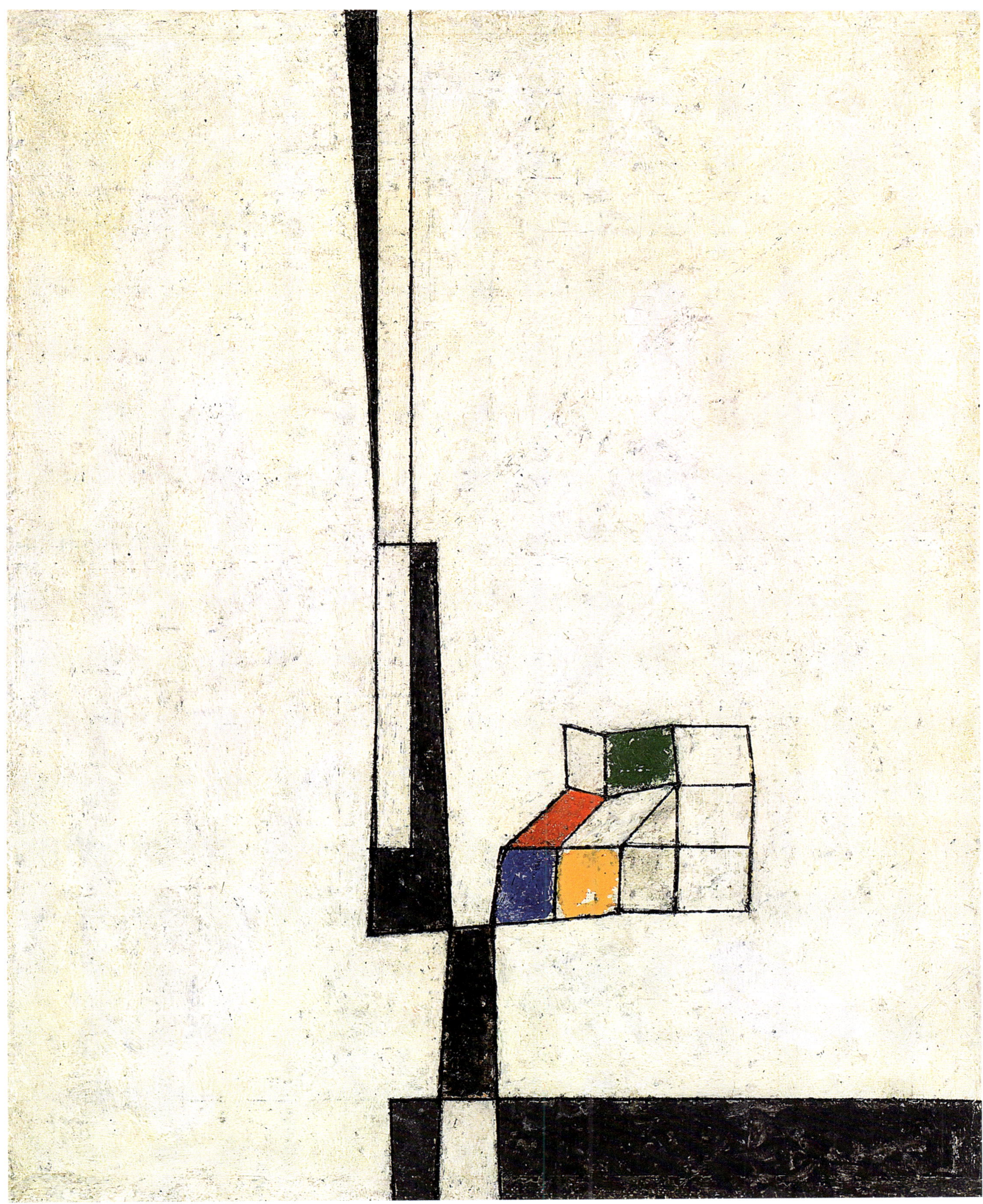

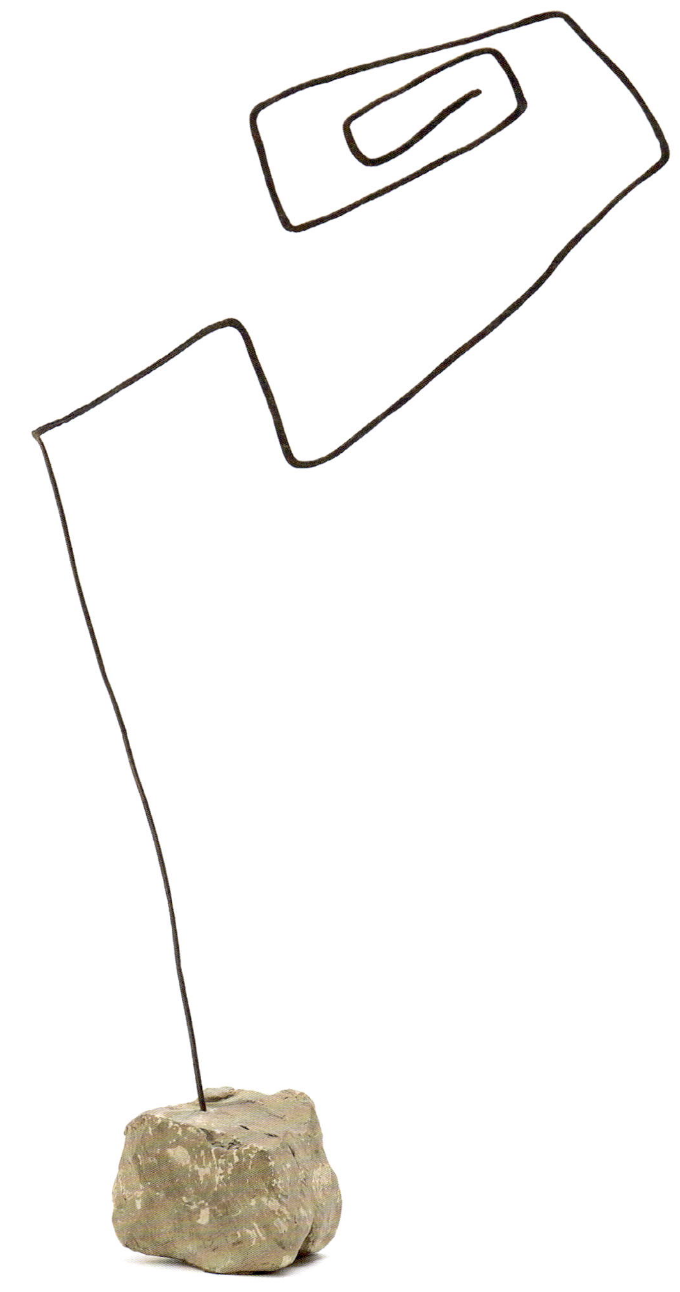

Lucio Fontana
ABSTRACT SCULPTURE
(SCULTURA ASTRATTA)
1934
wire and clay
33 × 19 cm
Fondazione Lucio Fontana, Milan
(34SC29)

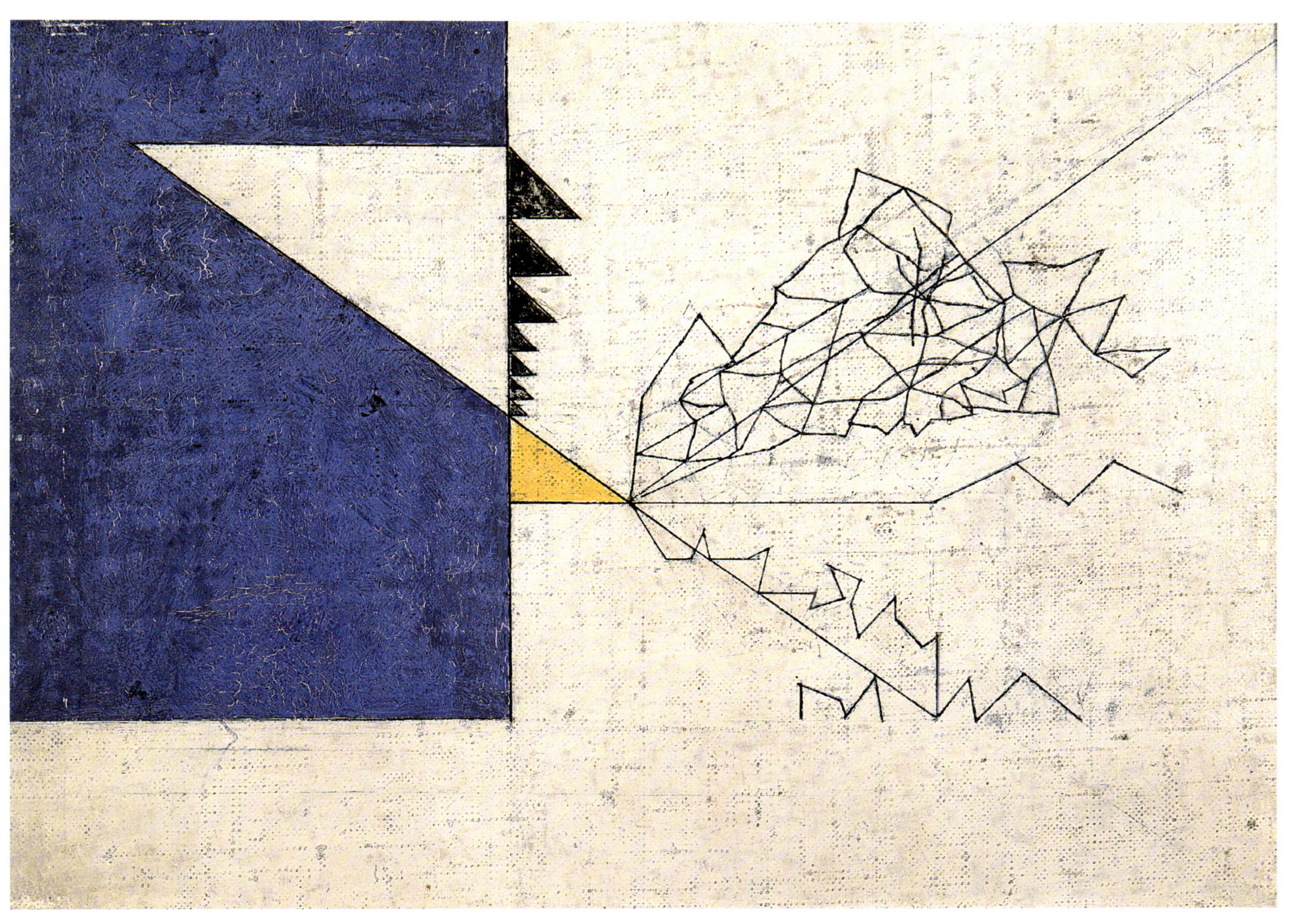

DRAGON
(DRAGO)
1933
oil on canvas
23 × 31 cm
Private collection,
courtesy Lorenzelli Arte, Milan

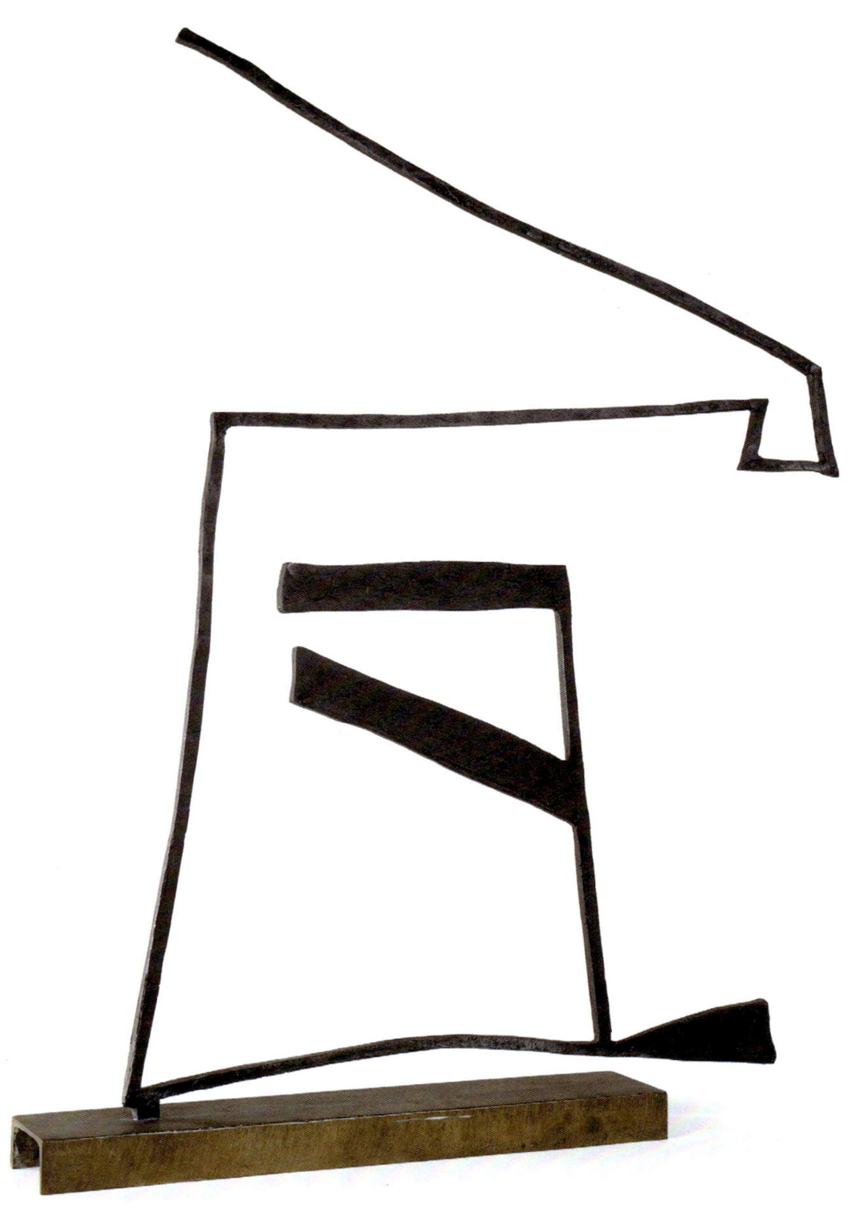

Lucio Fontana
ABSTRACT SCULPTURE
(SCULTURA ASTRATTA)
1935 (reconstruction, signed by the artist, 1950s)
iron and black paint on bronze base
60 × 50 × 7 cm
GAM, Galleria Civica d'Arte Moderna
e Contemporanea, Turin (34SC13)

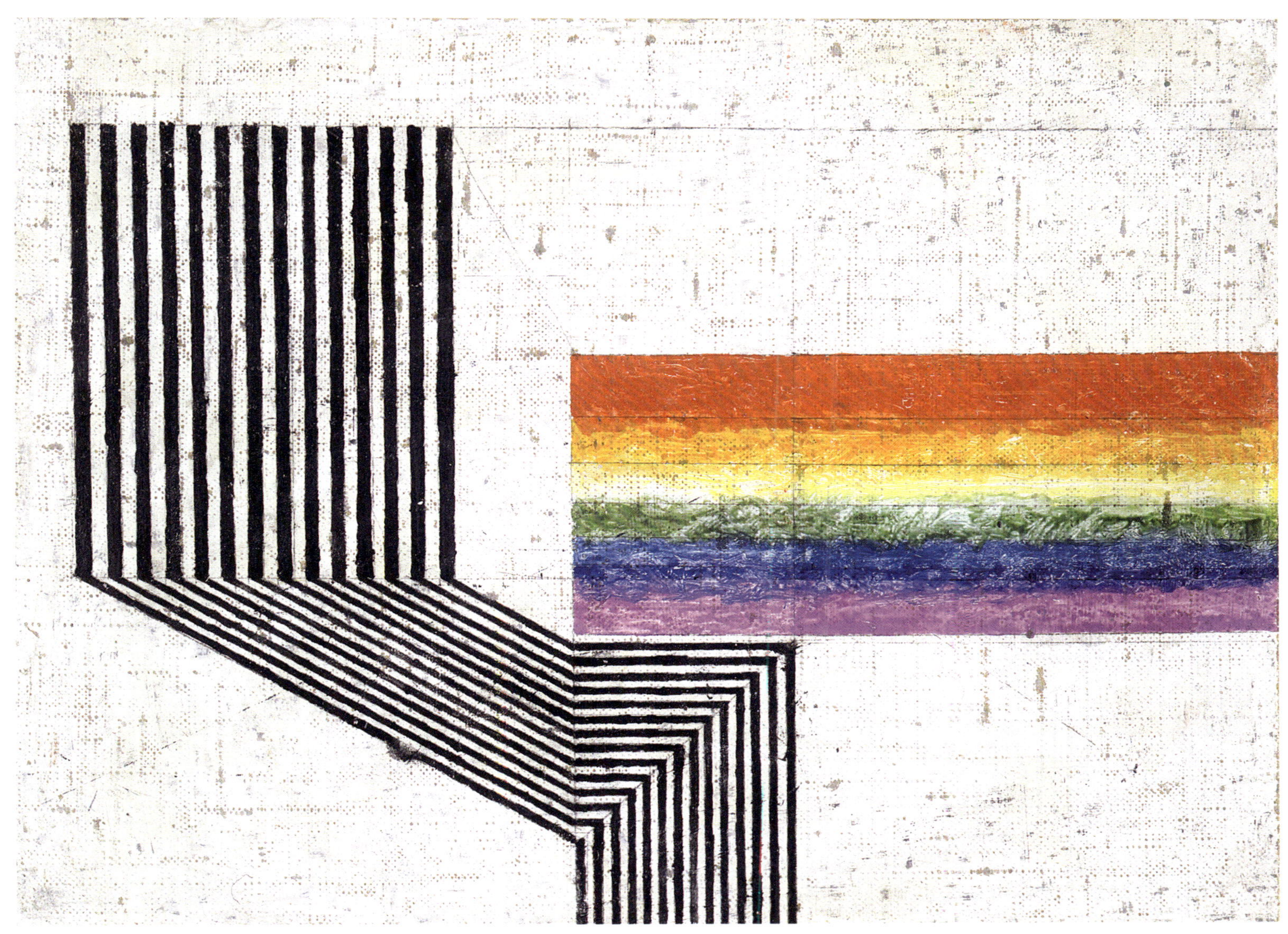

RHYTHM
(RITMO)
1933
oil on canvas mounted on board
21 × 29 cm
Collezione Museo d'Arte Contemporanea
di Villa Croce, Genoa

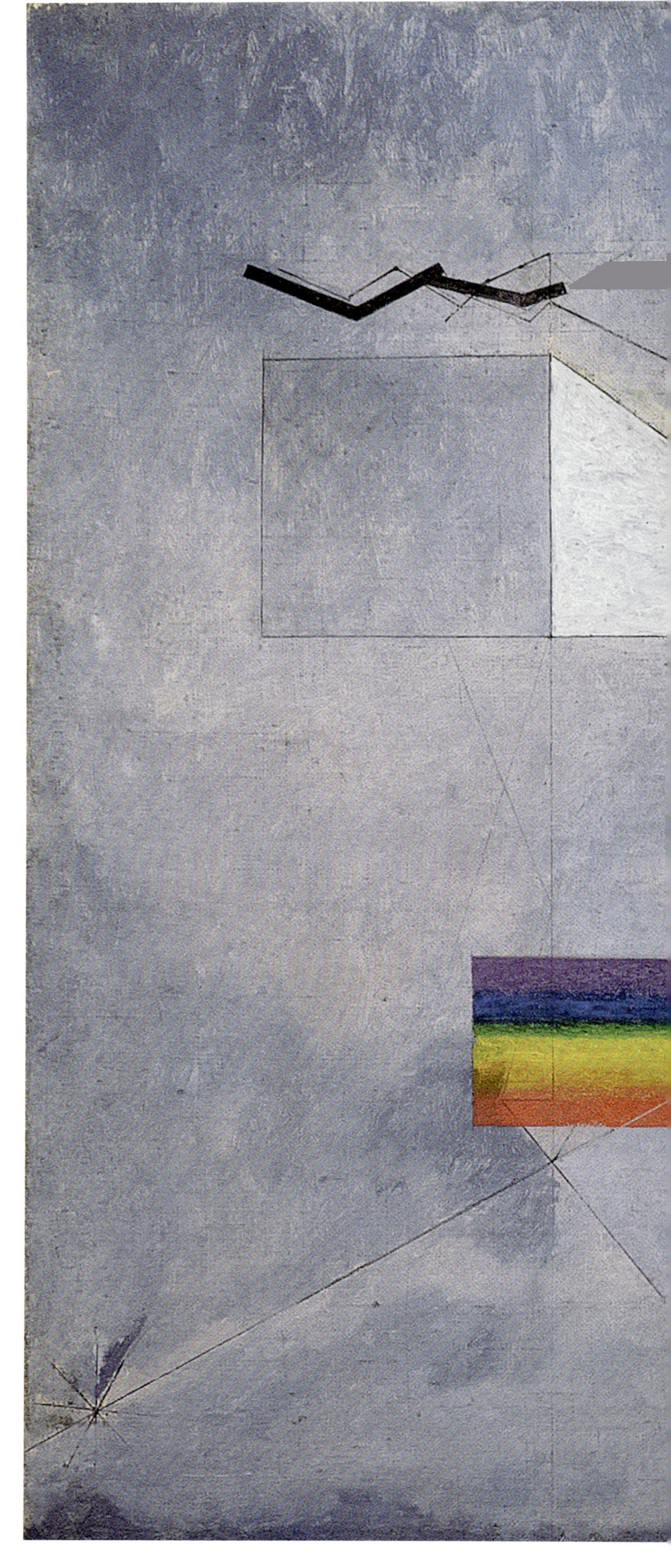

CASTLE IN THE AIR
(CASTELLO IN ARIA)
1933–36
mixed media on canvas
66.7 × 90.2 cm
Augusto and Francesca
Giovanardi Collection

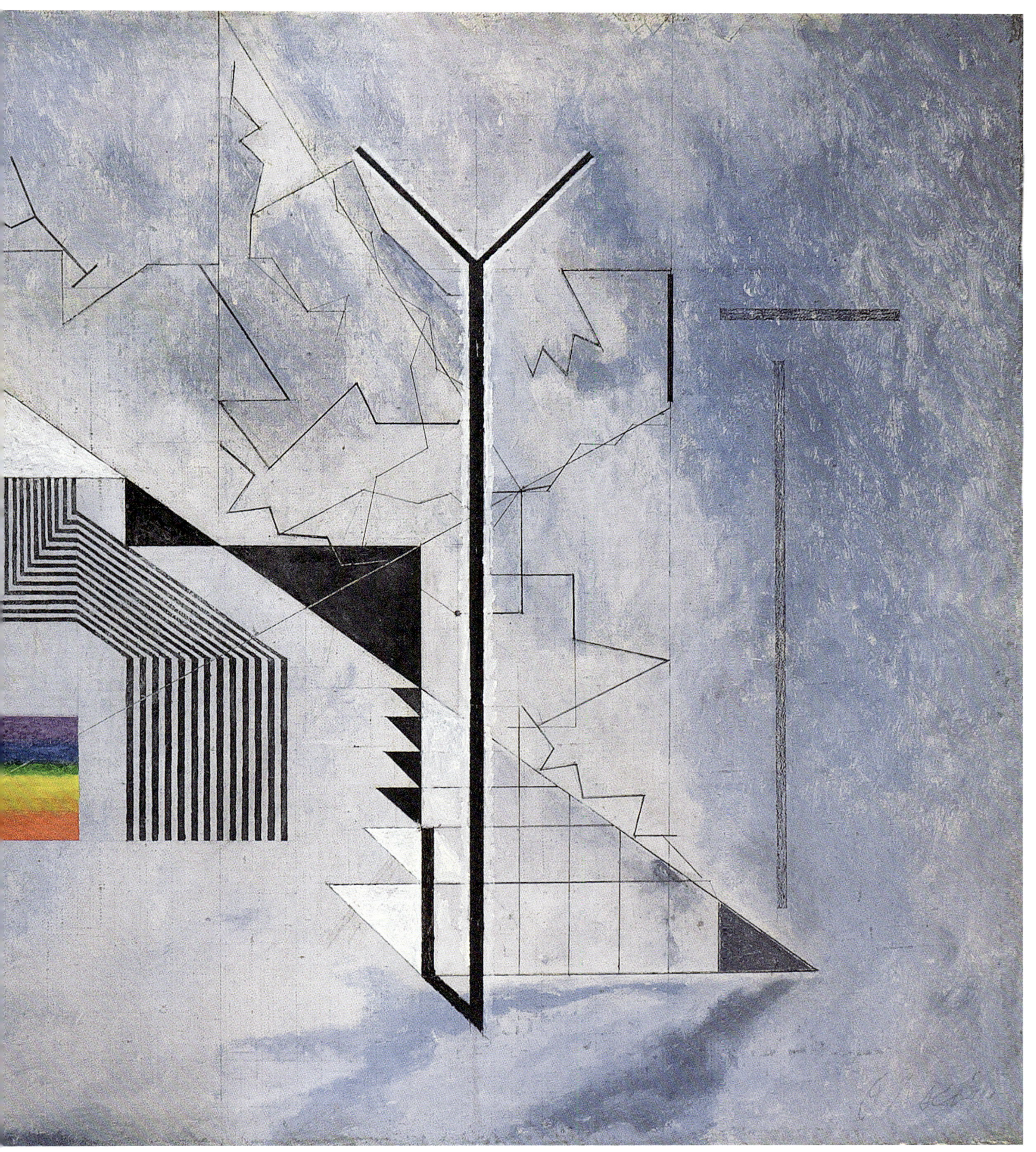

TASTING
(ASSAGGIARE)
1934–36
oil on canvas
22.8 × 27.6 cm
Augusto and Francesca
Giovanardi Collection

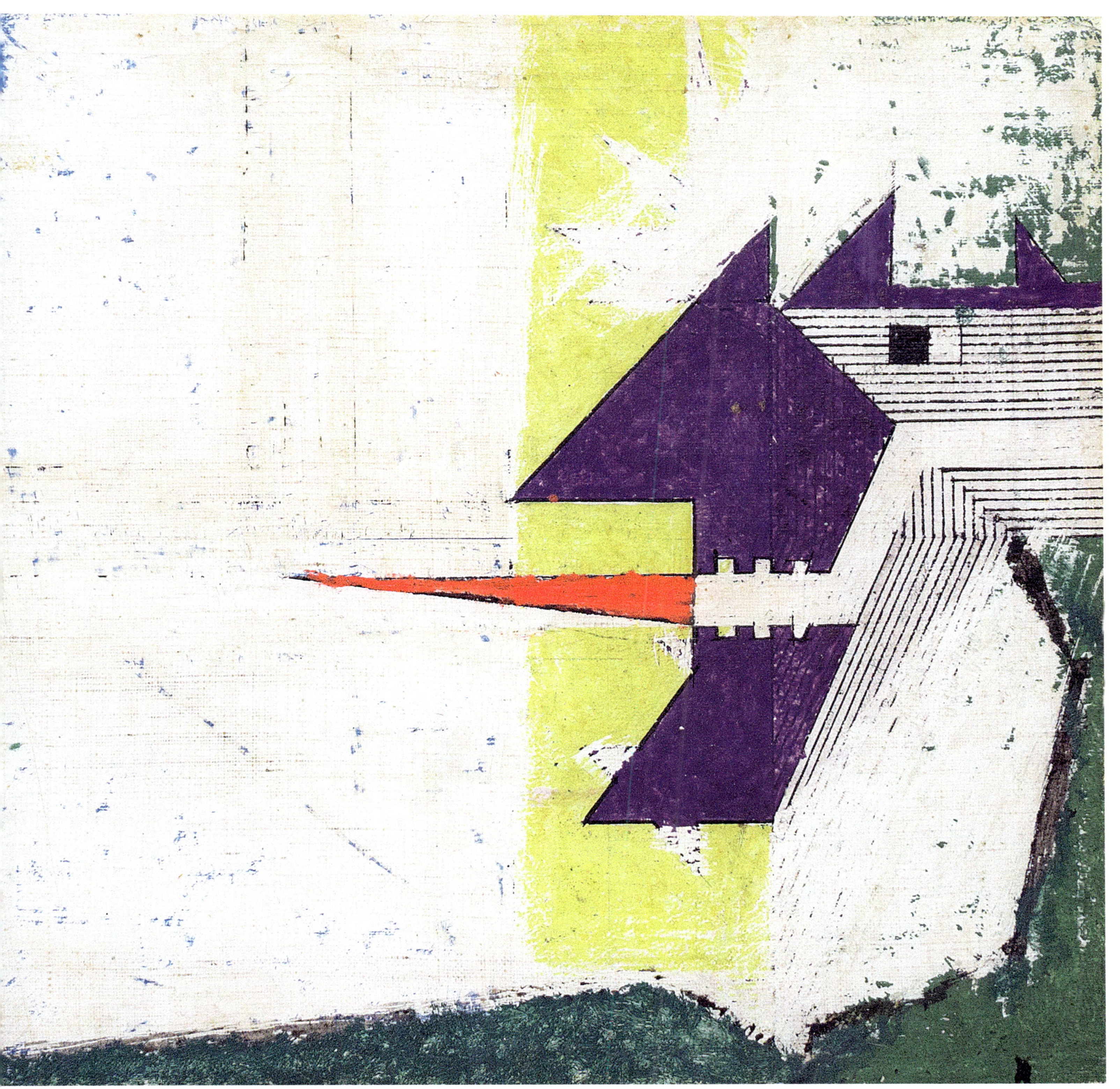

BITING
(ADDENTARE)
1935–36
oil on canvas
65.5 × 88.5 cm
Private collection

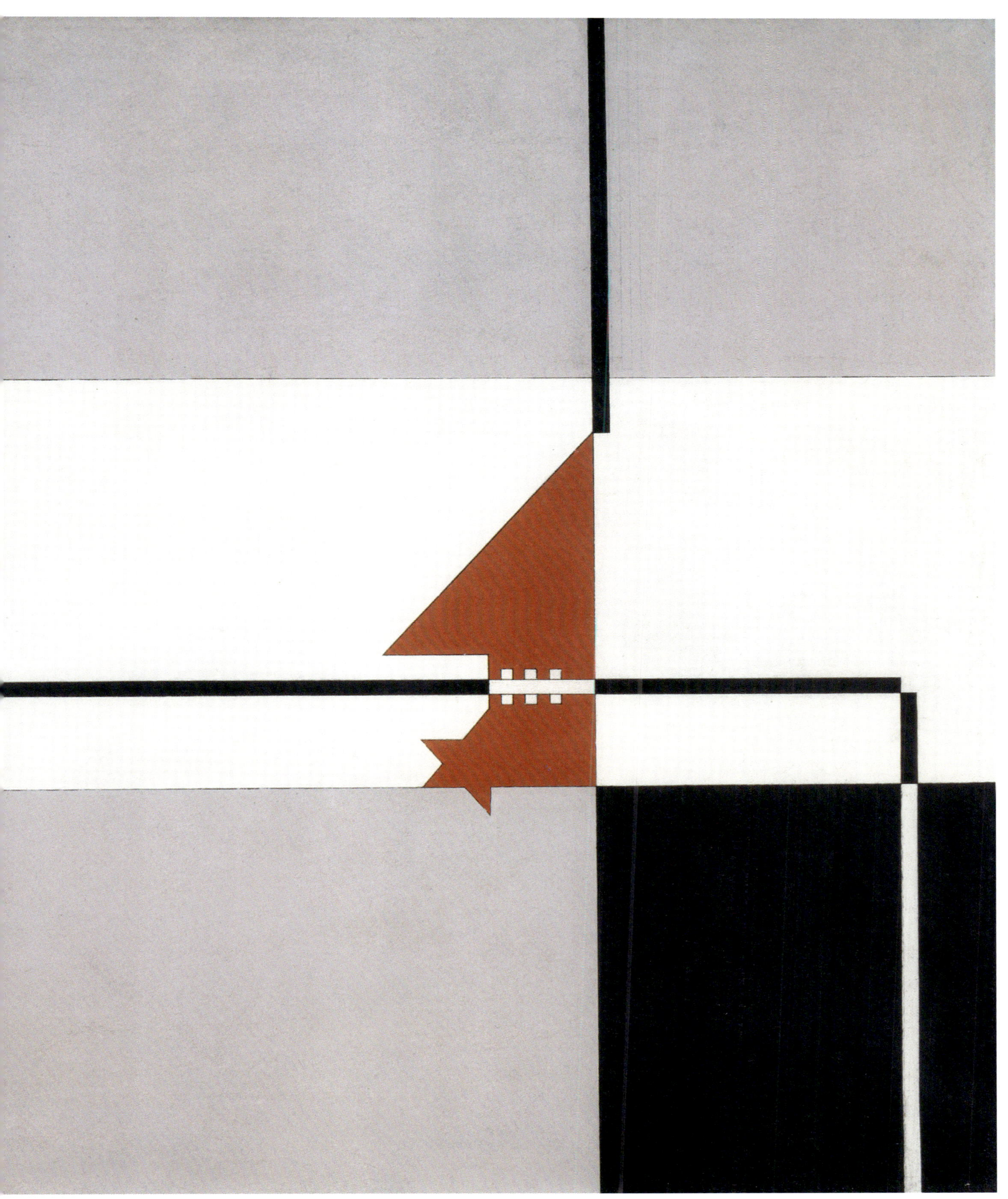

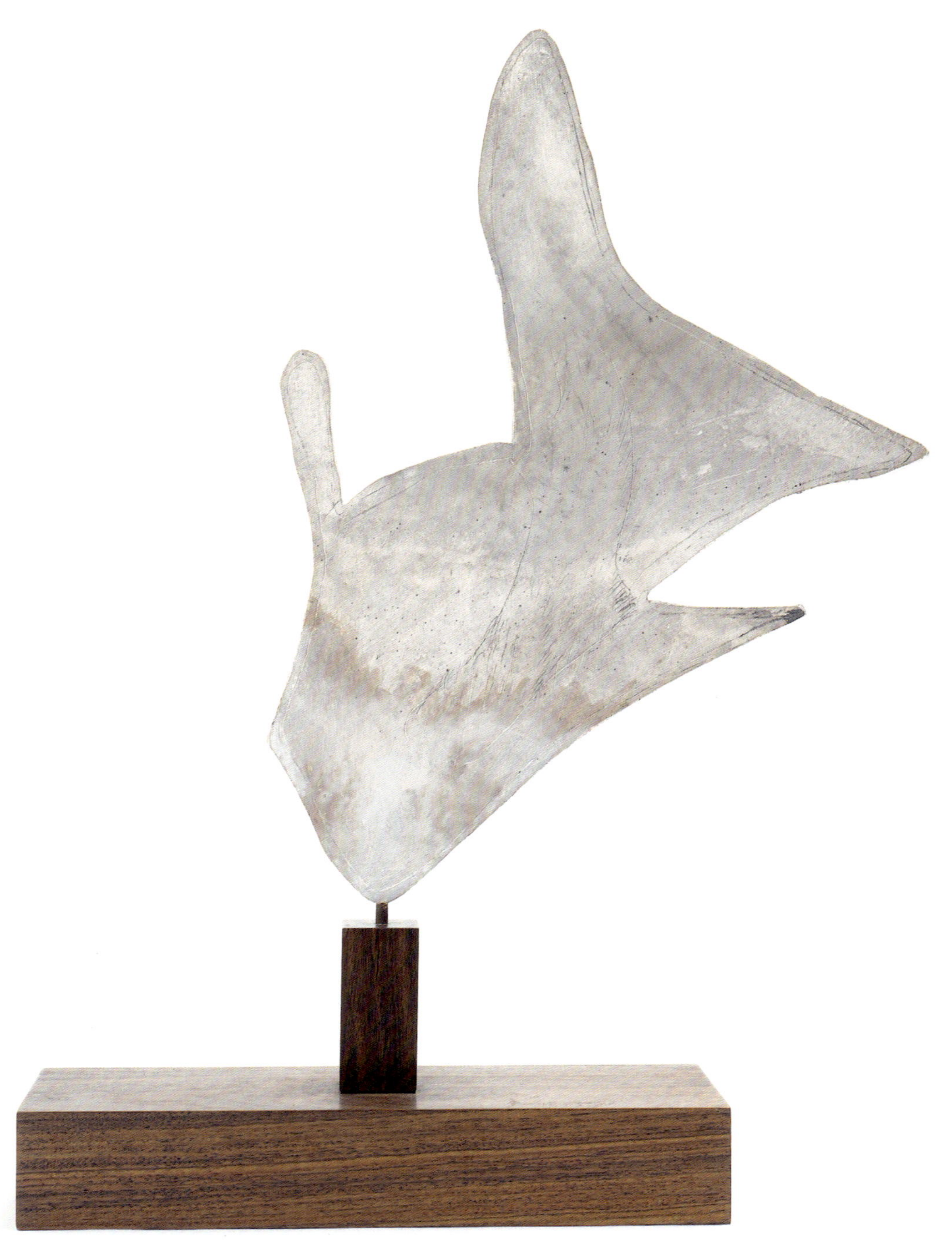

Lucio Fontana
ABSTRACT SCULPTURE
(SCULTURA ASTRATTA)
1934 (reconstruction, signed by the artist, 1950)
engraved white concrete
40 × 28 cm
Fondazione Lucio Fontana, Milan (34SC6)

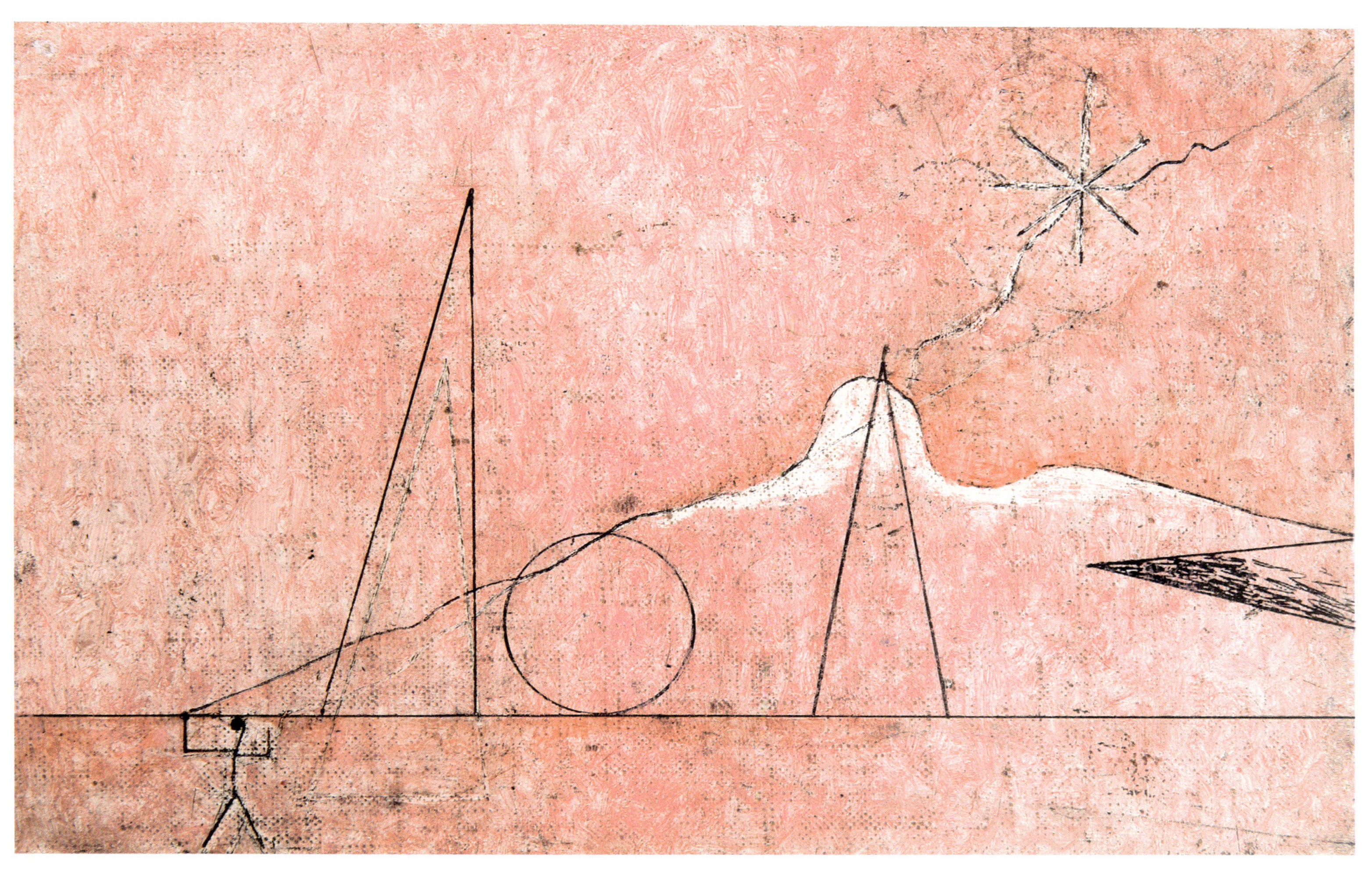

PINK KITE
(AQUILONE ROSA)
1935
oil on canvas
26 × 17 cm
Private collection

BIRD 2
(UCCELLO 2)
ca. 1936
enamel on board
74 × 94 cm
GAM, Galleria Civica d'Arte Moderna
e Contemporanea, Turin

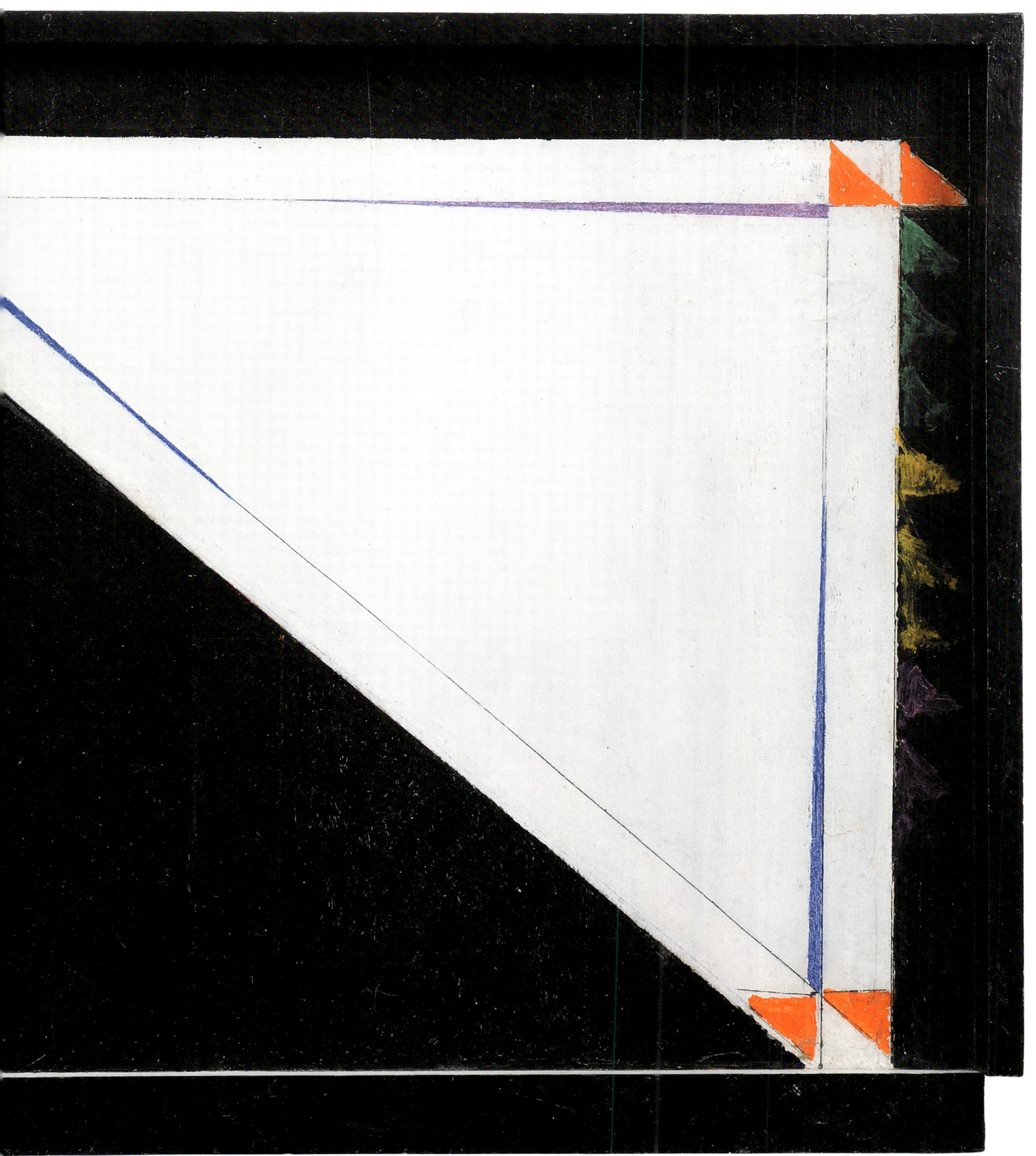

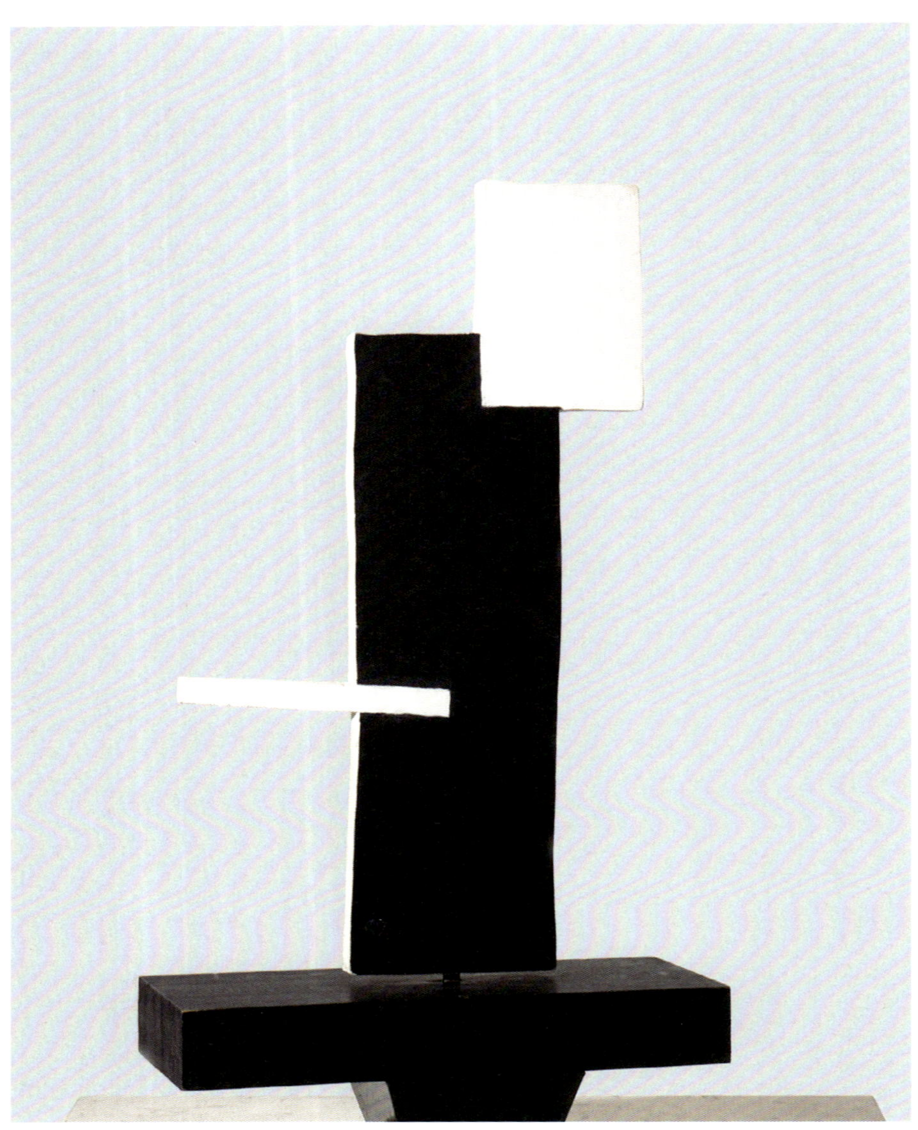

Lucio Fontana
ABSTRACT SCULPTURE
(SCULTURA ASTRATTA)
1934
reinforced concrete, black and white paint
41 × 25 × 1.8 cm
Private collection,
courtesy Fondazione Marconi, Milan (34SC24)

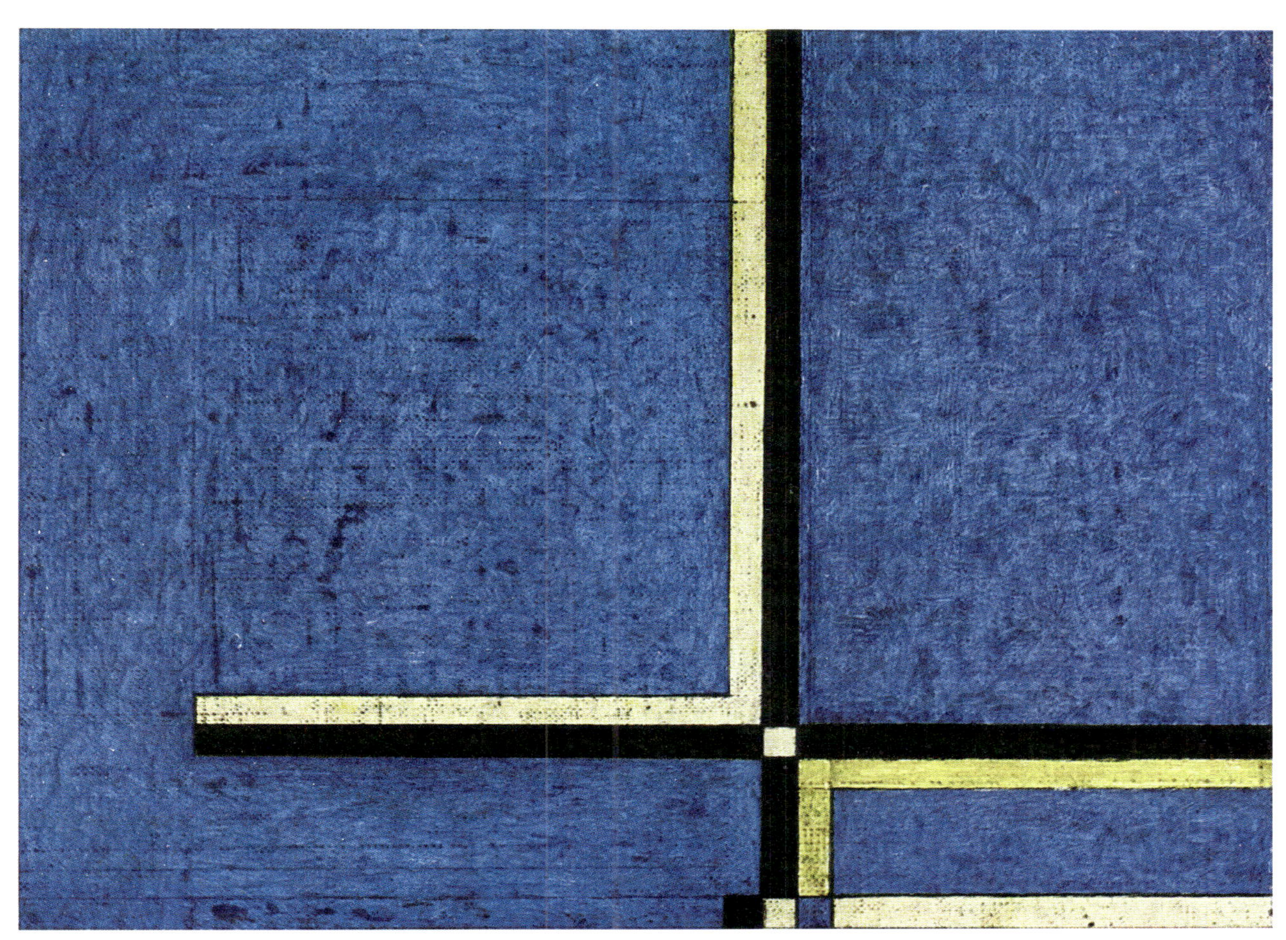

WINDMILL
(MULINO A VENTO)
1935
oil on canvas
21 × 27.5 cm
Sergio Casoli Collection

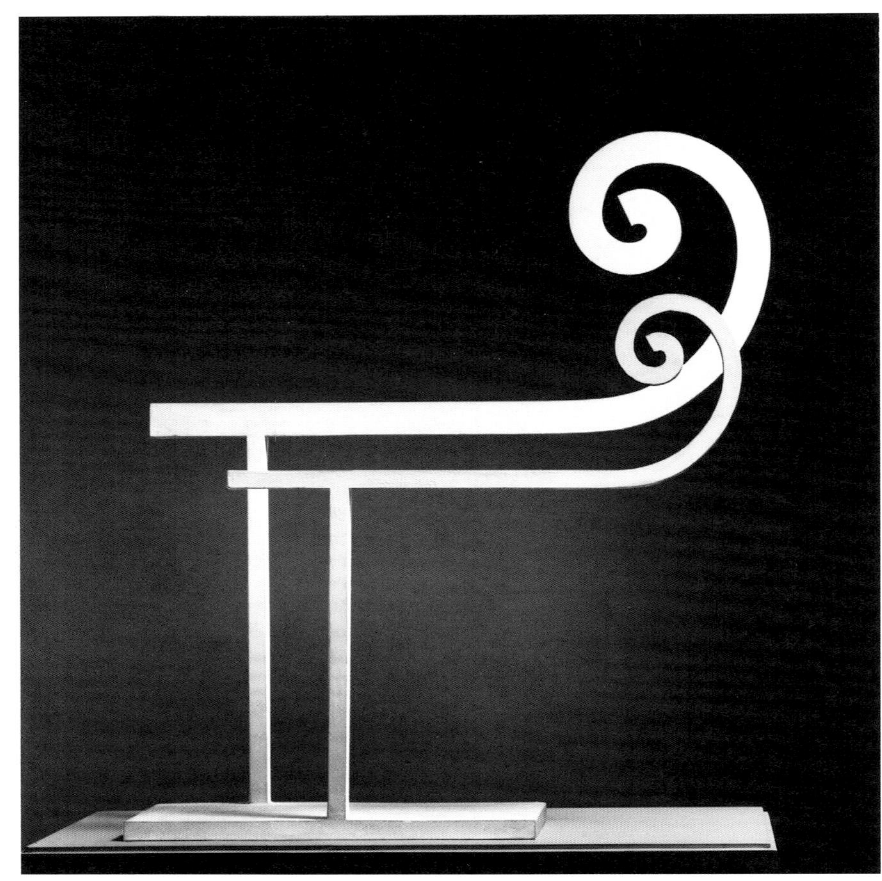

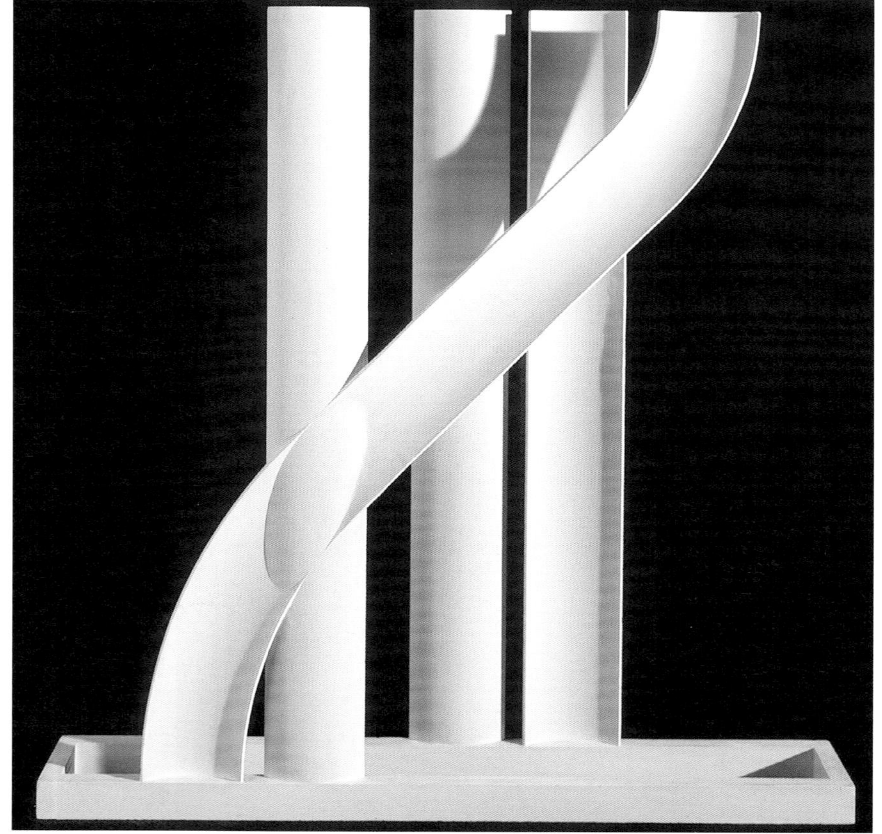

Fausto Melotti
SCULPTURE NO. 11
(SCULTURA N. 11)
1934
plaster
80 × 70 × 14.5 cm
Private collection

Fausto Melotti
SCULPTURE NO. 15
(SCULTURA N. 15)
1935
plaster
67.5 × 69.5 × 8 cm
Fondazione Lucio Fontana, Milan

ARCHIPAINTING
(ARCHIPITTURA)
1935
oil on canvas
91.5 × 72 cm
Private collection,
courtesy Lorenzelli Arte, Milan

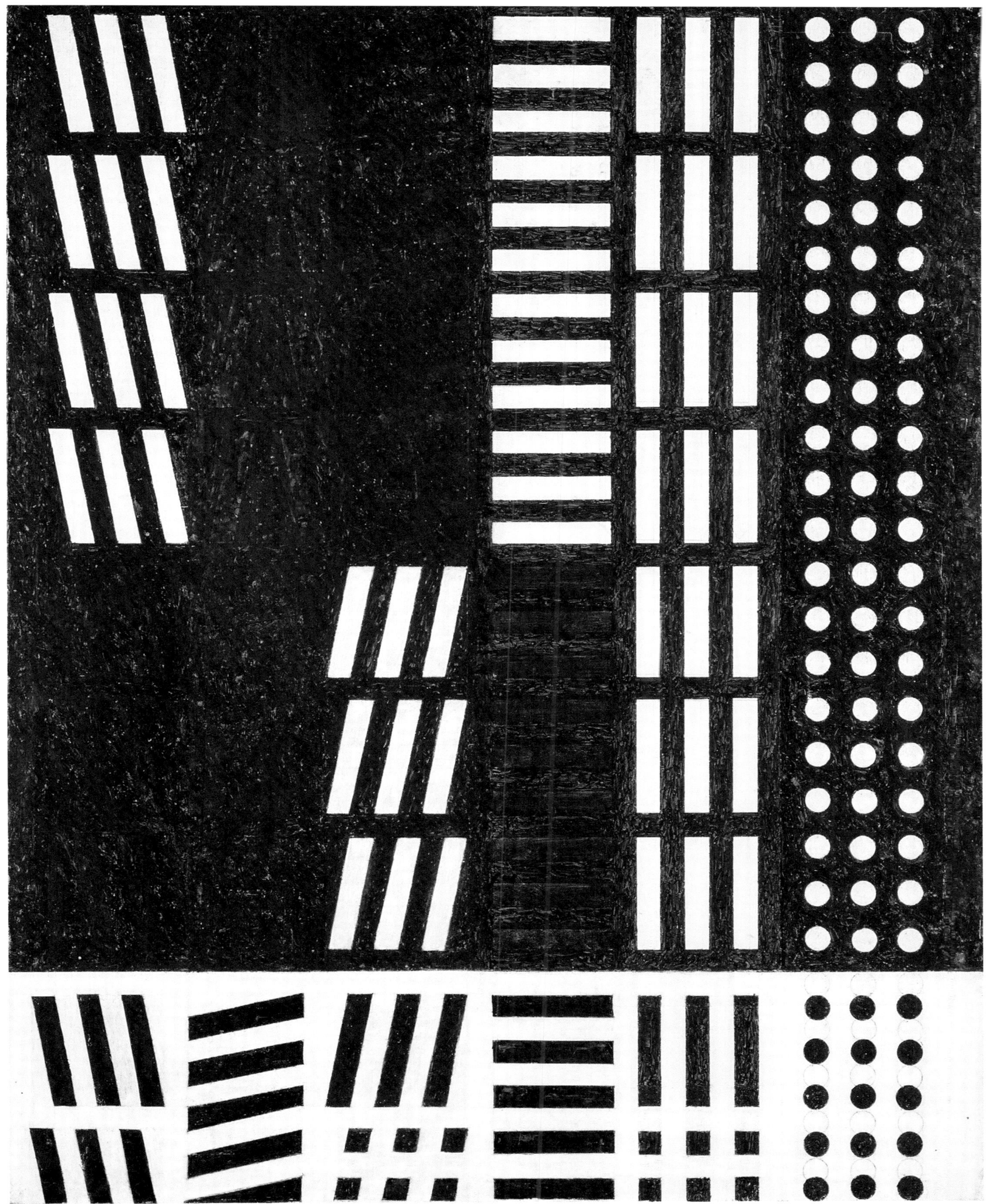

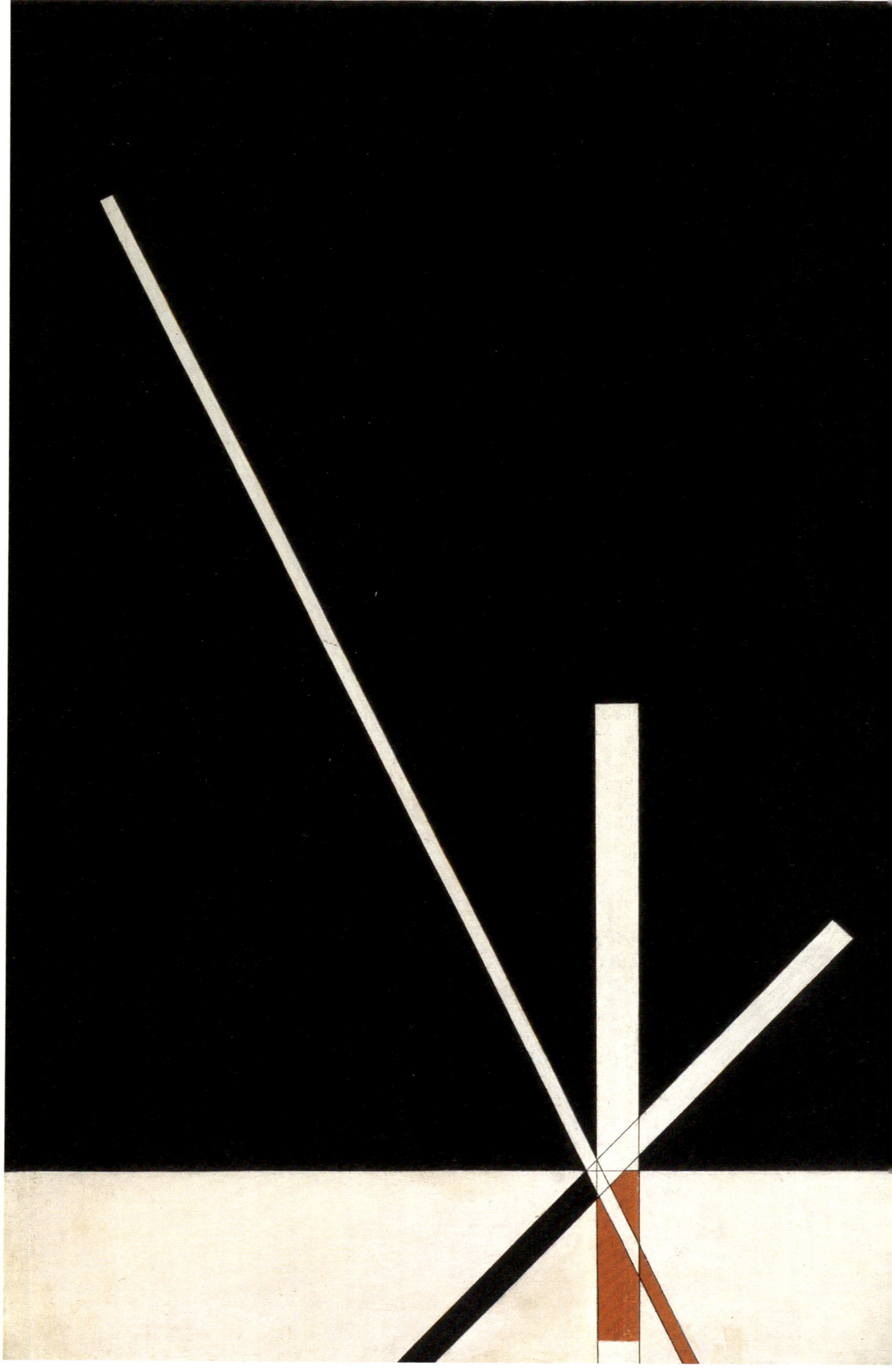

ARCHIPAINTING
(ARCHIPITTURA)
1936
oil on canvas
81 × 100 cm
Private collection

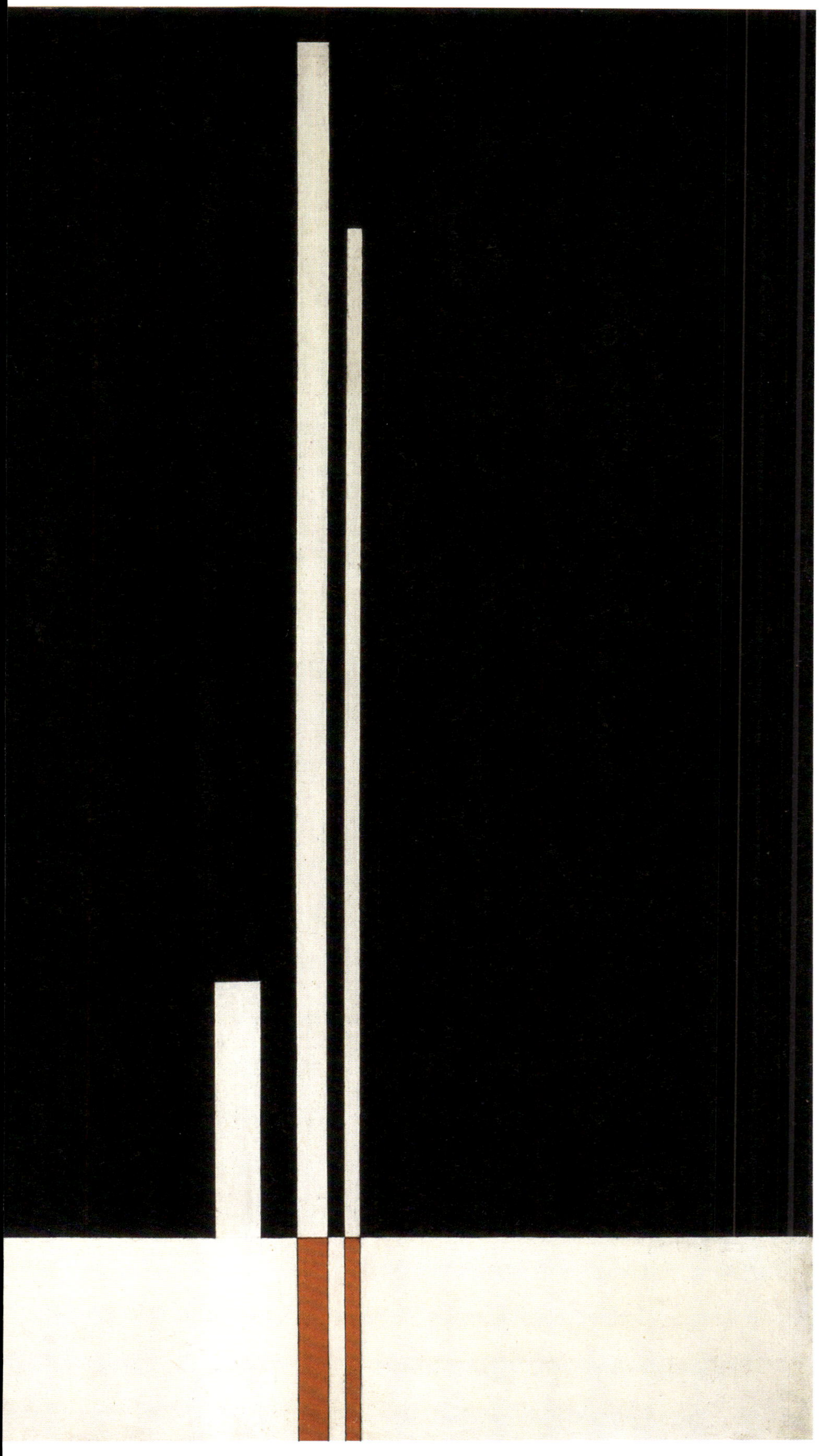

ARCHIPAINTING
(ARCHIPITTURA)
1937
oil on canvas
82 × 100 cm
Private collection

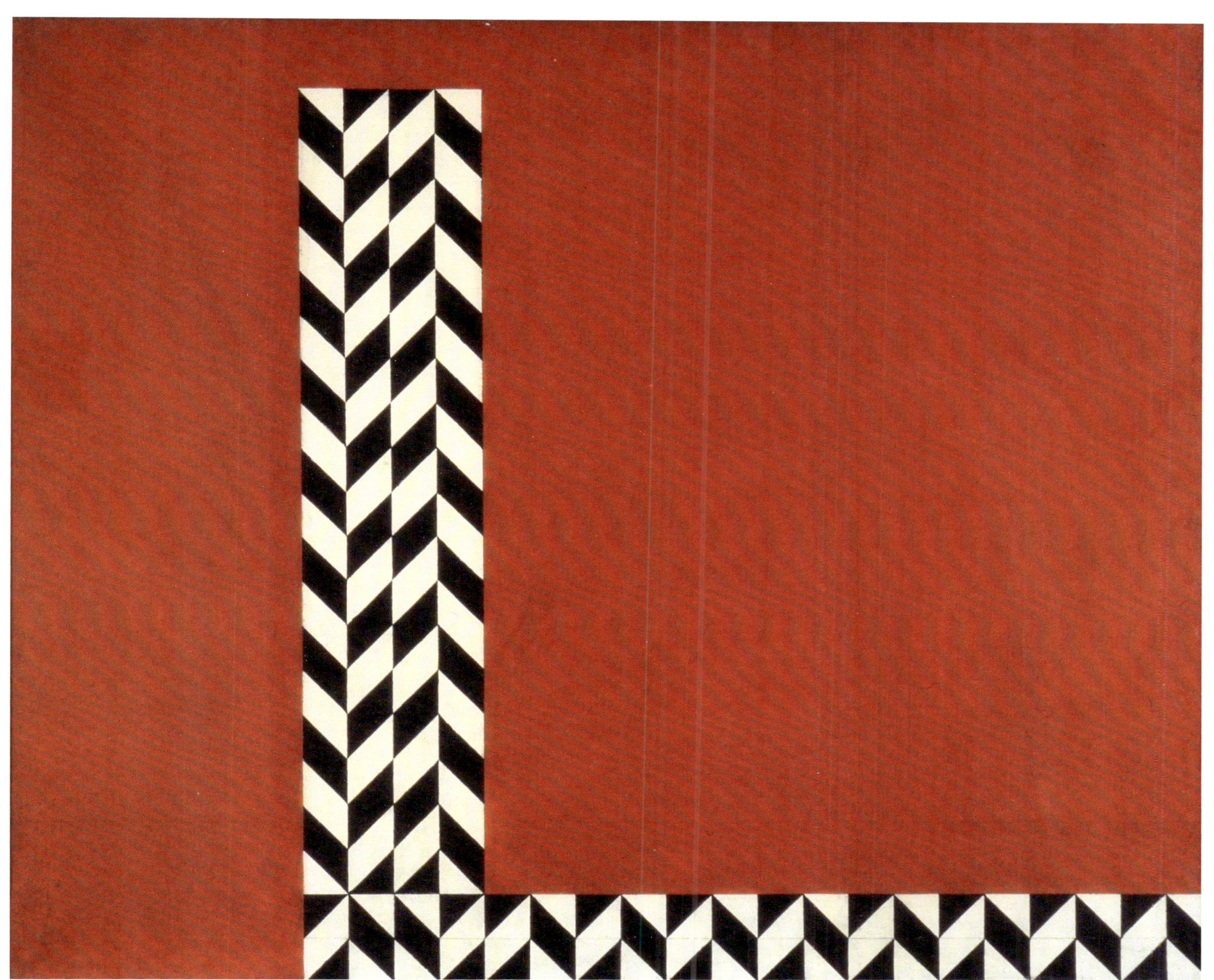

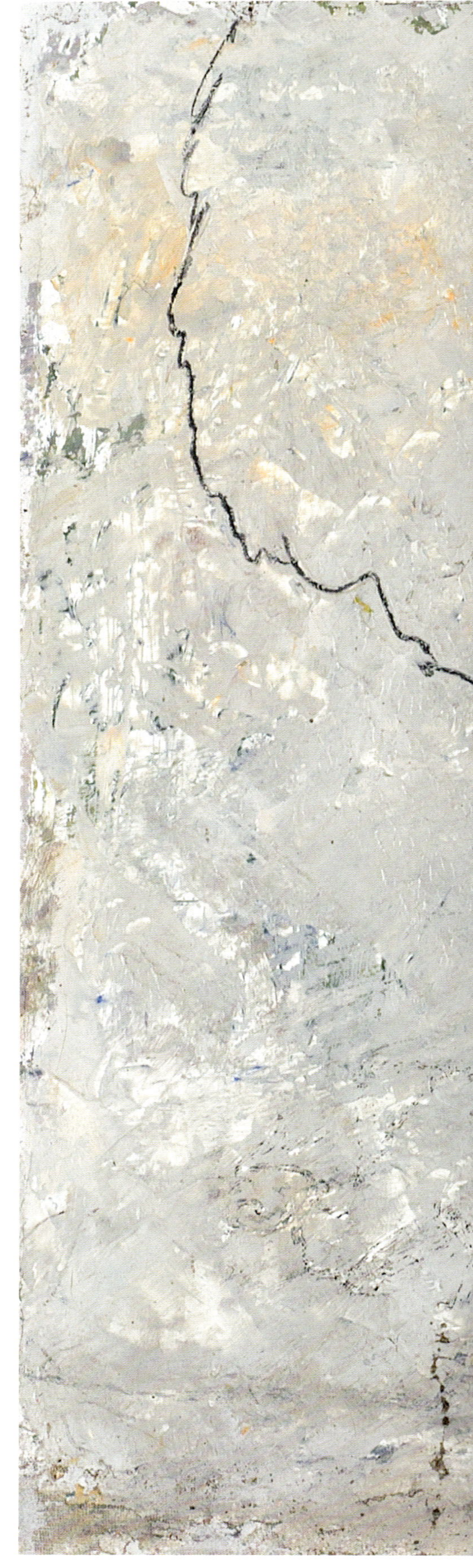

MEMORIES OF THE AFTERLIFE
(MEMORIE D'OLTRETOMBA)
1938
oil on canvas
38 × 47 cm
Private collection,
courtesy Lorenzelli Arte, Milan

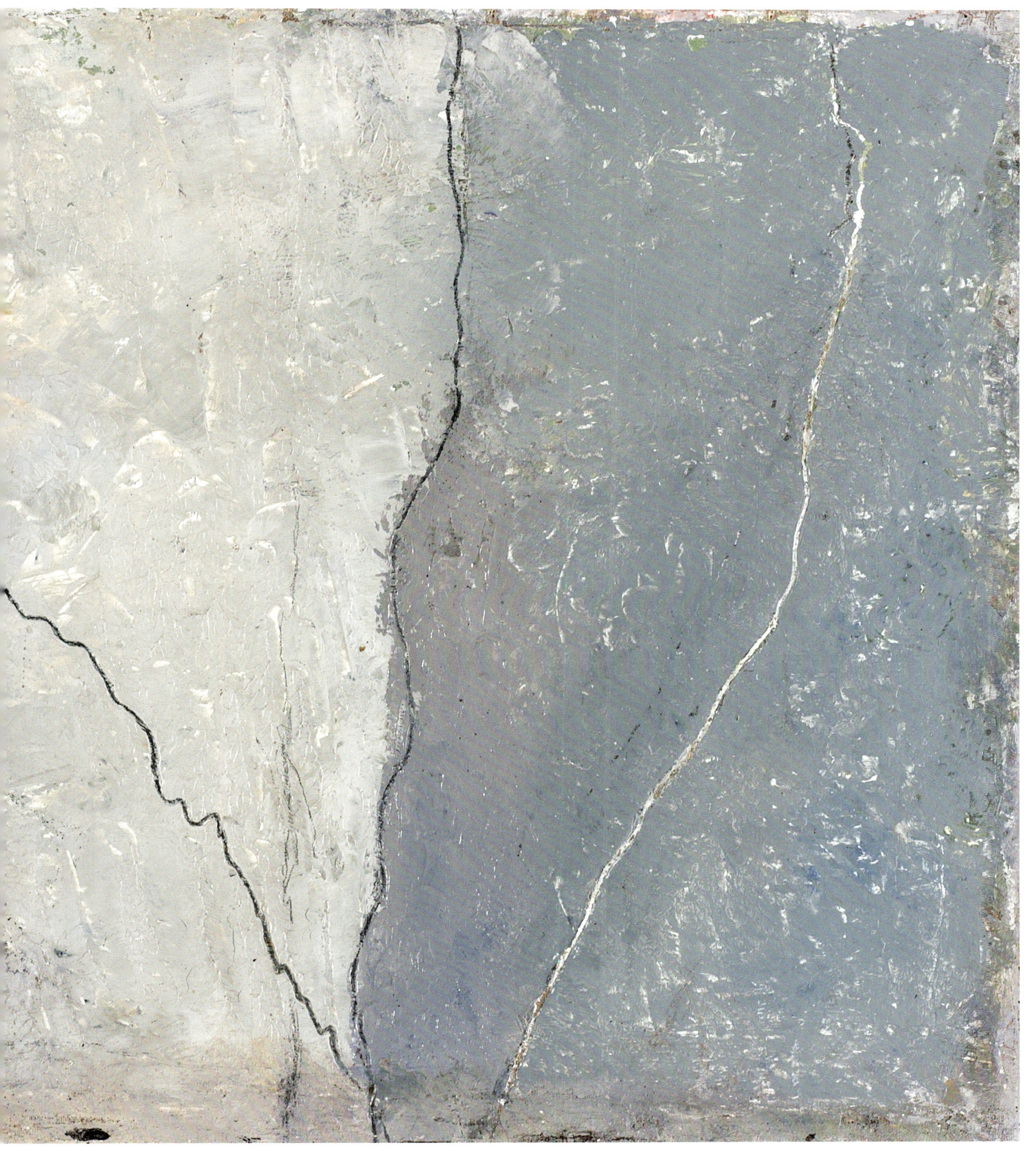

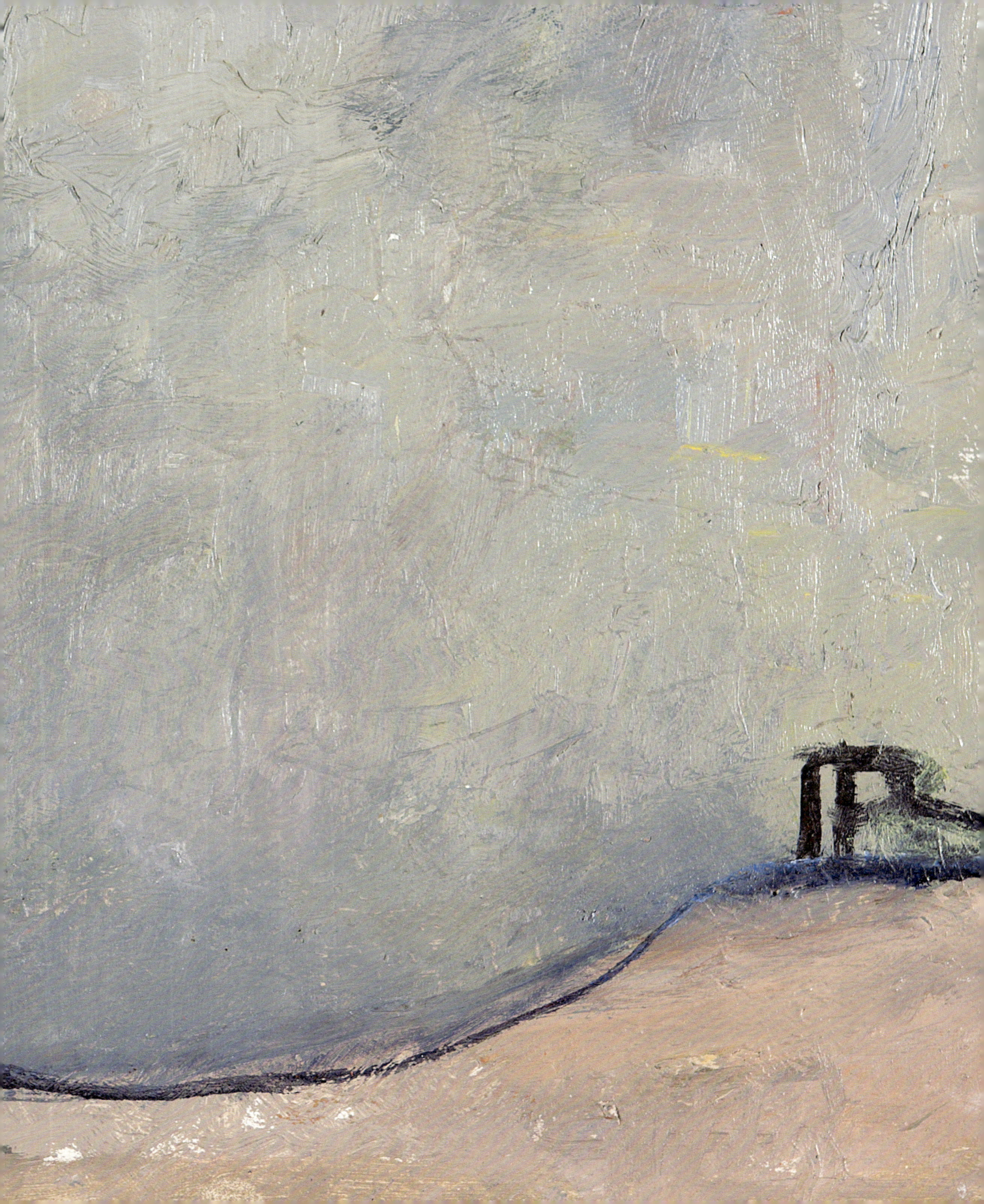

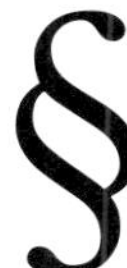

THE "ENIGMATIC WRITINGS" OF LICINI

The late 1930s marked a significant evolution of Licini's language toward a gradual surpassing of the elementary geometry of the abstract period. The encounter in 1938 with Ciliberti led him to further examine the theme of the "primordial" and of the symbolic and spiritual dimension of his painting. In a letter of 1941, we read:

> I write to you from the bowels of the earth, the "region of the Mothers" perhaps, where I have descended to preserve unsoiled certain immaterial, incontrovertible values that belong to the human spirit. In these still green depths, the originary land, perhaps, I will seek to recover the primitive secret of our purpose in the cosmos. As such, extinction of the contingent, for now.... Only then will I be able to show you my prey: those rare symbols that have no name; enigmatic alphabets and texts, totemic representations that only you with your science will be able to decipher.[37]

Licini took up some of the concepts expressed by Ciliberti in the periodical he founded in 1938, *Valori Primordiali*: he theorized a detachment from the contingent dimension in order to ascend to the universality of "the One" and to embrace only the "profound"—the "region of the Mothers," the "originary land," from which "the singular individuality draws, in the unexplored mystery."[38] However, this search for a dimension of higher purity and perfection in Ciliberti's philosophical reflection never translates into a conquest, but represents a constant aspiration that encompasses both the moment of the inevitable fall and the renewal of the desire to ascend. This tension finds correspondences in Licini's search, in the nagging thoughts that drive him to constantly return to his earlier works with an aspiration that is never satisfied

A CHARACTER IN GRAY (PERSONAGGIO IN GRIGIO)
1944
oil on canvas
36.2 × 47 cm
Private collection on long-term loan to Casa Museo Osvaldo Licini, Monte Vidon Corrado
detail

and, as such, represents the strength of his painting. The dualism of Ciliberti's thought is also found in many of Licini's works, from the precarious geometric figures to the angels. The dialogue between the artist and the philosopher is founded, then, upon a shared sensibility and a similar spiritual tension. From this perspective, as Bracalente pointed out, the "enigmatic writings" in his paintings—more frequent as the decade draws to an end—can be read at times through the Pythagorean interpretation of numbers, a theme discussed by Ciliberti in his writings and lectures of the time.[39]

One of the first works to include numbers and letters is *Mouth* (*Bocca*) (p. 121), which can plausibly be dated a few years later than the traditional attribution of 1934.[40] The number *2* seems to be used not toward cryptic ends, but in its visual resemblance to an eye, set in a still abstract face. Along with *Composition—Mouth* (*Composizione – Bocca*) (1934–36, p. 120), the painting indicates a crucial evolution of linguistic signifiers toward visual signifiers when Licini questions the geometric vocabulary that will take him from the *Archipaintings* to the *Characters* (*Personaggi*). Licini is working on the formulation of a personal cabala, which will soon erupt into highly personal graphemes. The immediate precedent is to be found in the art and the "words in freedom" of the Futurists, with whom Licini resumes contacts, supporting Marinetti's defense of modern art and joining, in 1941, the Gruppo Primordiali Futuristi sponsored by Ciliberti. Abstraction and late Futurism seem to be joining forces against the rhetoric of magazines such as the Roman *Il Tevere*, which in 1938, the year racial laws were instituted in Italy, defined avant-garde art as "foreign, Bolshevik, Jewish."[41]

In *Figure T3* (*Figura T3*) (1932–45, p. 123)—the dating is problematic due to a series of modifications to the painting—a letter and number delineate a nose and an eye inside a form/face deriving from the *V* encountered in *Capriccio No. 2*, *Memories of the Underworld*, and *Millionaire*: the sign sinks into the picture plane, it closes onto itself but remains wide open. Essentially, Licini is building a new anatomy, an otherworldly, spatial anatomy of celestial and terrestrial creatures.

The title of *Good-Luck Charm—Shit (Portafortuna – Merda)* (1939–41, p. 125) harkens back to the last of the *Racconti di Bruto* ("La merda che fuma" [Smoking Shit]) in a circularity between written word and painting, never programmatic, that has always been a feature of Licini's artistic production.[42] It also refers to the popular belief whereby unpleasant things are rendered positive by turning them into good luck charms, as the title of the painting explains. Various dates can be attributed to the painting, the most likely of which places it at the end of the 1930s, as can be seen from the comparison with other works of that time, leading us to place it in between *Millionaire* and the *Characters* series, with which it shares the anthropomorphic arrangement of letters to suggest a human figure. The background on the left side also recalls the landscapes of the 1920s: the blue sky and the horizon defined by the sinuous profile of a hill have become central features of extraordinary new works such as the *Flying Dutchman*, *Characters*, *Amalasuntha,* and *Rebel Angel* series.

In *A Character on a Yellow Background* (*Personaggio su fondo giallo*) of 1944 (p. 131), a large *C* surrounds the letters *I*, *M*, and *A*, which together form the word *CIMA*, meaning "peak," as if to transpose the hills and mountains into ideogrammatic form and thus identify the character with the high perspective from which to observe the horizon. *CIMA*, like *FMA*, *TMA*, *PMA*, and *QMA*, is one of the numerous combinations used by Licini in the construction of his word-characters, such as the Flying Dutchman in *Flying Dutchman, Blue* (*Olandese volante azzurra*) of 1944 (p. 129).

According to a legend of Norse origin, the Flying Dutchman is a sailor condemned to navigate eternally for having challenged God by sailing past the Cape of Good Hope. Made famous in the nineteenth century by Richard Wagner's opera, *Der fliegende Holländer*, the myth interprets the archetype of travel as an attempt to overcome human limits. He can be considered an alter ego of the artist who has chosen the existential dimension of "wandering" as one of the touchstones of his artistic and personal path. Licini's self-definition as "errant, erotic, heretical," which he wrote in the guestbook of a restaurant in Burano after dining there with Marchiori in 1934, is a common thread through his entire oeuvre, but reemerges with a forceful sensuality and renewed irreverence in the works of the 1940s.

With the *Flying Dutchman* paintings, Licini achieves a compositional completeness that anticipates the *Amalasuntha* and *Rebel Angel* series. On the one hand, he shows a great poetic rigor, intended not as rigidity but as a structured synthesis of word and sound; on the other, he constantly returns to unreality. Licini deploys this unreality to represent the inscrutability of space-time, such that his work is as unreal as it is timeless, completely removed from the contemporary world. While his art had previously followed the flow of the present, at least in part, from now on—that is, from the devastating years of the war—it is absolutely unrelated to current events, suspended in a timeless realm between earth and sky. Licini embodies the anarchic individualism of the poet: a being who exists in his own time, in order to rise above or sink into that tension of opposites that characterizes his work. And the emblem of this damnation, of this eternal limbo, is the Flying Dutchman, compelled to wander for all eternity. ▸

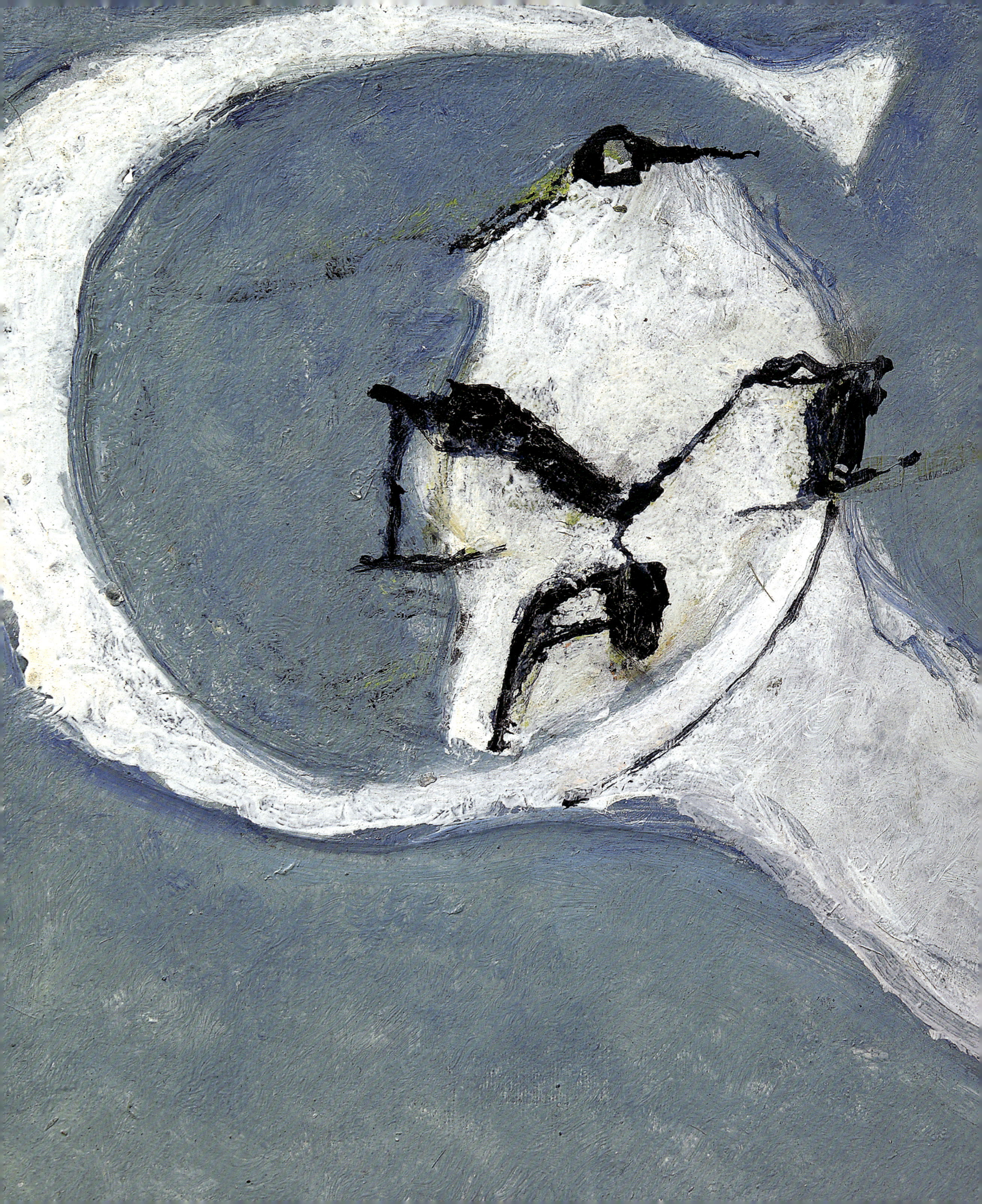

FLYING DUTCHMAN, BLUE (OLANDESE VOLANTE AZZURRA)
ca. 1944
oil on canvas, mounted on cardboard
20 × 25 cm
Silvia Poli Licini collection
detail

37. Letter from Osvaldo Licini to Ciliberti of February 1, 1941, in Licini, *Errante, erotico, eretico*, 161.
38. Franco Ciliberti, "Sul primordiale," *Valori Primordiali*, no. 1 (February 23, 1938).
39. See Bracalente, "5R=(2+3) →∞ …"
40. See Giorgio Magnoni, "Licini, secondo noi…," in *Licini secondo noi…*, exh. cat., Milan, Lorenzelli Arte, November 15, 2001–January 15, 2002 (Milan: Skira, 2001), 47.
41. "Straniera, bolscevizzante, giudaica," *Il Tevere* (Rome), no. 23, November 24–25, 1938.
42. On this theme, see Francesco Bartoli, "Figure dell'incastro e metafore dell'aria nel linguaggio di Licini," in Licini, *Errante, erotico, eretico*, 43–61.

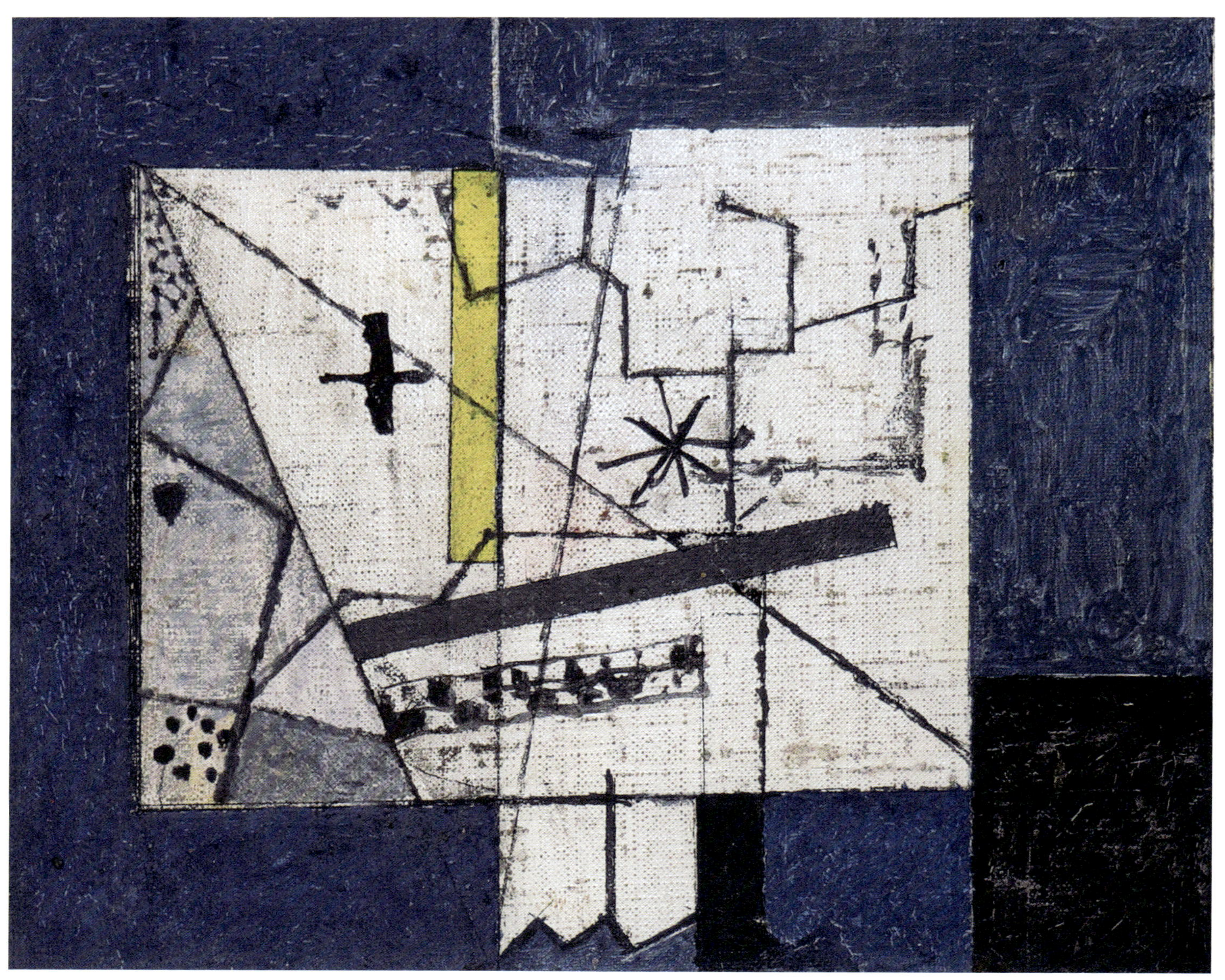

COMPOSITION—MOUTH
(COMPOSIZIONE – BOCCA)
1934–36
oil on canvas
21.8 × 29.5 cm
Augusto and Francesca
Giovanardi Collection

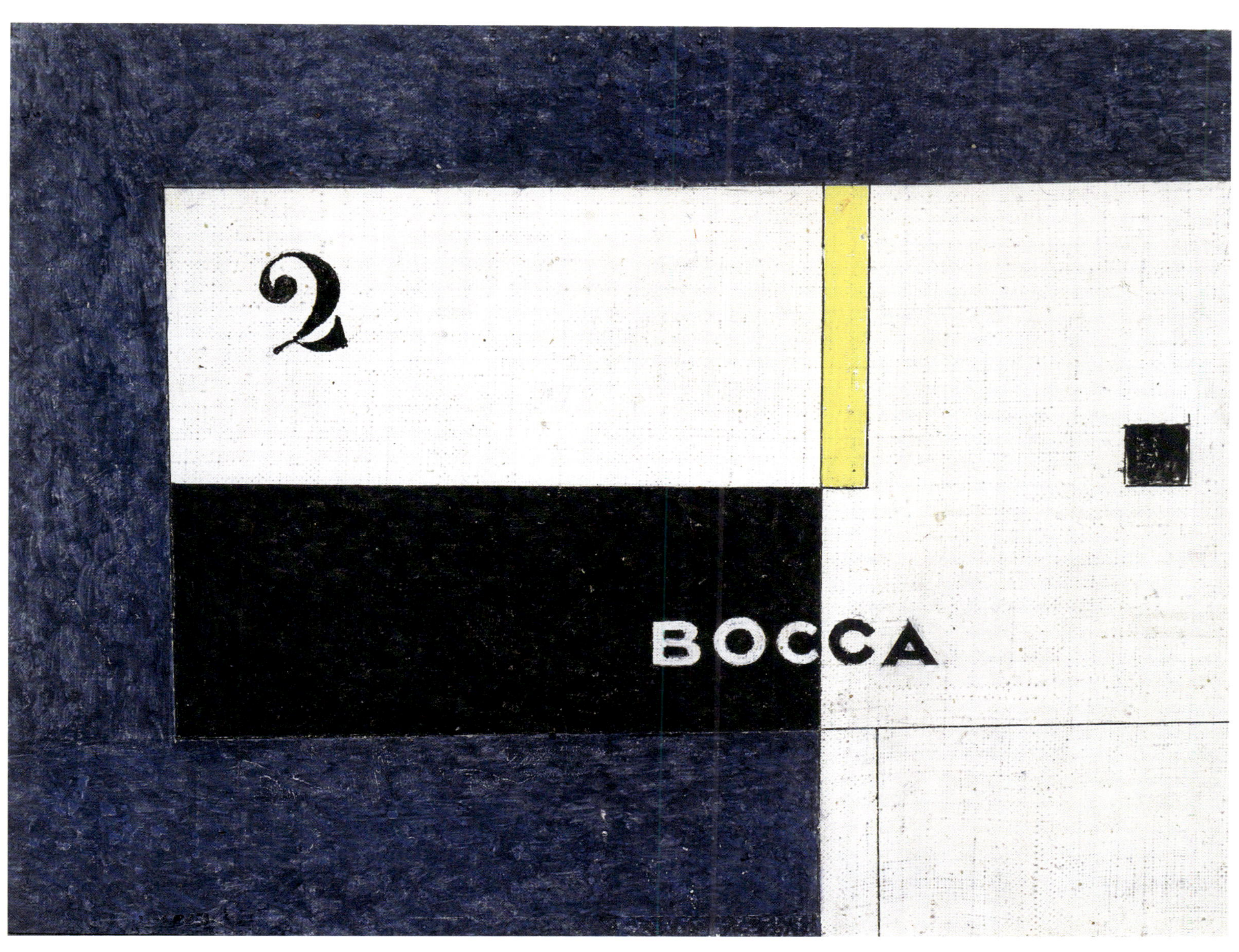

MOUTH
(BOCCA)
1934
oil on canvas
21.3 × 28.3 cm
Private collection

FIGURE T3
(FIGURA T3)
1932–45
oil on canvas
25 × 19.5 cm
Private collection, Milan

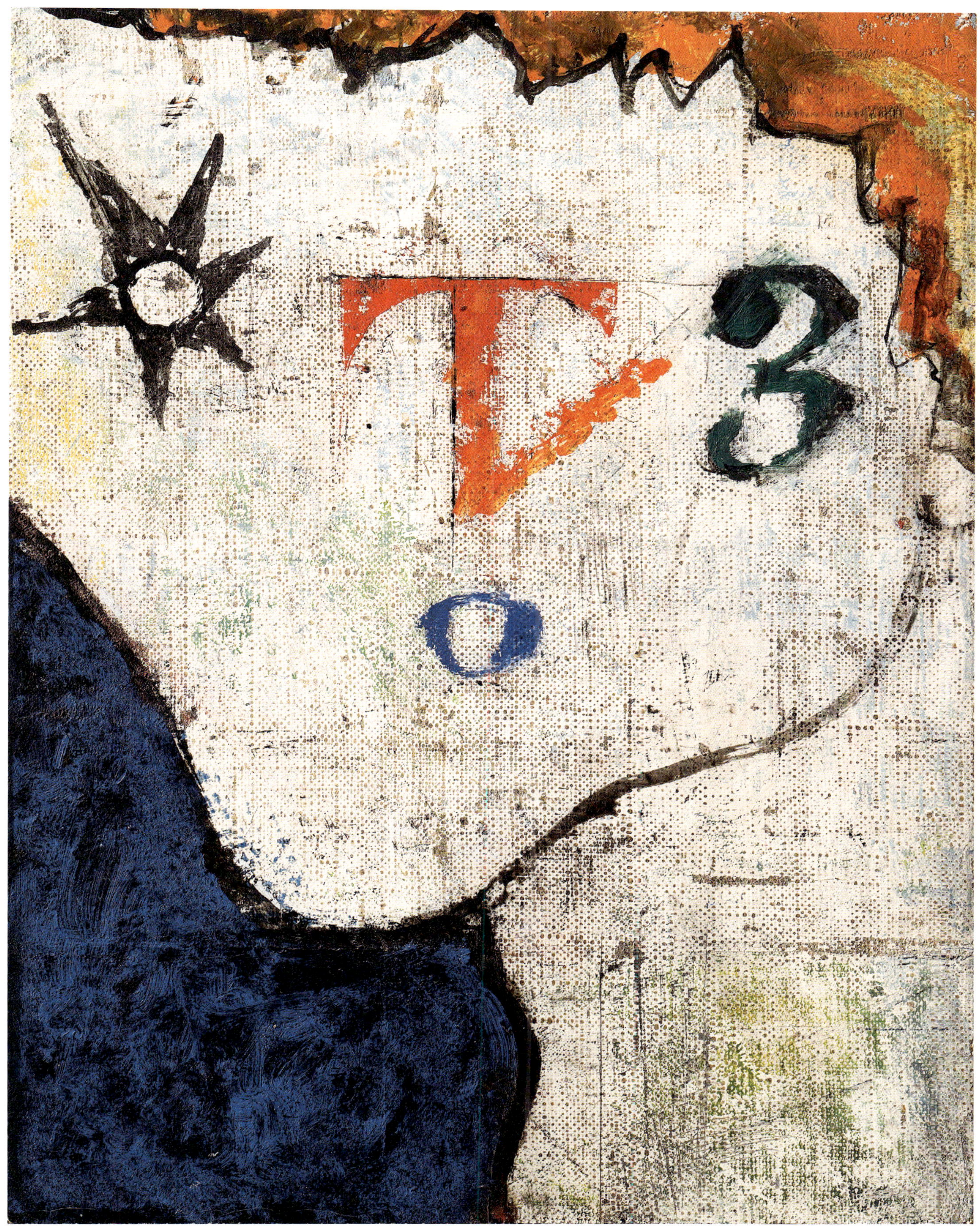
T
3

GOOD-LUCK CHARM—SHIT
(PORTAFORTUNA – MERDA)
1939–41
oil on canvas
23.5 × 18 cm
Private collection, Milan

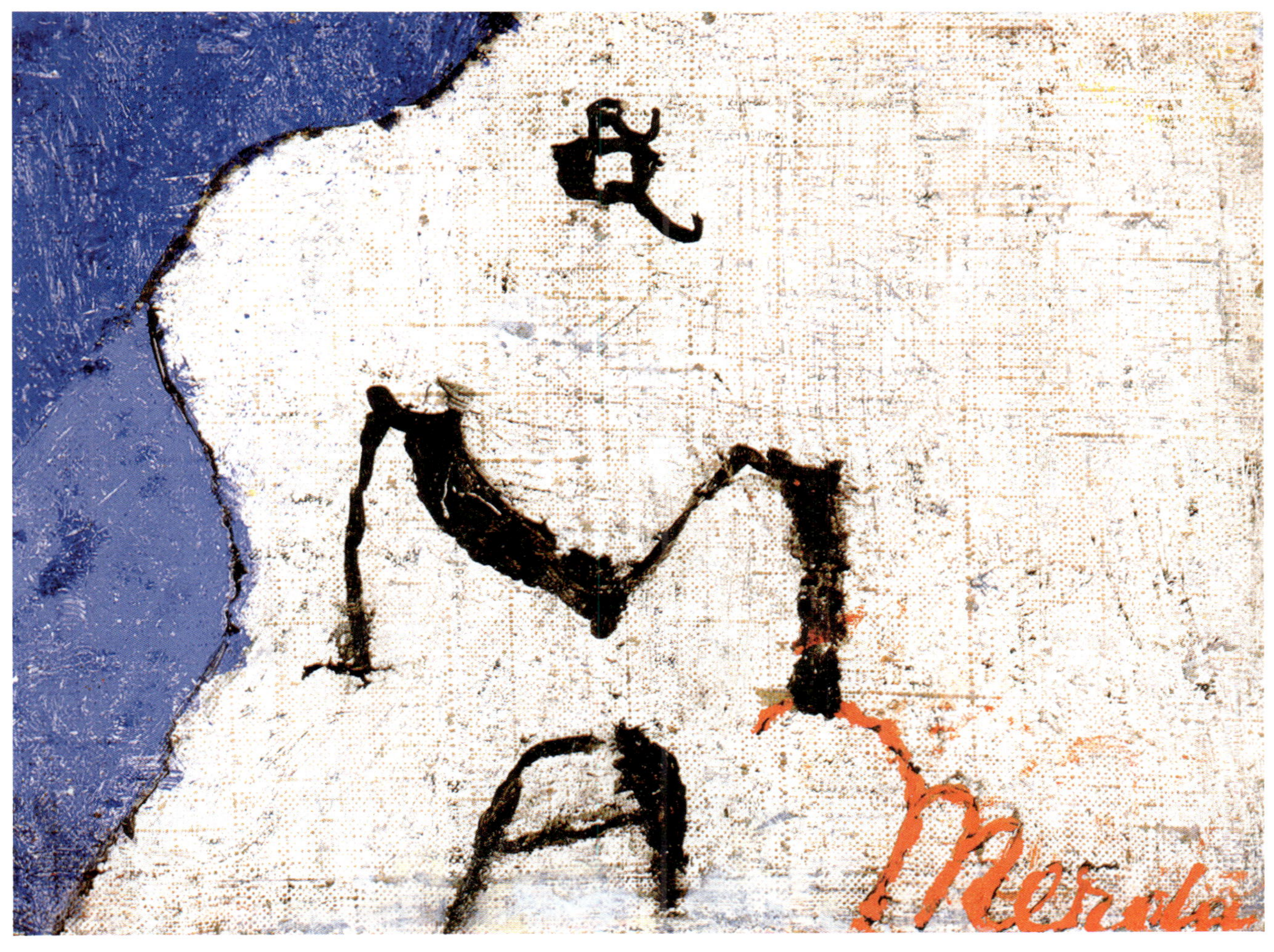

THE MILLIONAIRE
(IL MILIONARIO)
1938
oil on paper
17 × 37 cm
Private collection,
courtesy Lorenzelli Arte, Milan

A5362
8

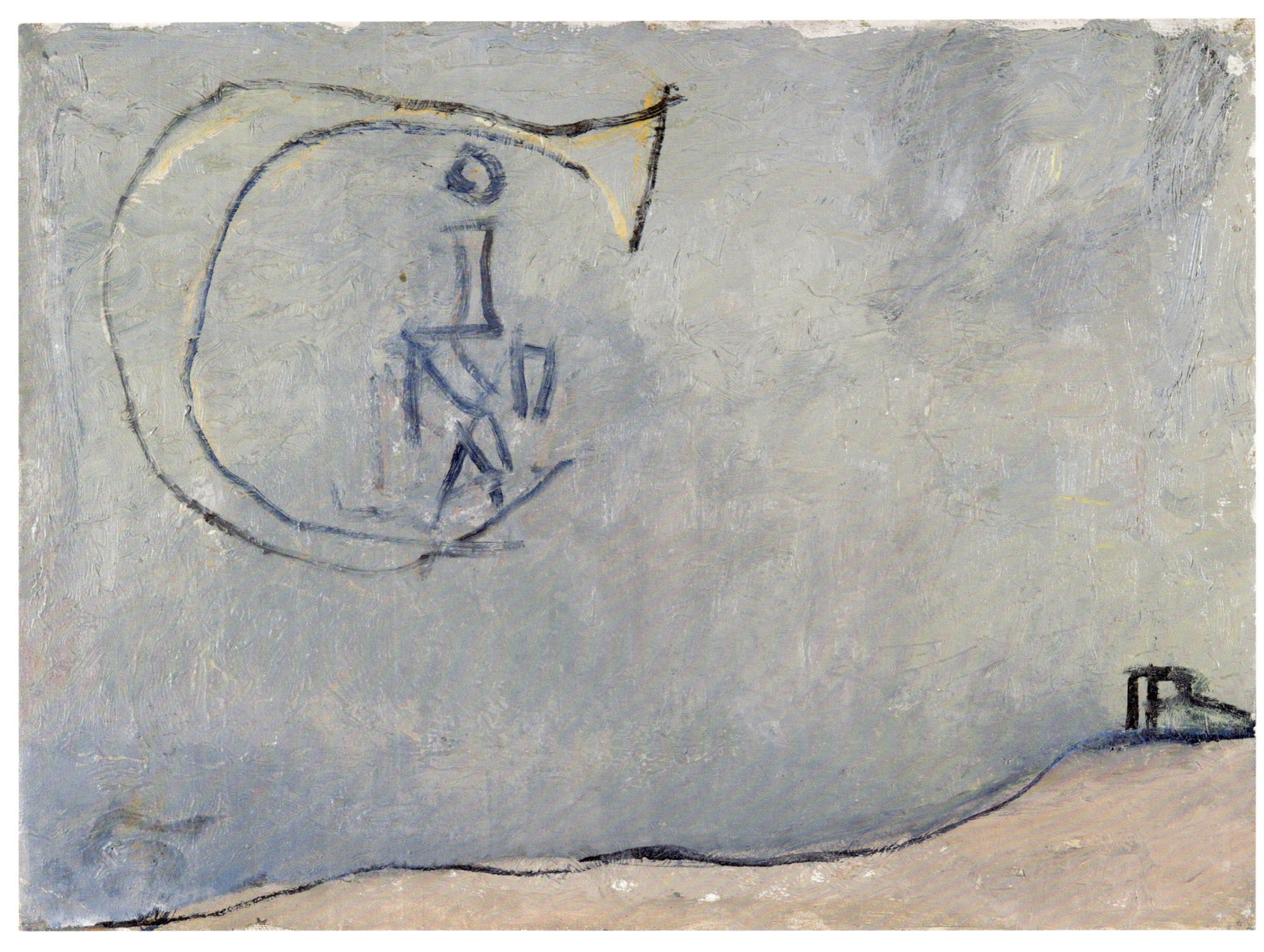

A CHARACTER IN GRAY
(PERSONAGGIO IN GRIGIO)
1944
oil on canvas
36.2 × 47 cm
Private collection on long-term loan
to Casa Museo Osvaldo Licini,
Monte Vidon Corrado

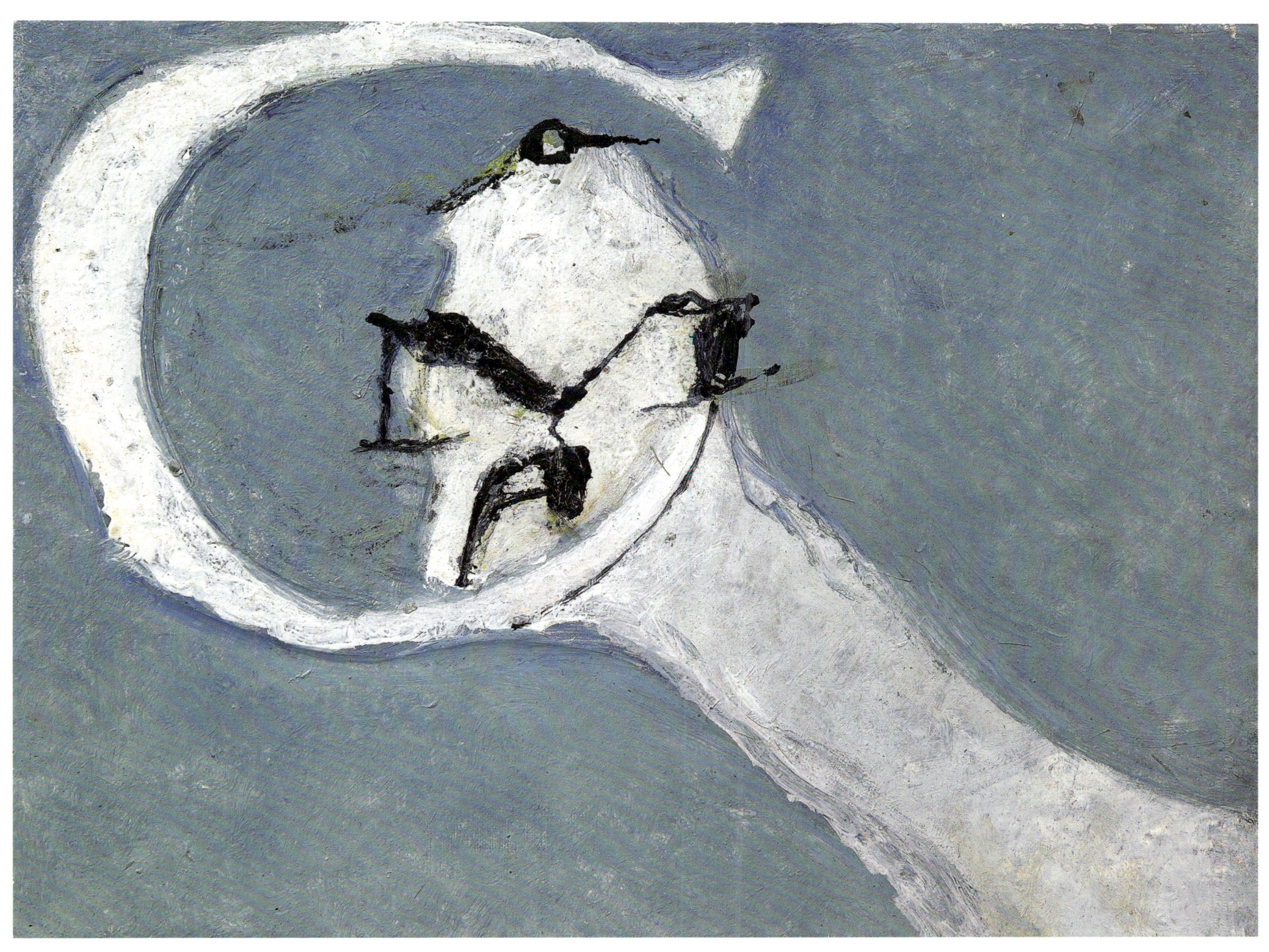

FLYING DUTCHMAN, BLUE
(OLANDESE VOLANTE AZZURRA)
ca. 1944
oil on canvas, mounted on cardboard
20 × 25 cm
Silvia Poli Licini collection

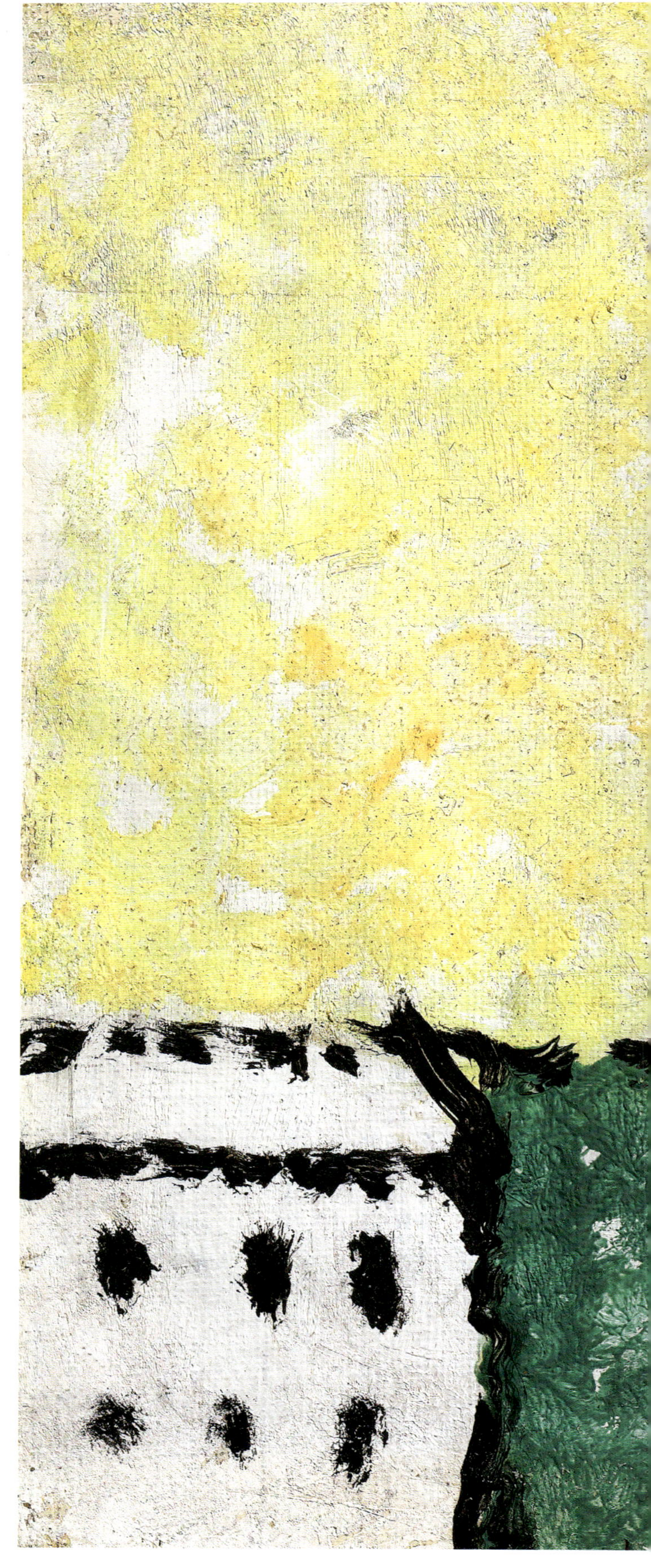

A CHARACTER ON A YELLOW BACKGROUND
(PERSONAGGIO SU FONDO GIALLO)
1944
oil on canvas mounted on canvas
23.2 × 30.6 cm
Private collection, Fermo

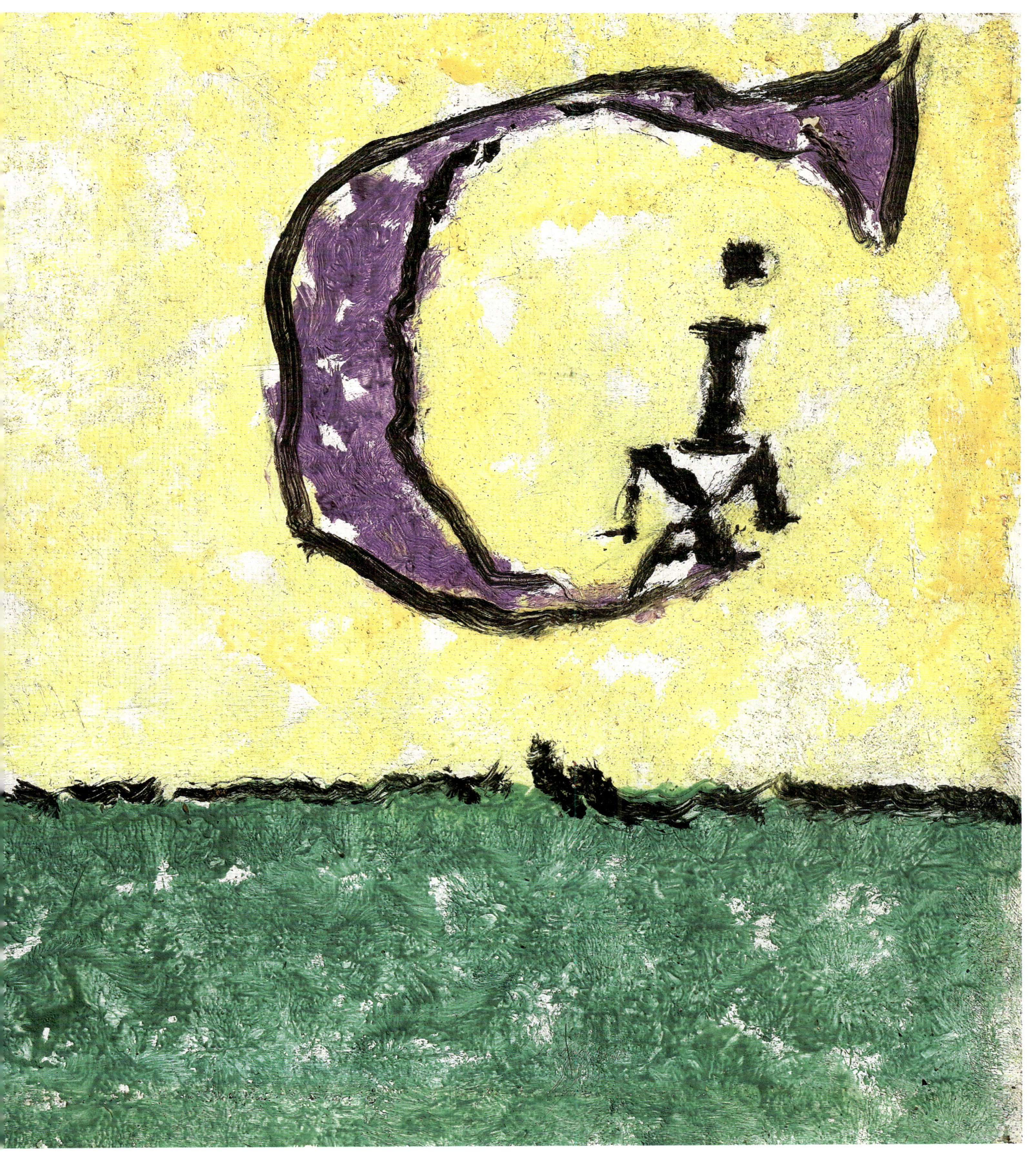

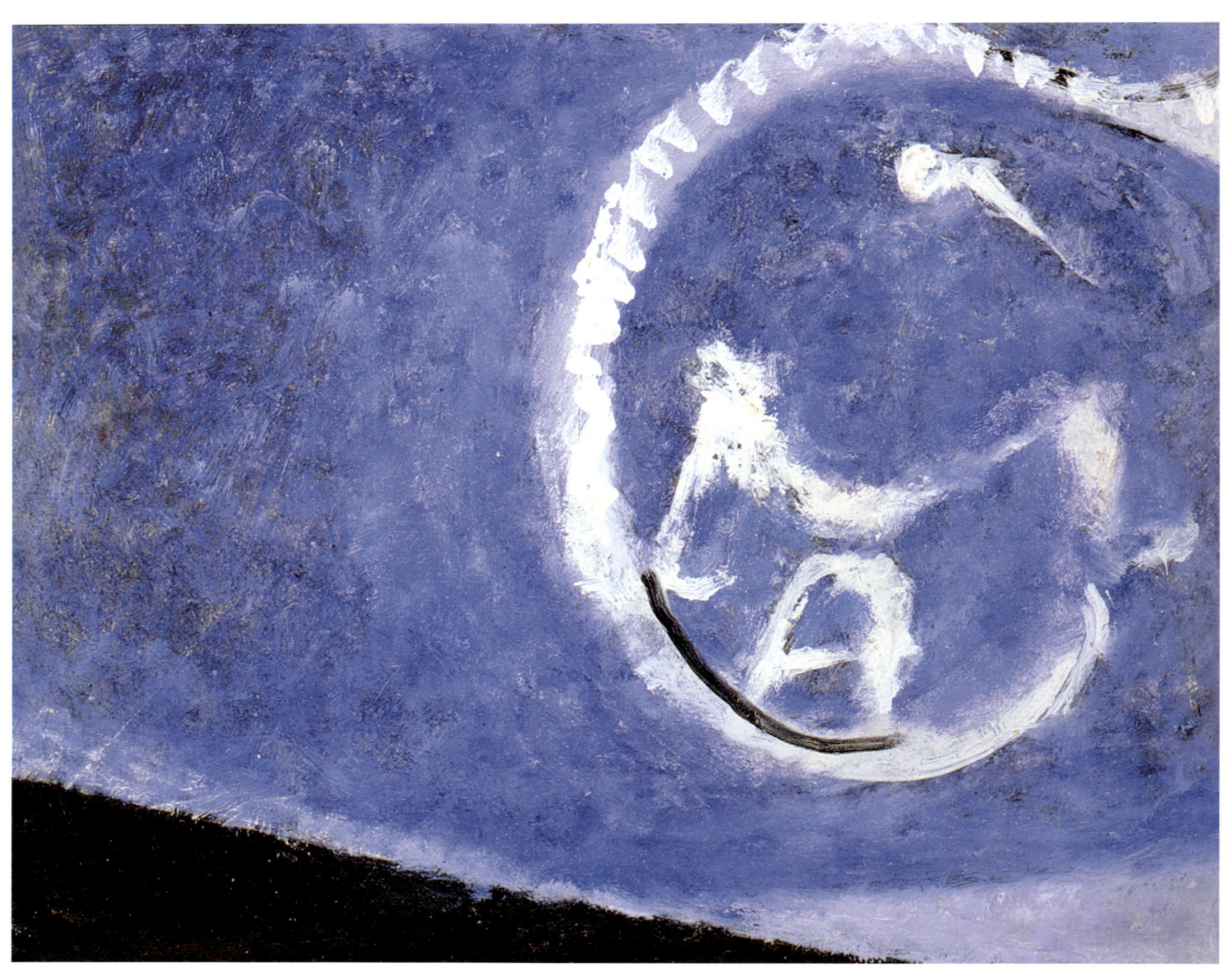

A LARGE CHARACTER
(PERSONAGGIO GRANDE)
1945
oil on canvas
23 × 29 cm
Private collection, Milan

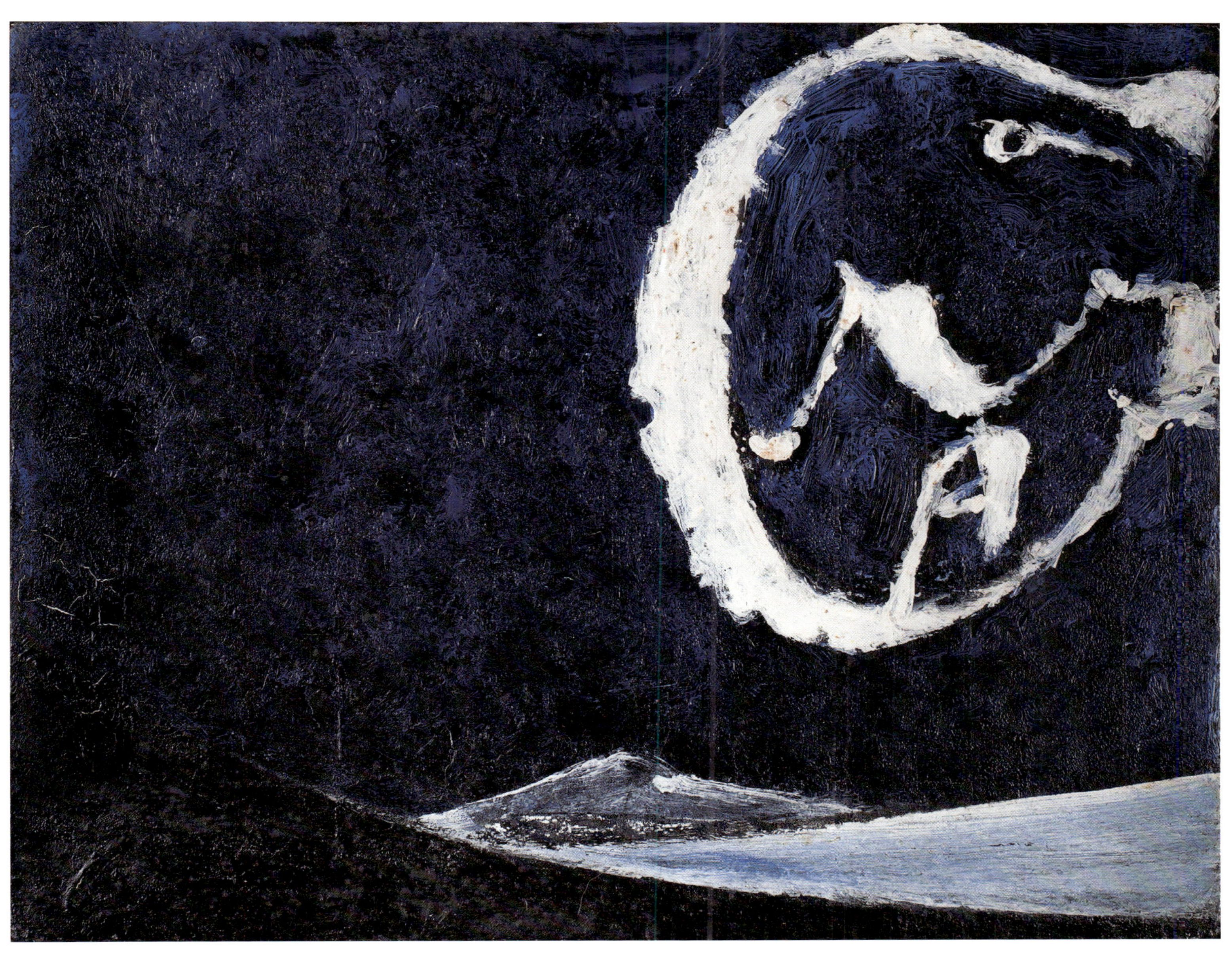

A CHARACTER
(PERSONAGGIO)
1946
oil on board
20.5 × 26 cm
Private collection, Porto San Giorgio

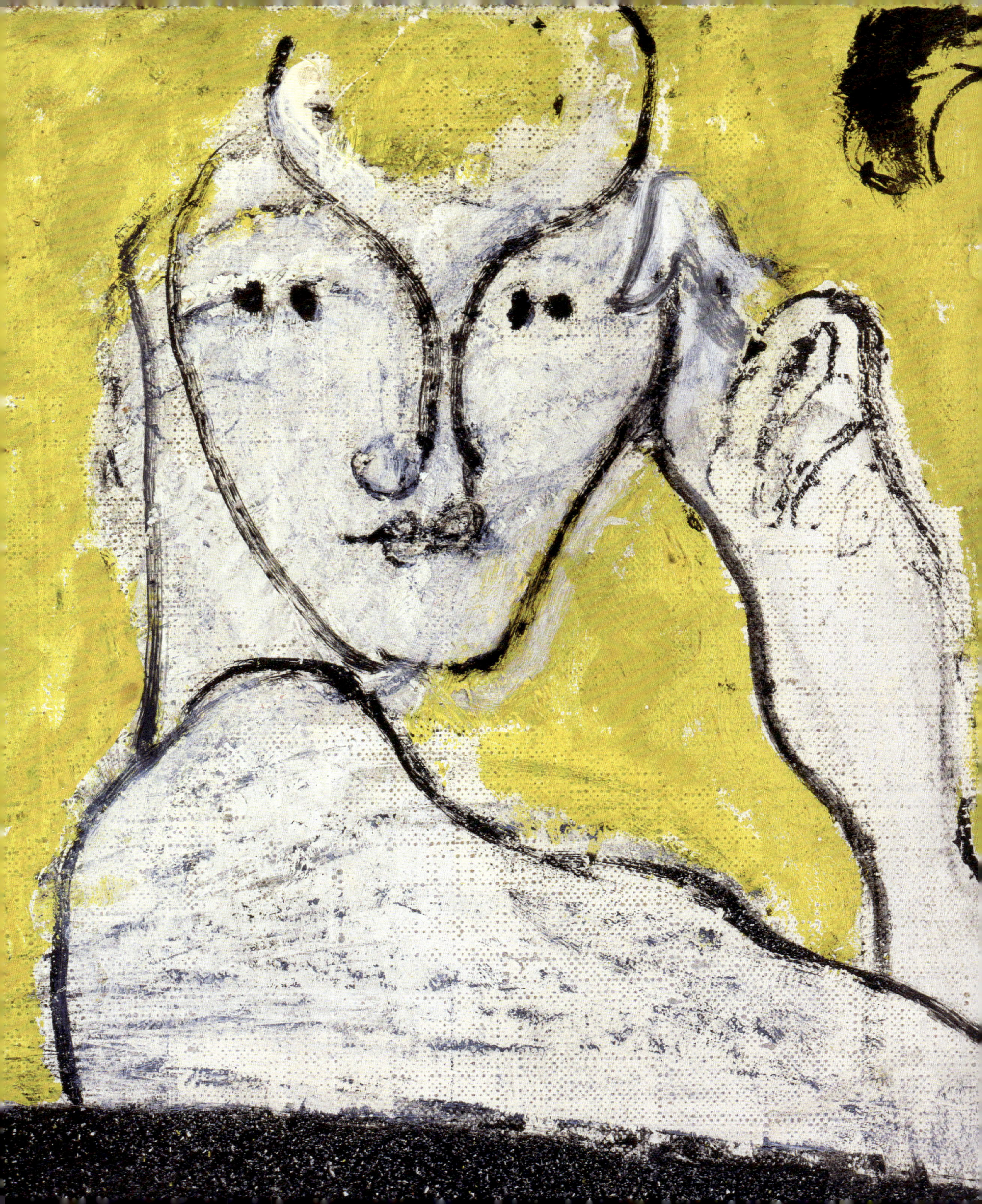

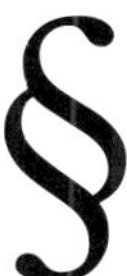

THE ICONOGRAPHIC INVENTIONS OF LICINI'S MATURITY: THE AMALASUNTHA AND REBEL ANGEL SERIES

"Amalasuntha is our beautiful moon, guaranteed silver for eternity, personified in few words, friend to every weary heart."[43] On the occasion of the 1950 Venice Biennale, when he exhibited nine *Amalasuntha* (*Amalssunta*) paintings, in a letter to Marchiori Licini explains the meaning of his new figure, born after the war out of the progressive metamorphosis of the *Characters* and the *Flying Dutchmen*. The name, borrowed from Amalasuntha, queen of the Ostrogoths, takes on a different meaning in Italian through a sequence of subtle phonetic and semantic shifts that recall the spirit of Lautréamont, whereby the Marian trope of the Vergine Assunta is inverted to become *mal Assunta*, or "badly ascended." At once moon goddess, crowned queen, Christian and pagan divinity, Amalasuntha embodies the eternal feminine, the female principle of Nature, the archetype of the "great mother" or "great Venus" common to all cultures. Licini is once again rigorously atemporal, thoroughly uninterested in keeping up with artistic currents, which in those years his Italian peers pursued compulsively through variations on the Picasso model, embroiled in a heated debate between Neorealism and abstract art. Licini was completely extraneous to this dynamic and continued on his own path as a radical outsider.

The horizon line in these new works assumes a dual significance: on the one hand, it maintains the idea of a rational and deliberate line, as in *Amalasuntha on a Red Background* (*Amalassunta su fondo rosso*) of 1950 (p. 154), while on the other it acquires an unusual organic morphology, where the hill becomes a sensual breast in a revealing connection to the way the artist had treated the nude in previous decades. The sky-dwelling Amalasunthas exist in constant dialogue with the earth: their ascent, their flight, often appears perched on the horizon line; other

THE SNOWMAN
(L'UOMO DI NEVE)
1952
oil on canvas
25.5 × 32.5 cm
Private collection
detail

times the horizon partially obscures them, almost as if by osmosis. They are all daughters of an ambiguous imbalance, of an ironic shift whereby they can smoke a cigarette, twist their face into a scowl, and strike fully human poses while at the same time undergoing enigmatic metamorphoses: the lines of their faces are often transformed into those of a hand-crown, elongating to become a foot, while from the horizon emerge the sinuous forms of breasts, or of hands holding a heart. These anatomical fragments have both a symbolic and graphic function in Licini's paintings, revealing the artist's poetic universe through the filter of irony. In *Amalasuntha No. 1* (*Amalassunta n. 1*) of 1949 (p. 153), for example, a crescent moon seems to direct the viewer's attention to the lower left corner of the painting, where there appears a hand holding a heart between the fingers, while in *Great Friend No. 2* (*La grande amica n. 2*) of 1948–50 (p. 147) a hand/foot is depicted in flight against a bold red background to become a scenario of erotic desire. These are essentially the same symbols that populate his youthful *Racconti di Bruto*, at once "heretical" and "erotic," in which the protagonist, contemplating his own heart in his cupped hands, was overcome by the irresistible impulse to give it "perhaps to the first man he met on the street."[44]

In continuity with the first *Character* paintings, mysterious numbers define the faces and seem to confirm the indecipherable nature of things, but they are first and foremost pictorial "signifiers" inserted into the body of a color that is never flat or uniform, but vibrant and often rarefied, as we see in *Amalasuntha 66–66* (*Amalassunta 66–66*) and *Amalasuntha on a Blue-Green Background* (*Amalassunta su fondo blu-verde*) of 1949 (p. 144). The Amalasuntha would earn Licini national and international acclaim, epitomizing the entire course of his artistic investigations to become his most recognizable formula. And with this, the myth of the shy and reclusive artist was revived, though with a different connotation compared to another well-known solitary artist, Morandi. In Licini, the constant return to the same subject is never a pictorial gymnasium, as in Morandi, but rather an endless struggle to reconcile painting and poetry.

In a fundamental essay of 1974, Francesco Bartoli highlights how "the great angelic, lunar, and celestial metaphors around which the relations between small symbols, emblems, and isolated images are established acquire a decisively synthetic and coagulatory role.... The painting is not merely a perfect assembly machine. It is also an exposition of myth and a scenic narrative."[45] Describing *Evening (Large)* of 1950 (p. 163), he writes:

> Everything is said in a few words, but everything is also articulated in a multiplicity of representative interconnections .... First of all, the surface is partitioned by a curve of earth (a concave horizon turned up-

side down, as if the gaze comes from outside), while the aerial zone is bisected into two horizontal bands, which are complementary in their chromatic function: yellow and green. This demarcation of space, however, is immediately negated by the line that draws the components, as its path runs seamlessly from top to bottom, eventually revealing the complex and ambiguous figure of an Amalasuntha: complex because it results from the conjunction of several components (hand, foot, profile), and ambiguous because it has an excess of attributes, such as the wings and the angelic body, which belong instead to Licini's other theme of demonic rebellion.… the recitative syntax of the work is based … on the signifiers of transformation: rotation, chiasmus, doubling, complementarity, pairs of opposites, balance, simultaneity.[46]

While *Evening (Large)* (*La sera [Grande]*) (p. 163), announces the theme of the rebel angel, *The Snowman* (*L'uomo di neve*) (p. 149) of 1952 is a figure that merges the Amalasuntha and the angel with echoes of the goat from *Imaginary Landscape* of 1927, which could perhaps have been taken up again later on, as often happened in the course of his career. In *Amalasuntha No. 3* (*Amalassunta n. 3*) (p. 157), for example, beneath the red background Licini allows a geometric construction to show through like a skeletal substructure, confirming once again the personal nature of the temporal dimension in which the artist's works exist.

Evening Twilight (*Crepuscolo della sera*) of 1951 (p. 179) is a very unusual work that seems to incorporate and summarize Licini's entire lexicon—geometry, poetry, symbolism, matter, horizon, color—in a rare dramatic synthesis that anticipates the evolution of his work between 1953 and 1958. The title is inspired by a poem from *Les Fleurs du mal* by Baudelaire, an author much loved by Licini, even if the dark-winged "demons" described by the poet are incompatible with the soft colors and lyrical atmosphere of Licini's work. The figure that stands out disruptively against the landscape introduces the theme of the Rebel Angel, anticipating the synthetic development of these figures in later works while at the same time retaining similarities with the earlier abstract period.

In the second half of the 1940s, in a sky much higher and more occlusive than that of the Amalasuntha paintings, the Rebel Angel appears. In this figure, which seems to span the space of the canvas, the line expresses a concrete idea of muscularity and power. The effort and struggle of the angel are the equivalent of the artist's own arduous quest to make the background into a sort of chromatic tone poem, anything but monochromatic, which evokes both the deepest darkness and the fullest, most abstract luminosity. The drama of the angel corresponds in a certain way to a new synthesis of the figure, in which two instances coexist: that of the representation of the realm of unreality, and that of creation, which Licini would develop until arriving at the cycle of the *Lunar Missiles* (*Missili lunari*).

The theme of the angel, which Federica Pirani discusses elsewhere in this catalogue, runs through all of Licini's work, starting from the *Archangel Gabriel* of 1919 up to the *Rebel Angel* series, which reveal a new visual narration of the *topos* of overcoming the limit of the biblical struggle and consequent fall, resulting in the loss of the rebels' angelic status. *Rebel Angel on a Yellow Background* (*Angelo ribelle su fondo giallo*) of 1949 (p. 165) appears to allude precisely to this dimension in the projection of the figure downwards, which recalls the work *Miracle of Saint Mark* (*Miracolo di San Marr…co*) of 1948, presented that same year at the Venice Biennale. As the Italian title humorously alludes, with the doubling of the *r* and the suspension of the final syllable of the name "Marco," the painting borrows the pose of the saint in the famous work by Tintoretto, *The Miracle of the Slave* (1548), in the collection of the Accademia in Venice.

In *Rebel Angel on a Yellow Background* (*Angelo ribelle su fondo giallo*) of 1952 (p. 171) and *Rebel Angel with a Red Heart* (*Angelo ribelle con cuore rosso*) (p. 172) of the following year, we find the iconographic theme of the heart, which, as Marchiori writes, is finally returned "to its place." Describing the blue background of the latter work, Marchiori points out that:

> This, for Licini, is a vast space, like the Sistine Chapel. Indeed, the angel is a figure of final judgment, menacing and solemn, despite the calligraphic signs that almost seem an ironic commentary on that majestic posture. Finally, with the arrival of this dominating angel, the heart has returned to its place after so many symbolic peregrinations.[47]

The work was exhibited at the important retrospective that Marchiori curated at the Centro Culturale Olivetti in Ivrea in early 1958, and again that same year at a solo show at the Venice Biennale, where Peggy Guggenheim was photographed surrounded by Licini's paintings. The international jury of the Biennale awarded him the Grand Prize for painting, an important, albeit overdue recognition of the centrality of his work in twentieth-century art. Of Licini the man, Palma Bucarelli wrote, "… both for the limited volume of his production and the singularity of his reticent nature, he remained in the shadow of noisier and more garish figures."[48] In Venice he presented a wide selection of paintings, from the 1920s to the most recent works of 1958–59, including *Saint Domingo Angel* (*Angelo di San Domingo*) (1957, p. 185) and *Rebel Angel* (*Angelo ribelle*) (1958, p. 191).

In the *Nocturnes*, Licini creates an abstract synthesis of tight rhythms that prefigures the *Lunar Missiles*. A humorous reference to the imagery inspired by the earliest explorations of space in the late 1950s is found in a letter to Marchiori dated October 6, 1957: "We shall meet again in

Turin on October 20. I will bring the sulfur and you the fuse, to launch into the space of the heavens a new sun (made of sh*t ...), such that henceforth every 'satellite' will tremble!"[49] *Saint Domingo Angel*, similarly to *Saint Rose Angel* (*Angelo di Santa Rosa*) (1957, p. 187), is representative of the fatefully conclusive convergence of the various threads of Licini's artistic enquiry: a hybrid kite-angel crowned by a small crescent moon hovers delicately in an intensely blue sky, holding the number *5* in its hand, interpreted by some as the union of the opposites 2 and 3, according to Pythagorean symbolism; in the lower left, an *o* and an *l* are merged in a single floating sign that is also found in numerous other works and can be read as Licini's signature.[50] But it is the *Rebel Angel* of 1958 that emblematically encapsulates the entirety of his artistic vision: from the landscape and the letters to the stars, the missiles, and the angel, which has by now become the ideogram of itself, composed of kites and destined to become a legend. ■

43. Letter from Osvaldo Licini to Giuseppe Marchiori of May 21, 1950, in Licini, *Errante, erotico, eretico*, 148.
44. Licini, "Il cuore in mano," in Licini, *Errante, erotico, eretico*, 148.
45. Francesco Bartoli, "Figure dell'incastro e metafore dell'aria nel linguaggio di Licini," in Licini, *Errante, erotico, eretico*, 60.
46. Francesco Bartoli, "Figure dell'incastro e metafore dell'aria nel linguaggio di Licini," in Licini, *Errante, erotico, eretico*, 60–61.
47. Giuseppe Marchiori, catalogue entry for the 1958 exhibition in Ivrea, curated by Marchiori, cited in *Osvaldo Licini. Tra le Marche e l'Europa*, 200.
48. Palma Bucarelli, "Licini e Mastroianni primi premi della XXIX biennale," in *La Sera di Roma*, June 18, 1958, 21.
49. Letter cited in Giuseppe Marchiori, *I cieli segreti di Osvaldo Licini* (Venice, 1968), 29.
50. Magnoni, *Licini, secondo noi...*, 47.

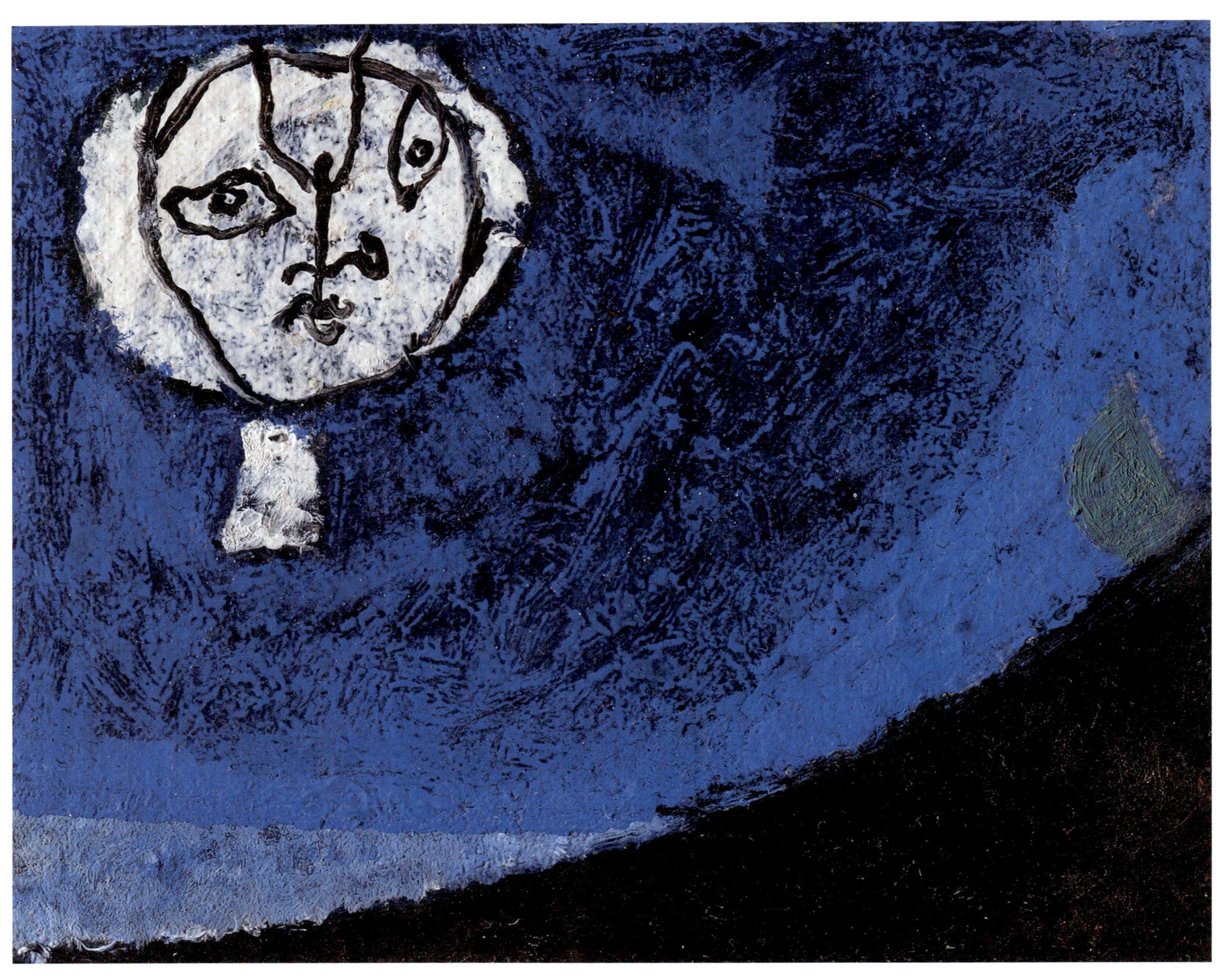

AMALASUNTHA MOON
(AMALASSUNTA LUNA)
1946
oil on board
17 × 13.8 cm
Private collection

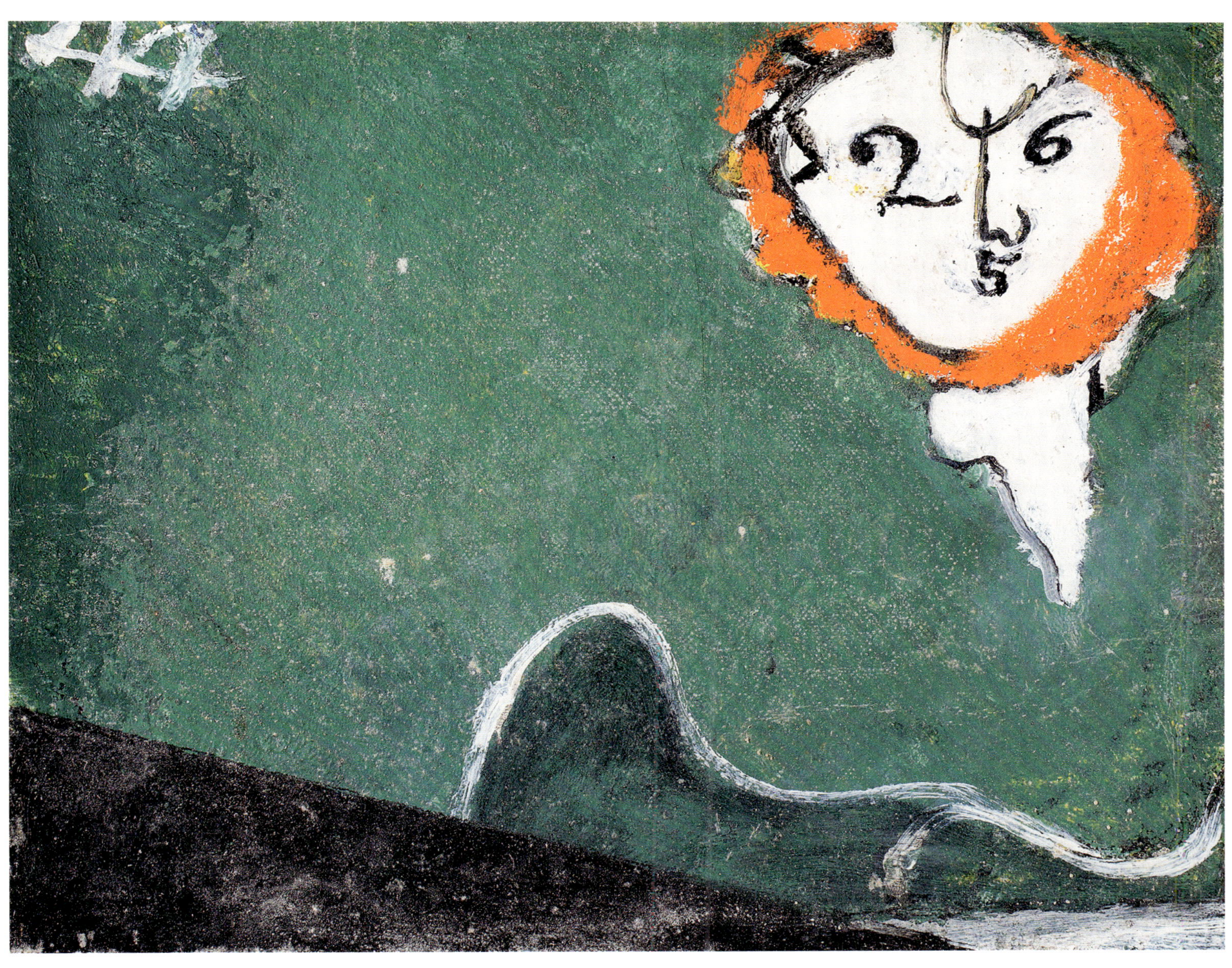

AMALASUNTHA WITH A RED AUREOLE
(AMALASSUNTA CON AUREOLA ROSSA)
1946
oil on canvas
20,5 × 27 cm
Private collection, Porto San Giorgio

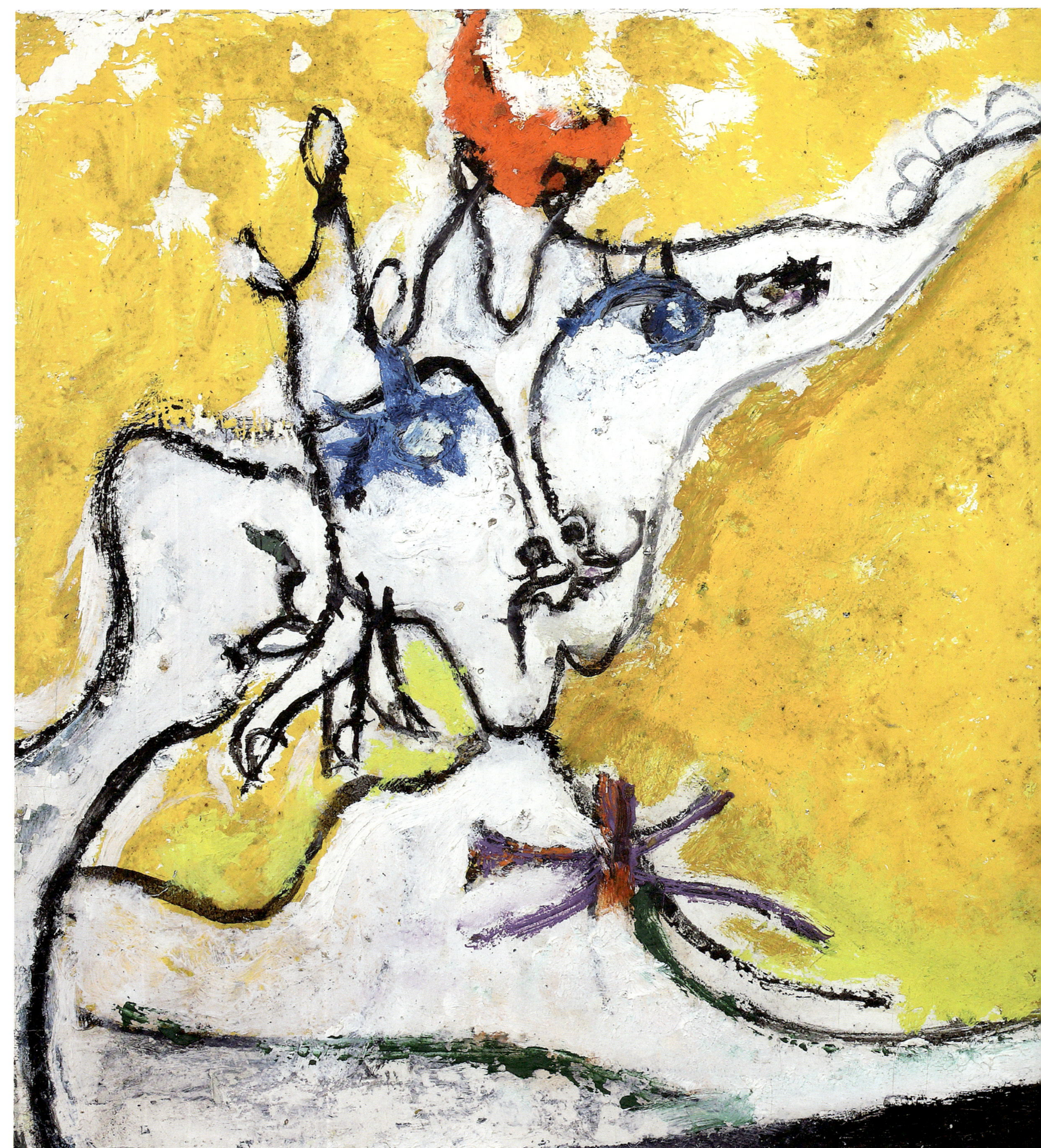

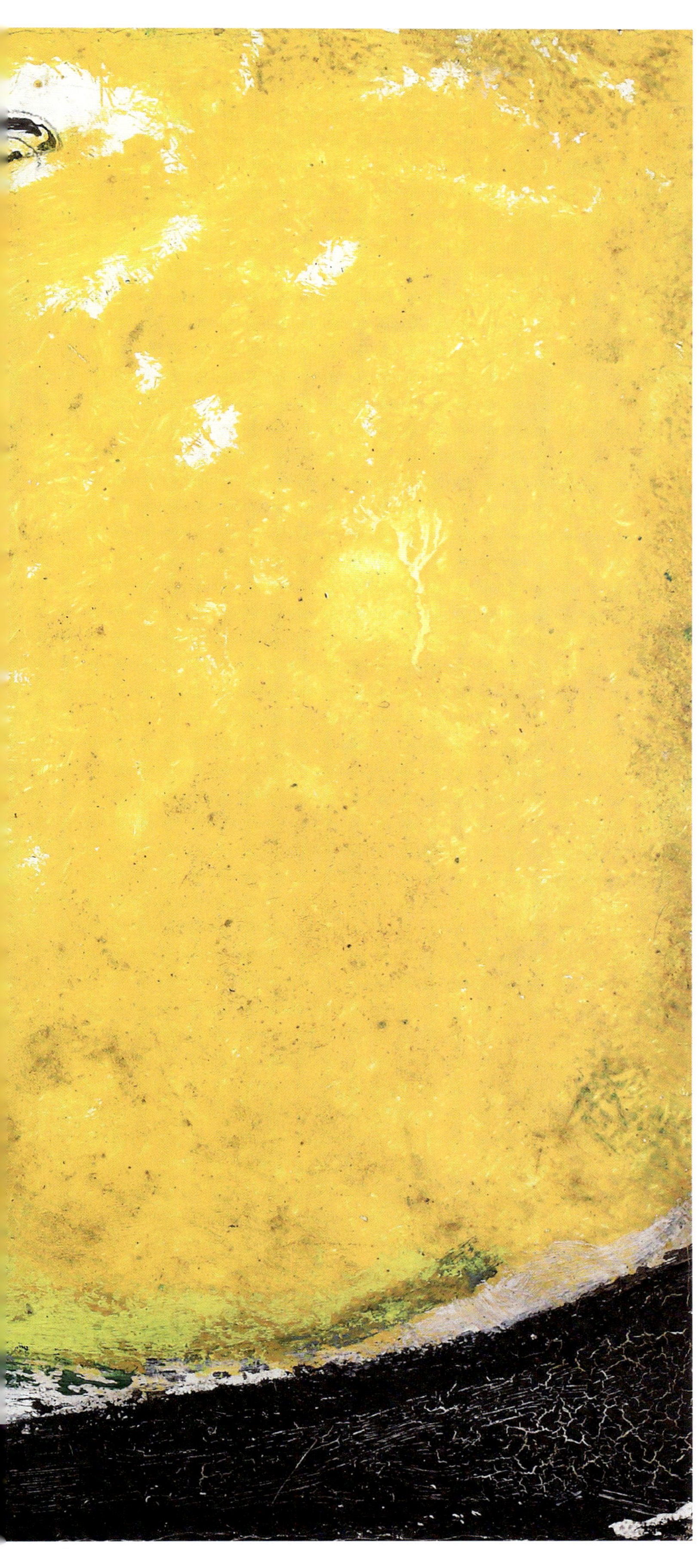

a character and the moon
(personaggio e la luna)
1949
oil on canvas
27.5 × 36 cm
Private collection, Rome

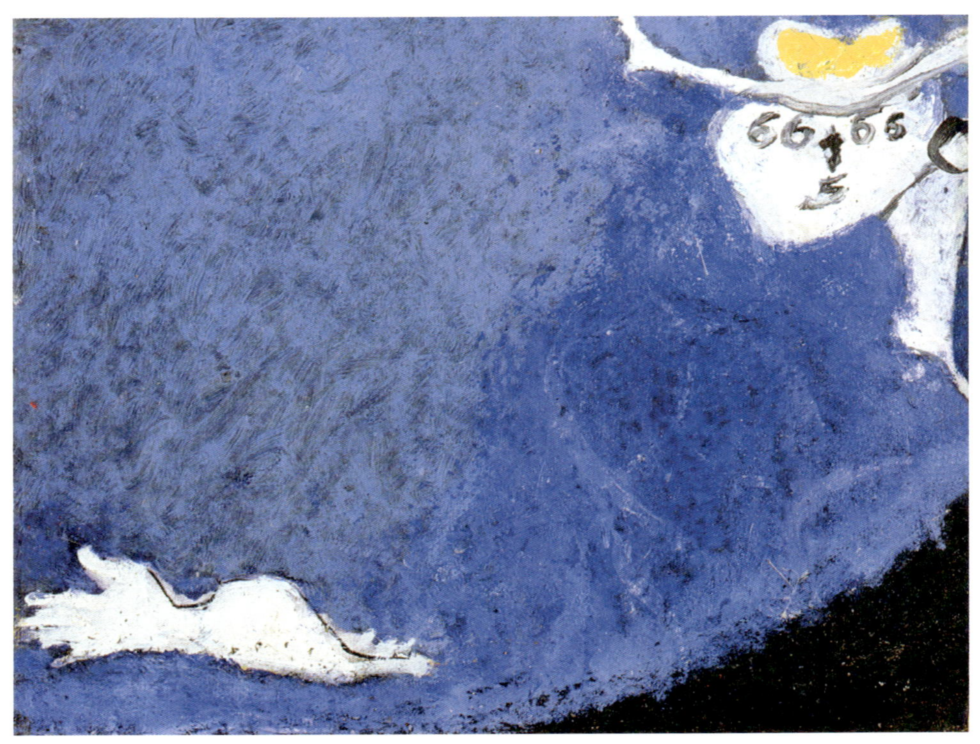

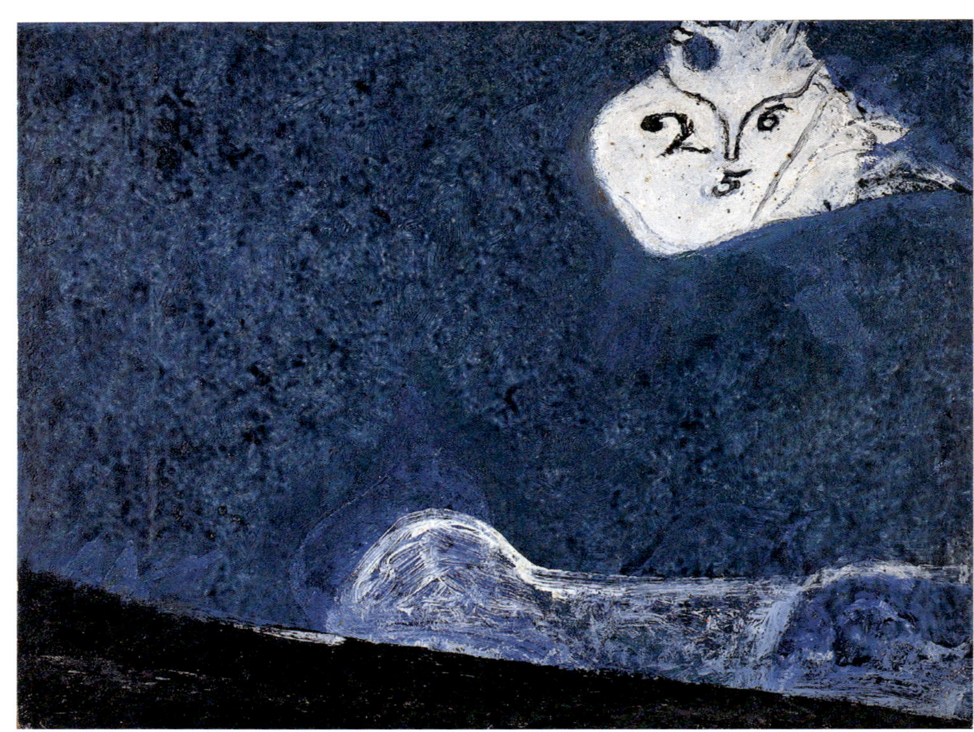

AMALASUNTHA 66–66
(AMALASSUNTA 66–66)
1949
oil on canvas
19 × 23.5 cm
Private collection, Milan

AMALASUNTHA ON A BLUE-GREEN BACKGROUND
(AMALASSUNTA SU FONDO BLU-VERDE)
1949
oil on canvas
23.6 × 32 cm
Private collection, Milan

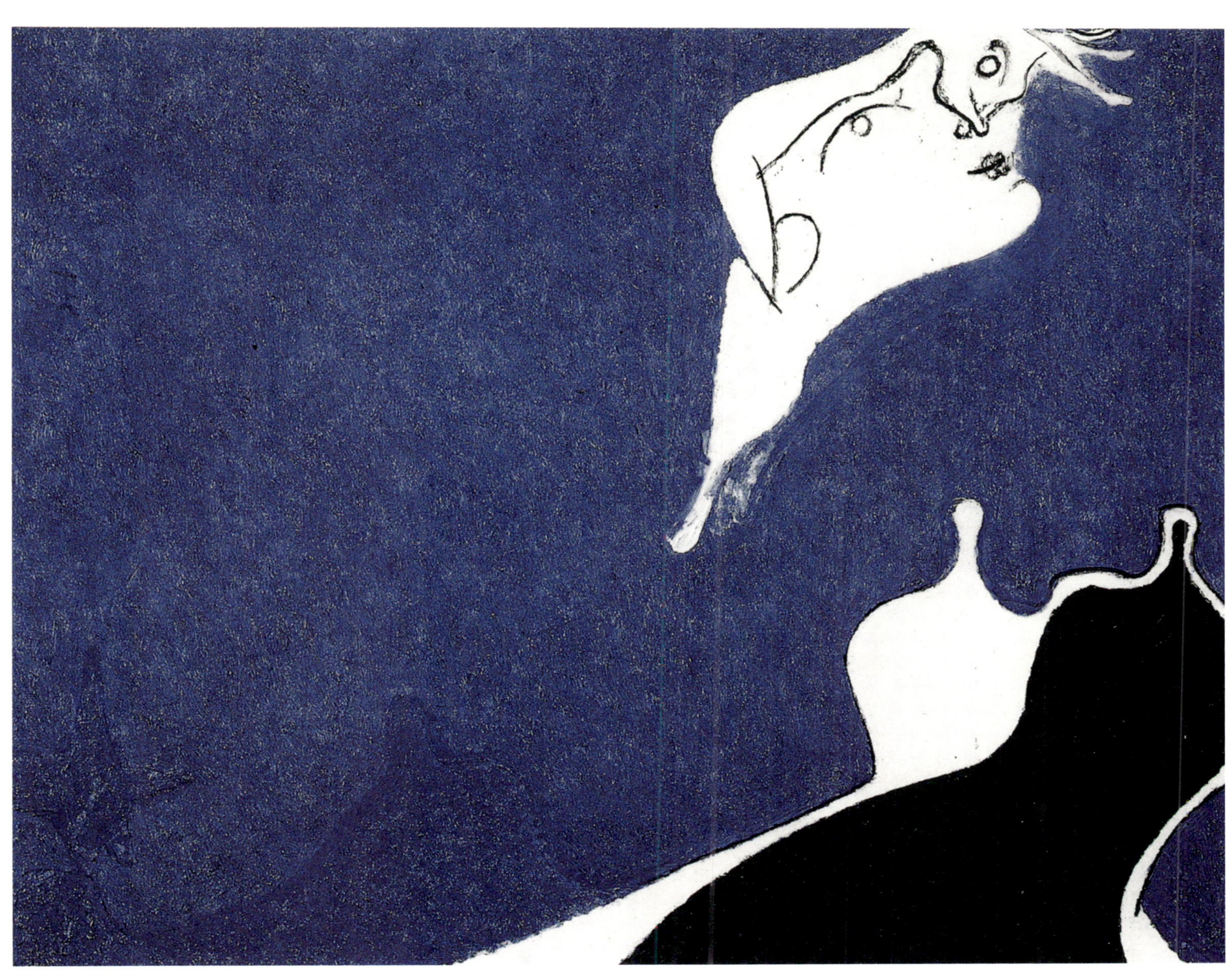

PATHÉTIQUE
(LA PATETICA)
1949–50
oil on canvas
81 × 100 cm
Private collection,
courtesy Lorenzelli Arte, Milan

GREAT FRIEND NO. 2
(LA GRANDE AMICA N. 2)
1948–50
oil on canvas
94 × 117 cm
Private collection,
Lorenzelli Arte, Milan

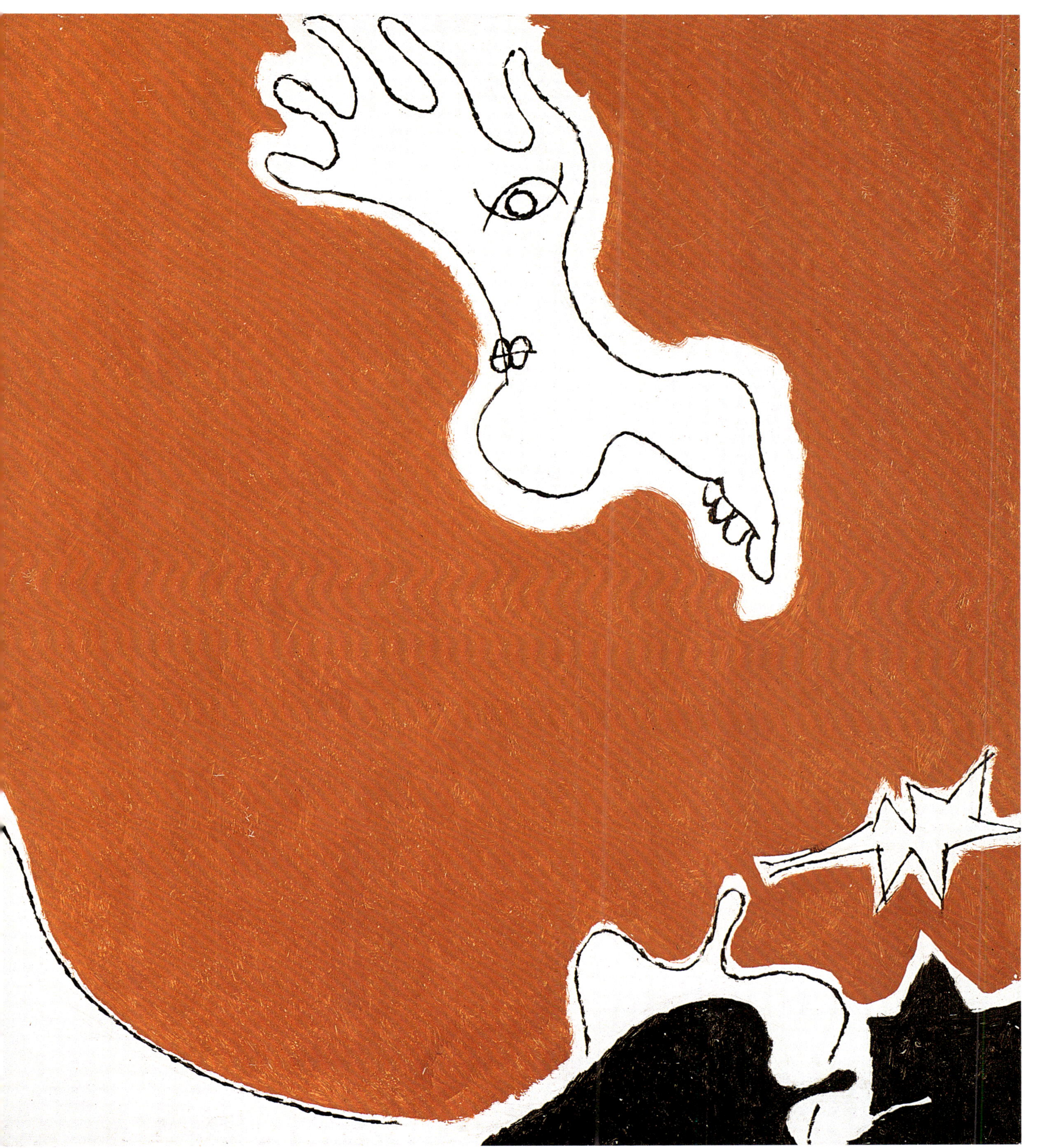

THE SNOWMAN
(L'UOMO DI NEVE)
1952
oil on canvas
25.5 × 32.5 cm
Private collection

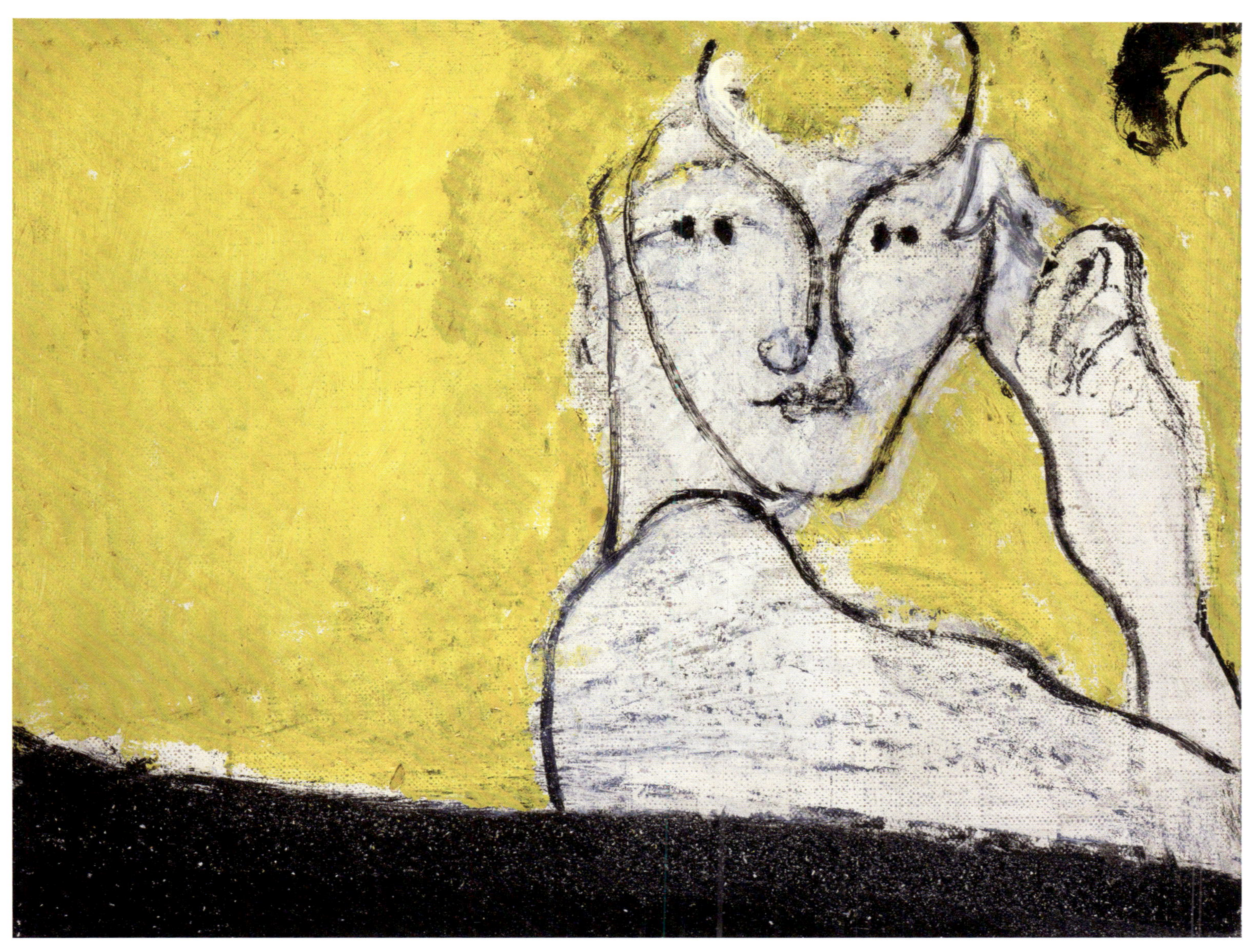

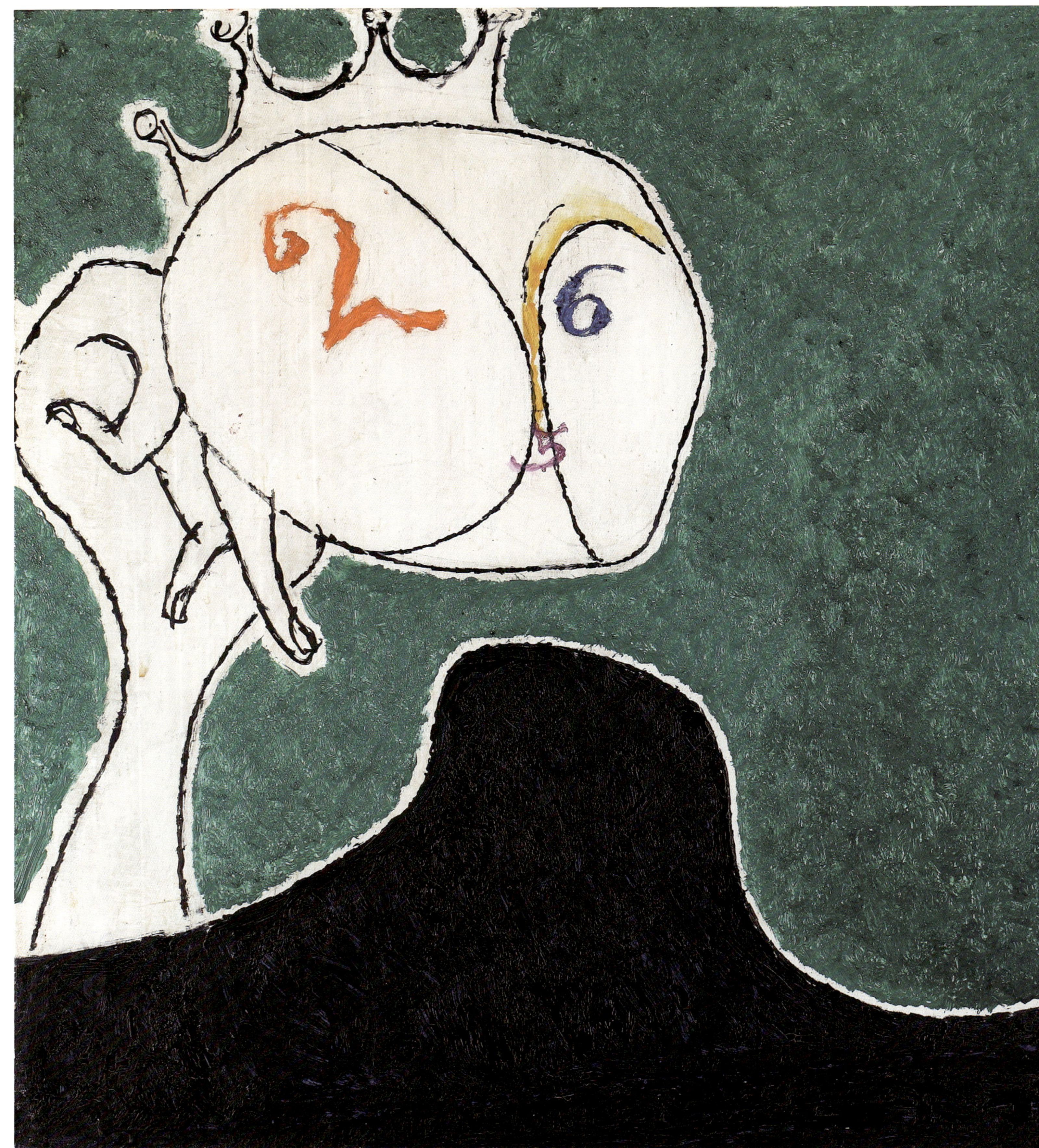

AMALASUNTHA ON A GREEN BACKGROUND
(AMALASSUNTA SU FONDO VERDE)
1949
oil on canvas
80.5 × 100 cm
Gori Collection,
Fattoria di Celle, Pistoia

AMALASUNTHA NO. 1
(AMALASSUNTA N. 1)
1949
81 × 100
oil on canvas
Maramotti Collection,
Reggio Emilia

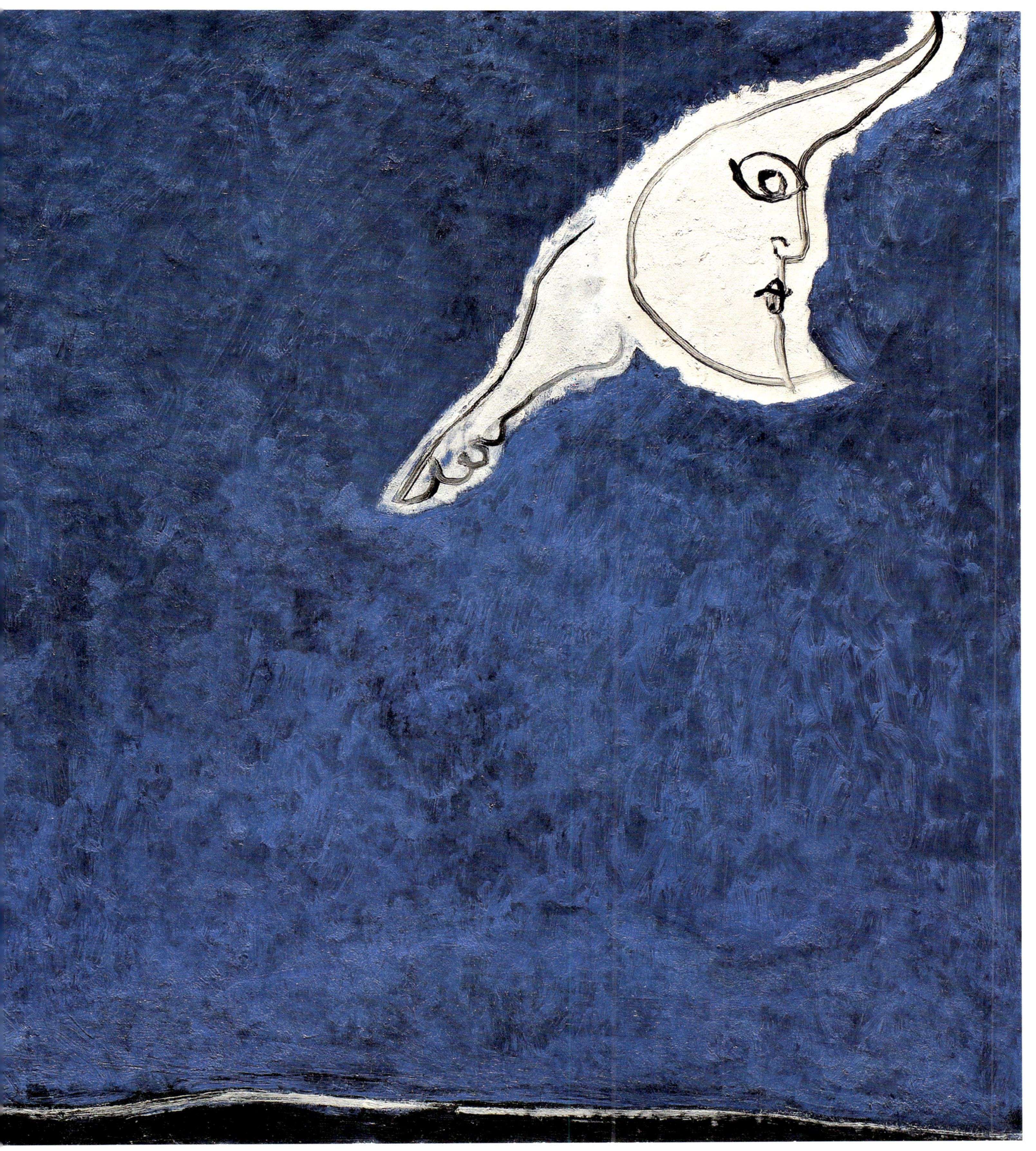

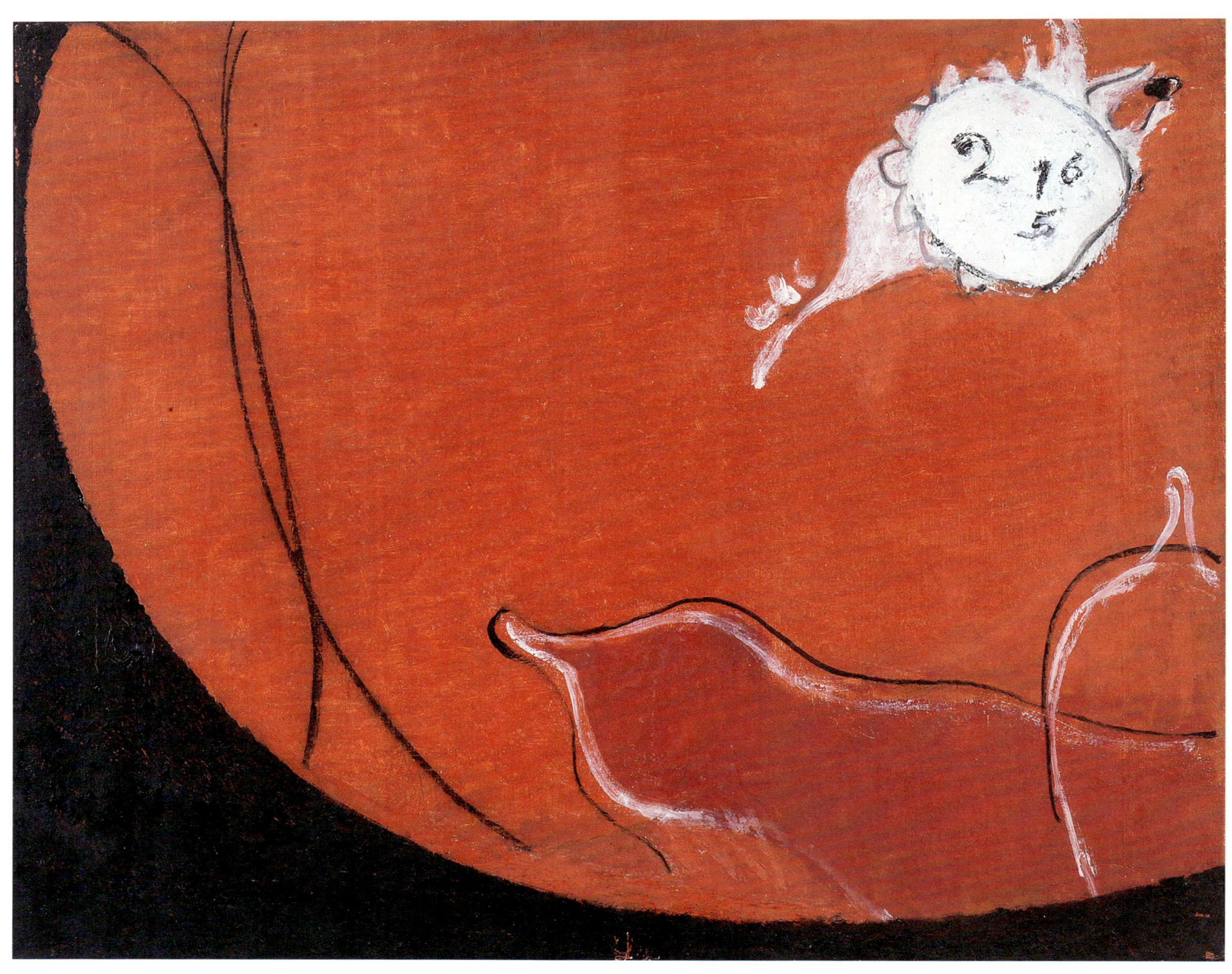

AMALASUNTHA ON A RED BACKGROUND
(AMALASSUNTA SU FONDO ROSSO)
1950
oil on canvas
64.5 × 81 cm
Private collection

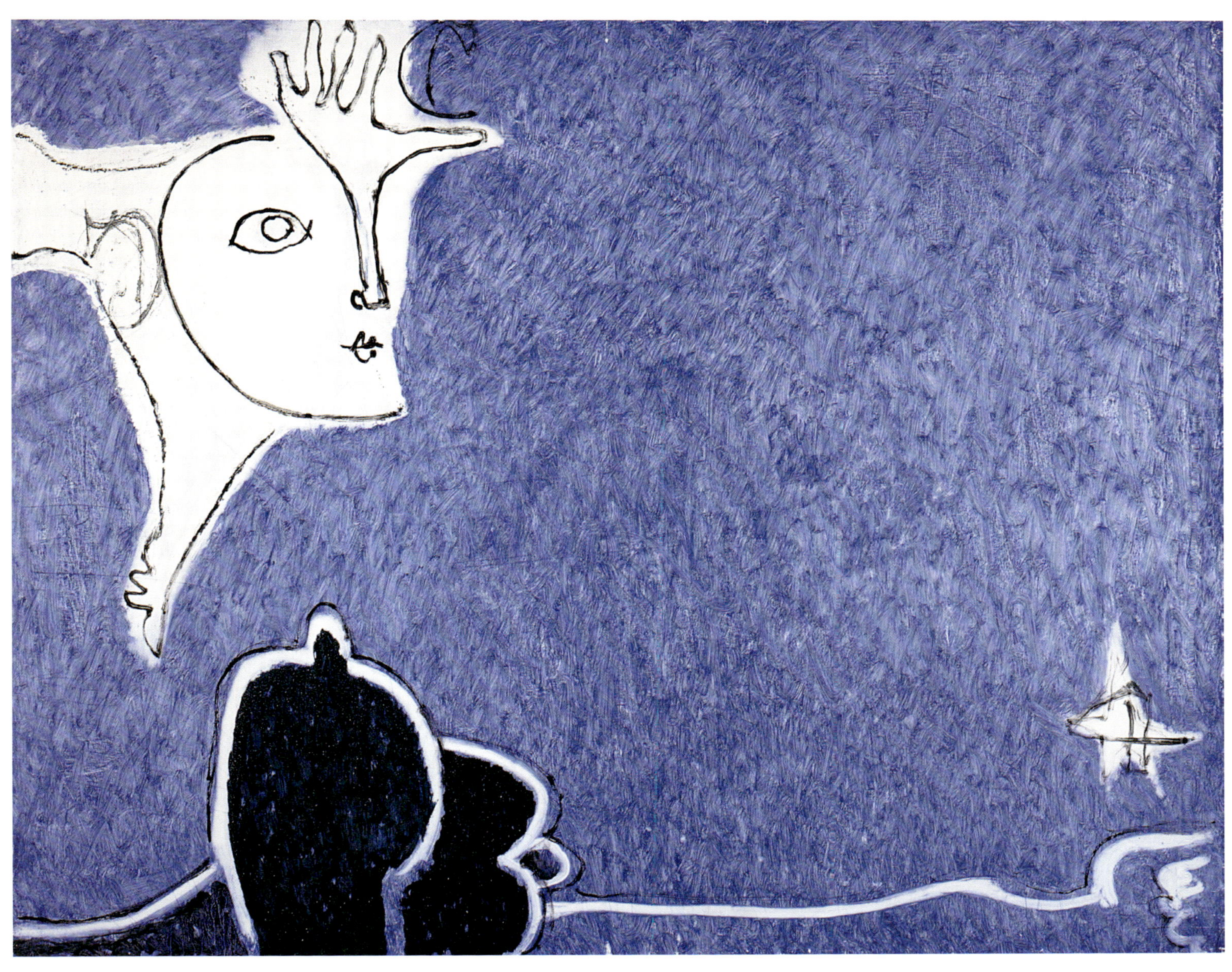

ITALY
(ITALIA)
1950
oil on canvas
93.5 × 117 cm
Private collection,
courtesy Lorenzelli Arte, Milan

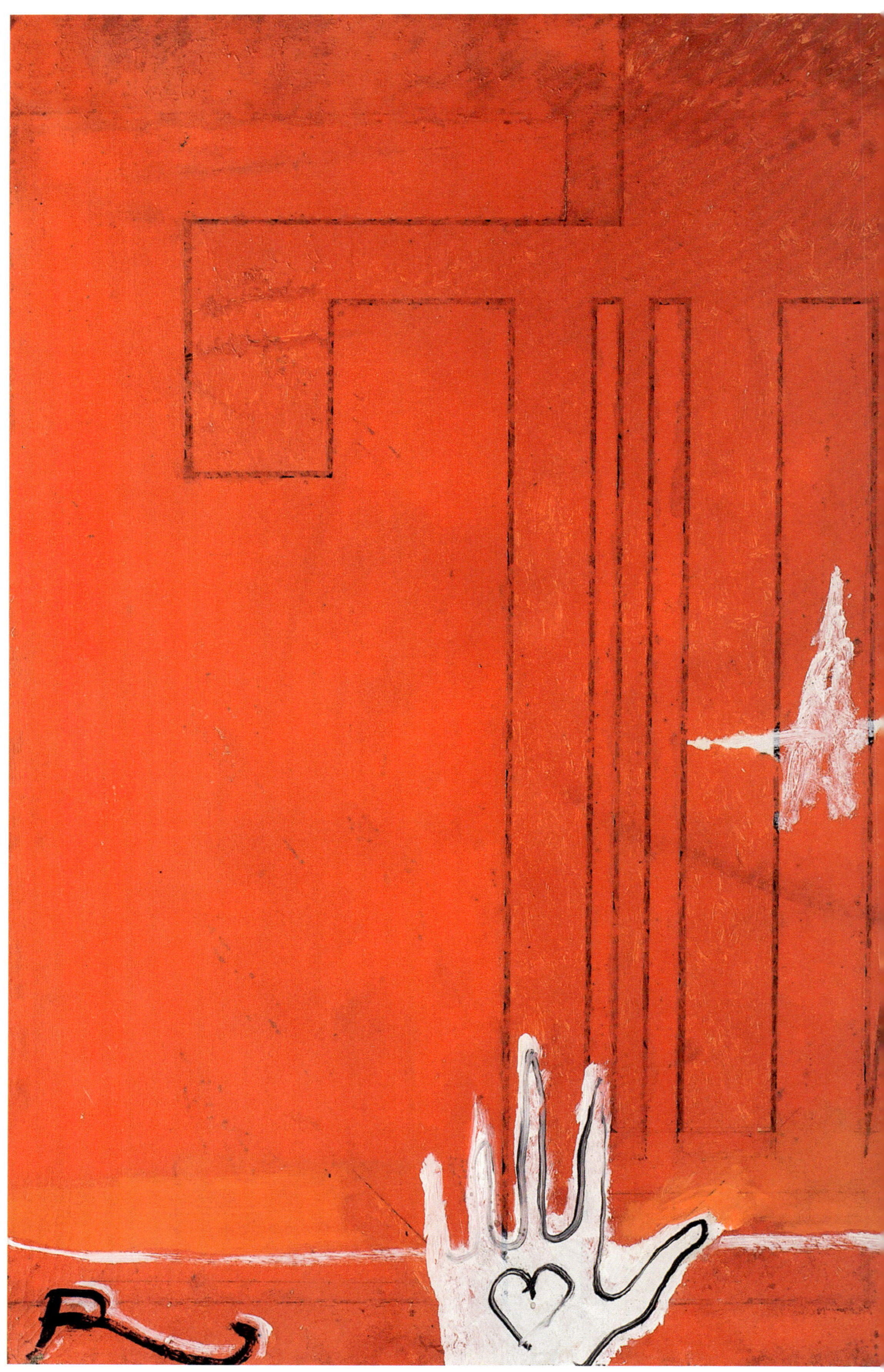

AMALASUNTHA NO. 3
(AMALASSUNTA N. 3)
1950
oil on canvas
80 × 100 cm
Private collection,
courtesy Lorenzelli Arte, Milan

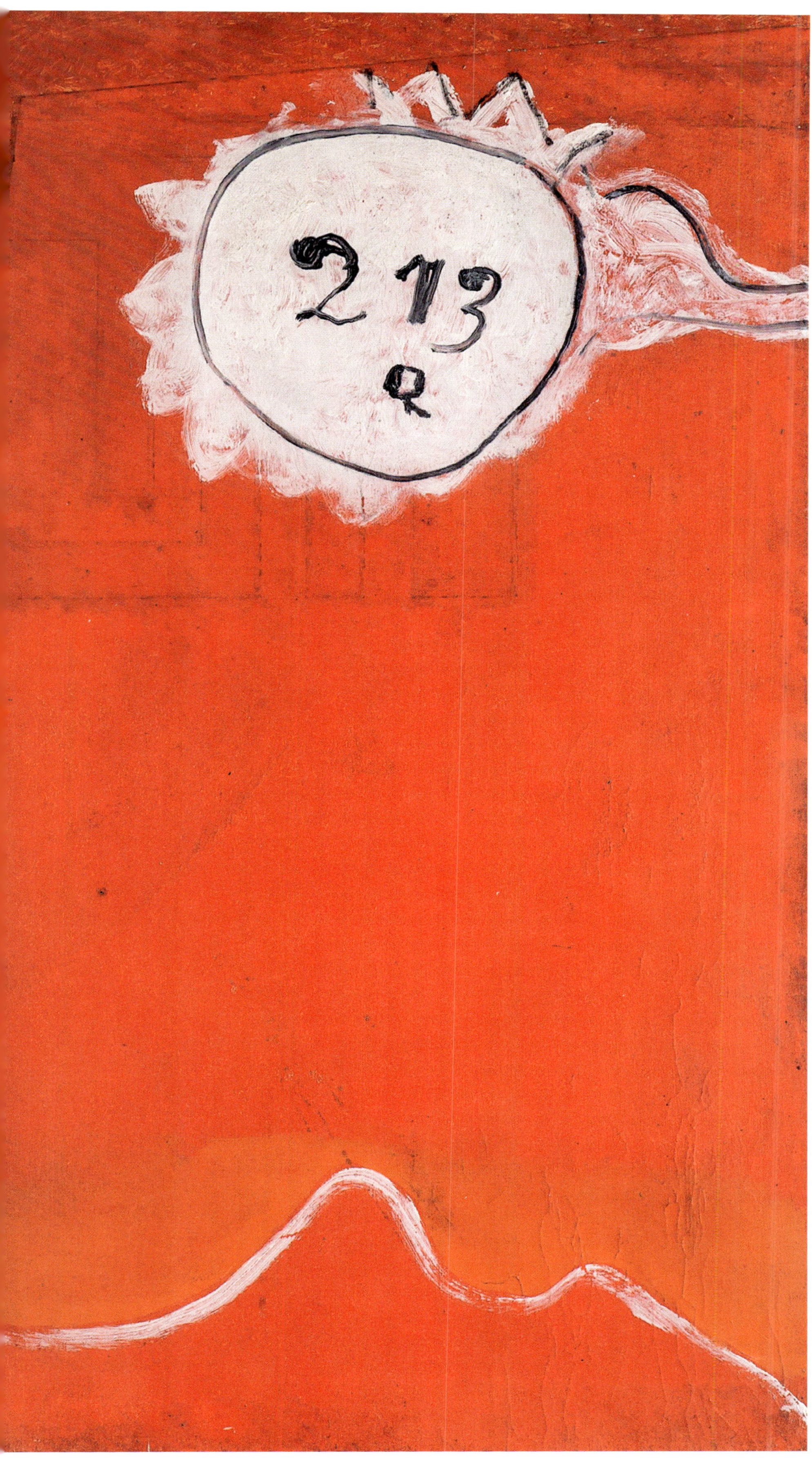
2 13

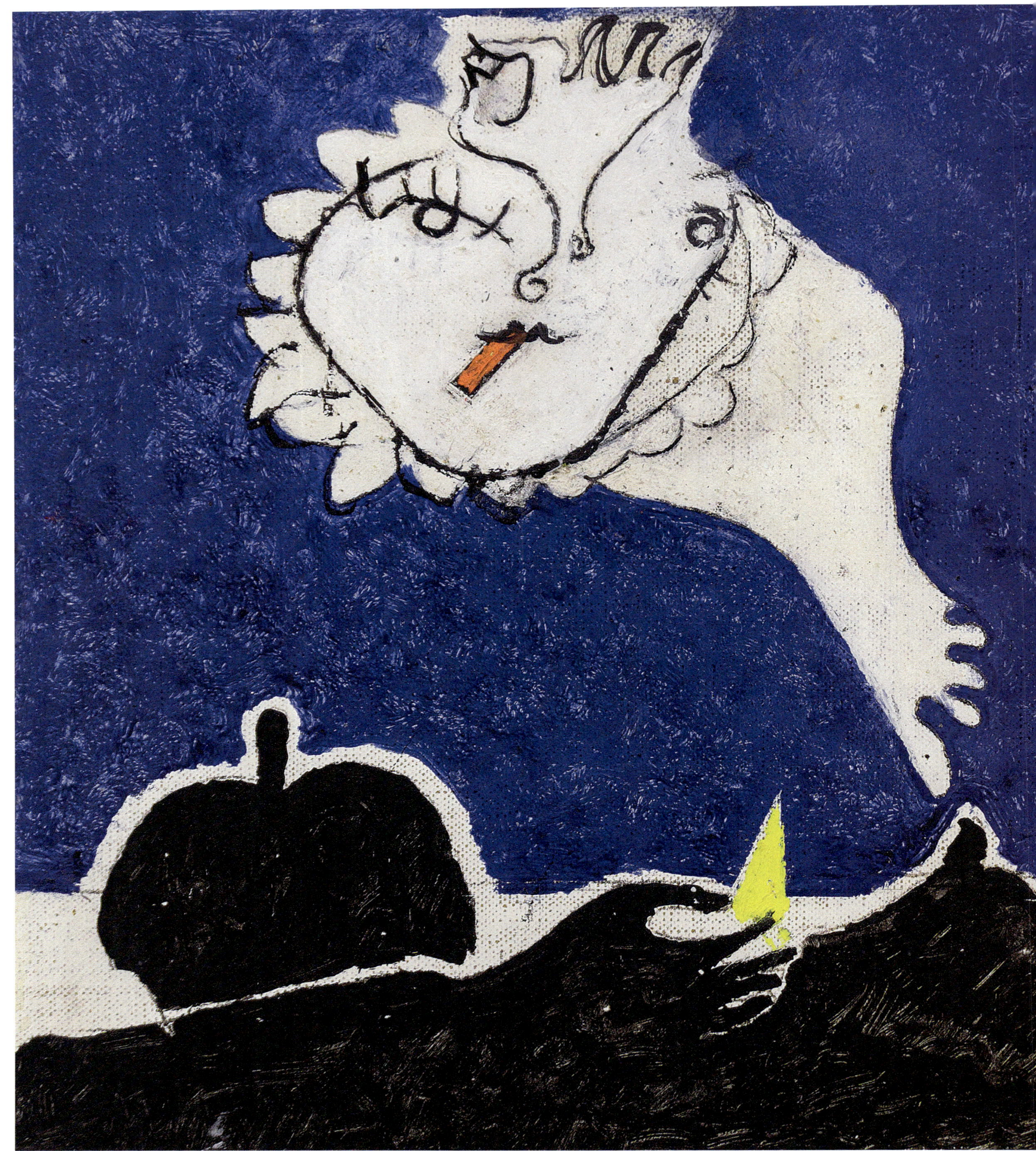

AMALASUNTHA WITH A CIGARETTE
(AMALASSUNTA CON SIGARETTA)
1951
oil on canvas
27.4 × 35.4 cm
Augusto and Francesca
Giovanardi Collection

AMALASUNTHA WITH A YELLOW EYE
(AMALASSUNTA OCCHIO GIALLO)
1950
oil on canvas
20.9 × 26.5 cm
Augusto and Francesca
Giovanardi Collection

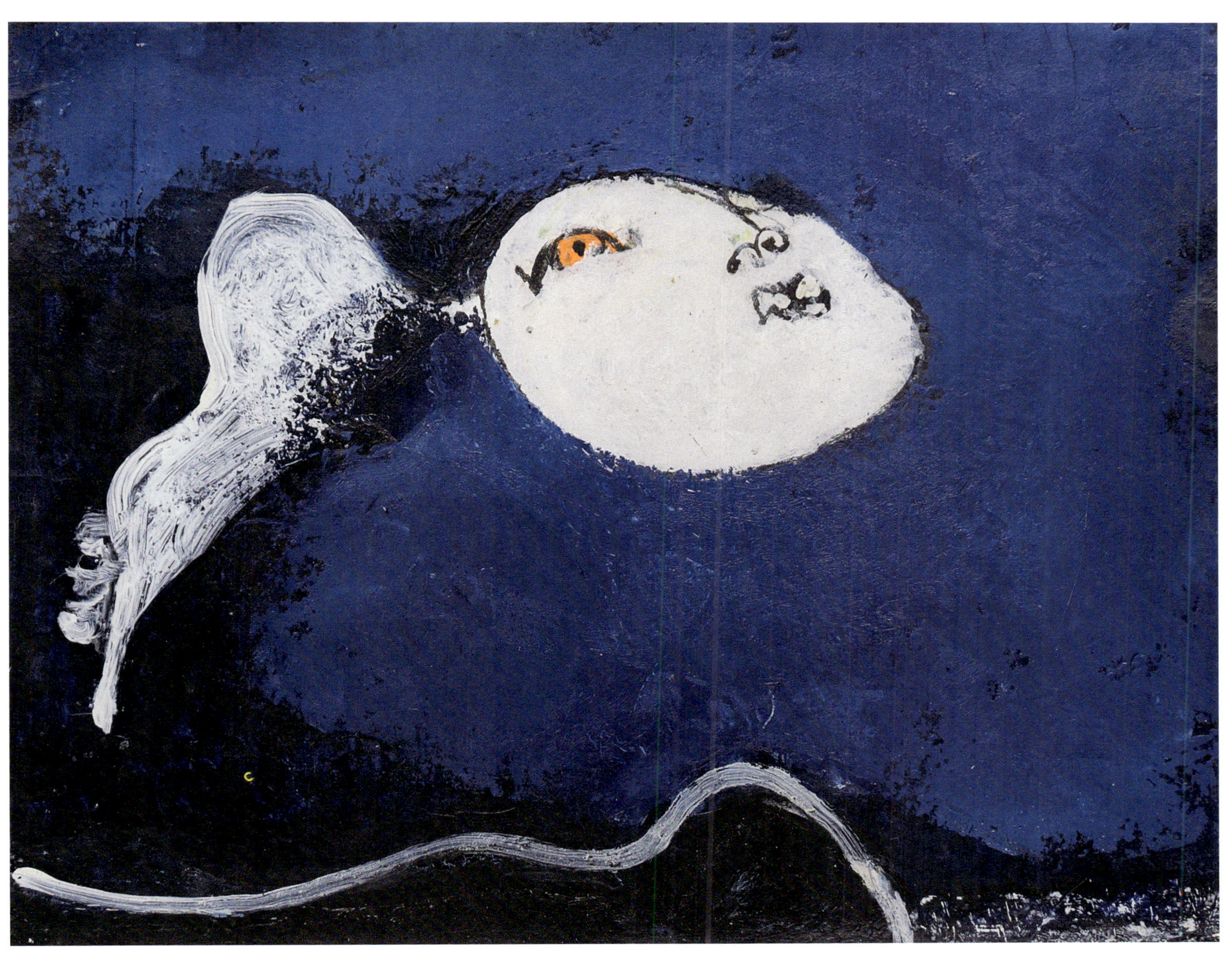

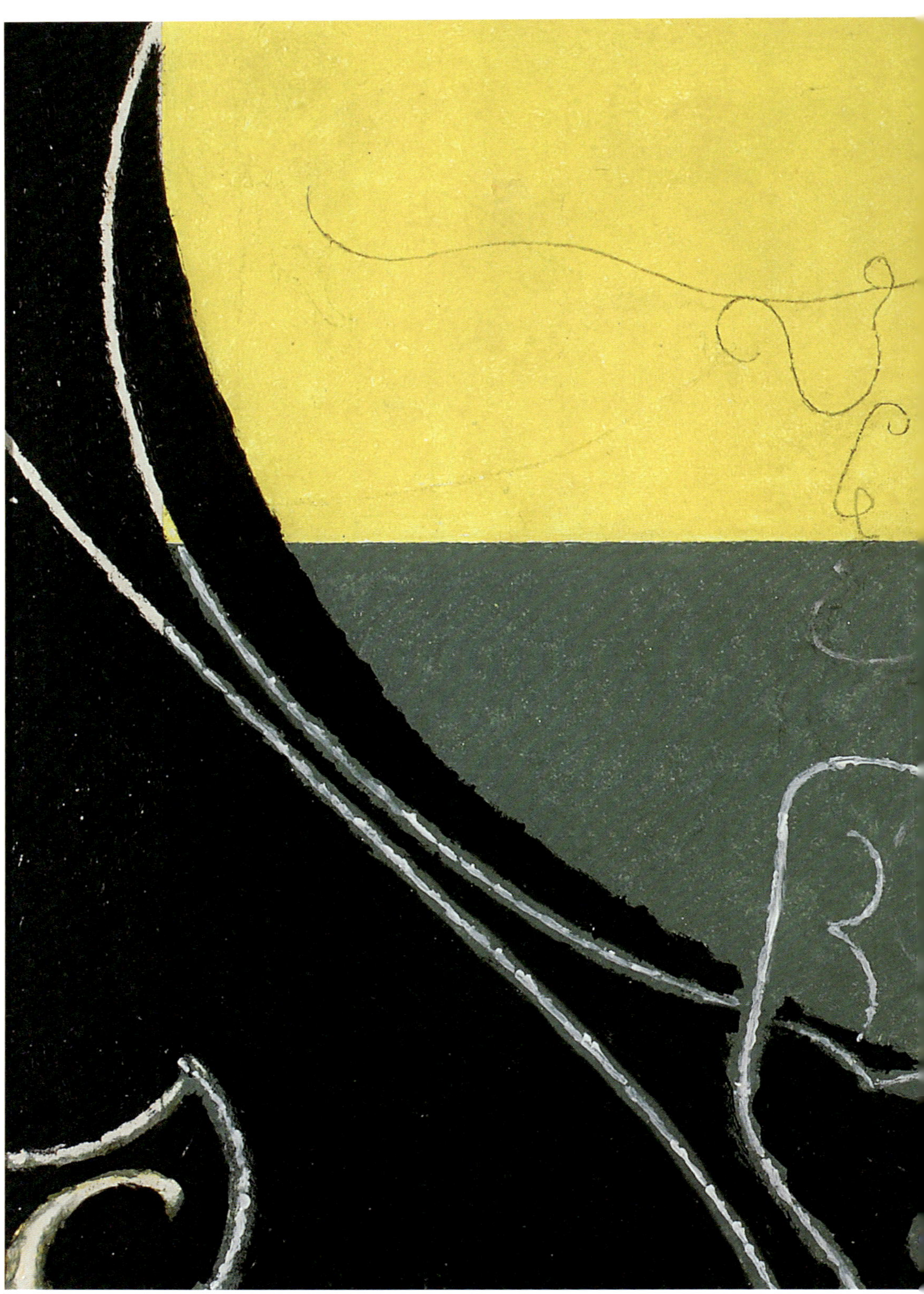

EVENING (LARGE)
(LA SERA [GRANDE])
1950
64 × 114 cm
oil on Masonite
GAM, Galleria Civica d'Arte Moderna
e Contemporanea, Turin

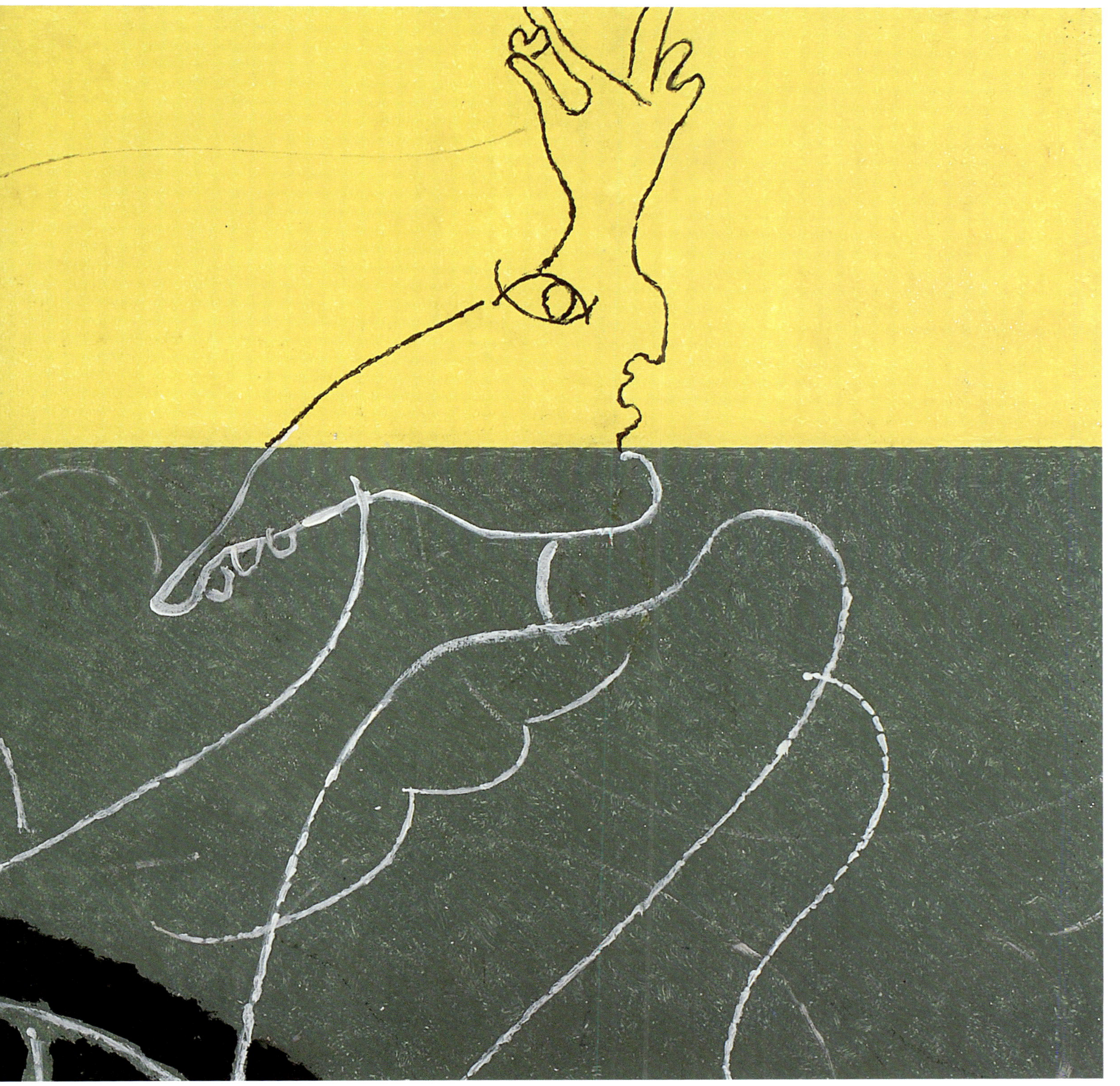

rebel angel on a yellow background
(angelo ribelle su fondo giallo)
1949
oil on canvas
26 × 32.5 cm
Private collection

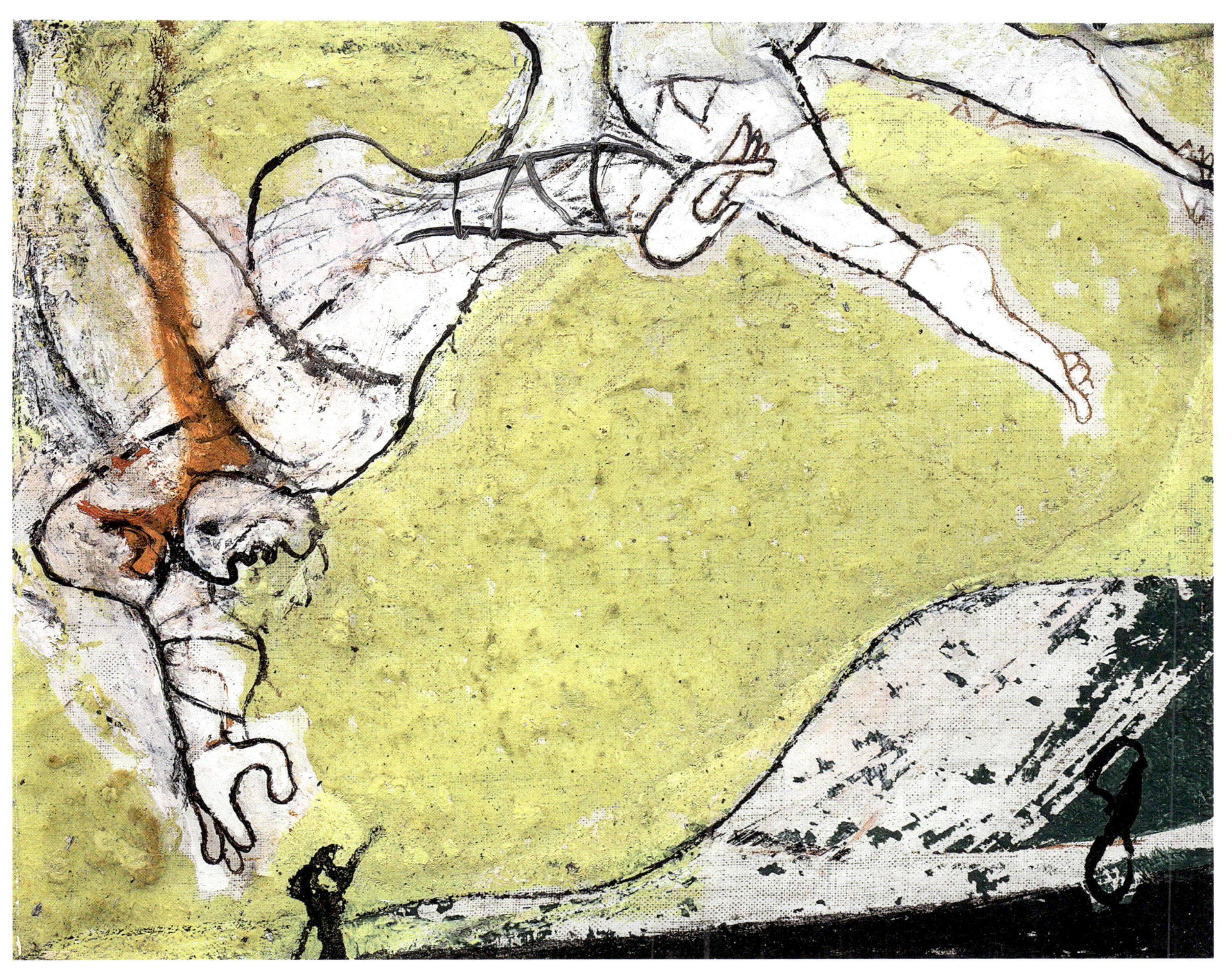

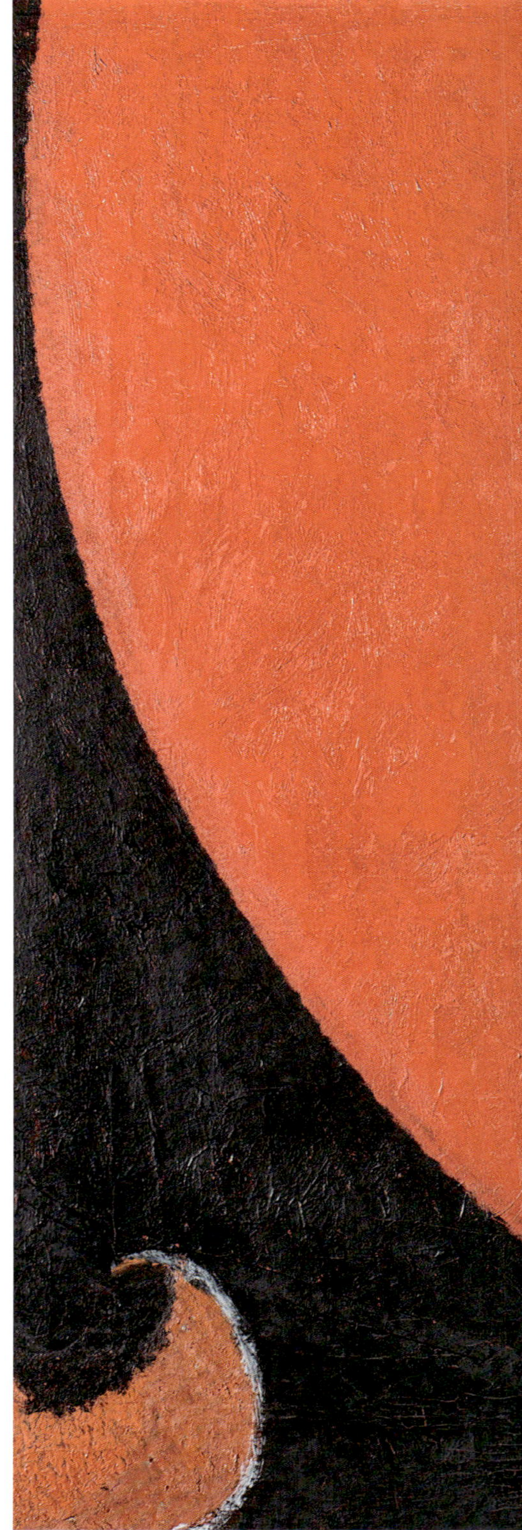

REBEL ANGEL ON A DARK RED BACKGROUND
(ANGELO RIBELLE SU FONDO ROSSO SCURO)
1946
oil on canvas
72.5 × 91.5 cm
Galleria d'Arte Contemporanea
Osvaldo Licini, Ascoli Piceno

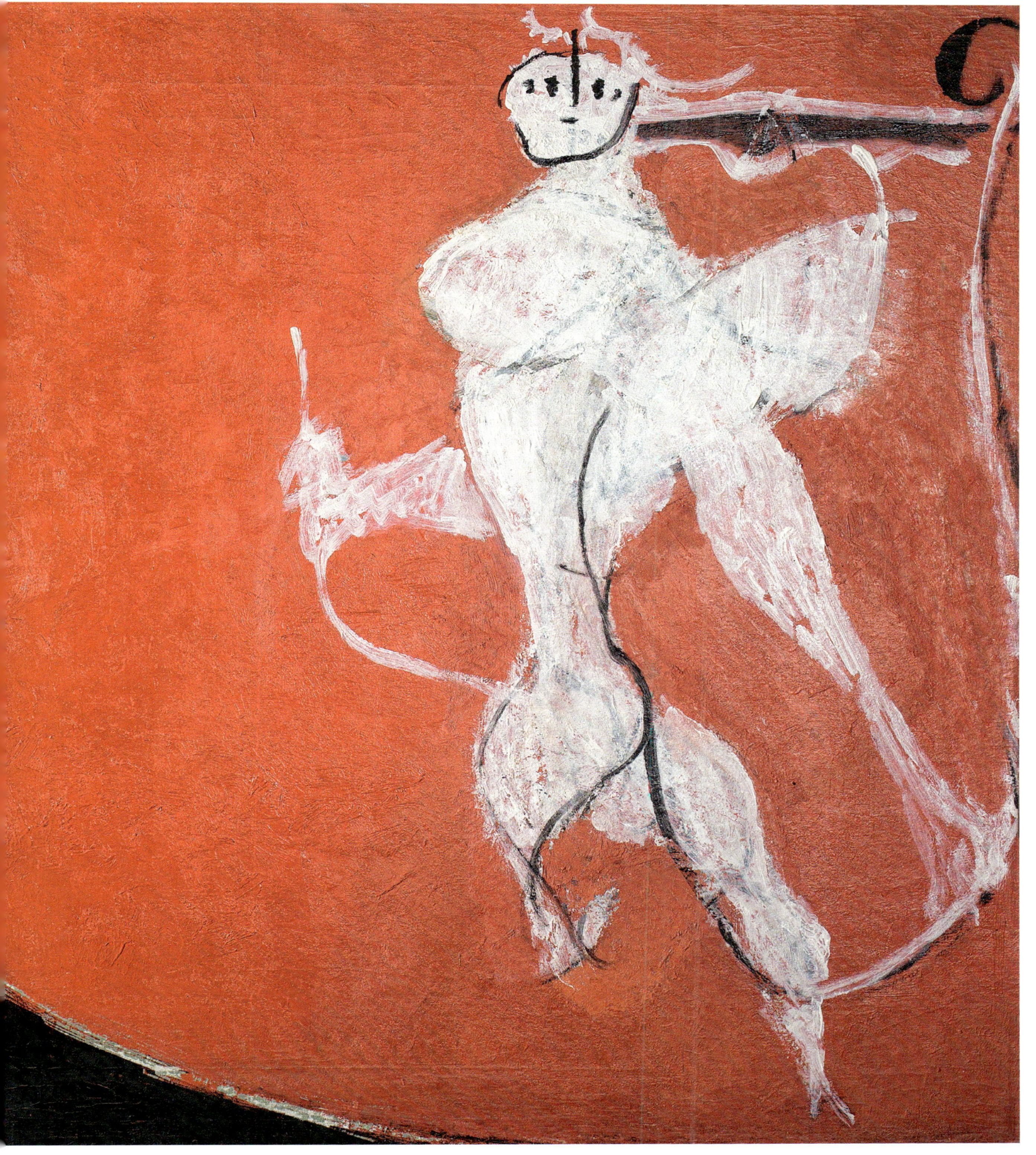

REBEL ANGEL AND MOON
(ANGELO RIBELLE E LUNA)
1947
oil on canvas
90 × 116 cm
Private collection, Turin

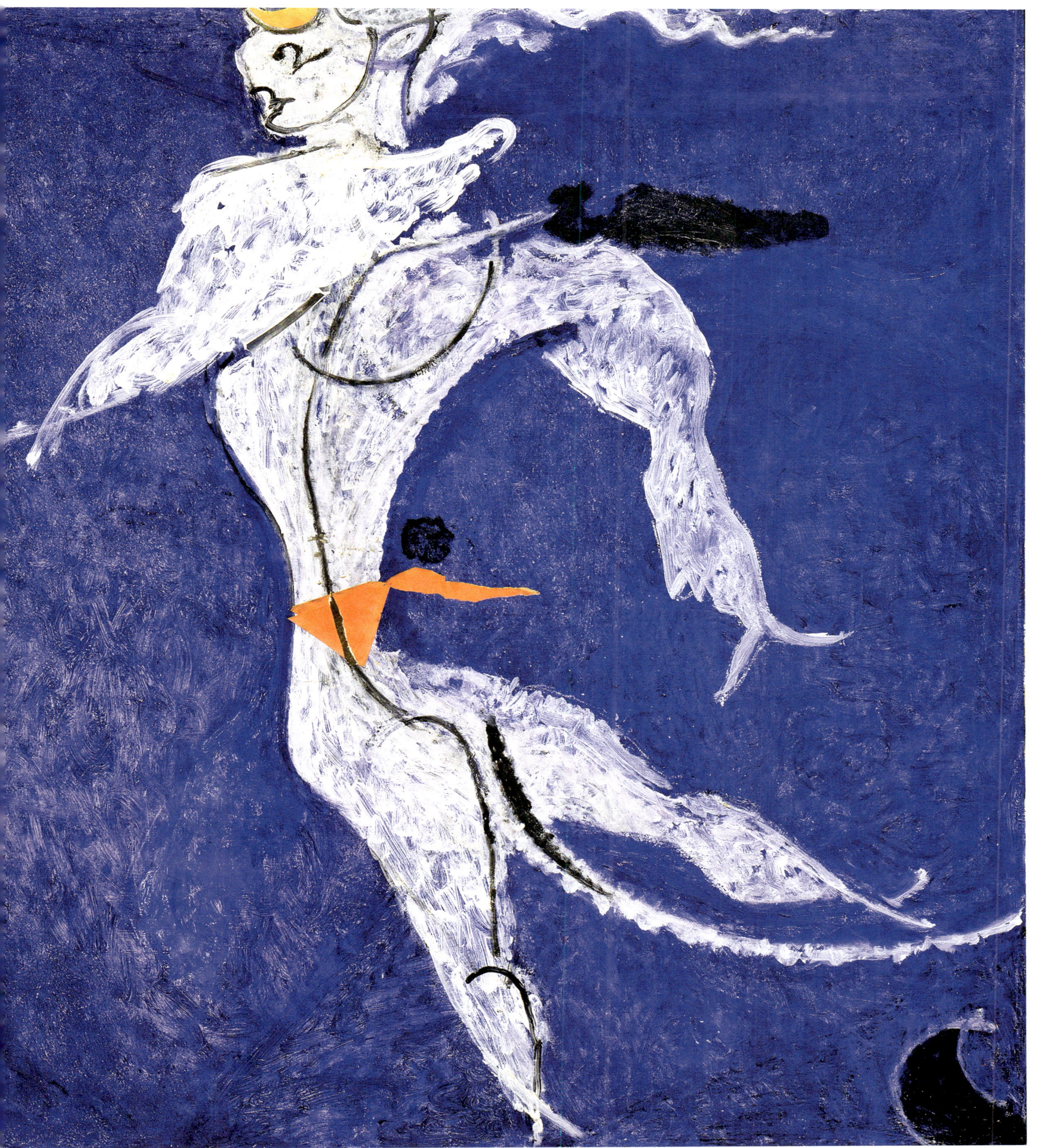

REBEL ANGEL ON A YELLOW BACKGROUND
(ANGELO RIBELLE SU FONDO GIALLO)
1952
oil on Masonite
92.5 × 114.5 cm
Museo del Novecento, Milan

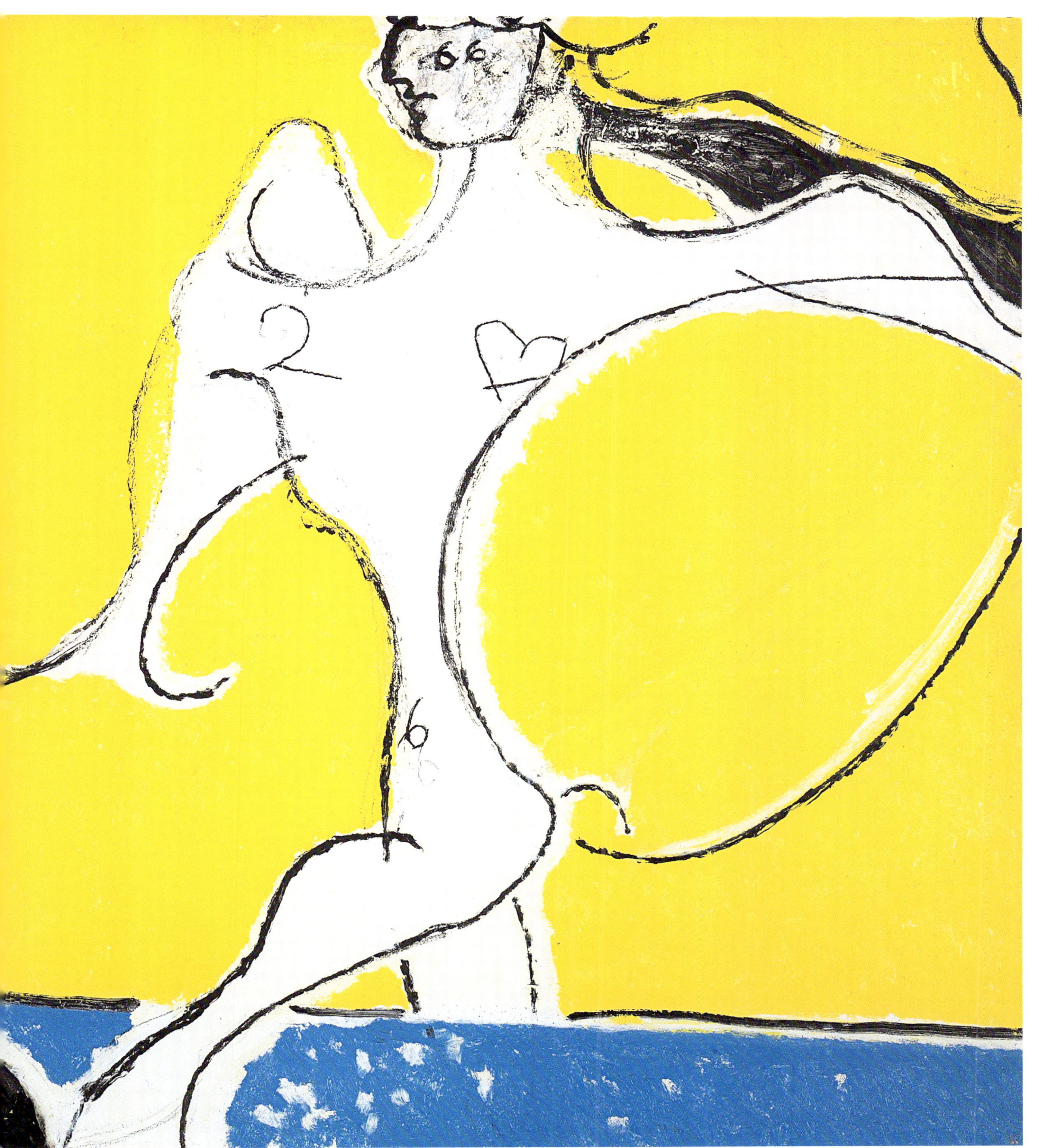

REBEL ANGEL WITH A RED HEART
(ANGELO RIBELLE CON CUORE ROSSO)
1953
oil on canvas
88 × 116 cm
Private collection

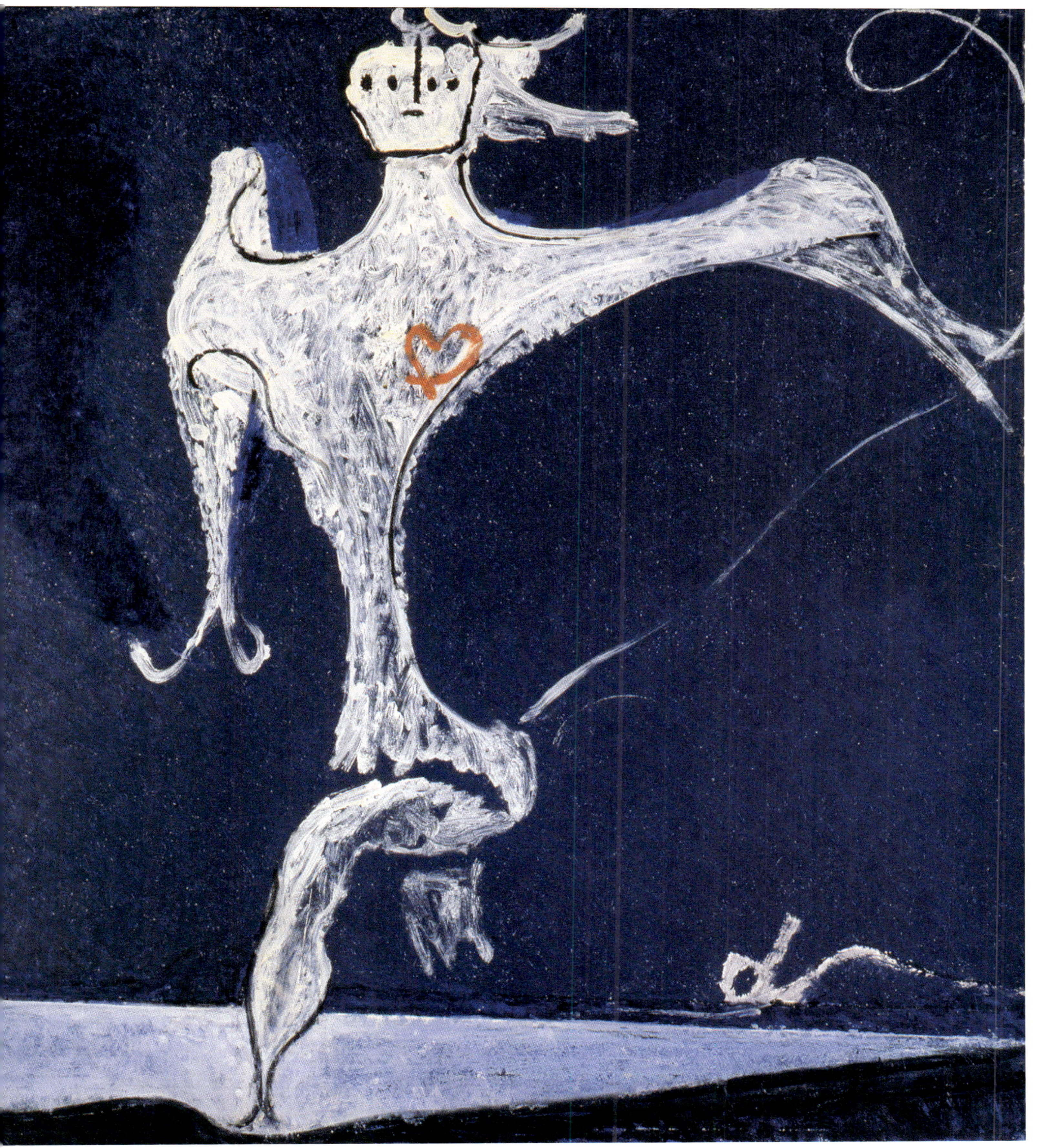

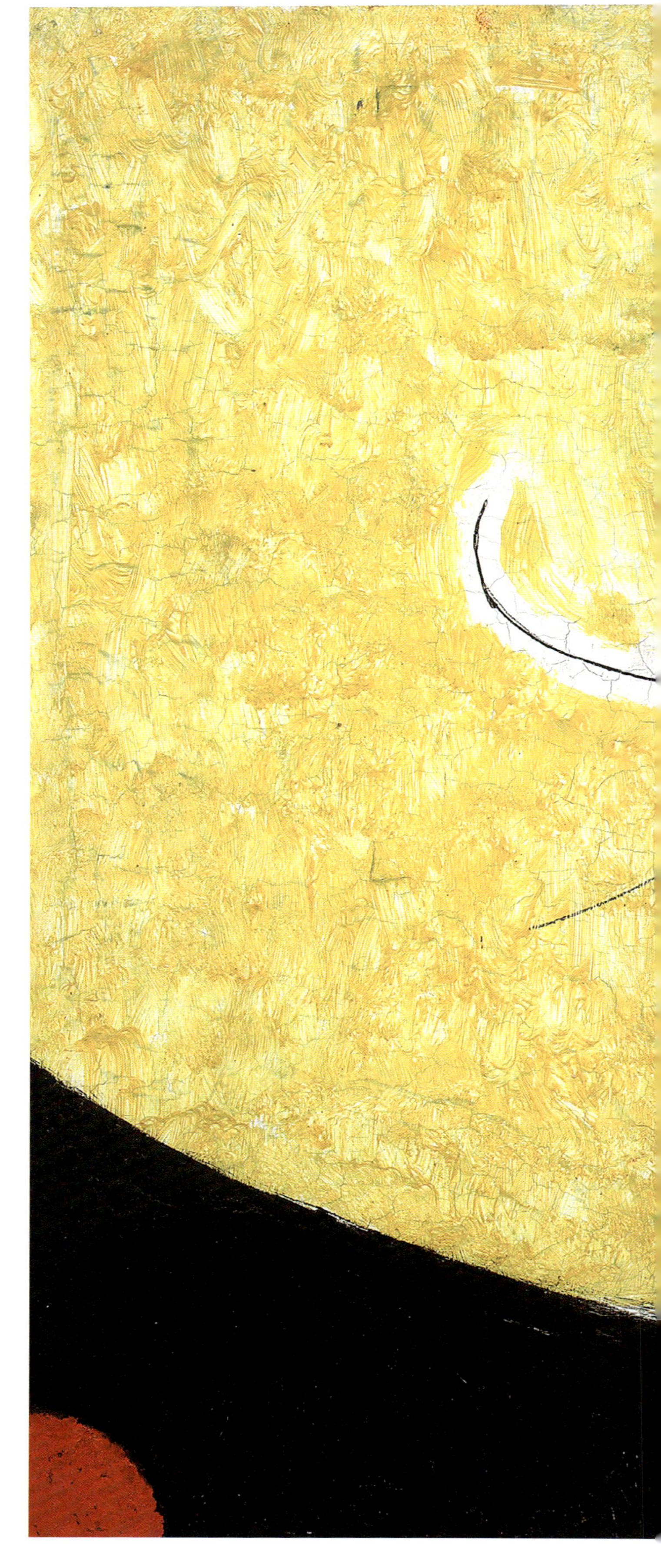

ANGELS, FIRST LOVE
(ANGELI PRIMO AMORE)
1955
oil and collage on canvas
47.5 × 64 cm
Private collection

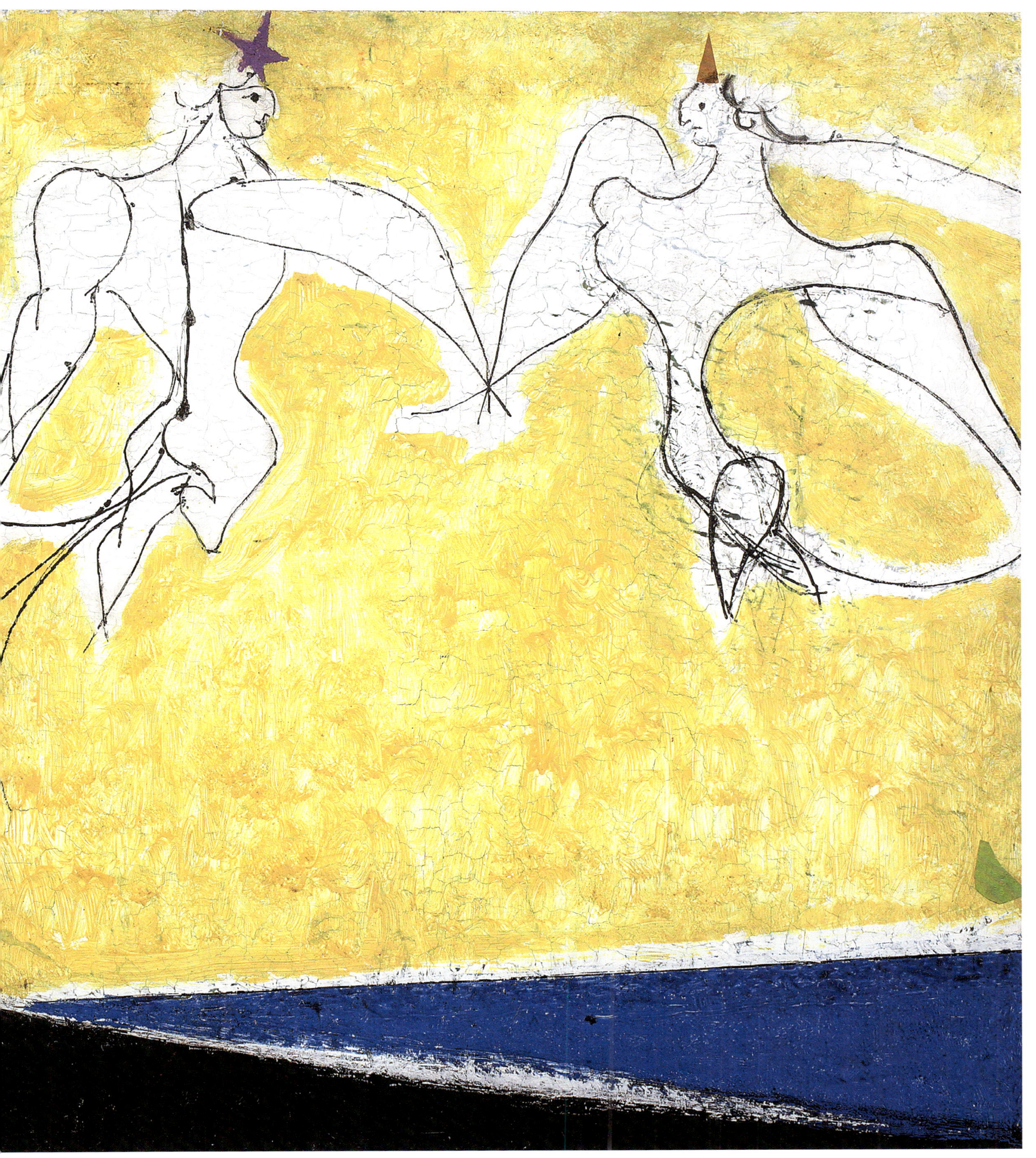

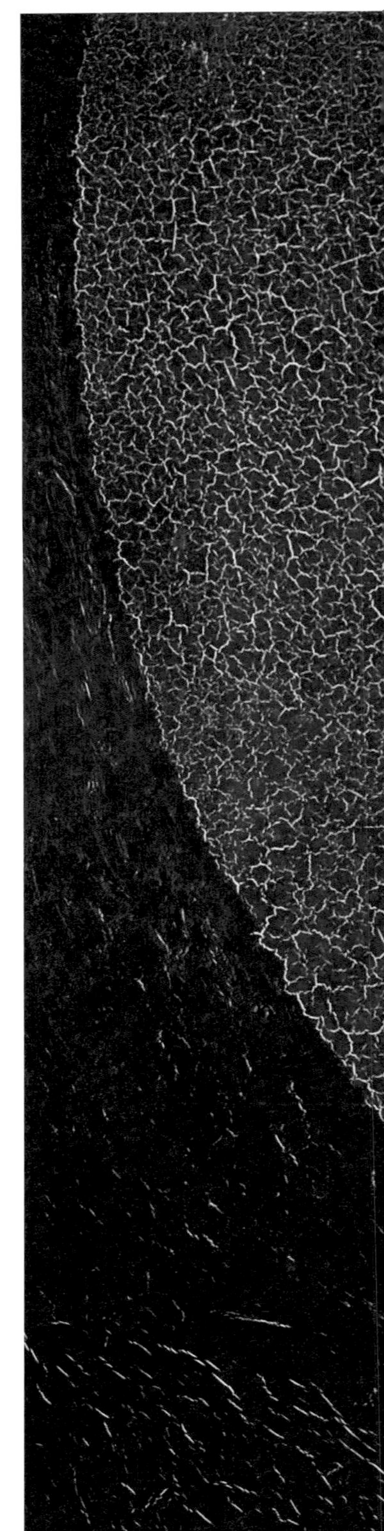

REBEL ANGEL ON A DARK BLUE BACKGROUND
(ANGELO RIBELLE SU FONDO BLU CUPO)
1956
oil on Masonite
93 × 125 cm
Private collection, Milan

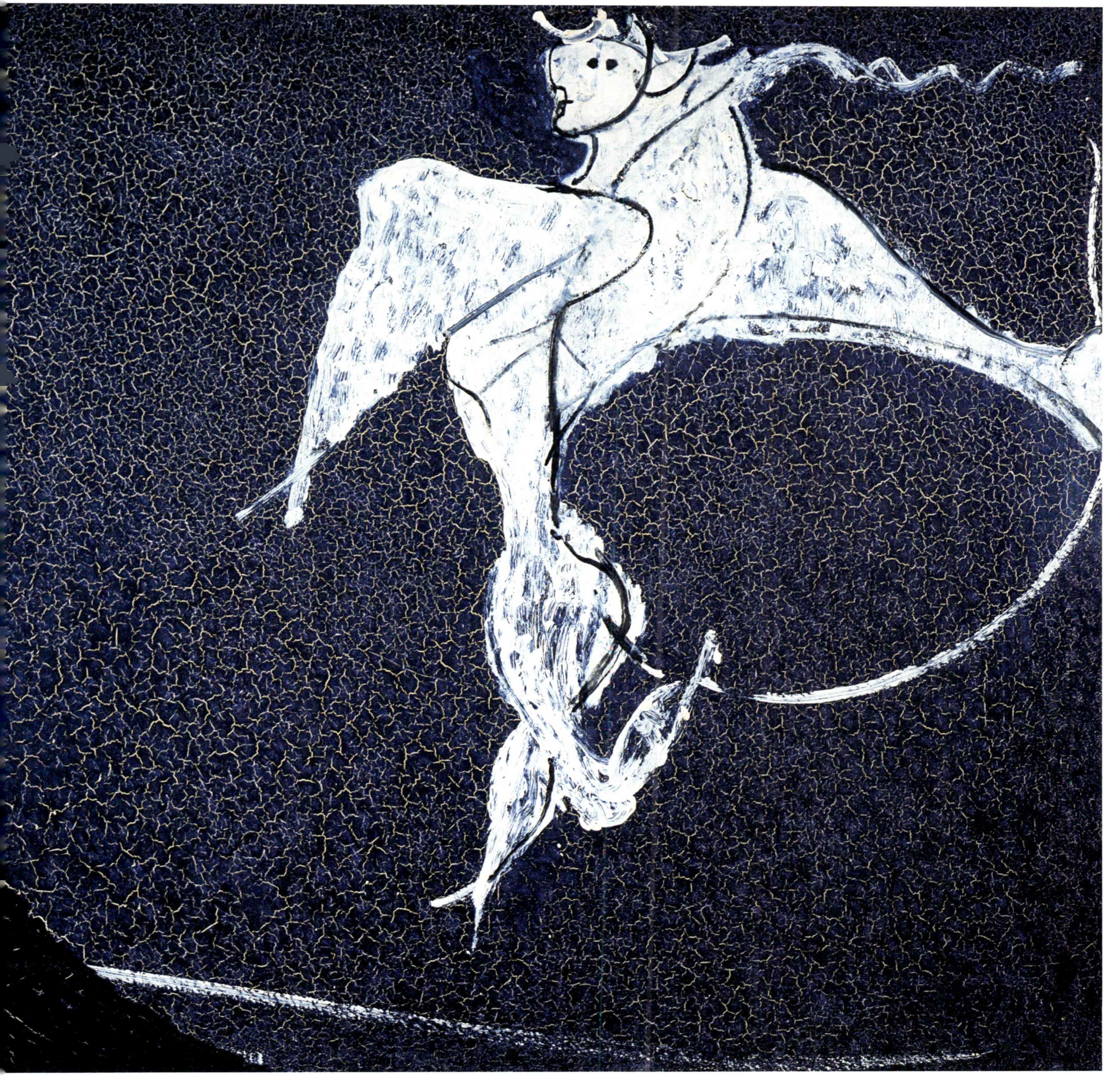

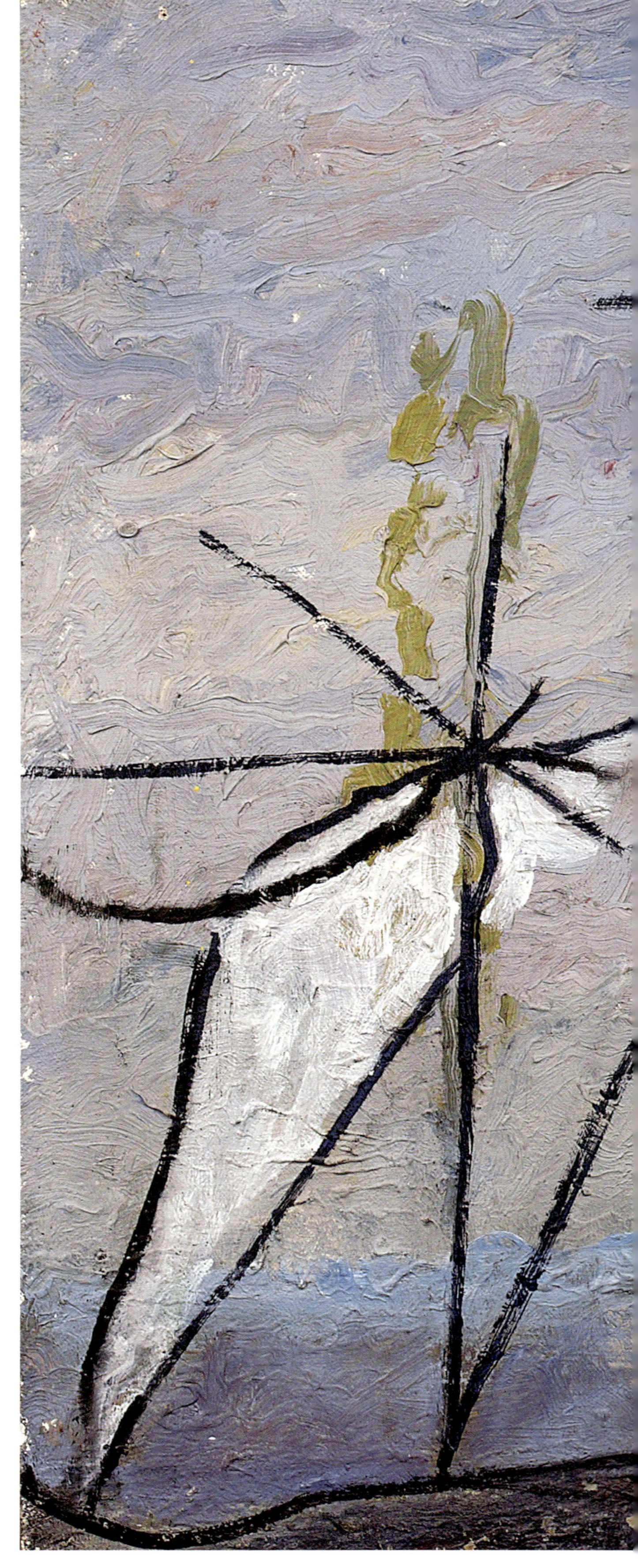

EVENING TWILIGHT
(CREPUSCOLO DELLA SERA)
1951
oil on canvas
49 × 65 cm
Lorenzo Licini collection

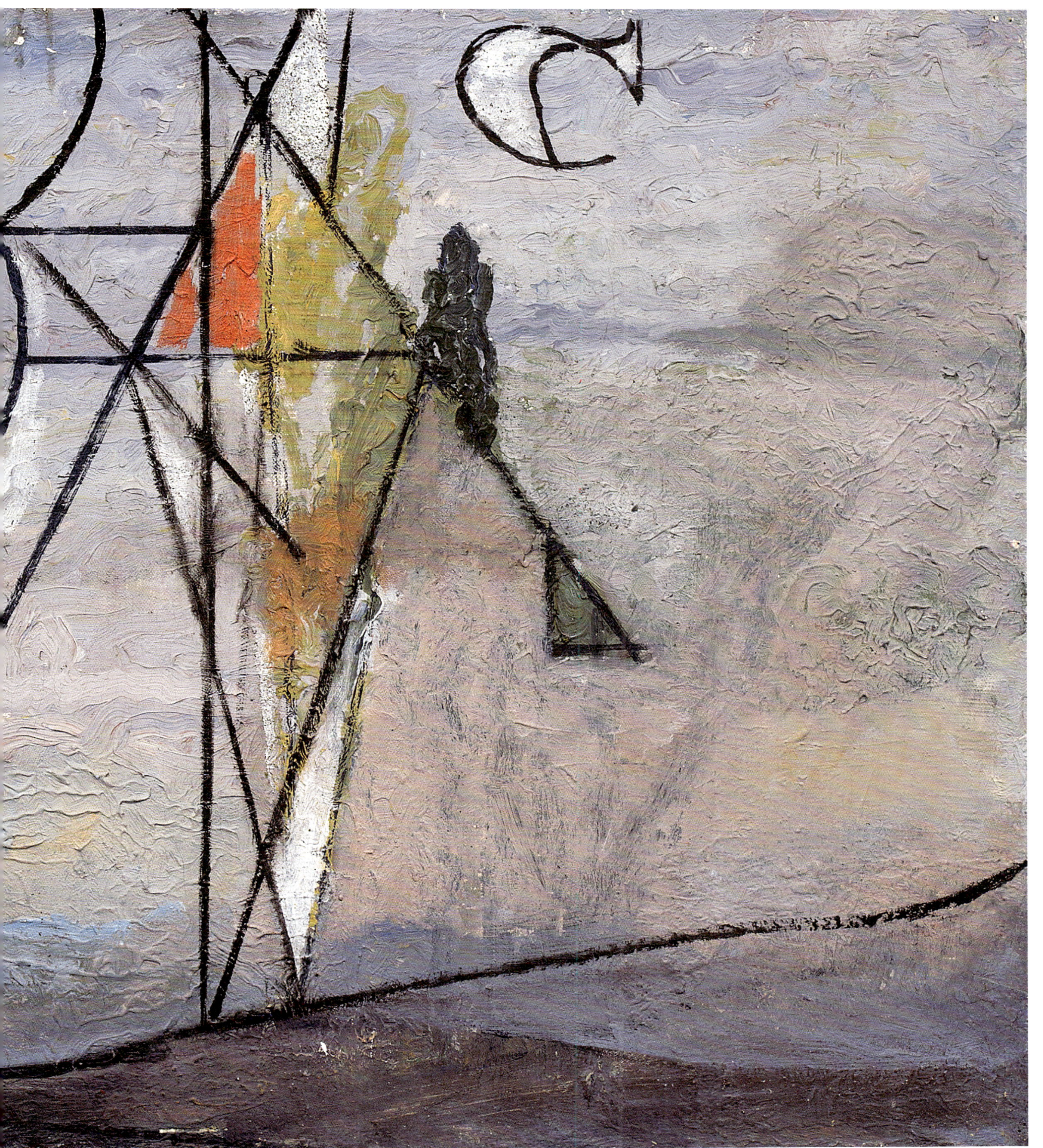

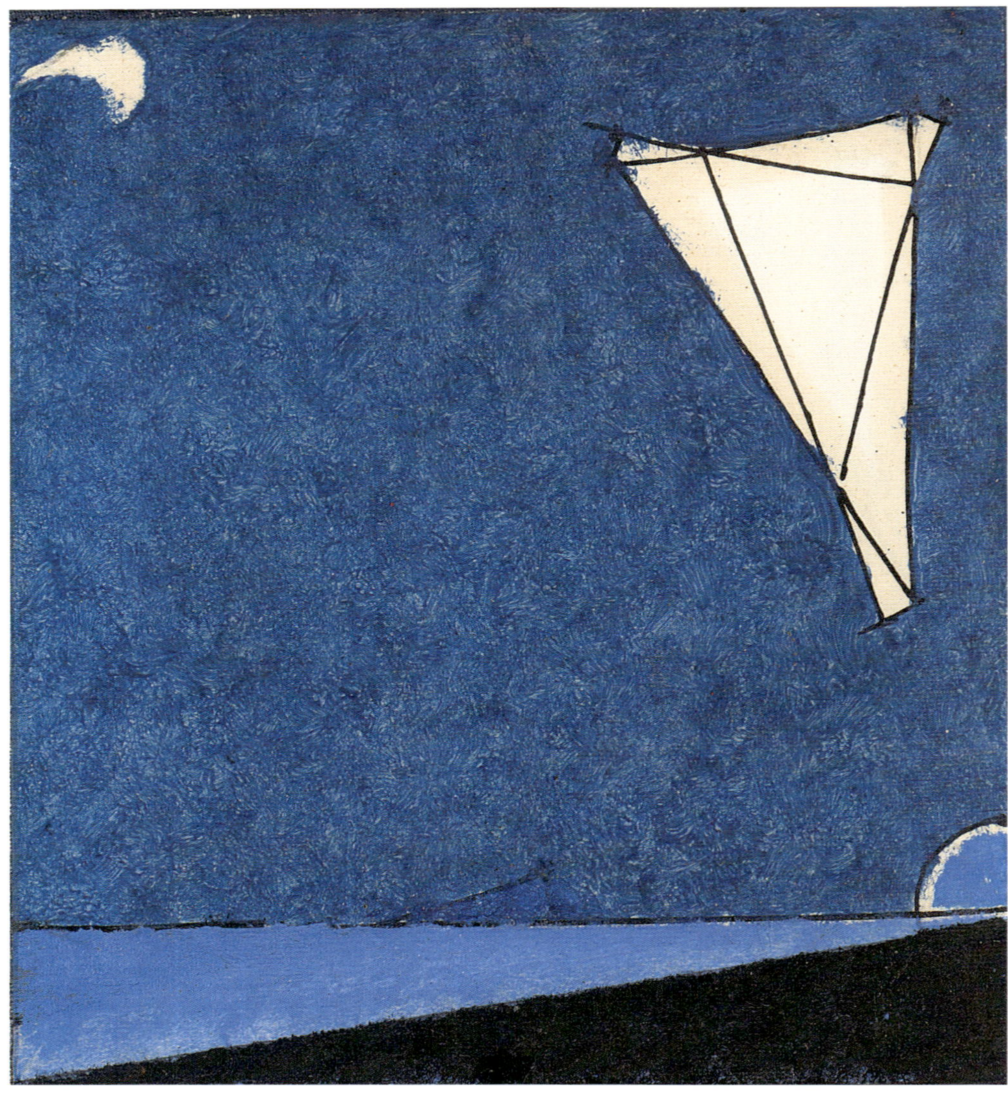

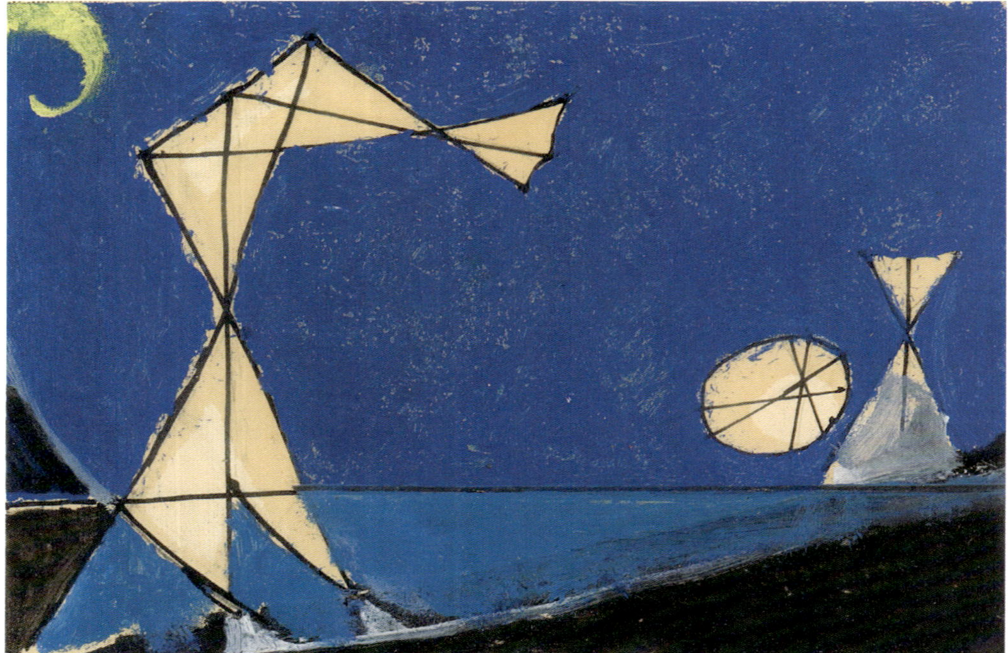

NOCTURNE
(NOTTURNO)
1955
oil on paper mounted on canvas
25 × 22.4 cm
Private collection, Fermo

SEASCAPE (NOCTURNE)
(MARINA [NOTTURNO])
1955
oil on paper
18 × 25.6 cm
Gori Collection,
Fattoria di Celle, Pistoia

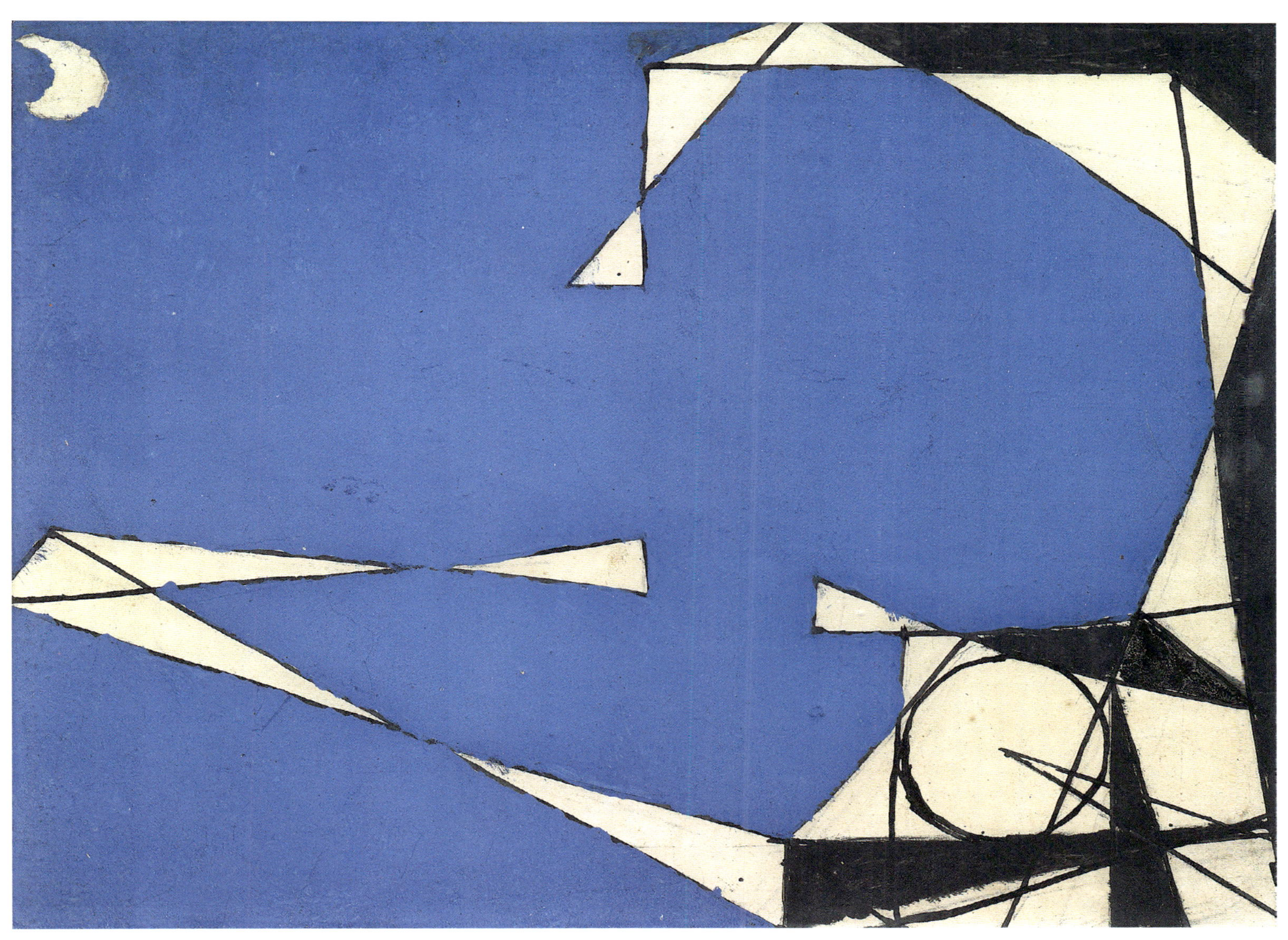

NOCTURNE
(NOTTURNO)
1953
oil on cardboard
33 × 24 cm
Private collection

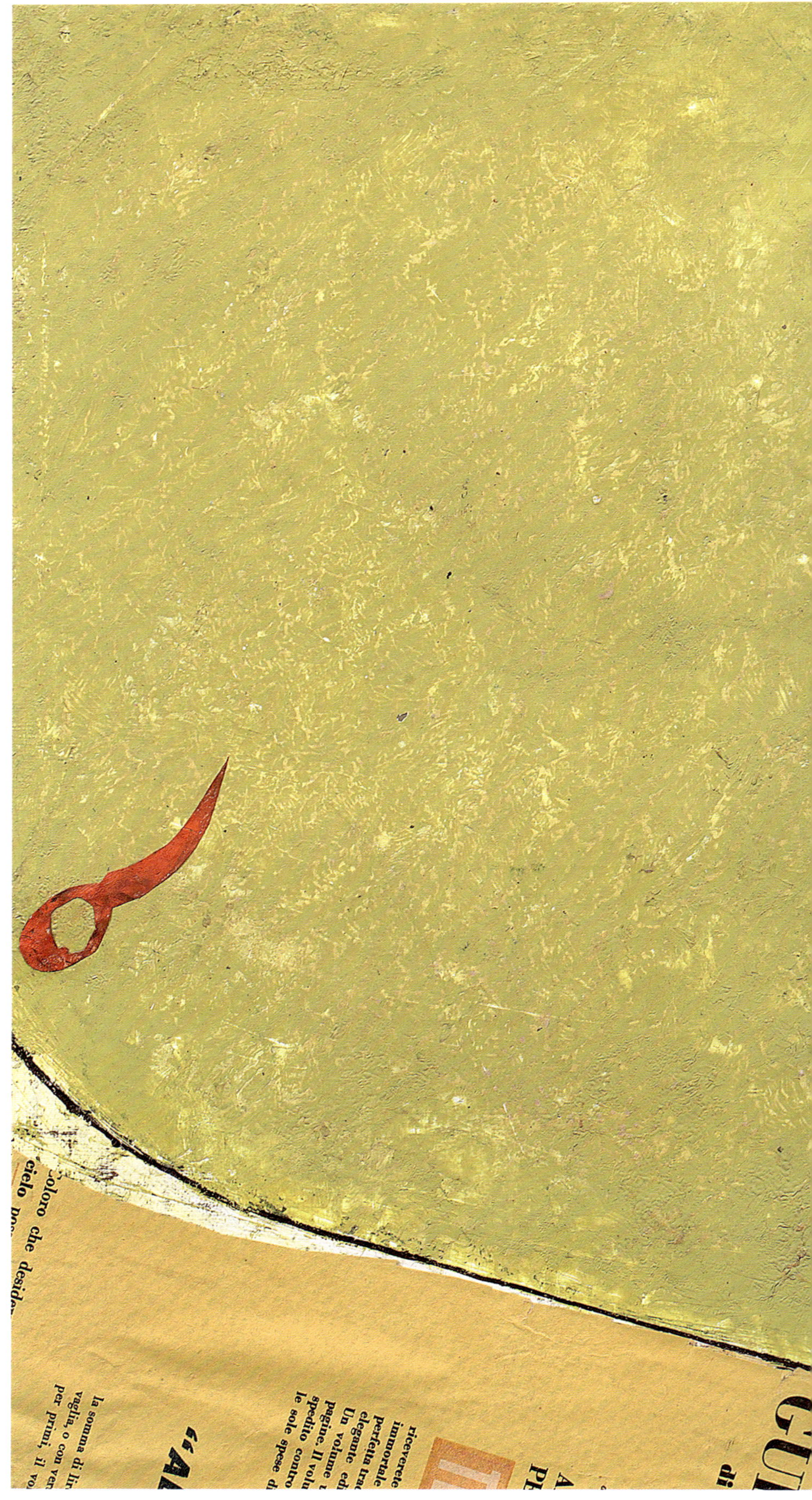

SAINT DOMINGO ANGEL
ON A YELLOW BACKGROUND
(ANGELO DI SAN DOMINGO
SU FONDO GIALLO)
1956
oil and collage on canvas
39 × 57 cm
Silvia Poli Licini collection

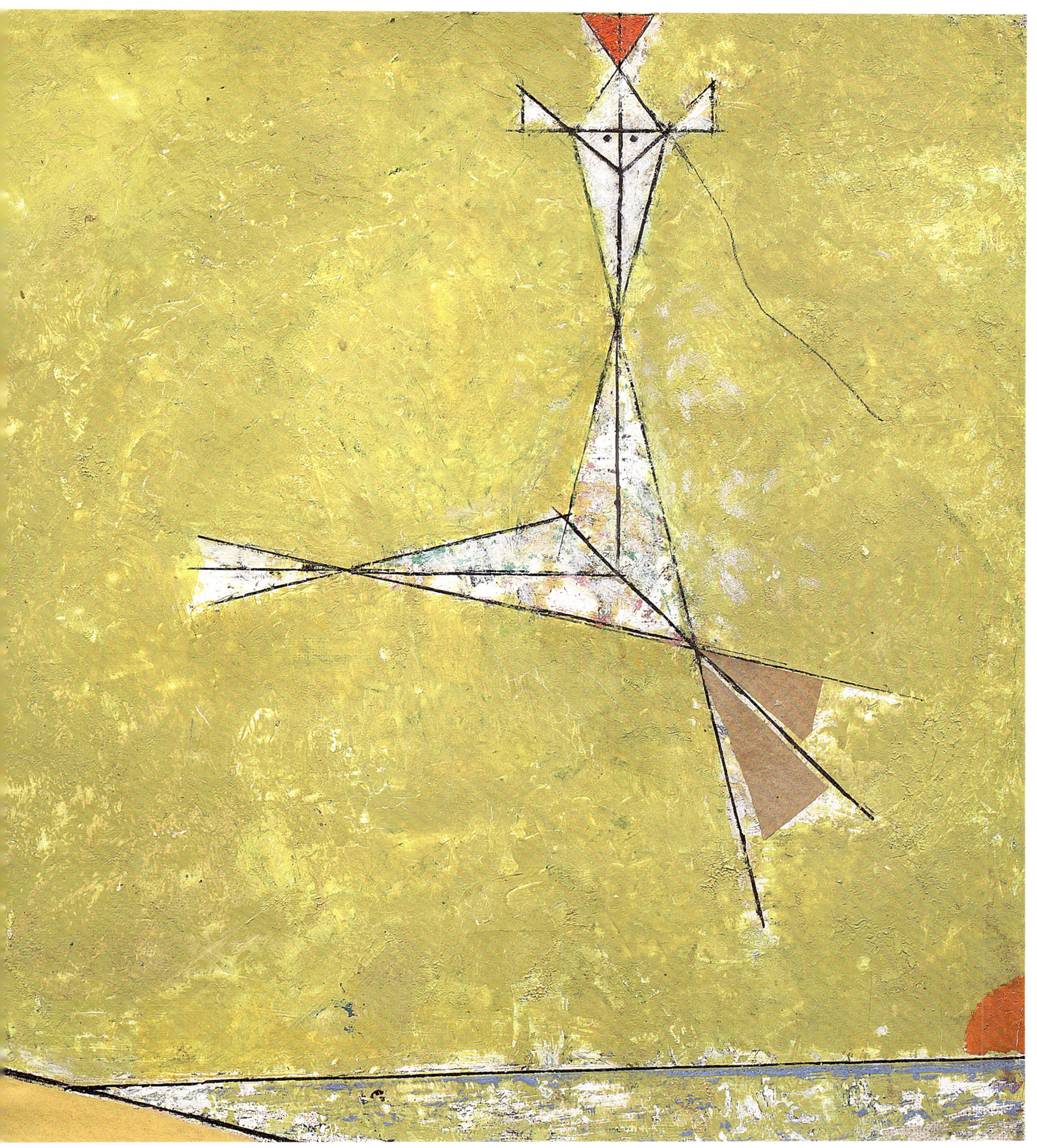

SAINT DOMINGO ANGEL
(ANGELO DI SAN DOMINGO)
1957
oil on Masonite
62.2 × 72.8 cm
Gori Collection,
Fattoria di Celle, Pistoia

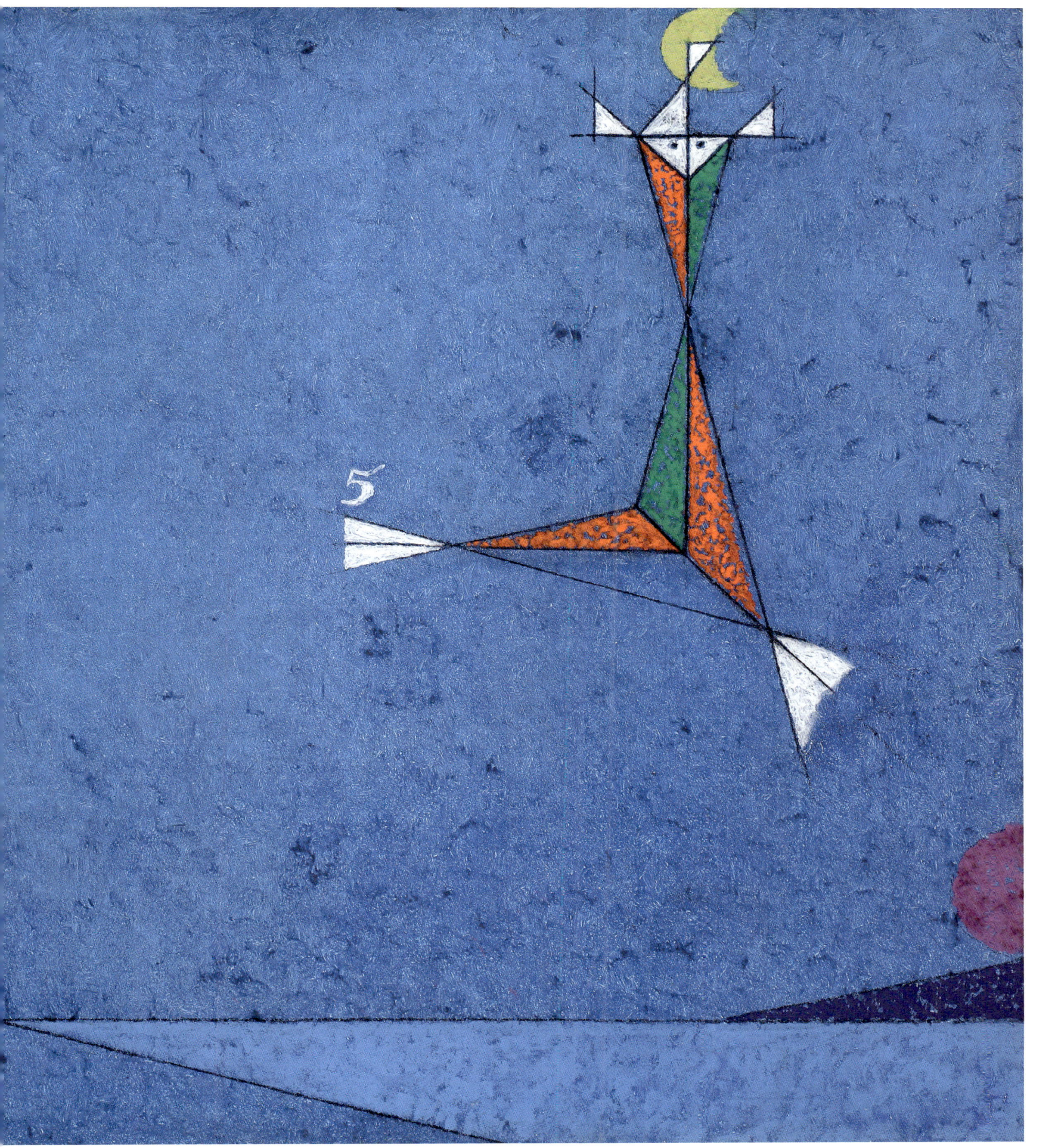
5

SAINT ROSE ANGEL
(ANGELO DI SANTA ROSA)
1957
oil and collage on canvas
56 × 68 cm
Private collection,
courtesy Lorenzelli Arte, Milan

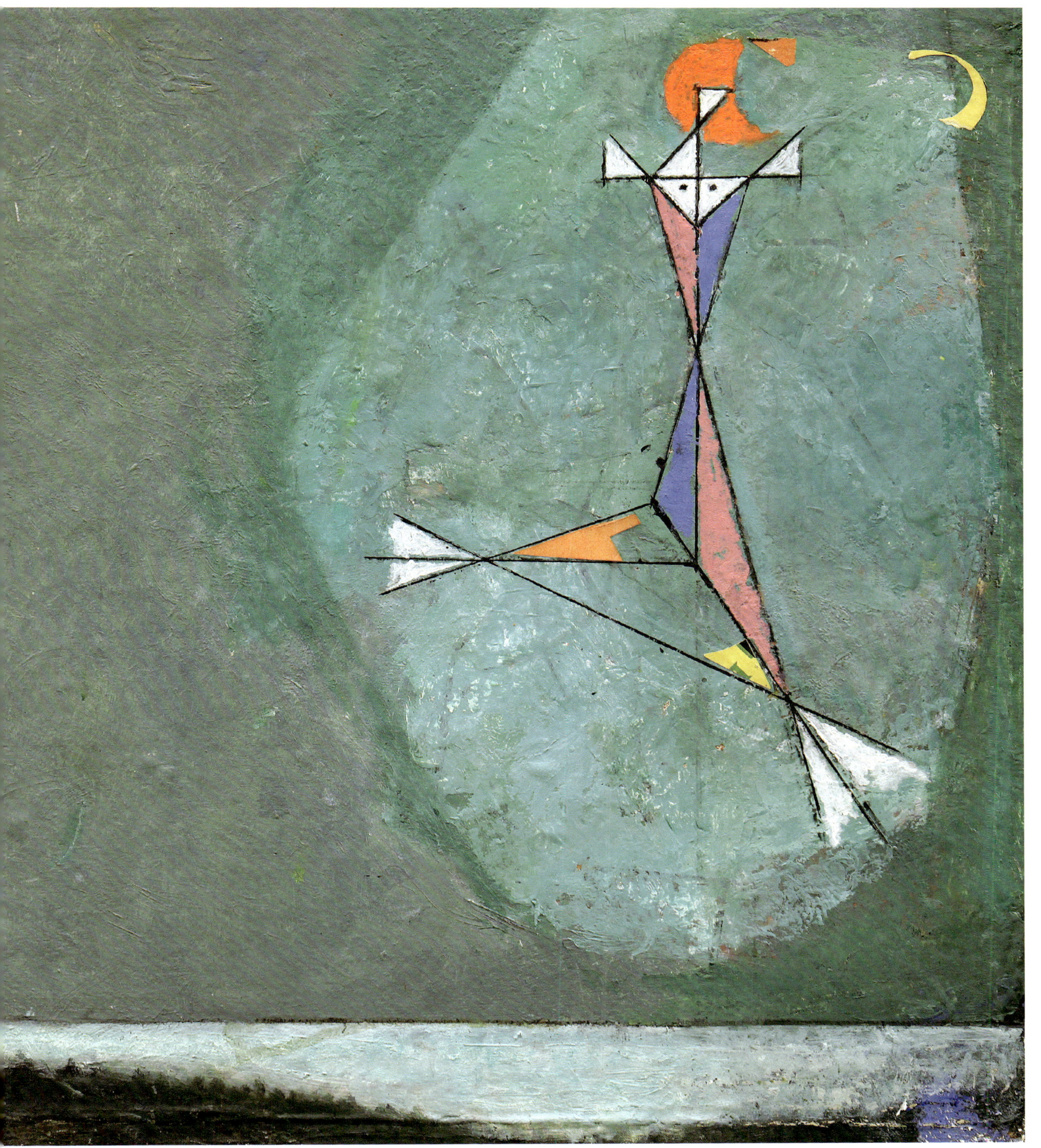

RHYTHM
(RITMO)
1958
oil on cardboard
24 × 33 cm
Private collection

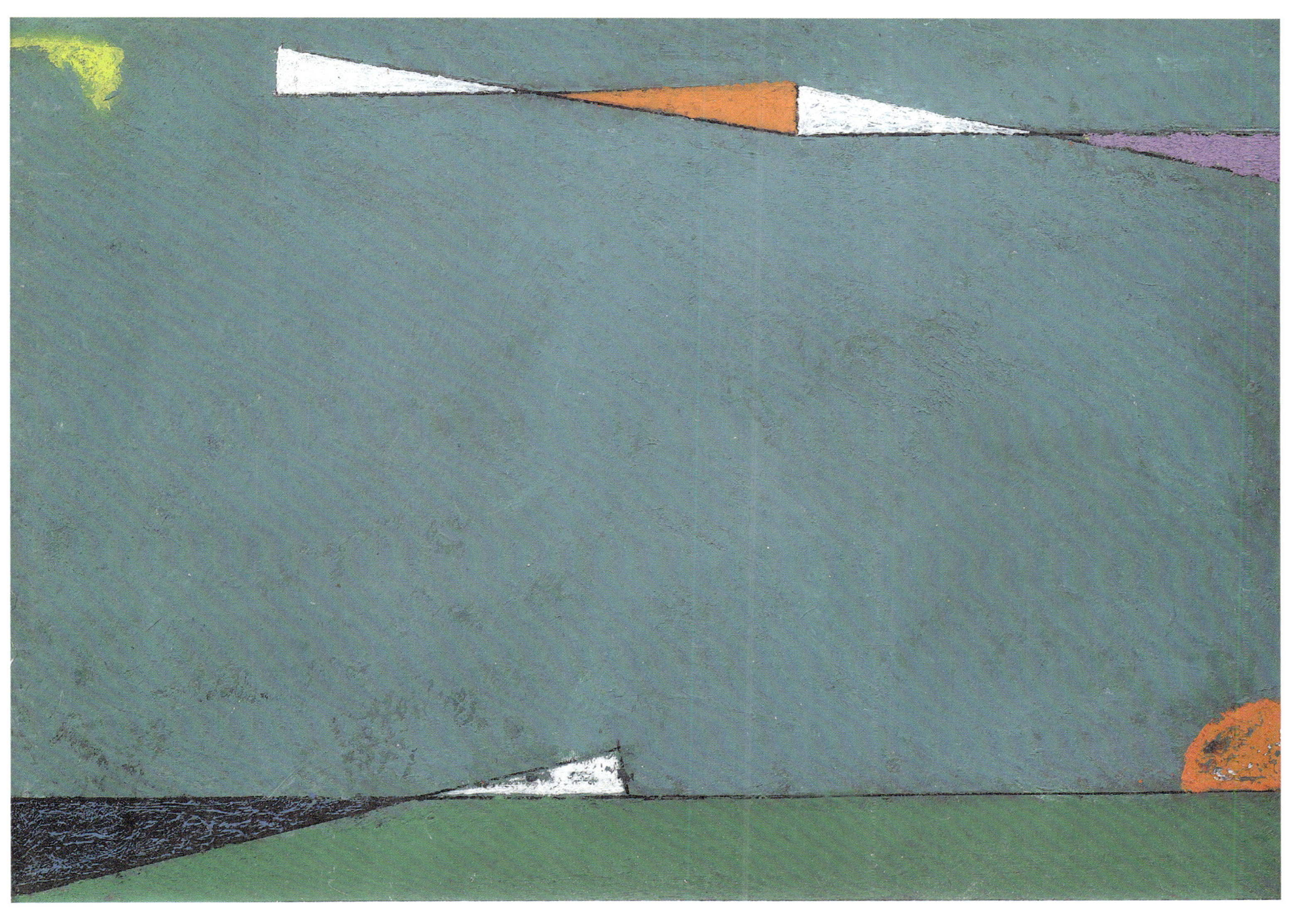

REBEL ANGEL
(ANGELO RIBELLE)
1958
oil on canvas
45 × 72 cm
Private collection,
courtesy Galleria Tega, Milan

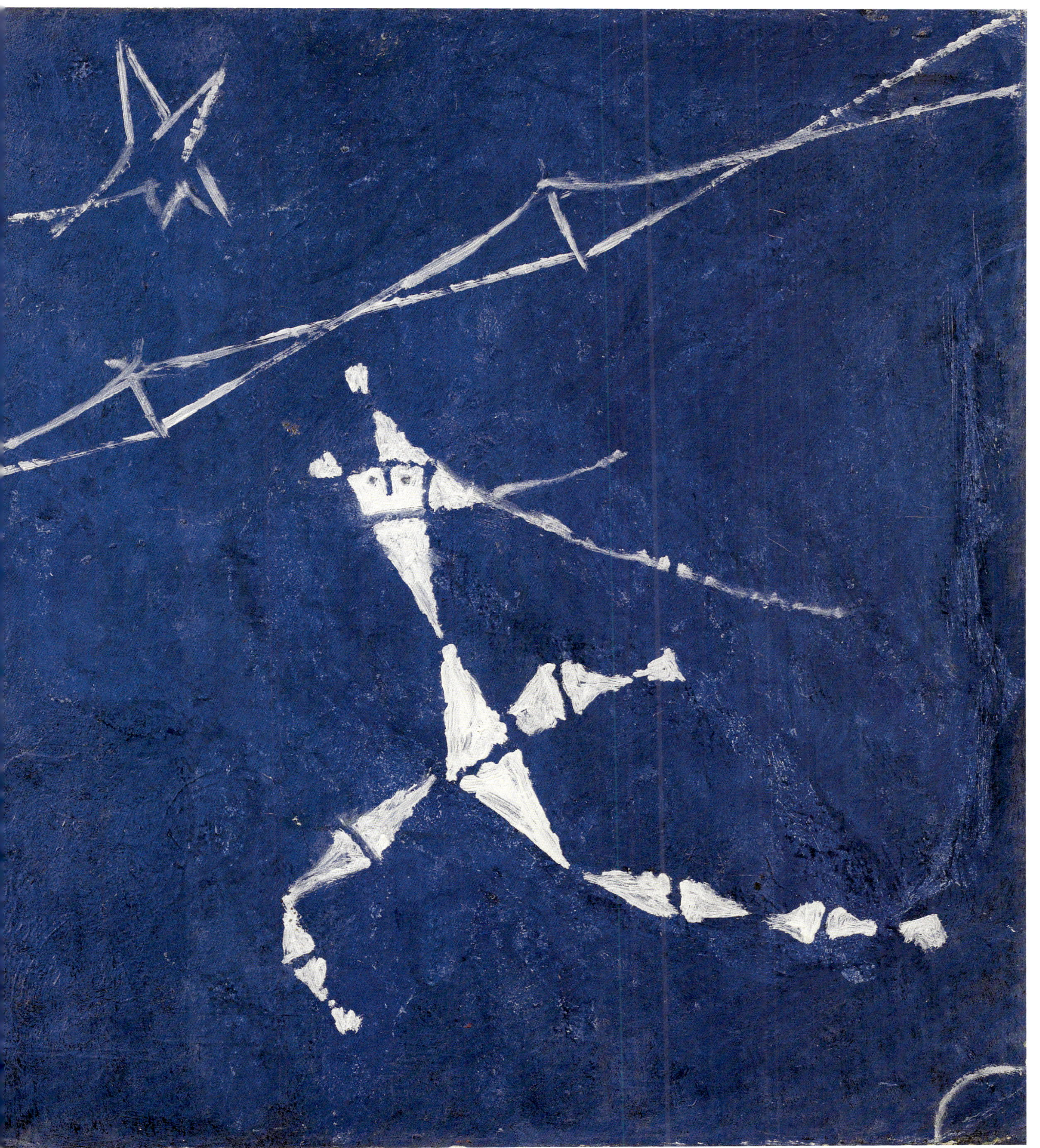

OSVALDO LICINI'S METAPHORS OF AIR: BETWEEN MEMORY AND OBLIVION

FEDERICA PIRANI

Metaphors of air and figures pertaining to the ethereal realm form a significant presence in the poetic imagination and paintings of Osvaldo Licini—a consistent iconography throughout his career, from his earliest to his final works. Though veiled or deliberately hidden, the theme of flight evolves in style according to specific and well-defined moments, from abstraction to Surrealism in the later years, with formal metamorphoses that do not affect its symbolic meaning.

The earliest representations of angels date to 1919, in works like *Archangel Gabriel* (*Arcangelo Gabriele*) and *Archangel* (*Arcangelo*) (pp. 30–33)[1]—although flying figures also appear in the contemporaneous series entitled *War Episodes* (*Episodi di guerra*). In the former, in an apocalyptic and fiery landscape, the Archangel Gabriel descends to earth while seeming to injure himself with his own sword pointed to his side, a wound that is also perhaps a necessary contamination of the impurity of existence.[2] In *Archangel*, a nude figure runs along a river towards the horizon while dense stylized clouds reflect the air inflamed by the blazing sun, almost as if to symbolically encapsulate the four elements of an ancestral cosmogony in a single image.

Both paintings were reworked in the early 1930s; in *Archangel* specifically, on the right side of the painting Licini added a figure with its back turned, an inscrutable warrior holding a shield.[3] In *Italian Soldiers* (1917, p. 25), from the *War Episode* series, an angel plunges from the sky wielding a sword, while in *The Clash* (*Lo scontro*, 1915),[4] a figure holding a fiery shield runs towards the center of the scene.

War Episodes is a group of stylistically similar works. They share a monochromatic, sometimes dichromatic palette, overt formal stylization, a concise and highly dynamic pictorial structure through the deployment of shadows and geometric faceting that seem an echo of Cubism, and the use of lateral wings that are explicit citations of theatrical set design. While certain affinities can be identified with the work of Giorgio Morandi, such as his *Bathers* (*Bagnanti*) of 1915 (p. 26), analogous connections could be drawn with the Cubist experimentations of Alexander Archipenko, Robert Delaunay, and Raoul Dufy, and with the drawings and sketches of Fortunato Depero for the Ballets Russes.

In spite of their formal similarities with the *War Episodes*, the unusual iconography that characterizes both *Archangel Gabriel* and *Archangel* seems to derive from other sources, and in particular from the text and illustrations of *The Marriage of Heaven and Hell* by William Blake, published in French in 1900, and from the poetry of Charles Baudelaire, Lautréamont, Guillaume Apollinaire, Paul Valéry, Arthur Rimbaud, Stéphane Mallarmé, Jean Cocteau, and Blaise Cendrars, all of whom Licini certainly knew and admired from his numerous trips to France.

Literature was in fact a treasure trove for the artist, an archive of myths he perfectly assimilated by reading the original texts. Together with his poetry, they constitute a substrate, an undercurrent from which he drew ideas. Written on scattered papers, letters, envelopes, and magazine covers throughout his entire life, Licini's poems and literary writings were difficult to assemble, largely due to the loss of many of the author's notes and annotations.[5] Only by reading between the lines of his reticence, which seems to have been Licini's prevailing attitude even in his most intimate moments, can we perceive the significance and the value he attributed to those poems.

Licini's letters are playful, full of jokes, burlesque expressions, and wordplay in the manner of Aldo Palazzeschi, revealing an immediate depth of thought. However, it is in his poetry that the figure of the angel frequently appears.[6]

Angels seem to disappear from Licini's pictorial language as he shifts to abstraction in the 1930s, when he claimed to have taken the works created earlier and "burned them at the stake." In truth, it was only a formal interruption, part of a complex process where memory and apparent oblivion alternated in the reworking of paintings, only to find its innermost motives in a mirror reflection of profound and persistent themes and mythologies.[7]

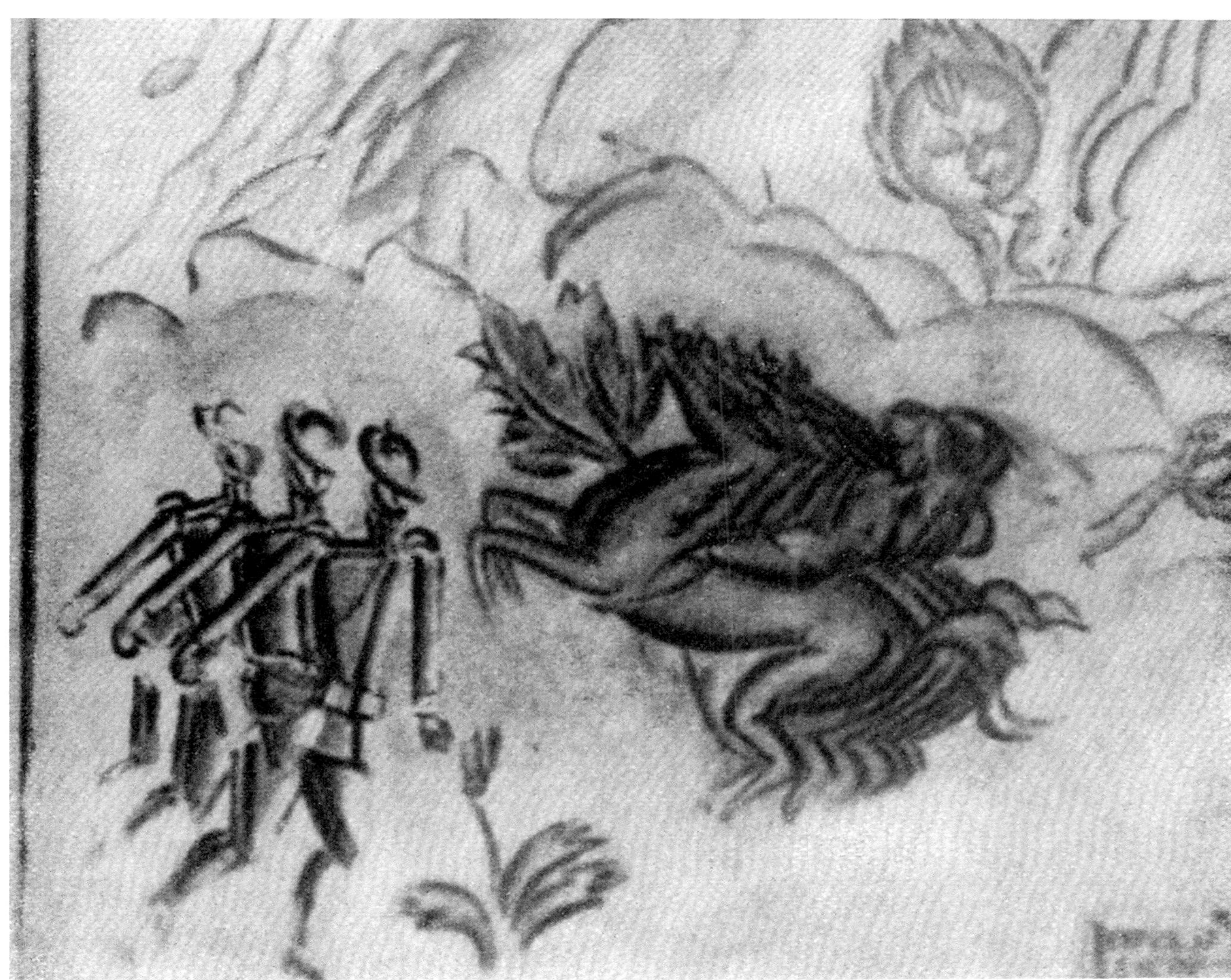

CLASH
(LO SCONTRO)
1915
Private collection

In his introductory text for his first exhibition at the Galleria Il Milione in Milan in 1935, Licini wrote: "Painting is the art of freely conceived color and form, and it is also an act of volition and creation, and contrary architecture, it is an irrational art with a predominance of fantasy and imagination, which is to say, poetry."[8] The eccentricity of Licini's thought transpires in this declaration: rather than a sterile adherence to the rationalist credo, Licini sublimated geometric modularity in aerial and unstable pictorial architectures; his images, instead of assuming a purified and aseptic appearance, seem to transform themselves into symbolic elements, just as the titles of his works were not limited to the simple definition of "compositions"—as abstract artists were wont to do—but invariably retain a degree of fantasy, pointing to an unusual density of meaning. A letter written to Giuseppe Marchiori in January 1935 is eloquent in this regard: "I believe that the ghost of God loses all virtue, even that of resigning himself to life, and that we will have to create other ghosts and chimeras and illusions to make us momentarily forget the boredom of the world and the ugliness of existence. This is why, for the last five years, *my kingdom is the air.* I sent three irrational paintings to the Quadriennale, taking all the responsibility that this heresy entails: *Castle in the Air, Stratosphere,* and *Archangel Gabriel* ... They are works painted at 500,000 meters of altitude, in the celestial realm ... Long live irrational painting."[9]

Licini, therefore, initially planned on presenting *Archangel Gabriel* at the second Rome Quadriennale after having reworked it, by modifying the compositional structure and adding, as mentioned

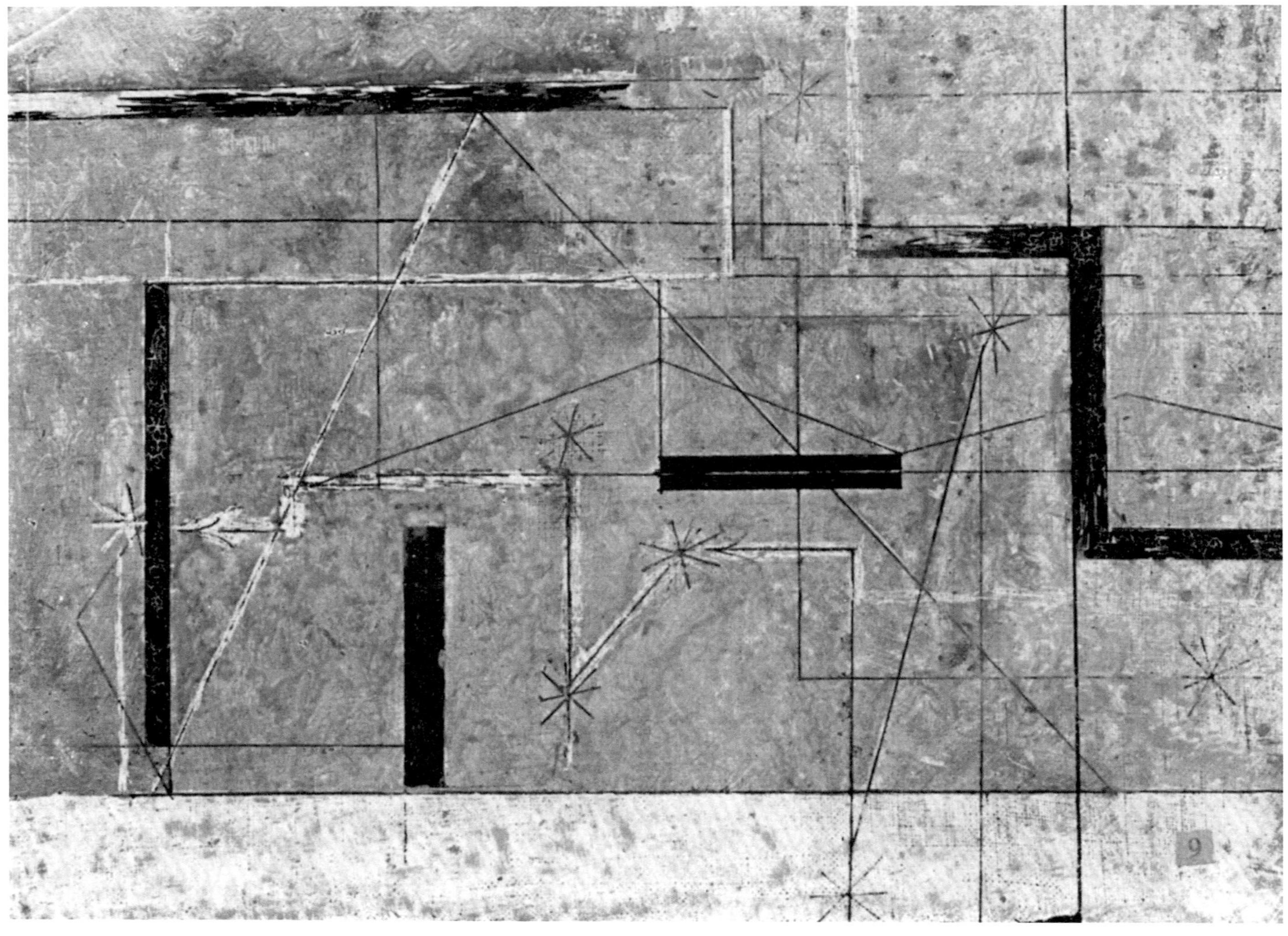

SAGITTARIUS (SAGITTARIO)
1933
oil on board
23 × 31 cm
Private collection

earlier, a new figure of a warrior angel. However, he then decided to show instead *Precarious Balance* (*Il bilico*, 1934, p. 75), a work apparently more in line with the dictates of abstraction. This episode is significant, if only because in all likelihood Licini's desire to rework those "primordial" paintings was motivated by one of his favorite art periodicals, among the most original and interesting in the Parisian panorama of the early 1930s, *Documents*, whose subheading was "Archéologie, Beaux Arts, Ethnographie, Variétés."[10] Headed by Georges Bataille, along with Georges Henri Rivière, deputy director of the ethnographic Musée du Trocadéro, and with the poet, musicologist, and art historian Carl Einstein, the magazine brought together the most eccentric refugees from the Surrealist movement, along with archaeologists, art historians, musicians, critics, poets, anthropologists, and philosophers. In the sixth issue of 1930,[11] Michel Leiris dedicated his "Dictionnaire" column to the word *angel* (*ange* in French) and connected it to numerous philosophical and literary sources. They were surely not unfamiliar to Licini, but in this particular context may have provoked his reimmersion into themes he had already investigated in part. Leiris cited several passages from *Heaven and Hell* by the mystic philosopher Emanuel Swedenborg, dedicated to angels and inspired by Neoplatonic and cabalistic thought.[12] He then addressed the inherent ambivalence in the angelic imagery of Blake and John Milton and described the characteristics of the archangel Gabriel, who

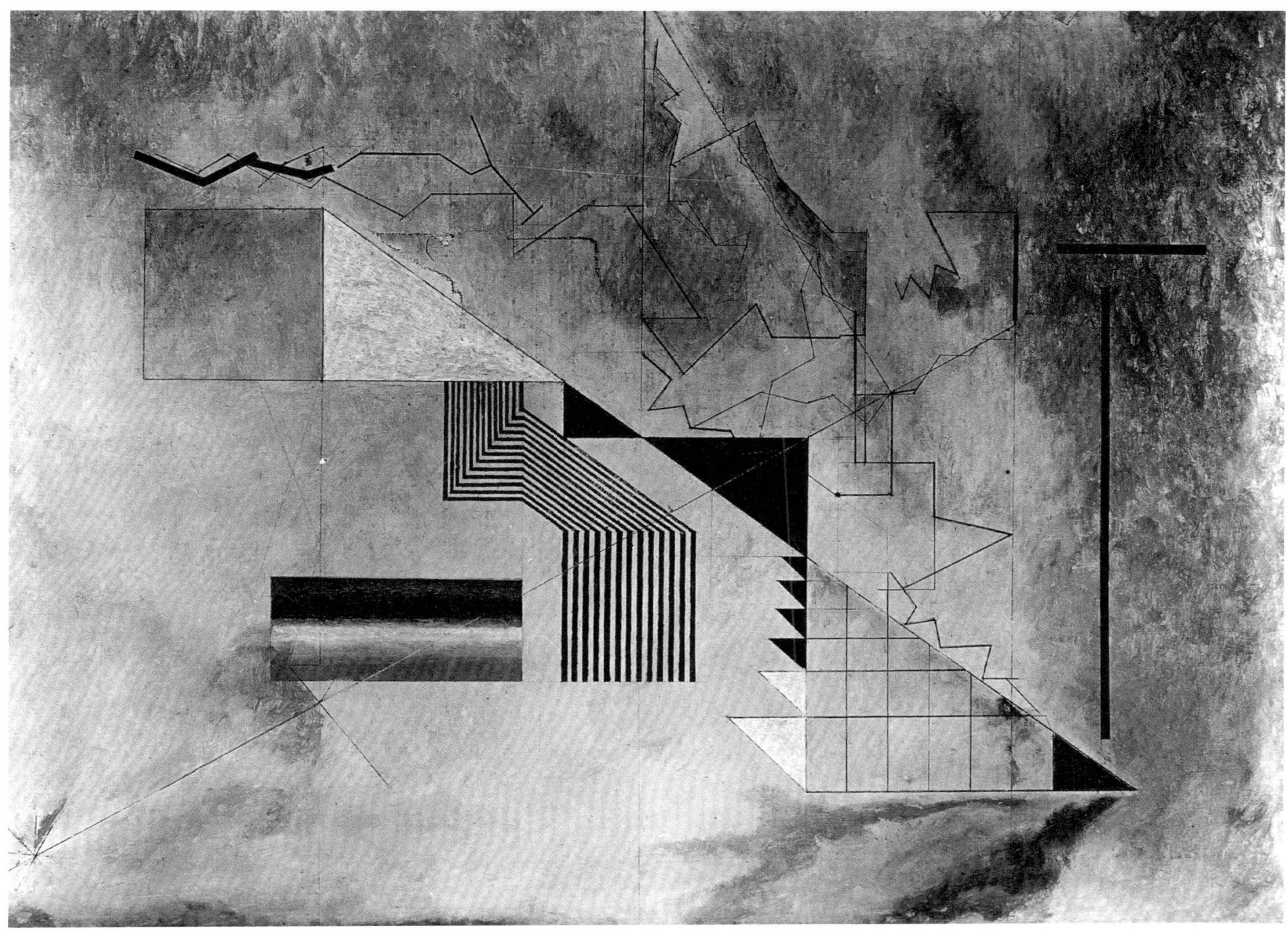

CASTLE IN THE AIR (*CASTELLO IN ARIA*), 1933–36 (PP. 94–95), WHEN IT WAS EXHIBITED AT THE SECOND ROME QUADRIENNALE IN 1935

represents the planetary genius of the moon in astrology. He also wrote about the *Book of Enoch*, an apocryphal book of the Old Testament, among whose stories is the one where Gabriel displays "the instruments of death to the sons of men, the shield, the breastplate, and the sword," concluding with the other archangels leading the heavenly armies against Lucifer and the rebel angels.

Given the depth and breadth of the arguments addressed, Licini's familiarity with the magazine, of which seven issues were published in 1929 and eight in 1930, may well have been a source of inspiration and theoretical foundation for the quest for "surreality" that was so important to him. Moreover, in the third issue Leiris wrote that "not only language, but all intellectual life is based on a game of transpositions, of symbols that can be defined as metaphorical." And it is precisely in the metaphorical transposition of the image that the figure of the angel persists in new forms in Licini's poetics during his abstract years.

On the other hand, the titles of the paintings of the 1930s and their compositional forms highlight a continuous and persistent meditation on the themes of instability and balance, strongly correlated with those of ascent, flight, and lightness.

The quintessential instrument of ascent and the attribute of perfection for all beings is, of course, the wing. In *Bird 2 (Uccello 2)* of 1936 (p. 103), Licini painted a triangle, clearly intended as a wing, rather than the creature itself. "One should be light like a bird, not like a feather," wrote Valéry, because light-

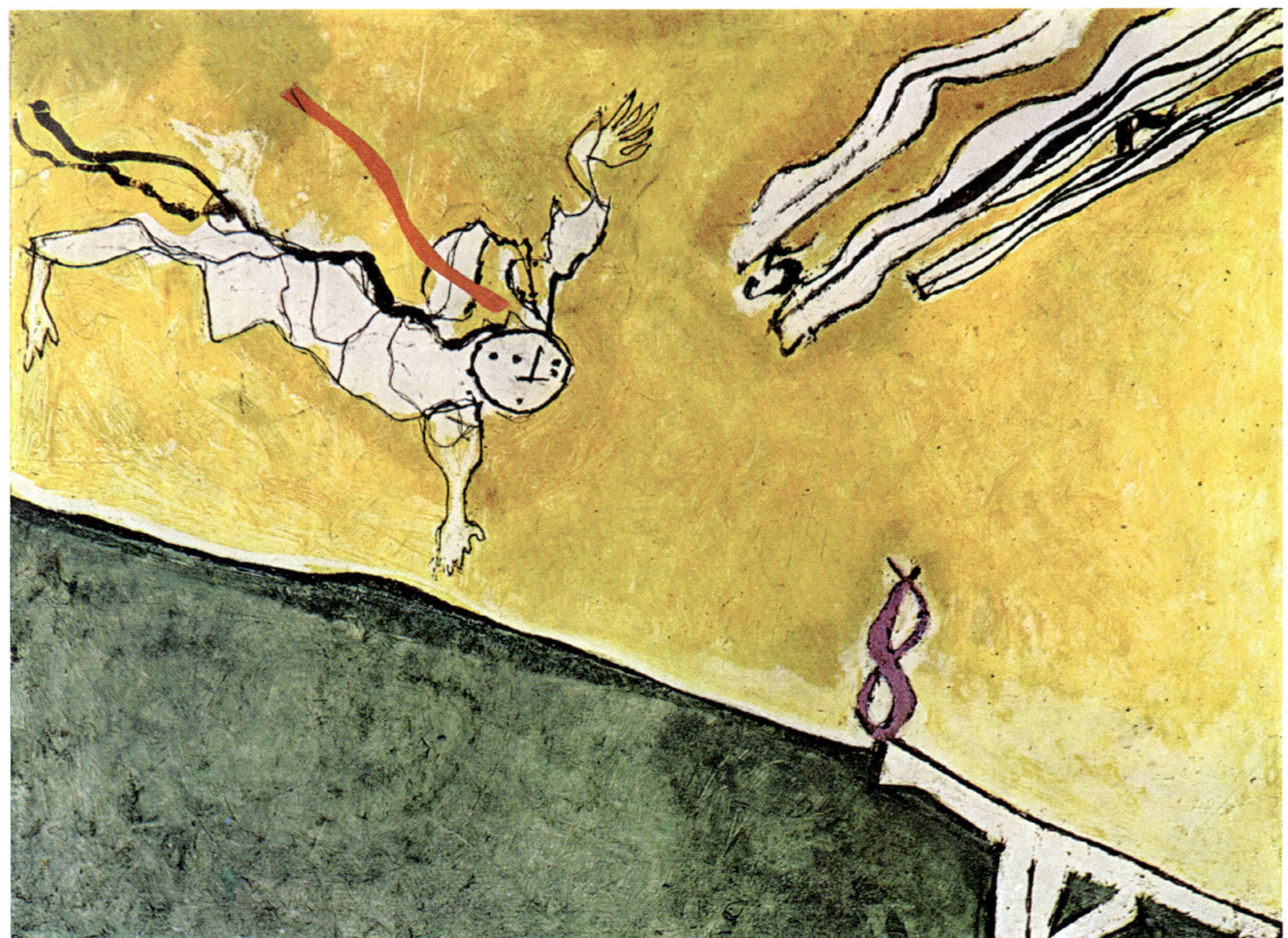

ness is the result of precision and determination and cannot be left to chance.[13]

Sagittarius (*Sagittario*) of 1933 is another transformation of the angelic image in which the natural attribute of the wing is replaced by the technological one of the arrow, and the amplification of the movement transforms ascent into momentum. The arrow is a projection of flight, of the impulse to overcome the resistance of gravity in order to make the flight last a bit longer than usual, as long as possible.[14]

The fear of gravity is countered by the virtues of the tightrope walker[15] (*The Tightrope Walker* [*L'equilibrista*], 1932), and the "miraculous" balancing of forms (*Capriccio No. 2* [*Capriccio n. 2*], 1932, p. 83; *Precarious Balance* [*Il bilico*], 1934).

In his essay "What Are Poets For?" Martin Heidegger defined balance as "that state in which something can resolve in one way or another.... What is so ventured is, of course, unprotected; but because it hangs in the balance, it is retained in the venture.... The venture is the force of gravity."[16] If we were to follow the line that connects the image of the angel and the tightrope walker, the image of balance and that of instability, of gravity and its defeat, we would also discover the figure of Friedrich Nietzsche's Zarathustra, for whom elevation and flight are the attributes of physical perfection, to which corresponds moral perfection, while gravity is associated with the devil.

For Licini, the years that spanned the beginning of World War II were a time of reflection and silence. "I reject mankind," he wrote to Marchiori in 1940, "I declare that I begin to feel ashamed to be a man, to still be reciting this farce."[17]

In the self-imposed isolation of Monte Vidon Corrado, he once again returned to the figurative

ANGEL WITH TAIL (THE MIRACLE OF SAINT MARK) [ANGELO CON CODA (IL MIRACOLO DI SAN MARCO)]
1948
oil on canvas
38 × 48 cm
Private collection

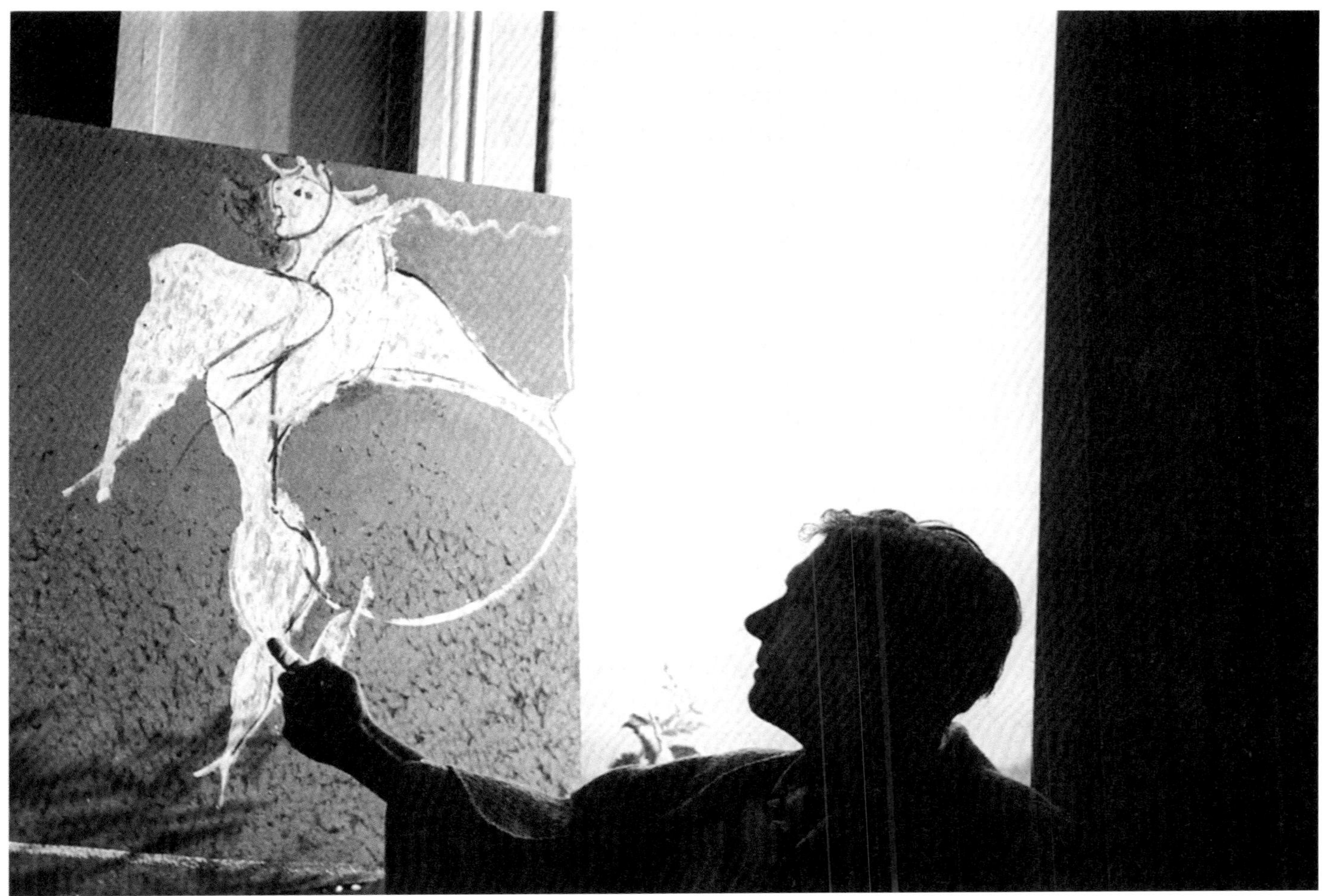

OSVALDO LICINI IN FRONT OF *REBEL ANGEL ON A DARK BLUE BACKGROUND* (*ANGELO RIBELLE SU FONDO BLU CUPO*)(1956, P. 177), 1952

paintings abandoned years before along with his abstractions, and he reworked them, overlaying layers of color and new images. "From the real to the abstract. And from the abstract I am now flying, in foliage and flowers, towards the boundless and the supernatural. Certainly this solitude is of great benefit to me," he wrote to his friend Maria Cernuschi Ghiringhelli.[18]

Thus, between the early 1940s and the following decade, new and fantastical characters were born and, again, despite a profound formal metamorphosis, they appeared endowed with the aspiration to fly. From the Wagnerian *Flying Dutchman* (*Olandese volante*) to the homage to *Baron von Münchhausen*, whose adventures are a constant challenge to the laws of gravity, from the *Amalasuntha Moon* (*Amalassunta luna*) to the *Rebel Angels* (*Angeli ribelli*) and the *Lunar Missiles* (*Missili lunari*), the painter's "secret skies" come alive with extraordinary figures of the kingdom of air.

However, Licini's imagery is also characterized by the coexistence and inseparable dialectic between the will to ascend, which is always associated with the risk of falling, and the contamination of the impure and the corporeal. This first appeared in his early literary work *Racconti di Bruto* (Tales of Brutus) written in 1913. If melancholy is "sadness that has taken on lightness, so humor is comedy that has lost its bodily weight,"[19] a melancholic and saturnine temperament like that of Licini could not have been without a certain inclination to humor.

In the *Racconti di Bruto*, which Licini himself described as "brutal cynicism," the Futurist matrix, the exaltation of the gratuitous gesture, and a declared, albeit unmotivated cruelty identify this character as a take on Jules Laforgue's Pierrot, "a less neu-

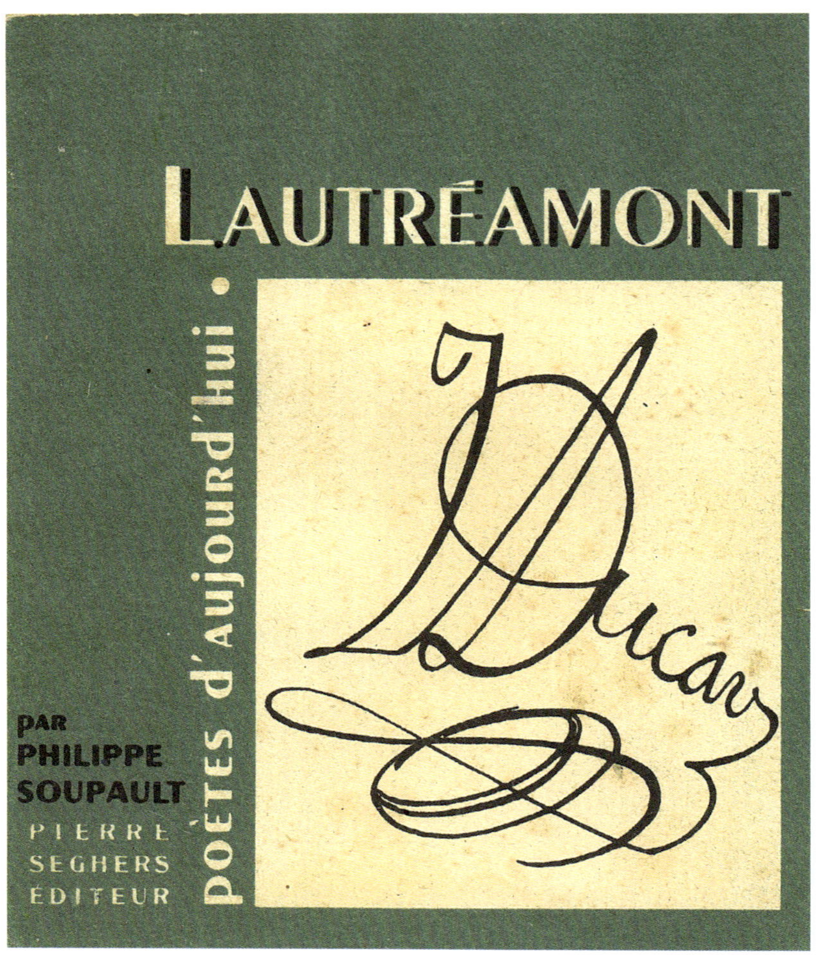

rotic and lunar variation on the taste for surprise" between *Ubu Roi* and Palazzeschi, suspended between violence, tightrope walking, and eroticism.[20] Brutus, moreover, as an autobiographical archetype of rebellion, is ancestor to the rebel angels carrying their hearts in hand that would appear forty years later in his paintings.

On closer inspection, the earliest angels are also marked by ambiguity: like the ones painted in the catacombs or carved on early Christian sarcophagi, they are not endowed with the celestial attribute of wings, they resemble avengers or warriors with unsheathed swords, angels of the Apocalypse in a landscape of sulfur and flame.

Licini understood the "human, all too human" risk, the unbridled vitality, even the violence and the gratuitous gesture. He was aware they were part of his own being and knew existed, in different degree, in all men. His angels, therefore, belong to the same tribe as those of Lautréamont, master of ambivalence and metamorphosis, and Apollinaire—both poets played a fundamental role in Licini's artistic evolution.[21]

In the famous episode of the struggle between Maldoror and the guardian angel in the Temple, the latter fights with an invisible sword while the former tries to bite the angel's face to infect him with his impurity. And although the angel succumbs, the final exchange of gazes between the angel ascending to heaven and Maldoror plunging into the abyss connects the two characters intensely: "What a look passes between them! All that humanity has thought in sixty centuries and much more that it will think could easily have been contained in that supreme farewell! ... That look binds them together in an eternal friendship."[22]

LAUTRÉAMONT (1953) FROM THE PRIVATE LIBRARY OF OSVALDO LICINI

The ambivalence of this extraordinary angelic figure, already explored by Blake, was particularly in the focus of Surrealism, the French literary movement so deeply loved by Licini.[23] One need only think of the writings of Jean Cocteau: "Selflessness, selfishness, tender pity, cruelty, sufferance of human contact, purity in his vices, a mixture of a violent taste for earthly pleasures and a disdain for them, naive amorality, do not be fooled: these are the signs of what we call angelitude and that every true poet possesses, all those who write, paint, sculpt or sing: few will admit it, because few can feel poetry. Until further notice, Arthur Rimbaud remains the archetype of the angel on earth."[24]
The angelic figures appearing in Licini's paintings in the late 1940s and through the following decade are often *Rebel Angels*, who reunite the celestial and the demonic, and whose ascensional movements of purification alternate with ruinous and ironic falls, as in *Angel with Tail (The Miracle of Saint Mark)* (*Angelo con la coda [Miracolo di San Marco]*) of 1948. They are angels, but with their original demon tails, as in *Angels, First Love* (ca. 1955, pp. 174–75): "Now I shall flutter away on my own, into the skies of fantasy: a rebel with a tail, which I sometimes amuse myself by biting."[25]
The character of Amalasuntha—the personification of the moon—also becomes the pretext for a significant play on words: Amalasuntha is the "badly ascended" (*assunta male*), and therefore a relative of Lautréamont's Maldoror and Apollinaire's Mal-Aimé. Moreover, Amalasunthas often assume bizarre attitudes: they smoke, they play the trumpet, they have a heart drawn on their hand that they seductively extend to the observer, and they fly just above the hills that have the erotic contour of female breasts.
In nearly all of Licini's poetry, there appears the figure of the angel with whom the artist often battles.[26] Here again is an ambivalent angel, like those of Baudelaire, Apollinaire, Cocteau, Lautréamont, and, earlier still, Blake. Licini wrote: "Because I know that soon / an angel made of everything / will descend to take me / whether angel or demon / it is the same / and matters little." These are figures that the artist has seen "finally arrive on foot and on horseback / from the sky with their swords of silk / flaming in midsummer in full midday / pointed at my heart as to seem angels / strange to a world dressed in blue."[27]
If the angel is symbol and residue of the transcendent, even as a dual entity, it is only through its gaze that one is allowed to penetrate the invisible and look towards the infinite, beyond the opacity of "a world dressed in blue."
The silence of things, the paralysis of language, the inadequacy of words are all elements of the modern consciousness. The angel as messenger[28] and image of creation is transformed for the contemporary artist into a sort of muse, embodying the aesthetic possibilities, the poetic capacity of the contemporary era. But these possibilities are subject to the risk of falling, of losing oneself.
As in Cocteau's *Orpheus*, it will be the angel who allows the poet/Orpheus to return to hell with the memories of what he has seen intact.
Indeed, only the poetic function offers the possibility of crossing the boundary between the two worlds and freely returning without facing the perils of the river Lethe. Although death has always been configured as the land of forgetting, the song of Mnemosyne, mother of the Muses, is a deciphering of the invisible, a geography of the supernatural. As such, unlike the soothsayer whose relation to time is geared more towards the future, the function of the poet mainly concerns the past, not only the world "of the dead and unborn,"[29] but the quest for the origin, for a primordial time.
This is the moment of creation for poets and painters. This is the time of Licini as revealed to Franco Ciliberti: "I write to you from the bowels of the earth, the 'region of the mothers' perhaps, where I have descended to preserve unsoiled certain immaterial, incontrovertible value that belong to the human spirit. In these still green depths, the moor of the origin perhaps, I will seek to recover the primitive secret of our purpose in the cosmos ... Only [after the descent to the inferno] will I be able to

show you my prey: those rare symbols that have no name; enigmatic alphabets and phrases, totemic representations that only you with your science will be able to decipher."[30] But the purity of the negative sign of the angels/demons, or the ambiguity of the other metaphors of air, are gradually replaced by the cosmic absolute of the subsequent paintings. Licini reaches the end of his journey with the supreme symbolic icons of the *Saint Domingo Angel (Angelo di San Domingo)* and the *Saint Rose Angel* (*Angelo di Santa Rosa*) (both from 1957, pp. 185, 187), but especially with *Nocturne* (*Notturno*) of 1958, where the blue shadow of a winged figure emerges from the saturated spaciousness of the sky: the silence of the cosmos, charged with expectation and mythic origins.

1. The two works might have been painted in 1917, as suggested by infrared reflectography conducted by Paolo Spezzani in 1988 and more recent IRR analysis published by Mattia Patti. See Mattia Patti, *Tracce disperse e segni nuovi. Osvaldo Licini attraverso la riflettografia infrarossa* (Pisa: Scuola Normale Superiore, 2006) and, by the same author, "Catalogo delle opere" in Fabrizio D'Amico and Marco Goldin, *Licini. Opere 1913–1929* (Treviso: Linea d'Ombra, 2006).

2. The archangel descending from the sky is wrapped in a fluttering, pleated drapery that seems to recall the sinuous forms of the vestment worn by the angel of Caravaggio's famous masterpiece *Rest on the Flight into Egypt* in the Galleria Doria-Pamphilj, Rome. I thank Marco Bussagli, among the foremost experts on the iconography of angels, for having pointed out this possible formal correspondence. Among his many publications on the subject, see Marco Bussagli, *Storia degli angeli. Racconto di immagini e di idee* (Milan: Bompiani, 1995). On a philosophical and theological reading of angels in Judaic and Christian traditions up to the twentieth century see Massimo Cacciari, *The Necessary Angel* (Albany, NY: SUNY Press, 1994).

3. Infrared analyses also demonstrated the presence of two figures, seen from behind and brandishing swords. See Patti, *Tracce disperse*, 14.

4. I identified *The Clash* among the works published in Vincenzo Costantini, *La pittura italiana dalla fine dell'Ottocento ad oggi* (Milan: Hoepli, 1934). Licini wrote about this painting in a 1933 letter to Acruto Vitali, in which he dates it 1915. See Osvaldo Licini, *Errante, erotico, eretico. Gli scritti letterari e tutte le lettere*, ed. Gino Baratta, Francesco Bartoli, and Zeno Birolli (Milan: Feltrinelli, 1974), 130. In a 1929 interview with Giovanni Scheiwiller, Licini described this group as "war episodes" (see Licini, *Errante, erotico, eretico*, 97–98). The works show a predilection for the fantastic, as well as an element of the irony typical of his poetics.

5. The poems were published for the first time by Giuseppe Marchiori, in *L'angelo ribelle* (Ancona, 1955), and later collected and organized in Licini, *Errante, erotico, eretico*.

6. See Licini, *Errante, erotico, eretico*, esp. 83, 87, and 89.

7. D'Amico pointed out that for Licini "caesuras are banished and returns are frequent and almost always fatal; ... [his work] is not a tense and linear journey, but rather one that finds its place as if straddling a sinusoid, in which new headways drag along legacies, perhaps regrets about what has been. In [his] work, nothing seems to be completely consumed, or to burn forever. Probably in this attitude of the intellect as well as the soul is a part, not a small one, of the artist's need, which will touch upon all his years, to go back to many of the paintings he had already completed." In "Remakings, Revisions, Returns: Licini's Exacting Path," in *Osvaldo Licini. Masterworks*, ed. Danilo Eccher (Milan: Electa, 2010), 139.

8. Osvaldo Licini, "Lettera aperta al Milione," *Bollettino della Galleria del Milione*, no. 39 (1935).

9. Osvaldo Licini, letter to Giuseppe Marchiori, January 7, 1935, in Giuseppe Marchiori, *I cieli segreti di Osvaldo Licini, Col catalogo generale delle opere* (Venice: Alfieri, 1968), 18.

10. In the winter of 1930 Licini wrote to a friend of his from the Marches, Ermenegildo "Checco" Catalini, and invited him to subscribe to *Documents*, "an art journal that is truly alive and very well done." See Licini, *Errante, erotico, eretico*, 114. In the magazine's program, one reads, are, among other things: "The most annoying works of art, not yet classified, and certain incomplete productions heretofore neglected will be subjected to studies as rigorous and scientific as those of any archaeologist.... We will generally focus on the most unsettling facts, those whose consequences have not yet been determined. In these various investigations, the sometimes absurd nature of the results and methods, far from being concealed, as always happens out of deference to the rules of social decorum, will be deliberately emphasized, in the interest of both humor and our aversion to banality."

11. Michel Leiris, "Ange," in *Documents*, no. 6 (1930): 367.

12. In 1926 Licini married Nanny Hellström, a Swedish painter known in France. The couple traveled to Sweden many times.

13. "Il faut etre léger comme l'oiseau, et non comme la plume." See Italo Calvino, "Lightness," in *Six Memos for the Next Millenium* (Cambridge, MA: Harvard University Press, 1988), 16.

14. See Gilbert Durand, *Le strutture antropologiche dell'immaginario* (Bari: Dedalo, 1972), 131–32.

15. A nod to Jean Starobinski, *Ritratto dell'artista da saltimbanco* (1970) is inevitable here. During his visit to the second Rome Quadriennale, the French ambassador asked Licini how it was possible for two triangles to remain balanced on opposite vertices, and the artist responded, "Par miracle!"

16. Martin Heidegger, *Poetry, Languange, Thought*, trans. Albert Hofstadter (New York: Harper & Row, 1971), 101–02.

17. Osvaldo Licini, letter to Giuseppe Marchiori, April 24, 1940, in Licini, *Errante, erotico, eretico*, 147.

18. Osvaldo Licini, letter to Maria Cernuschi Ghiringhelli, January 15, 1940, in Licini, *Errante, erotico, eretico*, 173.

19. Calvino, "Lightness," 19, and more generally, Raymond Klibansky, Erwin Panofsky, and Fritz Saxl, *Saturn and Melancholy* (New York: Basic Books, 1964).

20. The stringent and illuminating analysis of the figure of Brutus is in Gino Baratta, "Il paradossismo di Bruto," in Licini, *Errante, erotico, eretico*, 33–42.

21. An explicit reference to Apollinaire's angels is to be found in Licini's letter to Marchiori of January 13, 1953: "You must simply deliver a message for me on behalf of the angels of Apollinaire, from those angels of whom our pockets are full, I agree, but who unfortunately, on that blessed day, came out of our pockets to cross their swords with our souls, in our study, a stone's throw from Saint Mark's Basilica, at precisely the right hour, the hour of clairvoyance," in Licini, *Errante, erotico, eretico*, 149.

22. Comte de Lautréamont, *Maldoror (Les Chants de Maldoror)*, trans. Guy Wernham (New York: New Directions, 1950), 96.

23. On this topic, see my "Licini e l'Europa: La nascita dell'iconografia angelica," in *Licini*, ed. Mariano Apa, Francesco Bartoli, Paolo Licini, and Toni Toniato, exh. cat. (Milan: Mazzotta, 1988), 39–49; "L'angelo del Novecento," in *Art e Dossier*, no. 38 (September 1989): 16–20; "Poesia e pittura in Scipione e Licini," in *Abitare l'immagine*, ed. Mariano Apa, exh. cat. (Rome: Campisano, 2002), 76–90; "Licini e il demone della gravità. Da Bruto all'Angelo passando per Leopardi," in *Il segno marchigiano nell'arte del Novecento, Scipione, Licini, Cucchi*, ed. Francesca R. Morelli, Ludovico Pratesi, and Federica Pirani (Milan: Skira, 2008), 33–40. On the theme of the angel, see my "Gli angeli di Klee," in *Paul Klee, uomo, pittore, disegnatore*, exh. cat., curated by H. C. von Tavel (Milan, 2004), 53–61. On Licini and Klee see the dissertation by Ilaria Bettucci, "Osvaldo Licini e l'Europa: i rapporti con Paul Klee," Università degli Studi di Roma "La Sapienza," 2012–13.

24. Jean Cocteau, *A Call to Order*, trans. Rollo H. Myers (London: Faber and Gwyer, 1926).

25. Osvaldo Licini, letter to Corrado Levi of April 27, 1958, in Licini, *Errante, erotico, eretico* (see note 4), 169.

26. "In the shadow of a rose / outside the sea are sleeping / a thousand and one nights / which I battle in my sky / with angels made of nothing / and I almost no longer know / what it means to say good day / without thinking myself too disgraced / because I know that soon / an angel made of everything / will descend and take me / whether angel or demon / it is the same / it matters little / … / And a miracle / tell me something that is not / a miracle," in Licini, *Errante, erotico, eretico* (see note 4), 83. Baudelaire writes in his *Hymn to Beauty*: "From God or Satan, who cares? Angel or Siren / Who cares, if you make,—fay with the velvet eyes, / Rhythm, perfume, glimmer; my one and only queen! / The world less hideous, the minutes less leaden?" (*The Flowers of Evil*, trans. William Aggeler [Fresno: Academy Library Guild, 1954]).

27. See Licini, *Errante, erotico, eretico*, 87.

28. It is thus no surprise that in the famous *Angelus Novus* by Paul Klee, the head of the angel, where we would expect to see curly hair, is surrounded instead by rolls of parchment upon which a message may be written. See Gerschom Scholem, "Walter Benjamin and His Angel," in *On Jews and Judaism in Crisis* (New York: Schocken Books, 1976), 200.

29. The reference is to Klee's famous epitaph, "I cannot be grasped in the here and now. For my dwelling place is as much among the dead as the yet unborn. Slightly closer to the heart of creation than usual, but still not close enough." In *Paul Klee, 1879–1940*, ed. Susanna Partsch (Cologne: Taschen, 2003), 7.

30. Osvaldo Licini, letter to Franco Ciliberti, February 1, 1941, in Licini, *Errante, erotico, eretico*, 161. In 1936 Franco Ciliberti, the philosopher and theosophist, founded the Primordialist movement in Milan and in 1938 published the first issue of *Valori Primordiali*, with Adriano Ghiron, Piero Lingeri, and Giuseppe Terragni, a periodical dedicated "to the orientation of contemporary creation." In 1941 he published the *Manifesto del Primordialismo*, to which Licini, along with the abstractionists of Como and Milan, adhered. See, among other sources, *Franco Ciliberti. Storia degli ideali*, ed. Elena Di Raddo (Como: Archivio Cattaneo, 2003).

OSVALDO LICINI AND ART CRITICISM

SILENO SALVAGNINI[1]

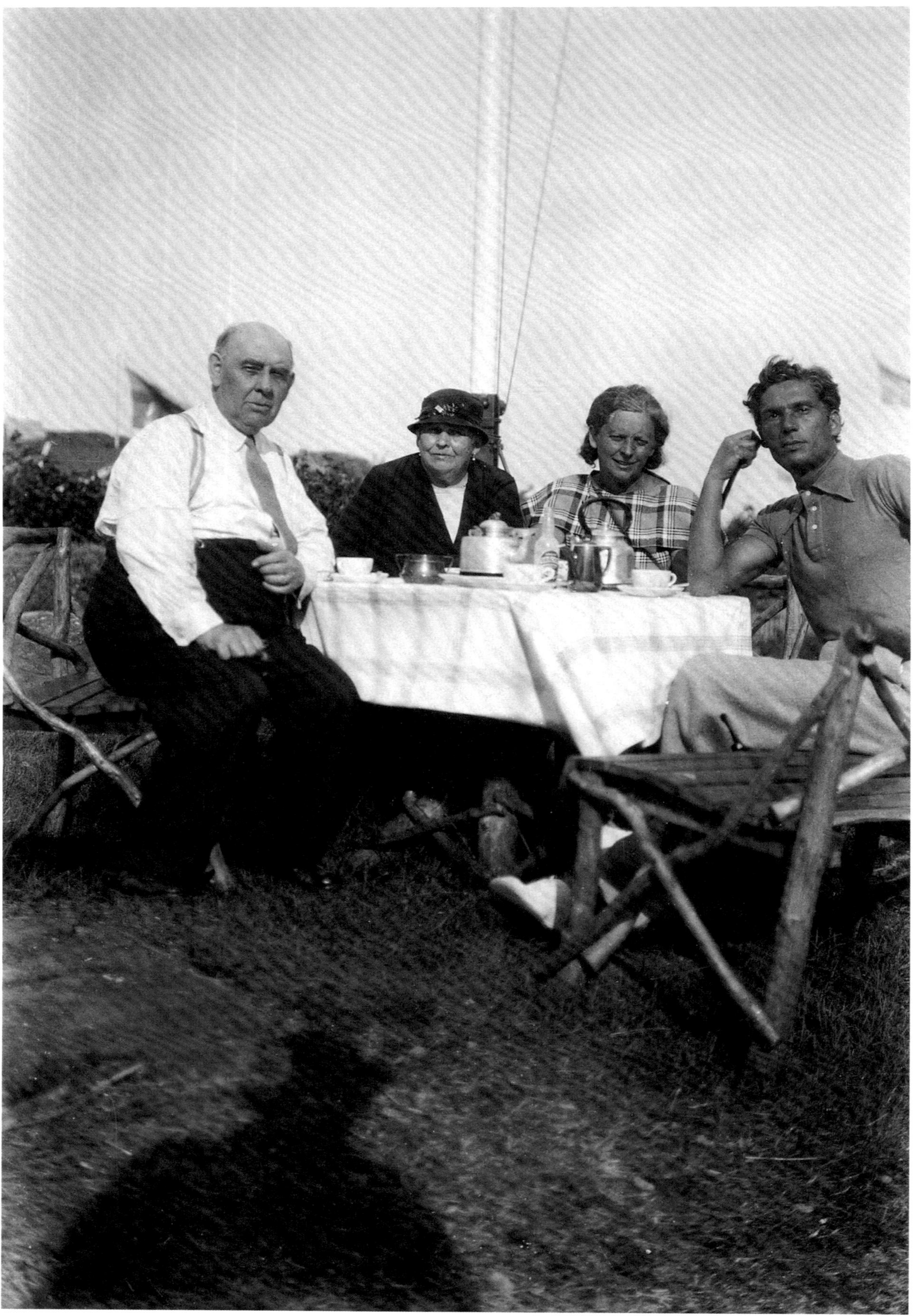

The most complete study on Osvaldo Licini ever published was released in September 1974. In addition to numerous poems and unpublished letters by the painter, *Errante, erotico, eretico* (Errant, Erotic, Heretic) also included three introductory essays by its curators: the sensitive art critic Zeno Birolli, the fine literary critic Gino Baratta, and the acute semiologist and theater critic Francesco Bartoli.[2] The book was immediately given a favorable review by Paolo Fossati, who in the *Corriere della Sera* expressed the hope that it might be—together with the exhibition at the Museum Ostwall in Dortmund directed by Eugen Thiemann (also the first, in 1971, to introduce Fausto Melotti, an Italian sculptor and the author of the preface to the Licini exhibition, to the rest of the world)—the start of a new debate on an artist who had not always received positive assessments in the past.[3] Fossati was thus underscoring a concept that had been championed forcefully a few years earlier in *L'immagine sospesa*, an essential book on Italian abstract art of the 1930s. According to the author, Licini, both the "abstract artist" and the inventor of the *Amalasunthas* (*Amalassunte*) and the *Rebel Angels* (*Angeli ribelli*), was not to be interpreted in a geometric key, or even worse, in a Constructivist one ("some have described a certain point of Licini's activity, his abstract work, as Constructivist synthesis, but have been terribly wrong"). Licini did not set out from preconceived, a priori schemes, but rather freely varied in an almost automatic manner—in the Surrealist sense of the term—naturalistic motifs and other overtly unreal ones, while substantially remaining within the strategies of painting itself.[4]
Thanks also to new information unearthed by the three scholars, Licini increasingly was recognized as a complex artist, and not simply explained away by banal, empathetic interpretations of his work:

OSVALDO LICINI WITH NANNY HELLSTRÖM AND HER PARENTS IN SWEDEN
1935

> Not just Surrealism and Cocteau, Jouve and Superville, or, by contrast, Man Ray and obviously Picasso, for instance (Matisse was also cited at length, a name to which we should return when dealing with Licini), but a France that had already entered Italy from a critical point of view. Of core importance is Licini's reading of Lionello Venturi's *Il gusto dei primitivi*.[5]

One month after Fossati's article in the *Corriere*, a very positive review by Vanni Scheiwiller—his father, Giovanni, was one of the first to draw attention to Licini in Italy—appeared in *Il Settimanale*, in which he pointed out the value of both the book and the exhibition in Dortmund. His article also mentioned the excellent foreword by Melotti.[6]
One day later, however, and rather unexpectedly, Pier Paolo Pasolini panned *Errante, erotico, eretico* in the Rome newspaper *Il Tempo*. In his review Pasolini compared it with *Hermaphrodito* by Alberto Savinio, which had been published by Einaudi the same year. Pasolini admitted he was not familiar with the artist, even though the few reproductions "offer a notable image of him"; on the contrary, "it appears to me that his writing simply does not exist. It is merely an invention of his rediscoverers." What was it about Licini the writer that Pasolini disapproved of? First of all, his "gesticulation," his intention to shock the bourgeoisie with his writing; the sort of "ideological syncretism" typical of Italy in the 1910s and 1920s:

> ... that amalgamates nothing except perhaps in words, or in a certain generic "sentiment of scandal" (which explodes in all its emptiness in Futurism). It suffices to "belong" to a certain type of culture, to have more or less read a certain list of authors, especially when they are French, and those idiotic Italian provincials are served. There was something terrorist-like in all this that couldn't help but develop into Fascism .... And Licini was played (naturally) by the Fascist illusion. You could bet on it. Since first I read his texts, and then the information about them,

> from the very first lines of *Racconti di Bruto* (I pray the reader believes me) I thought to myself: "What we no doubt have here is a writer who let himself be played by the Fascist illusion." The information I read later, albeit in a reticent manner, proved I was right. The content-oriented style, empty and available to all—whose only task is to gratify Licini's narcissism and the ensuing need for scandal—naturally ends up "molding" Licini's writings ...[7]

As a natural corollary the fact that, albeit gifted as a painter, he was "not intelligent enough and substantially not erudite enough to really be of interest. His young followers didn't realize that his work is based on 'silence, moods, and sullen generosities,' he remains 'solitary and reserved,' he is old, old, old, he has all the age of Italian provincialism, so dear to Falqui, may he rest in peace. His shit does not stink."

Pasolini offered a cruel comparison between Licini's text and Savinio's. To his mind, the gesticulation was not something in and of itself, something empty, but rather a poetic choice, realized by a man "whose primary goal was expression. Hence, the shocking rules of the gesticulation were all part of a stylistic system."

We could raise doubts about Pasolini's panning of the text, but two of the points he makes are of particular interest here. First of all, that it is absurd to compare a painter, who also dabbles in literature essentially to create some good painting, to a writer like Savinio, who dabbles in painting as well but is first and foremost a great writer—Savinio's painting not being equal to his written pages nor, to be truthful, even close to Licini's painting, in terms of value. With fine irony, Giuseppe Marchiori—a great friend of Licini and the first to write enlightening texts about him, followed, in 1968, by a *General Catalogue* of his works—in a "review" of Pasolini's "review" instead had positive things to say about the three young critics who had undertaken the huge task that resulted in *Errante, erotico, eretico*, even if this had given "Pier Paolo Pasolini the chance to describe my friend Osvaldo, the Communist Mayor of Monte Vidon Corrado, as a 'pre-Fascist goliardic brute.'" Marchiori's greatest criticism of Pasolini was that of not having understood that the texts were not meant to be read as full-fledged literary writings, but rather as poems "serving as a commentary to the pictorial inventions." Marchiori also refused to endorse Pasolini's description of Licini as a person who was "not intelligent enough and not erudite enough." Marchiori believed the judgment to be "too severe, distorted as it was by the assumption of considering a painter to be a 'man of letters,'" where instead he had "shown intelligence and culture in his own field: the field of painting." Marchiori ended his review with a bittersweet reproach to the writer:

> I nonetheless hope that the book, curated by three young critics, will become a pretext to stimulate Pasolini's ever-vibrant curiosity to familiarize itself with and learn to love the art of Osvaldo Licini, perhaps not a writer, but a truly European painter.[8]

Truth be told, I believe that Pasolini's aversion to Licini's "literary" creations, and non-realistic art in general, was somehow linked to the teachings he received from his teachers at the University of Bologna, that is to say, Francesco Arcangeli and Roberto Longhi. The latter would also publish the first version of *Ragazzi di vita* (*Il ferrobedò)* in *Paragone – Letteratura*.[9]

THE ORIGINS (1894–1929)

The most relevant information on the early years of Licini's biographical bibliography can be found in the many writings by Marchiori, in *Errante, erotico, eretico*, and in a rather rich year-by-year account by Enrica Torelli Landini.[10]

Giuseppe Marchiori "LA VERA VOCAZIONE DI LICINI," *LA VOCE REPUBBLICANA*, MAY 17, 1975

Born in 1894, from 1902 Licini lived with his grandparents in Monte Vidon Corrado because

Pag. 7 / Sabato 17 maggio 1975

La Voce Repubblicana

Diario di un critico

La vera vocazione di Licini

Incominciamo dal titolo: «Licini, errante erotico eretico», che deve esser corretto così: «errante, eretico, erotico», con un crescendo, molto più proprio a quel «Bruto», personaggio in cui Licini voleva riconoscersi, con goliardico spirito bolognese, a vent'anni.

Lo so: le reazioni ribelli di allora al cosiddetto filisteismo borghese erano di parole, anzi di parolacce, dette un po' alla ventura, ma sempre con l'intenzione segreta di far arrossire le vergini del primo decennio del secolo (la percentuale era abbastanza alta in quei tempi) e di far uscire dai gangheri gl'innumerevoli moralisti, che dominavano col terrorismo repressivo nelle famiglie patriarcali, rimaste fedeli, nonostante i primi annunci del secolo nuovo, alle sacre tradizioni dell'obbedienza e del rispetto.

Pasolini, in una acuta e spietata analisi del libro, in cui sono raccolti scritti, lettere e poesie di Licini (I), afferma di non conoscere l'opera del pittore di Monte-Vidon Corrado. Forse, se l'avesse conosciuta, non avrebbe dato al «Bruto» liciniano l'importanza di un testo letterario, mentre si trattava invece di uno sfogo parolibero del tutto gratuito e anche di scarso valore documentario, sia per un giudizio sulla letteratura del tempo, sia soprattutto sulla personalità di Licini, artista singolare che non deve nulla al futurismo, nei primi anni della sua formazione simile in questo al compagno di accademia e amico, Giorgio Morandi.

Le origini dell'uno e dell'altro sono comunque molto diverse. Per quanto riguarda Licini, la sua vera vocazione va collocata in quel dominio dell'arte fantastica nutrita, all'inizio del secolo, di simbolismo e di surrealtà.

In seguito Licini fu sensibile all'influenza di Matisse, rafforzata più tardi dalla parentesi cezanniana, suggerita, forse, dagli schemi costruttivi del paesaggio morandiano, dopo il breve e straordinario periodo metafisico del maestro.

Dal futurismo non vi è traccia, nell'arte del pittore marchigiano, né prima né quando egli decise di risolvere, dal 1930 in poi, i problemi che non aveva risolto nei paesaggi e nelle nature morte, accettando i principi fondamentali dell'arte astratta. Soltanto nei «Racconti di Bruto», Licini aveva creduto, con una certa ingenuità, di provocar scandali, di fare opera rivoluzionaria.

«I provinciali italiani imbecilli», dei quali parla Pasolini, avevano subissato con urli furibondi e con lanci di prodotti ortofrutticoli uomini come Carrà, Boccioni e Palazzeschi (Sant'Elia, che fu un rivoluzionario sul serio, non era abbastanza pittoresco per «gl'imbecilli» che affollavano i teatri, sino al 1915, per contestatare i futuristi con rumorose chiassate).

Anche il giovane Licini (aveva vent'anni quando espose con Morandi all'Albergo Baglioni a Bologna) aspirava forse al facile martirio del lancio dei pomodori anziché a quello delle frecce, scagliate dagli arcieri contro il nudo corpo dell'efebico San Sebastiano. Ma futurista non era, e futuristi non erano i suoi compagni, a cominciare da Morandi.

Inoltre Licini dava ben poca importanza alle sue poesie, che Pasolini giudica «decisamente scadenti», e che dovevano invece commentare le invenzioni pittoriche, definite in modo improprio «gestuali».

Quando poi Pasolini afferma che le lettere di Licini hanno «un assai scarso interesse culturale», il suo giudizio appare troppo severo, viziato com'è dalla premessa di considerare «letterato» un pittore, definito persino «poco intelligente» e «poco colto», mentre invece aveva dimostrato intelligenza e cultura nel campo che gli era proprio: quello della pittura.

In quanto alle lettere, almeno le più importanti, dirette a me, che ho conosciuto bene Licini e che ho scritto di lui sin dal 1935, e sempre senza intendimenti apologetici, credo di poter affermare con assoluta certezza che esse mi hanno sempre aiutato a interpretare le sue opere più astruse degli anni tra il 1938 e il 1957, cioè dopo il periodo che apre e conclude l'esperienza liciniana dell'arte concreta (1931-37).

Tutte opere che dimostrano quale fosse la vera «cultura» di Licini, legata a un momento particolarmente vitale nella storia dell'avanguardia europea. La parola «cultura», nel suo caso, non può avere altri significati. E le sue lettere quindi, a mio parere, hanno un valore culturale di straordinario interesse.

Pasolini non accetta la definizione di «solitario e schivo», data da Birolli all'«uomo» Licini, poiché «uno scrittore che si fonda su *silenzi, umori e generosità scontrose*» è «vecchio, vecchio, vecchio», «ha tutta la vecchiezza del provincialismo italiano, caro alla buonanima di Falqui».

Un processo di tal genere mi sembra ingiusto nei riguardi di un uomo, che era uno strano tipo di «solitario», poiché viveva per mesi e mesi nell'ambiente piuttosto animato, di Montparnasse, dove certamente non era e non si sentiva solo e che, prima di tornare alla sua casa di Monte Vidon Corrado, passava altri mesi fra Göteborg e Stoccolma o viaggiando, con la moglie svedese, lungo i più famosi itinerari artistici europei.

Non erano giri turistici, ma viaggi di studio, interrotti dai lunghi soggiorni a Parigi, dove frequentava moltissimi amici. Così sino al 1958, l'anno della sua morte immatura.

Lasciando in pace la «buonanima di Falqui», parliamo invece di Modigliani e di Soutine, di Kandinsky e di Magnelli, di De Pisis e di Campigli, per citare soltanto i primi nomi che mi vengono alla mente, insieme a quelli di Seuphor, di Cendrars e di Raynal, cioè di gente che ha fatto «cultura» e che gli «imbecilli» italiani di allora, e non solo di allora, hanno ignorato. Ma il «solitario» Licini non li ignorava, insieme con tanti altri che gli erano amici.

Alla fine Pasolini conclude, in modo imprevisto, con una frase, che simbolicamente allude alla «vecchiezza» dello «scrittore». Questa: «La sua m... non puzza».

Licini, invece, trascurando l'allusione olfattiva, si era servito della parola per disarticolarla, inserendola, attraverso le lettere che la compongono distribuite non a caso nello spazio delle sue visioni fantastiche e sempre con la stessa funzione grafica, attribuita ai numeri e alle sigle imposte alle «Amalassunte», vaganti nei cieli come astri impazziti.

I «bravissimi giovani» — Baratta, Bartoli e Birolli — animati dal loro ardore documentario, hanno creduto di rendere un buon servizio alla memoria di Licini, pubblicando i «Racconti di Bruto» fra le lettere e le poesie, che hanno offerto a Pier Paolo Pasolini l'occasione di definire il mio amico Osvaldo, sindaco comunista di Monte Vidon Corrado, un «teppista goliardico prefascista».

Mi auguro tuttavia che il libro, curato dai tre giovani critici, diventi anche un pretesto per stimolare la curiosità sempre viva di Pasolini a conoscere e amare l'arte di Osvaldo Licini, pittore (anche se non scrittore) davvero europeo.

Giuseppe Marchiori

OSVALDO LICINI: «Errante, erotico, eretico», a cura di G. Baratta, F. Bartoli, Z. Birolli, Milano, Feltrinelli, 1975.

Biblioteca

La poetica musicale di Arnold Schoenberg

A distanza di 15 anni dalla sua prima pubblicazione in Italia, Feltrinelli ripropone nella collana «I fatti e le idee», nella traduzione di Maria Giovanna Moretti e Luigi Pestalozza, «Stile e idea» di Arnold Schoenberg: un'attenta rilettura della prima versione condotta sul testo inglese comprensivo di 15 scritti estetici, alcuni dei quali tradotti dall'originale tedesco. I titoli delle composizioni, le citazioni poetiche, ecc. sono stati lasciati dai curatori in tedesco solamente nei casi in cui Schoenberg non li ha tradotti in inglese. Alla raccolta degli scritti Schoenberghiani fa seguito un saggio di Luigi Pestalozza sulla vita e sull'opera del grande musicista austriaco.

Quando uscì in America, nel 1950, «Stile e idea» fu salutato come il libro in cui Schoenberg — al cui nome è legata la nascita e la prodigiosa crescita della dodecafonia — esponeva la sua poetica. Si tratta infatti di una raccolta di saggi scelti dallo stesso compositore tra i suoi numerosi scritti sulla musica, per rappresentare il frutto di 40 anni di attività intellettuale e artistica.

Proprio nell'ampiezza e nella varietà dei temi trattati, si delinea chiaramente la profondità del mondo di Schoenberg, e il volume ne assume il valore vero e proprio di una «poetica».

ARNOLD SCHOENBERG: «Stile e idea», Feltrinelli, pp. 270, L. 4.900.

Con una spesa di 60 milioni

Nasce a Bologna il giardino "psicologico"

BOLOGNA, 16. — Un giardino originale, forse l'unico nel nostro paese, è stato realizzato dal comune nella zona adiacente al teatro comunale denominata «Del Guasto». Si tratta — ha detto l'assessore Pier Luigi Cervellati, durante la presentazione alla stampa — di un progetto che cerca di rendere in termini moderni i concetti naturalistici del giardino destinato alla sosta, al riposo e al gioco dei bambini.

La nuova opera sorge su un'area complessiva di 3 mila mq. sulle macerie dell'antico palazzo Bentivoglio chiamato «Domus Aurea».

Il giardino si divide in due parti che hanno funzioni diverse: il «largo» Respighi, protetto da una rigogliosa alberatura, recuperato ai pedoni e attrezzato con panchine tradizionali per la sosta e il riposo e il bastione Del guasto, destinato al gioco dei bambini, con effetti spaziali, quinte, percorsi, passaggi, cavità e degradi, che facilitano i giochi liberi, fantasiosi e creativi. La realizzazione dell'opera è stata lungamente discussa con gli abitanti del quartiere Irnerio a dimostrazione della volontà del comune di rispondere sempre più compiutamente ai bisogni più sentiti della comunità. L'importo dei lavori, che hanno comportato anche la messa a dimora di 1.500 piante di circa 100 specie diverse, è di circa 60 milioni.

A Rafael Alberti il premio "Etna-Taormina" di poesia

TAORMINA, . . — La giuria del premio di poesia «Etna-Taormina» di un milione di lire, presieduta da Angelo Maria Ripellino, e con segretario generale Giancarlo Vigorelli, ha assegnato i premi a Danilo Dolci per l'opera «Poema umano» edizione Rizzoli; nella sezione riservata alla poesia straniera, che ha pure in dotazione un milione di lire, il premio è andato al poeta spagnolo Rafael Alberti per l'intero arco creativo del suo lavoro.

Dopo il furto alla Galleria d'arte moderna

Tentativi per prevenire la ricettazione dei quadri

Mentre le indagini della polizia stentano a trovare una traccia il Comune di Milano sta provvedendo alla stampa di un opuscolo sui quadri rubati

MILANO, 16. — A trenta ore dalla rapina alla galleria d'arte moderna di Milano, le indagini della polizia sono praticamente al punto di partenza. «Nulla di nuovo» dicono i funzionari che si interessano a questo secondo, clamoroso «colpo» ai danni del museo milanese. Per tutta la giornata di ieri sono continuati, nelle sale della Villa Comunale di via Palestro dove è ospitata la galleria i rilievi della polizia scientifica, allo scopo di scoprire eventuali tracce lasciate dai banditi che hanno agito nella notte fra mercoledì e giovedì aggredendo, armi in pugno, i due custodi che si trovavano all'interno delle sale stesse. Dell'esito di tali accertamenti nulla è trapelato.

E' stato possibile finora accertare che le opere rubate sono complessivamente trentasei. In un primo tempo, l'elenco ufficiale fornito dalla direzione della galleria alla polizia comprendeva trentotto quadri: un successivo controllo ha consentito di stabilire che due dei quadri che si ritenevano rubati «La principessa di Saint-Leger» di Daniele Ranzoni e «Vecchio mulino» di Eugene Laermans, erano stati soltanto spostati dalla loro abituale posizione.

E' stata l'unica notizia confortante nella depressione generale che ha colto i responsabili dei musei cittadini dopo l'episodio dell'altra notte. Sul valore del furto nessuno si pronuncia. «Davanti alla razzia, soprattutto come è stata compiuta questa volta — ha detto stamani la conservatrice dott.ssa Florio — il problema va ben oltre il valore dei quadri. Questa rapina è un affronto alle istituzioni ed alla stessa cittadinanza».

Come già fu fatto in occasione del furto del 17 febbraio scorso, quando furono asportate ventotto opere, recuperate il 6 aprile scorso, la ripartizione culture del comune di Milano, con la collaborazione del Sindacato mercanti d'arte, farà un'opuscolo illustrativo dei dipinti rubati che sarà distribuito in gran numero in Italia ed in vari paesi del mondo ai mercanti d'arte.

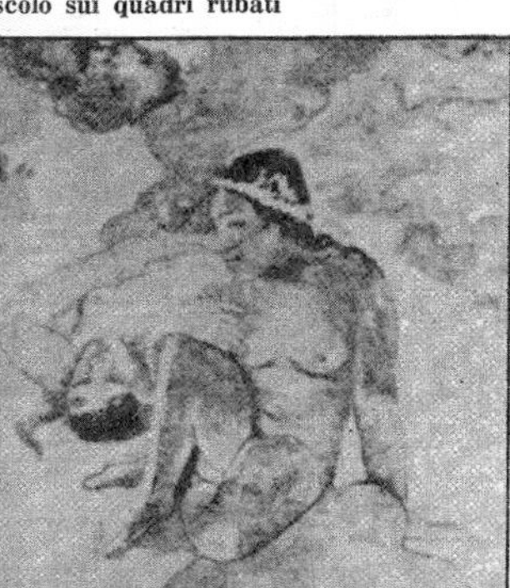

Uno dei due Gauguin rubati

«In tal modo — ha spiegato la conservatrice — contiamo di poter bloccare almeno quelli che sono i «canali di vendita» ufficiali, segnalando la possibilità che vengano offerte opere di provenienza furtiva».

Ieri i musei milanesi sono rimasti chiusi per una protesta dei custodi che hanno voluto manifestare solidarietà ai colleghi, rimasti vittima dell'aggressione e per rimarcare alcune carenze di personale e tecniche nei servizi di sorveglianza. L'agitazione prosegue oggi.

Smentita del ministro Spadolini al 'Messaggero'

Con una lettera al direttore del «Messaggero» il ministro per i beni culturali e ambientali, senatore Giovanni Spadolini, smentisce nel modo più assoluto la notizia, compresa in un servizio del quotidiano romano, che «il ministero stesso abbia partecipato a presunte trattative con i ladri per il recupero dei dipinti trafugati il 15 febbraio scorso presso la galleria civica di arte moderna di Milano, la stessa in cui si è verificato un secondo e più grave furto.

«In primo luogo — scrive il ministro Spadolini — il ministero per i beni culturali non ha alcuna competenza sui musei di enti locali, trasferiti alle regioni secondo il dettato costituzionale: musei che anche per la vigilanza e l'organico dei custodi dipendendo esclusivamente dalle regioni. In secondo luogo, il ministero non ha avuto alcuna parte nelle indagini che hanno portato al ritrovamento della refurtiva e che sono state condotte dalle forze dell'ordine, con le quali non c'è stato alcun contatto, nemmeno informale. L'Italia è uno Stato di diritto — aggiunge il senatore Spadolini —; e il ministro per i beni culturali non ha alcun potere né nello svolgimento delle indagini giudiziarie né nell'espletamento delle funzioni di polizia, esclusivamente rimesse alla guida e al controllo del ministro dell'Interno».

Il ministro Spadolini conclude la sua lettera ricordando al direttore del «Messaggero» che «la Camera dei deputati ha approvato proprio il 14 maggio e in sede di commissione deliberante praticamente alla unanimità, il disegno di legge sul potenziamento degli strumenti di prevenzione antifurto e antincendio presentato nel marzo scorso al consiglio dei ministri e che prevede nuovi ingenti fondi, da utilizzare immediatamente, non solo per i musei statali ma anche, almeno come concorso nella spesa per i musei locali o non statali. Non è possibile, conclude la lettera, fare miracoli, neanche miracoli «laici». E le inadempienze di un trentennio non possono essere cancellate in un giorno».

Telegramma di Bucalossi al prof. Luigi Donati

L'on. prof. Pietro Bucalossi, ministro dei Lavori Pubblici, ha inviato il seguente telegramma al prof. Luigi Donati, dell'ospedale maggiore di Milano, in occasione della presentazione alla stampa del primo bisturi-laser che abbia superato la fase sperimentale, lo «Sharplan», realizzato in Israele:

«Trattenuto Roma impegni governo per nuova legge sulla casa, plaudo iniziativa illustri medici italiani et internazionali, corso nuove tecniche chirurgiche stop Presentazione bisturi laser dopo lunga accurata fase sperimentale schiude nuove speranze in vari campi medicina particolarmente chirurgia plastica et antitumorale soprattutto lotta contro melanomi stop dunque da Israele il raggio della vita stop ciò dimostra ulteriormente assurdità misure discriminatorie prese da Unesco stop manovre Unesco rivelate in questi giorni risalgono 1972 dimostrando esistenza antica macchinazione, malcelata impostazione razzista.

Cordiali saluti,

prof. Pietro Bucalossi

Una prova simulata dell'incontro «Apollo» - «Soyuz»

Tra americani e sovietici l'abbraccio in cielo

Nel prossimo luglio avverrà per la prima volta nella storia della cosmonautica l'attracco in orbita fra un veicolo americano e uno russo

(Nostro servizio particolare)

HOUSTON, 16. — Astronauti americani e cosmonauti sovietici si sono scambiati un cordiale saluto nello spazio, a 225 chilometri dalla terra, ma solo per finta. Non perché mancasse la cordialità: mancava il volo spaziale. Gli uomini dell'Apollo e quelli della Soyuz stanno conducendo — a Houston gli americani, a Kaliningrad presso Mosca i sovietici — le prove di simulatore del volo congiunto che faranno in luglio, e che vedrà per la prima volta nella storia della cosmonautica, l'attracco fra un veicolo di fabbricazione americana ed uno di realizzazione sovietica.

«Saluti al popolo sovietico» ha detto il comandante dell'«Apollo», Tomas P. Stafford. Aveva appena completato una manovra simulata, quella di apertura dell'ultimo portello di separazione dei due veicoli agganciati nel cosmo. Stafford ha allungato una mano, stretto la mano della mano dell'inesistente cosmonauta. In teoria si trovava con lui Alexi Leonov, comandante della «Soyuz».

Il primo incontro di americani e sovietici nello spazio sarà contrassegnato da un cerimonia, qualcosa di simile ai convenevoli che precedono una partita di calcio internazionale. Ci sarà scambio di bandierine e di doni fra astronauti e cosmonauti. Per adesso lo scambio è stato simulato, americani e sovietici si sono soltanto salutati per telefono.

Qualche ora prima i sovietici avevano simulato, nel centro di volo di Kaliningrad, l'aggancio della loro cosmonave con l'«Apollo». I tecnici addetti alla elaborazione dei piani hanno immaginato un «problema» all'ultimo minuto, e questa loro iniziativa ha cambiato tutto. Anziché essere l'«Apollo» a svolgere il ruolo attivo nella manovra di attracco esso è stato affidato alla «Soyuz».

Con questi problemi di fantasia si provvede ad addestrare i cinque (tre americani e due sovietici a far fronte a quasiasi problema reale. Alan Bean, il comandante dell'equipaggio di riserva americano che lavorava al simulatore computerizzato, ha annunciato: «attracco ottimo, tutto a posto».

Le comunicazioni fra i due veicoli spaziali simulati e i rispettivi centri di controllo sono limitate alle fasi nelle quali sarà possibile il contatto durante il volo reale.

Dopo l'aggancio Bena e i suoi due compagni sono stati rilevati dall'equipaggio numero uno quello che farà il volo di luglio se non ci saranno inconvenienti tali da costringere a un cambiamento di squadra. L'equipaggio comandato da Stafford comprende Donald «Dekes» Slayton e Vance Brand. A Kaliningrad (il centro che i giornalisti occidentali hanno potuto visitare per la prima volta l'altro giorno) si trovano Alexei Leonov e Valeri Kuvasov. Hanno salutato gli astronauti dopo l'aggancio e l'apertura dei portelli. Gli addetti al centro di controllo e gli osservatori presenti nel salone di Houston non li hanno però potuti udire, per difficoltà tecniche.

b. e. h.

Simposio internazionale sui "pacemaker"

L'evoluzione tecnologica presuppone progressi ed aggiornamenti continui. La scienza medica se da un lato deve tener d'occhio il progresso e le sue prospettive, dall'altro non può essere condizionata, ragion per cui essa è legata soprattutto ad una esatta e corretta valutazione dell'oggi.

I problemi non sono solo medico-scientifici, ma anche tecnici.

Questo è emerso durante i lavori dell'importante simposio internazionale sui «pacemaker» apertosi ieri a Fiuggi Terme.

Il simposio è interamente dedicato ai problemi relativi a queste apparecchiature, e vi partecipano più di duecento scienziati ed esperti provenienti da tutto il mondo.

Per aiutare il cuore malato quando le medicine non bastano più, oggi che la scienza guarda ai trapianti ancora come ad un interrogativo, la tecnica moderna ha trovato una risposta elettronica, uno stimolatore cardiaco che fornisce al cuore il giusto ritmo di pulsazioni, stimolandolo in modo estremamente regolare e che supplisce per via elettrica a quello stimolo che non arriva più per via naturale.

Il «pacemaker» è un prodotto che investe una vasta gamma delle più sofisticate tecnologie.

Dall'aprile del 1970 ben 1000 stimolatori cardiaci e pile nucleari sono stati applicati nel mondo.

Durante il simposio di Fiuggi è prevista tra l'altro l'analisi dei risultati ottenuti con questi 1000 «pacemaker», che sarà compiuta dai congressisti francesi.

Il dottor Paul Laurens, che ha diretto per la Francia la équipe dei cardiochirurghi, aprirà con la sua relazione questa parte dei lavori.

I lavori del simposio, organizzato dall'«Ente Fiuggi» con la collaborazione tecnica della C.K. International, sono iniziati dopo il saluto rivolto ai congressisti dal prof. Antonio Cellupica, in rappresentanza dell'«Ente Fiuggi», e dall'avvocato Ennio Sirena in rappresentanza dell'amministrazione comunale. E' seguita la prima relazione, dedicata ai problemi della stimolazione elettrica. Durante questa seduta scientifica il prof. P. Maurice, direttore della clinica cardiologica della Università di Parigi, ha colto un interessante aspetto del problema riguardante la continua evoluzione in campo scientifico, che presuppone un continuo aggiornamento.

«Ciò che andava bene ieri — ha detto — è superato oggi, ciò che oggi è considerato utile ed adatto sarà certamente superato domani».

I problemi più importanti riguardano la disponibilità di una sorgente di energia elettrica che consenta all'apparecchio una vita sempre più lunga dopo l'impianto. Pacemaker alimentati con sorgenti nucleari sono disponibili ormai da diversi anni.

E' nell'energia nucleare, che sfrutti le radiazioni emesse da una sorgente di plutonio, il futuro prossimo dei «pacemaker».

Intervallo

Lettera di Pirandello a Romolo Valli

Signor Valli, nella rappresentazione del mio dramma (il benservito a un uomo, dopo che, a sua insaputa, gli si son fatte rappresentare, nel miglior modo possibile, e proprio per bene, tutte le parti: d'amico, di marito, di padre, di suocero): dramma che Lei replica, con successo incontenibile di pubblico, al teatro Eliseo di Roma, scopro che sono state censurate la bellezza di 18 battute e 12 didascalie. E questo, signor Valli, a mia netta insaputa, e senza nemmeno chiedere un parere alla signora Marta Abba.

Lei ben sa che io scrissi «Tutto per bene» per un grandissimo e accorato artista quale fu Ruggero Ruggeri, e questo avvenne tra il dicembre 1919 e il gennaio del 1920, assai prima, ordunque, della Marcia su Roma e della mia iscrizione al Partito. Le chiedo, ora, per quale oscuro zelo e disegno sciaguratissimo sia stato manomesso dal regista Giorgio De Lullo e da Lei, che il più intervistato e intellettuale attore d'Italia, proprio il terzo atto, in quel sublime ed algido iniziarsi: una scena emblematica, una chiave di volta, come scriverebbe il Garboli, una atmosfera di raggelante humour, a detta pure del Virdia e del Tian, una di quelle situazioni esemplari di una verità che getta la maschera e ammicca alle platee con drammatica spudoratezza, come sentenziò il Ripellino, che con il mai troppo compianto Ruggero sulla ribalta durava oltre il quarto d'ora, strappando al pubblico, sempre, convintissimi e sofferti applausi. Che forse, signor Valli, il gesto delle corna, cui mi riferisco nella didascalia che Le trascrivo: «Fa le corna, pallido e ridente, e le mostra al cameriere. Il cameriere lo guarda sbigottito. Pausa», il gesto delle corna, dico, Le par sconveniente, sconcio magari, per la festosa e assopita platea per cui Lei recita da più lustri il mio teatro? Veda, il Ruggeri con quel gesto, rivolto prima al cameriere, indi al pubblico medesimo, aveva dei «bravo» di cuore gridati a tutta gola, molto spesso da onorevoli socialisti presenti in sala da federali e da finanzieri sommi, e tutti verosimilmente si identificavano nelle disgrazie del mio Martino Lori.

L'Italia del delitto d'onore e dell'infedeltà muliebre, sempre da vendicare, massimamente quella con valore retroattivo, non va nascosta e mai sottaciuta, come ha fatto Lei tagliando una scena tipica del nostro più cocente e caratteristico costume, dalla Sicilia alle Alpi. Che forse, signor Valli, «le signorinette maritate di fresco», cui accenna il protagonista di «Tutto per bene», dico le «giovani mogli degli impiegati», le amanti dei politici e dei funzionari più abbietti non contano più nei cantieri e negli edifici del più disfrenato carrierismo nazionale, ieri come oggi? Il Fratini ben fece, in quel suo informato articolo che lessi sul «Caffè», a ravvisare l'inconcepibile taglio e a ricordarlo ai deboli di memoria drammaturgica. Per due pirandelliani ad oltranza, come Lei e il De Lullo vi proclamate, il fatto è abbastanza spiacevole e mi riservo, signor Valli, di perseguire il suo colpo di forbici nelle opportune sedi. Firmato Luigi Pirandello.

Ma certo. Così avrebbe scritto il Pirandello al Valli, dopo aver assistito quest'anno a quell'edizione che di «Tutto per bene» ha presentato «La Compagnia dei Giovani». Aggiungo che il dramma del consigliere di Stato ed e capo di gabinetto Martino Lori, il quale gronda di figliastri, di esecrande suocere e di adultere dissepolte, appartiene a un'insolente problematica da «profumi e balocchi». Come assistere alla secrezione di sentimenti già mummificati, al balletto di fantasmi lacrimosi e ricattatori. Il tutto condito con la acqua di colonia e i sali da bagno d'un falso istituto di bellezza.

Pirandello di «Tutto per bene» proclama santo e puro ciò che è turpe, cerca di trasformare piaghe purulente in incarnati botticelliani. Pirandello di «Tutto per bene» trucca da vergine e da educanda l'infetta psicologia d'una società borghese che solo Moravia, nel 1929, riuscì a vivisezionare con la lucentezza d'un adolescente chirurgo. Con Pirandello si resta, invece in un covo di spettri ripugnanti. Assistendo a «Tutto per vene» so che la vita sta aspettandomi fuori dal teatro, dopo la mezzanotte: potrò telefonare ancora agli amici, incontrare a Ponte Margherita «la belle dame sans merci. Fuggiamo da questo tribunale di morti. Dimentichiamo subito gli atroci ricatti del consigliere di Stato Martino Lori. E che almeno il fantasma si ricordi, come un automobilista sorpassato, di fare le corna, all'inizio del terzo atto».

Gaio Fratini

Prime del teatro

Un Molière partenopeo

Una curiosa riproposta molieriana del Teatro Alfred Jarry di Napoli

(t. c.) — Nel corso di una stagione in cui il nome di Molière è stato speso più volte e in più modi, ecco giungere da Napoli al Teatro Sangenesio la Compagnia del Teatro Alfred Jarry con una curiosa riproposta molieriana di Mario Santella: «Chelleta Sciacquagliosa».

Santella, notoriamente tra i più va'di esponenti della nostra avanguardia teatrale, ha rivolto già in precedenza le propie attenzioni ai classici mettendo in scena edizioni di «Macbeth», di «Faust» di Marlowe, di «Peccato che fosse una sgualdrina» di Ford, etc., edizioni segnalate a suo tempo dalla critica e accolte generalmente con un certo favore.

Questa «Chelleta Sciacquagliosa» (termine partenopeo che potrebbe significare «Piccola Commedia Scintillante») è un omaggio a Molière: un omaggio e non un libero accattamento, in quanto i rapporti tra il testo assunto a modello («Georges Dandin», salvo errori) e lo spettacolo che ne deriva sono volutamente esili ed evasivi.

Della commedia di Molière non rimane che la situazione, situazione del resto talmente canonica da essere propria del teatro di tutti i tempi. La storia del marito tradito e sbeffeggiato diviene, quindi, pretesto per un irresistibile carosello napoletano, carico di tutti quegli umori tipici del teatro popolare, di Scarpetta e di Petito, di Viviani e dei de Filippo, di Pulcinella e di Totò. Un omaggio, in fondo, a Napoli prima che a Molière.

Lo spettacolo di Santella mira conseguentemente più al divertimento del pubblico che non al rigore dell'avanguardia, anche se dell'avanguardia teatrale usa mezzi e stilemi: ne deriva una serata piacevole non priva di momenti esilaranti, con la riproposta sempre valida della tradizionale comicità napoletana da un lato e, dall'altro, un'operazione su Molière condotta rinunciando tanto agli orpelli accademici quanto alle velleità di certe facili riletture critiche.

Della compagnia, oltre Mario e Maria Luisa Santella, fanno parte Gianni Battaglia, Rosanna Benvenuto, Lidia Berrara, Berto Lama e Delia Morea.

vice

Alcune città finlandesi sarebbero minacciate dalle radiazioni di una base sovietica

WASHINGTON, 16. — In un articolo sulla «Washington Post» il giornalista Jack Anderson scrive che radiazioni emesse da stazioni sovietiche di localizzazione a microonde puntate contro basi missilistiche americane potrebbero essere all'origine di casi di attacchi cardiaci e di cancro in città all'interno della Finlandia. La stazione sovietica, scrive Anderson, si trova sulla riva orientale del lago Ladoga a nord-est di Leningrado e osserva basi missilistiche nella parte settentrionale degli Stati Uniti.

L'articolo così prosegue: «I raggi sono così potenti che gran parte dei cittadini sovietici nelle vicinanze, a quanto si dice, è stata trasferita. I sovietici ora contrallano il fascio di raggi — si ritiene — con un computer a grande distanza. A quanto si dice gli scienziati sovietici, a causa della pericolosa radiazione dei potenti raggi a microonde, dirigono il fascio di onde da un quartier generale distante. Ma i finlandesi al di là del confine sono stati colpiti da insolite malattie. Nelle città finlandesi di Kuopio, Joensuu e Ilimontsi, la città più vicina alla stazione a microonde, l'Organizzazione mondiale della sanità ha trovato tassi straordinari di malattie cardiache.

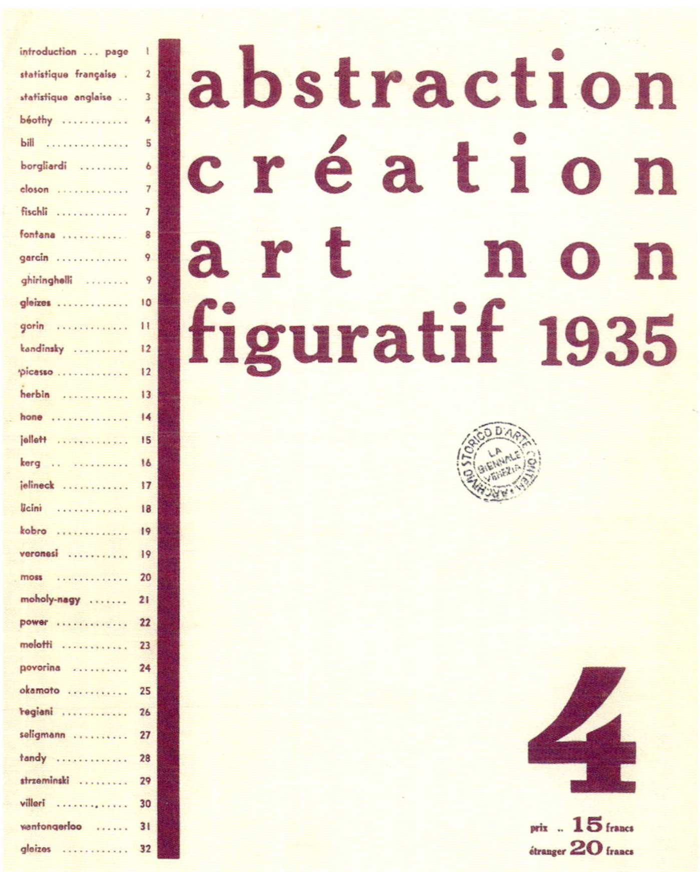

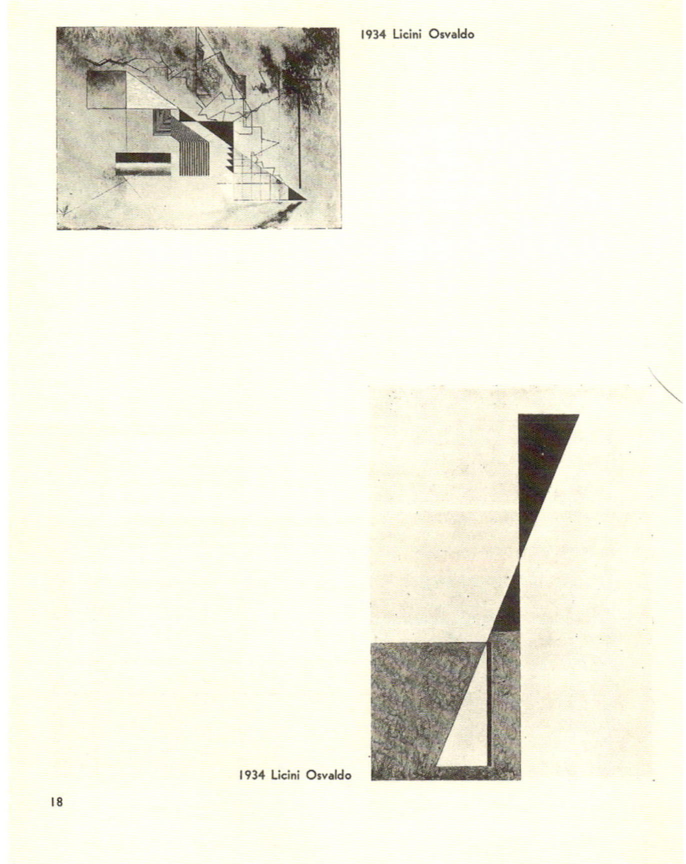

his parents had moved to Paris for work (his father was a poster designer and his mother was the manager of a fashion atelier). In 1908 Licini enrolled in the Accademia di Belle Arti in Bologna studying alongside the likes of Giorgio Morandi, Giacomo Vespignani (Giorgio and Giacomo in *Racconti di Bruto* [Tales of Brutus]), Mario Bacchelli, and Severo Pozzati.

Licini wrote his *Bildungsroman* at the age of nineteen, in 1913. The following year he transferred to the Accademia di Belle Arti in Florence. What exactly is Brutus? It might be described as a combination between Ardengo Soffici's *Lemmonio Boreo*, Alfred Jarry's *Surmâle, roman moderne*, and Filippo Tommaso Marinetti's *Roi Bombance*; in other words, a mixture of atheism, asociality, blasphemy, rapes, obscenities, supermanism, abysses of grotesque, and puppetlike humor—which are also reminiscent of *Candide* by Voltaire. It is a sort of lyrical and tragicomic monologue at the same time, with ripples of hyperbole and hilarity due to a *physique amusante* typical of fin-de-siècle side shows. In Baratta's words:

> ... those were already years when Pierrot and his monologue could merge with the superman and the Don Quixote of a Florentine sort, Lemmonio Boreo; the days when wayfarers and lovers of the stars sang their cocottesques: Licini would listen and was fueled by this lymph. From this were born his *Racconti di Bruto*.... Bruto was the paronomastic *Errante erotico eretico*, a sort of *pseudos* through which Licini talks about himself while renouncing the subject function, which he delegates to the character. Bruto is the action-word; or, if you wish, an action, a gesture, a behavior that becomes word. The impression of waste, of a certain temporariness that Licini's pages can at times arouse, must be explained in light

"ABSTRACTION – CRÉATION" NO. 4, 1935. *CASTLE IN THE AIR* (*CASTELLO IN ARIA*), 1933–36 (PP. 94–95), AND *PRECARIOUS BALANCE* (*IL BILICO*), 1932 (PP. 74–75) ARE ILLUSTRATED

> of a raging gesture that often cannot stand waiting to be embodied. Bruto, in fact, can only adopt the technique of violence, of chaos, or an overturning of things.

However, a few words of clarification are needed here. Whereas in the *Lemmonio Boreo* scandal, which soon became blind fury toward a bourgeois culture that continued to bask in a few stereotyped certainties, one might glimpse the incunabula of the Fascist "return to order," Brutus's destructive ferocity did not necessarily lead to this. An example of this is the frequent, ad nauseam, and exaggerated repetitive use of the word *shit*. More than leading to a "return to order," Brutus proved to be the interpreter of a virgin materiality as the inescapable moment of anarchism: of that materiality, in other words, that had represented the most provocative aspect—beyond the equivocation of his alleged idiocy—of *Bertoldino* by Giulio Cesare Croce.

For all these reasons, I do not at all agree with Torelli Landini when she tries to overestimate Licini's training as a Futurist, in her opinion unjustly underestimated by Marchiori.[11] The critic himself admitted the young Licini's Futurist apprenticeship by referring, in a 1958 catalogue, to a letter that Licini had sent him in 1939, in which he wrote: "With Morandi, when we were young, we drank from the early stages of Cubism, and with Morandi we fought for Futurism alongside Marinetti, before the war."[12] For Marchiori, however, what Licini was really trying to do was prove his own personal rebellion, more than his embrace of Futurist poetics: "'Secessionist' is, perhaps, a term that is more suited to Licini's rebellious, anarchic, intolerant character, at least when he was young, a character of programs and order, and Futurist only in the subversive language of the protest and the polemic against artistic and social conventions."[13]

When, along with Morandi, Pozzati, Vespignani, and Bacchelli, in 1914, Licini participated in an exhibition at the Hotel Baglioni in Bologna—the opening, thanks to the interest shown by the musician Balilla Pratella, to whom he had sent the first story in *Racconti di Bruto* hoping it would be published in *Lacerba*, was seen by Marinetti, Carlo Carrà, Umberto Boccioni, and Luigi Russolo—a review of the show unsurprisingly spoke of Licini as being not so much a Futurist, as a painter "with all the elements in his 'head in the right place' [seeing that] his paintings are devoid of rotations, revolutions, and interpenetrations."[14] Another text discussed how Licini's and Vespignani's painting had been rather admired by the exhibition visitors "for the sweet melancholy of the hues, for the sense of morning tide poetry, and for the dewiness and languor that permeated them."[15] In a third critical essay that is often overlooked, Pietro Mazzucato instead describes Licini as a Futurist:

> ... we shall place Giorgio Morandi, Mario Bacchelli, and Osvaldo Licini among the Futurists, Giacomo Vespignani, instead, and Severo Pozzati among the Passéists. I believe there is no reason to talk about the other three Futurists. I have determined that their expressions do not go beyond the "still lifes" of the Cubist Picasso, of Cézanne, and of Boccioni, where figures of tables, bottles, and glasses are disassembled in the void according to the refractions and the overturning of the planes.[16]

Two paintings included in the 1914 Bologna exhibition, one by Licini (*Self-Portrait* [*Autoritratto*], 1913, p. 23), and one by Morandi (*Portrait of a Woman* [*Ritratto femminile*], 1912, also known as "Portrait in the Style of Derain" [Ritratto derainiano], of his sister),[17] when compared, once again underscore the distance from Futurism of the two great artists at that time. Morandi's portrait shows a few rough similarities with the rigid squaring of some of Derain's figures (and this is the only affinity with Licini's work) and an analogous perception of color to Licini's self-portrait (the painting remained jealously preserved by his schoolmate

BLM 1952

Ur innehållet

A. M. DAHLQUIST-LJUNGBERG: *De sista kvinnorna. Dikt*

MARCEL PROUST: *Skandalen Marie. Novell*

ÅKE NORDIN: *Förvandlat landskap. Dikt*

SIGFRID SIWERTZ: *Studentgänget och den goda trätan*

VILGOT SJÖMAN: *Inifrån och utifrån*

BENGT HOLMQVIST: *Kommentar till en utvald*

GEORG SVENSSON: *Den nya Chaplin*

KOMMENTARER: *BLM:s rundfråga. — Teaterkrönika. — Filmkrönika. — Från bok till film, en debatt. — Bokrecensioner. — För boksamlaren. — Nya utländska böcker.*

November

Pris 2:50 Årgång 21 Nr 9

ALBERT BONNIERS FÖRLAG STOCKHOLM

BLM, NO. 9, 1952. LICINI'S NOTES ON GUILLAUME APOLLINAIRE ARE VISIBLE ON THE PAGE OF THE SWEDISH JOURNAL THAT DISCUSSES *L'HÉRÉSIARQUE ET CIE* BY APOLLINAIRE

Un giorno io aspettavo me stesso
io mi dicevo Guillaume
è ora che vieni

Rhen" och "Maj" har förlänats mycket av originalens egenartade charm — fastän åtminstone den förra utrustats med ett dussintal ord som originalet inte har någon motsvarighet till. I den stora dikten "Zone" har Linde fallit för frestelsen att överdriva överdrifterna och understryka det pojkaktiga i den naiva visionen av himmelsfärden, och kanske har rimmen blivit grövre och märkbarare på svenska än på franska, men uppgiften tillhör de exceptionellt svåra. Den lilla pärla som kallas "Annie" — ägnad Apollinaires första stora kärlek — verkar hos Linde en smula limerick vilket originalet inte gör. Större förtjänster har avgjort den vackra versionen av den underbara "Les colchiques" och trots ett par diskutabla detaljer "L'Amour, le Dédain et l'Espérance". Ett dunklare och krångligare slut än originalets har översättaren — tydligen i ambitionen att få med alla fina nyanser — givit åt den dikt som heter "Cortège" och som han kallar "Skuggornas tåg", men den viktigaste raden har dessbättre all sin kraft bevarad: "mot det lysande förflutna är morgondagen blek...".

"Cortège" är en av dessa dikter där Apollinaire är på jakt efter sin identitet:

En dag
en dag väntade jag på mig själv
jag sade mig Guillaume det är på tid du kommer
så jag äntligen får lära känna vem jag är
jag som känner alla de andra

Detta sökande som är så underligt förgäves, ger sin melankoliska ton, sin ton av förtvivlan och egendomlig mystik åt en livsbejakelse i nuet och i det förflutna som var enorm. En livsbejakelse som var så full av spontan tillgivenhet för alla människor och alla ting — en romantisk expansion utan gräns och en modern livskänsla utan gräns.

Jag känner dem med alla mina fem sinnen och några till

— — — — — — — — — — — — — — —

Jag behöver bara vädra vittringen av deras kyrkor
lukten på floderna som rinner genom deras städer
blommornas doft i de offentliga trädgårdarna
ja lukten av en liten hund skulle räckt o Corneilles Agrippa
för att jag troget skulle kunna beskriva dina medborgarbröder där i Köln
deras heliga tre kungar och ursulinernunnor i gåsmarsch
som gav dig anledning till ett så felaktigt slut beträffande hela kvinnokönet

Corneilles Agrippa? Här har översättaren tydligen missförstått Apollinaire. Den som drog egendomliga slutsatser om kvinnokönet var naturligtvis inte någon gestalt hos Corneille utan den märkvärdige ockultisten och filosofen Cornelius Agrippa från Köln, en av de sällsammaste företrädarna för den fantastiska riktning i senmedeltida vetenskap, enligt vilken människan kunde vinna en övernaturlig makt över de sinnliga tingen med hemliga medel, och författare till ett arbete "Om vetenskapens osäkerhet och fåfänglighet". Apollinaire var en man med många lektyrer...

Det märks också tydligt i hans ymniga produktion på prosa, ur vilken Ebbe Linde presenterar ett ypperligt urval, översatt med en livfullhet och entusiasm som är helt kongenial med Apollinaires författarglädje. Ett par lysande noveller ur "L'Hérésiarque et Cie" får inleda urvalet — i "Ärkekättaren", titelnovellen, firar Apollinaires snillrikhet och paradoxala humor sina finaste triumfer, samtidigt som novellen på ett mycket kätterskt och lättfärdigt sätt vittnar om det intresse han aldrig upphörde att hysa för katolicismen, för Ordningens religion. I "Möte i Prag", berättelsen om den vandrande juden, är det däremot Äventyrets mystik som fått verklighet och betvingande atmosfär. Berättelserna om Baron d'Ormesan ger prov på en vildare och hänsynslösare humor, något mitt emellan slap-stick och mardröm — en skräck förvandlad till gapskratt, ett gapskratt dämpat av fina aromatiska ångor. Det surrealistiska dramat "Brösten på Tiresias", som väl egentligen är oöversättligt och som enligt kännare lämpligen bör njutas till Poulencs musik, har Ebbe Linde också vågat sig på — men att bedöma en sådan bedrift i detalj skulle fordra en mindre avhandling. Oreserverat gläder man sig i stället åt pikareskromanen "Den dräpte skalden" — det låter så fornnordiskt, varför inte lika gärna "Den mördade poeten"? Romanen, som är översatt i sin helhet, berättar inte utan ett visst (nonchalant behandlat) självbiografiskt underlag om livet som en dröm, overkligt som en dröm, verkligt som en dröm. Hur en ung man råkar födas — av sällsamma föräldrar, hur han tillägnar sig erfarenhet, kärlek, poesi och teater tills han når den mognad som berättigar honom att bli offer för förföljelse och död — och till äreminne en "djup" staty av tom luft och till gravölet en lätt chanson.

Ingen som vill veta hur livgivande och full av egendomlig tjuskraft modernistisk litteratur var, när den var ung, får underlåta att läsa Guillaume Apollinaire.

ÅKE JANZON

che io finalmente possa
conoscere chi sono io
io che conosco tutti gli altri

Morandi). The similarity is especially evident in the bodies of both of figures, whose plastic nature is almost completely annulled by the light that is glimpsed through the brushstrokes, as if it struggled to make room for itself but wanted to come into view at all costs. Whatever the case may be, these were not Futurist paintings. Indeed Boccioni did not include Licini and other artists in the upcoming *Esposizione libera futurista* at the Galleria Sprovieri in Rome, although Licini, Morandi, and Baccheli had asked him to be considered.[18]

In 1915, Licini volunteered to fight in World War I. After he wounded his leg—he would limp for the rest of his life—in 1917, he went to stay with his mother in Paris. It was also the year when he attended the premiere of Jean Cocteau's *Parade*, with music by Erik Satie and stage designs by Pablo Picasso, and met Amedeo Modigliani. Until 1920, Licini traveled back and forth between Florence and Paris. From 1921 onwards, his stays in Paris grew longer. Mario Tozzi, who in just a few years was to become one of the promoters of the so-called Italiens de Paris (Filippo de Pisis, Giorgio de Chirico, Gino Severini, Savinio, Renato Paresce, Tozzi himself, Massimo Campigli), wrote as follows: "In Paris I soon ran into Licini, whom I had met along with Morandi in Bologna, my companions, albeit ahead of me, in the academy there.... I had left Licini a Futurist in Bologna, and here I found him a Post-Impressionist: Matisse + Dufy + Friesz in the landscapes and flowers; a bit à la Modigliani in the figures...."[19]

If we compare Licini's *Dancers* (*Ballerine*) (1917, p. 27) with Morandi's *Bathers* (*Bagnanti*) (1915, p. 26), the latter shows some vague similarities with many of Cézanne's *Bathers*—which, if we think about the black-and-white reproductions we are familiar with, he tended to charge with plastic density—while Licini's painting recalls in the forms but above all in the colors (a variety of dark and light blues) such paintings by Henri Matisse as *Interior with a Goldfish Bowl* (*Intérieur, bocal de poissons rouge*) (1914, Musée National d'Art Moderne, Centre Georges Pompidou, Paris), and above all *View of Notre Dame* (*Vue de Notre-Dame*) (1914, Museum of Modern Art, New York), which remained in Matisse's studio until 1954.[20]

In Paris during the 1920s, Licini showed his work at random locations and in more authoritative institutions, such as the Société Nationale des Beaux-Arts and the Salon d'Automne. He showed at the Salon d'Automne twice: in 1921, three paintings, and in 1922, three other works including *Portrait of Nerina* (*Ritratto di Nerina*).[21] Through Tozzi, Licini participated in both the *Les Italiens de Paris* and the *Novecento Italiano* exhibitions.[22] For the 1926 exhibition at the Palazzo della Permanente, in Milan, through Gian Emilio Malerba—one of the seven artists in the original group, with whom, in 1922, the Novecento Italian was born at the Galleria Pesaro under the critical approval of Margherita Sarfatti—Licini presented three works, a *Still Life* (*Natura morta*) (acquired at the opening by Mussolini, Torelli Landini tells us) and two *Seascapes* (*Marine*).[23] Licini's works were exhibited in Gallery V alongside those of Morandi, Felice Casorati, de Chirico, Leonardo Dudreville, and Anselmo Bucci (which shows how diverse the exhibition was). Licini's *Still Life* was reproduced in the catalogue and is proof of how distant he was from the contemporary works by Morandi. Three years later, an even larger Novecento exhibition was mounted at the Palazzo della Permanente and this time Licini did not pass unnoticed. These were Giovanni Titta Rosa's words in *Lavoro fascista*:

> In the third room, a Landscape [*Paesaggio*] by Licini, painted with fervor, in light and melodious hues, captures our gaze; of all his still lifes, at least one of them seems to emerge from the painting, but the other is made in a vigorous, frank, rhythmical style, though sometimes the painter indulges in his contemptuous bravura.[24]

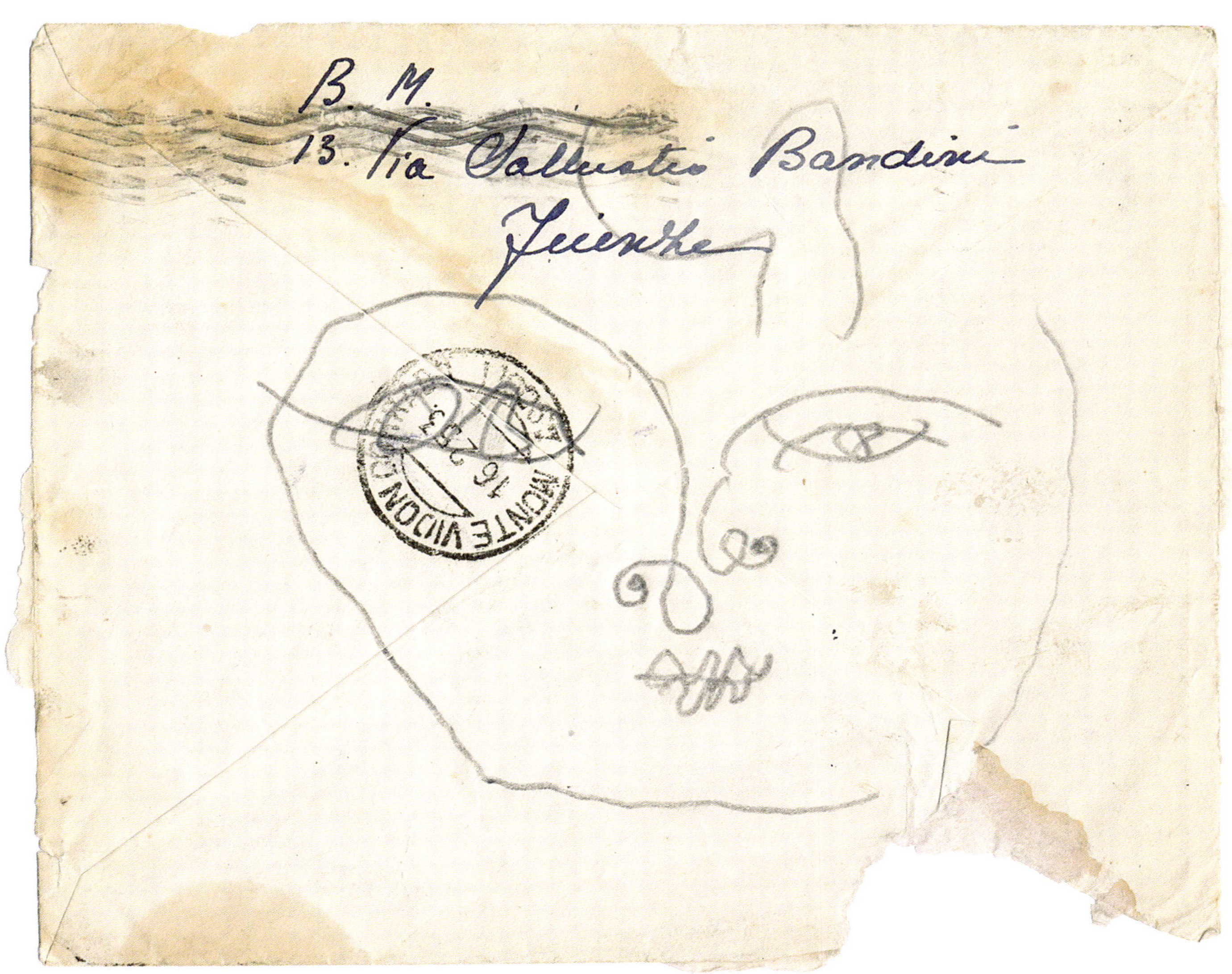

AMALASUNTHA
(AMALASSUNTA)
after 1953
pencil on paper

The only painting by Licini included in the catalogue was the *Landscape*, featuring marked luminosity reminiscent of the Neo-Impressionist, and anti-Novecento, taste of the group Sei di Torino promoted by Lionello Venturi, or perhaps more so in the style of de Pisis's *Still Lifes* made in that same period.[25]

The Italian and French critical reviews of the exhibition probably led Giovanni Scheiwiller—who was soon to head Hoepli's Modern Italian Art series—to undertake in that same year a sort of survey of contemporary Italian artists. When asked who his favorite artists were, Licini answered: "Giotto, Masaccio, Piero della Francesca, Giorgione, Titian, Tintoretto, Greco, Rembrandt, Goya, Courbet, Corot, Manet, the Impressionists, Cézanne, Utrillo, Modigliani, Renoir, Fattori." It is worthwhile noting that his list did not include any modernists. To the question about his "Studies related to your artistic evolution (indicate, if possible, the duration of such studies)," Licini replied: "1913–15 fantastic primitivism; 1915–20, war episodes (almost all destroyed); 1920–29 realism?" The question mark is especially striking. And then: "What is your definition of Modern Art?" To which the artist replied: "Force—Color—Human sentiment: Poetry." Indeed, his own personal poetics. In one of the last questions, Licini proved his understanding not only of the differences in style, but also of the fact that all the labels, in art, were mere conventions, including the Novecento: "Is the existence of the Novecento style a good thing or a bad thing?" Answer: "It is neither good nor bad. It is a manifestation of innocuous, disparate tendencies. I am only interested in the Artist when he is great."

FROM ABSTRACT ART TO THE END OF THE WAR (1930–1945)

The motives behind Licini's move, in the early 1930s, from a fundamentally realist painting style to abstract art have yet to be fully explained. No doubt the change took place between 1931 and 1932, and it coincided with the artist's travels to Scandinavia in the company of his Swedish wife to see the Italian exhibitions of the Novecento artists, promoted in Oslo, Stockholm, and Helsinki by Margherita Sarfatti. During the same trip Licini also stopped off in cities such as Hamburg and Copenhagen, and, on his way back to Italy, Paris. Particularly interesting are the observations of the Scandinavian press on the artist's works. For instance, in one Swedish newspaper a critic observed that:

> Italian painters can be divided into two large groups: one group is inspired by nineteenth-century Impressionist Realism, and a second group has left Futurism behind to embrace the Cubist school, in turn ending up in a modern type of "classicism" .... To these two groups a third one might be added, which seems to include free students of Matisse and his school. Belonging [to this trend] is one of the finest colorists of this exhibition, Osvaldo Licini, [who] uses green hues that are almost sickly and yet refined, such as in *Portrait of Nella* (*Ritratto di Nella*).[26]

During the journey Licini visited numerous museums. Having arrived at the Kunsthalle in Hamburg, where we "went in just to go in," he confessed to his friend Checco (Ermenegildo Catalini) on August 23, 1931:

> Imagine our surprise when appearing before our eyes was Manet's famous *Nana*, and on the back wall the *Comtesse d'Hornanville* ... the largest, the most spectacular canvas by Renoir! And then there was Picasso, Cézanne, Toulouse-Lautrec, Pissarro, Degas, etc. Awaiting us at the museum in Göteborg was Rembrandt's *The Knight with the Falcon*, another wonder! I would have liked to see you ... with me standing before this Rembrandt (which I had never seen, not even in a reproduction). What a masterpiece! We could have risen up together to the high places, the stratosphere ... I felt like grabbing people by the lapels and shouting in their faces just how great Rembrandt is! Perhaps it is the influence of the wet weather, or the light that comes from the stars, more than from the sun, or the breadth of those sunsets that makes Rembrandt seem so great to me. A hallucination ... The Dark Veronese ... [so I decided on my way back] to pass through Amsterdam and see *The Night Watch* and *The Syndics*.

Another letter written by Licini on October 1 to the same person gives us an idea of the extent of the metamorphosis in his aesthetic taste, as influenced by the new northern European landscapes. While in the previous letter he had been deeply moved by the Swedish coastline, which "is a labyrinth of stone and sea [where] between stone and stone, the rich vegetation described above grows," in the latter one he wrote:

> Dearest Checco, I would have liked to see you on the boat to Stockholm .... You must cross half of Sweden to get there. Where can I find the words to describe this marvel to you? Along a narrow canal of deep and shiny water the steam penetrated the gullies and the tall rock walls. We crossed the "embalmed forests," we met the Cytheras and the lagoons, and toward sunset the steamboat was reflected in a huge burgundy-colored lake. Immense cascades were faced by a sim-

> ple device, iron gates, and in a few minutes we were raised high atop the tallest peaks. At eight hundred meters above sea level, in the boat, above the mountains, the endless mythological forests below our feet, skies turn upside down in the water, alone on board, the moon in the sky like a madwoman! Where were you? Would you have let yourself be taken in like me in this great romantic net? Nibelung Kings appeared; the entire retinue of fairy-tale princesses: it is to the sound of horns that Wagner begins his great orchestra. This is what I experienced. Understand me, you who are lucky enough to live in the shadow of the *great* southern sun (by now you must be baked like Pisan-style chestnuts).

Described here are many of the visual suggestions that Licini would develop a dozen years later in the *Flying Dutchmen* (*Olandesi volanti*) and in the *Amalasunthas* (*Amalassunte*) series, although combined with the artist's memories of the great masters of French literature, such as the Comte de Lautréamont, Arthur Rimbaud, Guillaume Apollinaire, and the contemporary avant-garde artistic culture, that of *Abstraction-Création*, *Documents*, and *Cahiers d'Art*. No less important, however, is the final bitter irony. The "meridian sun" did not just allude to Vincenzo Cardarelli's *Il sole a picco*—mentioned in other letters as well—but to all those Italian critics "in classical style" who revolved around Ugo Ojetti, the *Borghese della Sera*—a parody of the *Corriere della Sera*—and to the "consumers of opiates": "The opiate, Oppo-ist, Neo-Verist inclination wanted by Ephysius the tutor-protector prevails.... The seven wise men, of solo (or monstrous) shows, who were given seven rooms, well represent this equivocal, pusillanimous, provincial, stinking inclination."[27]
It is reasonable to imagine that, when combined, these episodes encouraged Licini to abandon Mediterranean, Latin, realistic art, to immerse himself in "abstract" painting. I place the term in quotation marks because, upon closer examination, if ever Licini was an abstract artist, he was so in an entirely personal way. In his 1930 monographic text on contemporary Italian art, Giovanni Scheiwiller reproduced a *Landscape* and a *Still Life* with de Pisis-like bottles from 1928, upholding the idea of our art being a continuation of the Italian Novecento, whose major exhibition centers were in Milan and in Paris.[28] In 1934, Vincenzo Costantini again wrote: "Linked even to the 'Fauves' [before this he had mentioned de Pisis], more generically and I would say even more bashfully, is Licini's painting, which is at times fantastic (*Clash*) at others naturalistic."[29]
That same year, Licini published in *L'Orto*—a journal revived in 1932 by Marchiori—a "Ricordo di Modigliani" [In Memory of Modigliani] set in 1917, the year he spent convalescent in Paris after being wounded in the war. Marchiori wrote:

> I met Licini for the first time in 1934. He came to visit me in Venice after an exchange of letters ... his passport, so that I would recognize him, was a small painting, *Red Rhythm (Ritmo rosso)* (1932), slid into the pocket of his jacket. That small piece of cardboard ... traumatized me, it shook my bourgeois caution, and it became the symbol of a friendship that was born out of a divergence of ideas.[30]

We therefore also owe to the great painter the fact that Marchiori—at that time well informed about what was happening abroad—would in just two decades become the most knowledgeable art critic in all of Italy.[31]
The following year was crucial for Licini. In January, he wrote to Marchiori that he had provocatively sent to the "gran Fessarca" (Efisio Oppo, evidently taken from Apollinaire's "hérésiarque") three works "painted in the sidereal zone, which no Picard will ever be able to sully. Long live irrational painting!" The paintings included *Castle in the Air* (*Castello in aria*) (p. 95), *Archangel Gabriel* (*Arcangelo Gabriele*) (p. 30) later replaced by *Precarious Balance* (*Il bilico*, 1934), and *Stratosphere* (*Stratosfera*, 1933). Licini showed his work alongside that of Atanasio

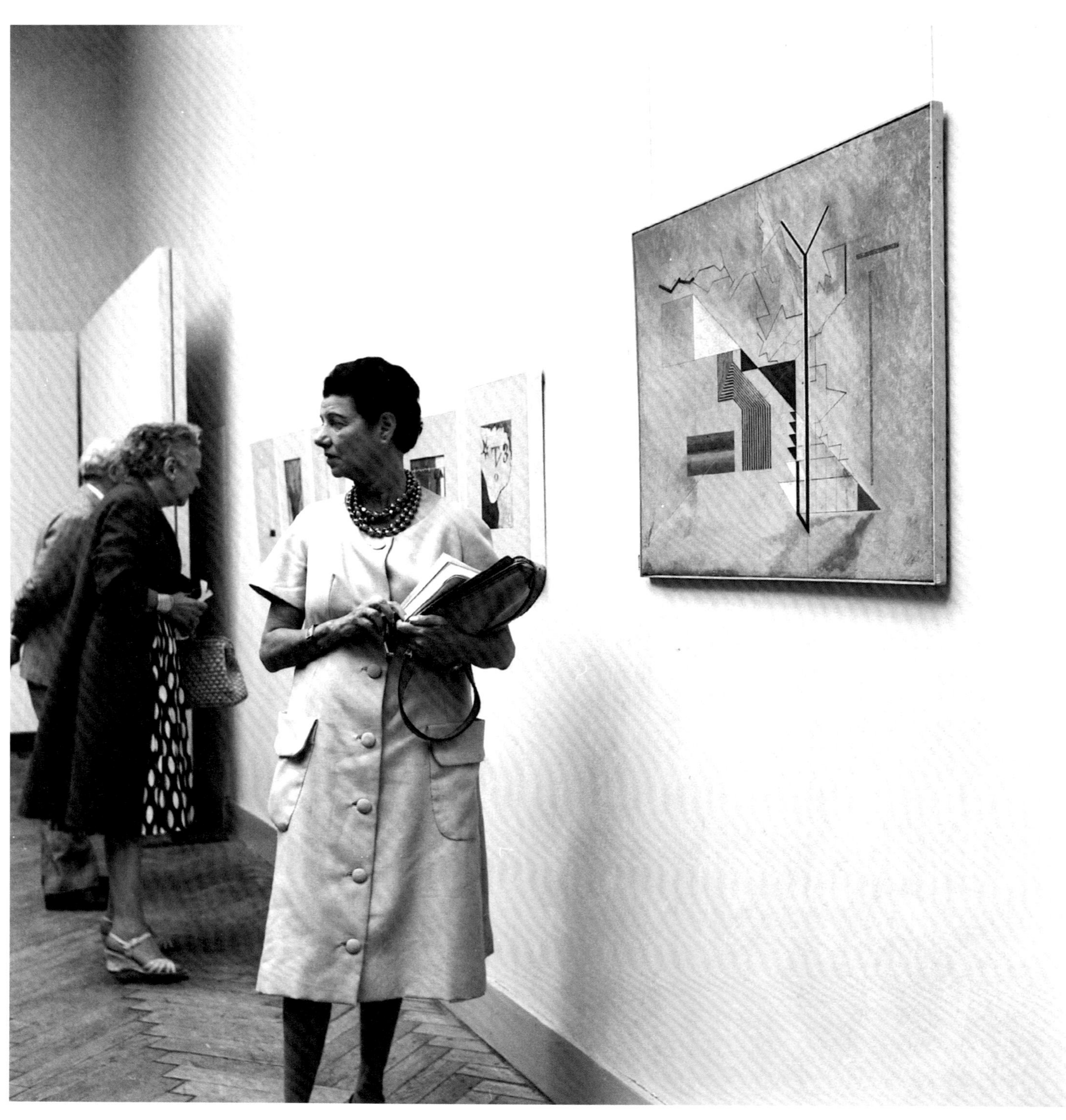

PEGGY GUGGENHEIM AT THE EXHIBITION OF OSVALDO LICINI NEXT TO CASTLE IN THE AIR (*CASTELLO IN ARIA*) (1933–36, PP. 94–95), 29TH VENICE BIENNALE, 1958

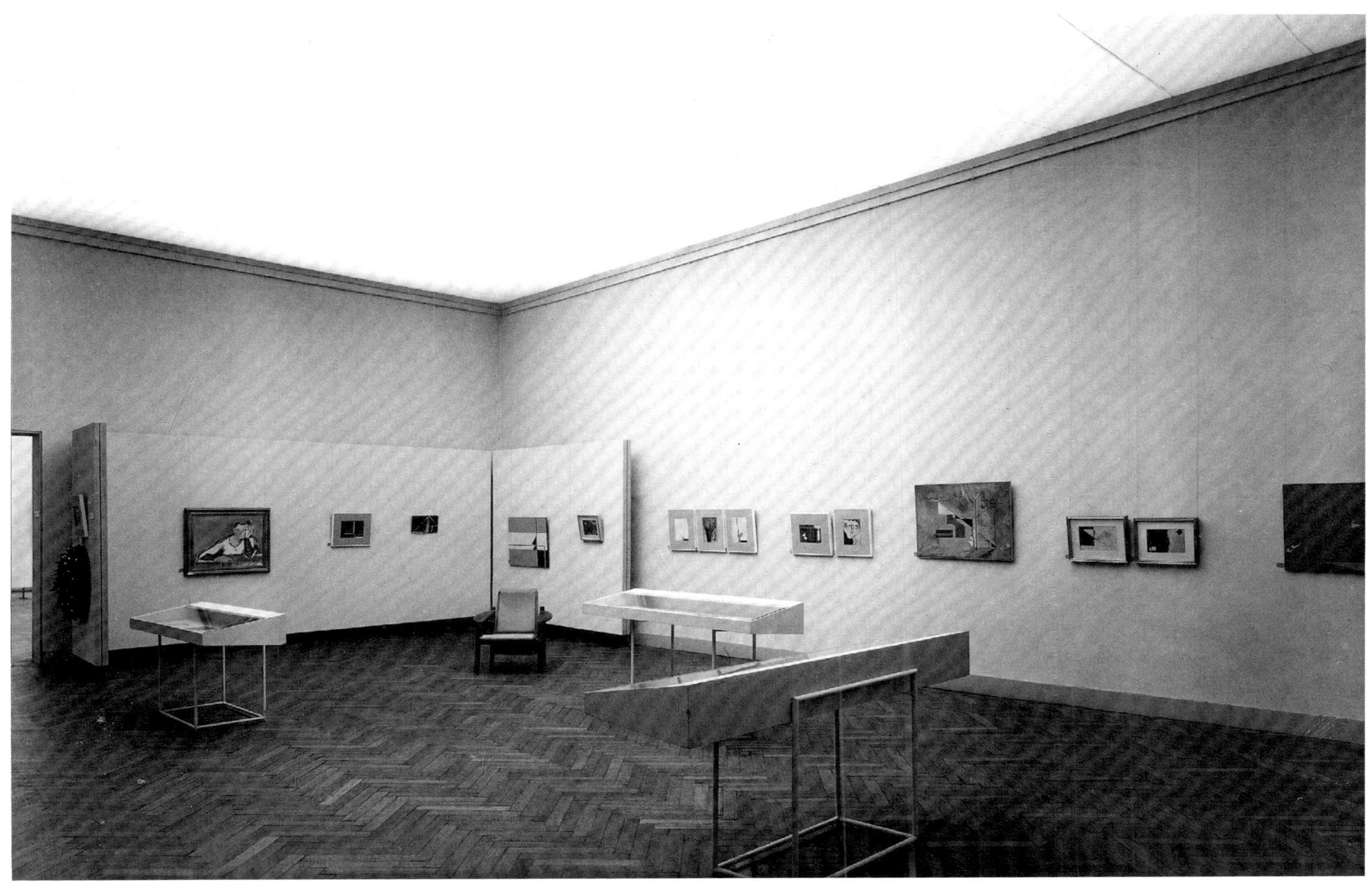

INSTALLATION VIEW OF THE EXHIBITION OF OSVALDO LICINI, 29TH VENICE BIENNALE, 1958

Soldati, Mauro Reggiani, Oreste Bogliardi, Alberto Magnelli, Gino Ghiringhelli, and Lucio Fontana. In February, Marchiori recalled that "with Licini, Belli, Fontana we spent several intense days of true intellectual exaltation in Rome. Our discussions would continue until daybreak, along the streets that by that time had grown deserted."[32] As Fossati later pointed out, Carlo Belli was the one to give way to that ambiguity or, better still, that double soul of Italian abstract art, which during World War II—my words—would also characterize Concrete Art: on the one hand, a "rationalist," architectural as well as graphic element; on the other, instead, an "irrational" component, linked to the most intimate drives of the soul, in the manner of Vasily Kandinsky (or Paul Klee, if you prefer), masterfully interpreted by Licini.

An equivocation favored by the title *Kn* itself, which was not an acronym for Kandinsky—who, among others, was cited by Belli along with Mondrian on several occasions—but something else: "The title of the book refers to neither Kandinsky, nor modern art tout court .... Just after the beginning of the book Belli writes: 'An exhibition of works without a title, without a signature, without a date, and with no human references, distinguished the one from the other by the simple algebraic indications K, K1, K2, ... kn. (We shall assume Kn to be the expression of this idea).'"[33]

Marchiori reviewed the abstract works at the Quadriennale in an article that also had reproductions of *Castle in the Air* and *Precarious Balance*: it was no doubt the first time an Italian newspaper was publishing paintings that were not figurative. While Marchiori often reproached other artists for having added motifs that were still naturalistic in their works, his words for Licini were much

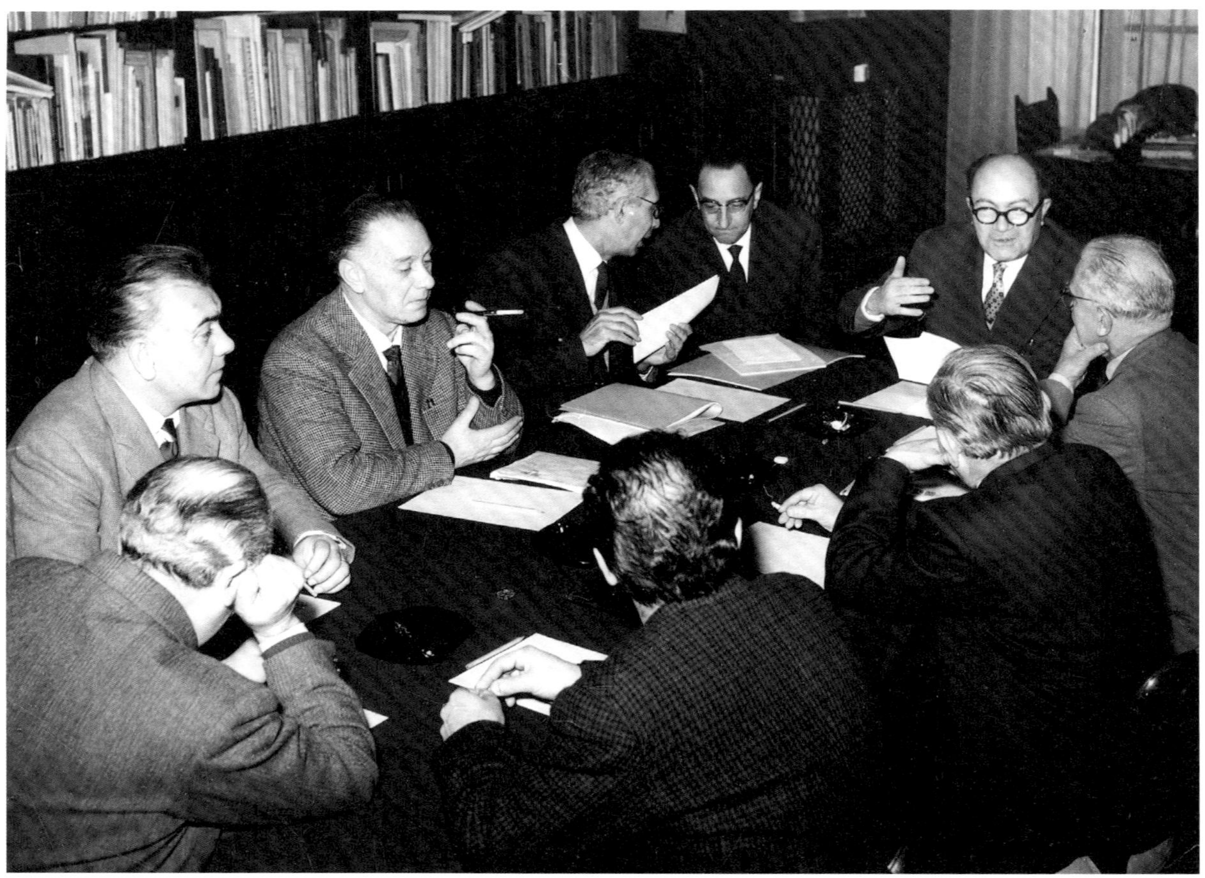

kinder: "A first example of his [Licini's] purification is *Precarious Balance*: an overturned triangle suspended on the vertex of another gray triangle, which rises up as an affirmation of unshakable certainty. This geometry will not convince the viewer steeped in positivist experiences: how can a triangle remain suspended this way? Licini, who is a solitary wise man of the mountains, and like all loners devoted to contemplation, is also a poet, will answer thus: 'By some miracle.'"[34]

A few days later Licini wrote to Marchiori. After thanking him and telling him that the fourth issue of *Abstraction-Création* had been published in Paris, including reproductions of *Castle in the Air* and *Precarious Balance*,[35] he confessed he had unwillingly accepted the invitation to have a solo show at the Galleria del Milione: "I didn't want to do it, but my Milan friends so insisted that I was forced to give in."

Licini showed figurative and abstract paintings, and drawings. In the *Autopresentazione* (Introduction) he repeated that he believed his "Milanese friends" to be travel companions, but also that he had some doubts about whether his positions and theirs were the same:

> We do not know each other, friends of the Milione. By chance we found ourselves in that ninth room at the Quadriennale .... And you have invited me to show my work in Milan. I must confess that I do so somewhat unwillingly. Because of your insistence I have yielded for the sake of that discipline that imposes our rule.... Up until four years ago I did all that I could to create good painting by representing what was real. Then I began having doubts. Being doubtful is not a weakness, it is a work of strength, like *forging*, Descartes once said. And I grew convinced, like many others today, that my painting was late, sur-

BIENNALE COMMITTEE, VISUAL ARTS, 29TH VENICE BIENNALE, 1958. Counterclockwise from the head of the table with glasses, Giovanni Ponti, Umbro Apollonio, Gian Alberto Dell'Acqua, Renato Birolli, Pietro Zampetti, Bruno Saetti, Pericle Fazzini, Sergio Bettini, Felice Casorati

> passed, old-fashioned .... Painting is the art of colors and forms, freely conceived, and it is also an act of will and of creation, and it is, contrary to what architecture is, an irrational art, dominated by fantasy and the imagination, that is to say, poetry. And so I took two hundred good paintings that I had painted based on what was real and stowed them away in the attic.[36]

Marchiori reviewed that show as well, suggesting that one could glimpse in Licini's work analogies with Morandi "owing to the purity and the beauty of the material, and to the same constructive rigor."[37] However, not all the opinions were positive ones. For instance, in *L'Ambrosiano* Carrà patronizingly reproached Licini for wanting to do away with all his previous art.[38] But perhaps the criticism that most distressed Licini was that of the Galleria itself in the *Bollettino* that served as an exhibition catalogue: "We shall not be the ones to spoil the good reader who will listen to Licini ... by intervening to specify the value of the term *rational* in architecture and of the apparently antithetical term of *irrational* in painting." According to the Ghiringhelli brothers, Licini "did not pose this radical question to himself," for if "this discipline that led architecture toward rationalism has an offspring in painting, then that offspring is abstraction: which is evident in its theories and in the works."[39]

Licini returned to the "buried harbor" of Monte Vidon Corrado, giving in now and again to flights to the great city of Paris. These were his words in a letter he wrote to Marchiori in December of the same year: "My Parisian life was disorderly, idle, and yet, I believe, well spent. From Kandinsky to Zervos I came to know almost all the viewpoints in art. I visited the studios of the best, I was lucky enough to see the Flemish art exhibition and, before leaving, a solo show of the work of Man Ray, at the Galerie des Cahiers d'Art, which was truly interesting. Picasso remains one of the strongest of all; I saw some marvelous pieces."

Less than two years later Marchiori involved Licini in the writing of a long article on modern art for the *Corriere Padano*. It was intended as a defense of modern art, which was increasingly in the eye of the storm due to anti-Semitism, and it included contributions by Carlo Belli, Licini, and Maurice Raynal. Licini illustrated it with his paintings and drawings and a work by Jean Hélion.[40]

The times grew darker: critics such as Ojetti, Telesis Interlandi, Romano Romanelli, and Giovanni Preziosi tended to consider modern art as a whole as being "Bolshevik" and "Judeo-Masonic." Particularly famous is an article that appeared in one of the most Fascist periodicals, *Il Tevere*, whose November 24–25, 1938, issue contained a page reproducing works by de Chirico, Terragni, Fontana, and the disturbing image entitled *Chaos* (*Caos*) (1937) by Renato Birolli. All of them were scathingly identified as artists and followers of a "Bolshevizing" and "Judaic" art. All this encouraged Licini to participate with the Futurists championed by Marinetti—one of the few to take the side against this infamy—at the third Quadriennale d'Arte Nazionale in Rome.[41] Licini explained the reasons for his decision in a letter to Marchiori:

> Before figures such as Soffici and Carrà, no one will be surprised if Licini goes to Rome to pay tribute to F. T. Marinetti, a man of courage, dynamic, coherent ... capable for the cause—art—of sacrificing himself to an extreme. Allow me to say that I am not officially a member of the Futurist moment [even though] you, in Rome, at the Quadriennale, will find me hanging on the walls reserved for the Futurists, and along with me Rho, Radice, and Soldati, seeing that at the very last moment both Ghiringhelli and Reggiani defected and deserted ...

Nonetheless, the equivocation had a footnote two years later when, at the height of the war, Licini

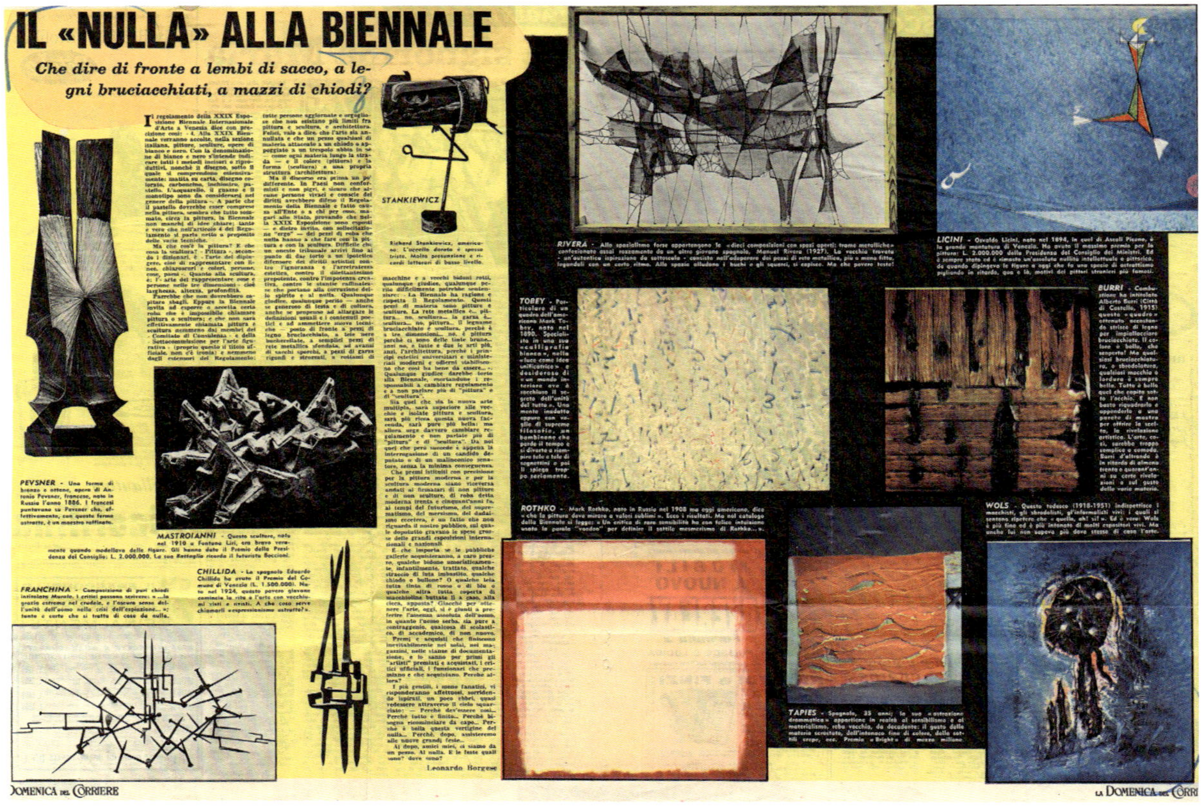

IL «NULLA» ALLA BIENNALE

Che dire di fronte a lembi di sacco, a legni bruciacchiati, a mazzi di chiodi?

STANKIEWICZ

DOMENICA del CORRIERE

found himself once again classified among the Futurists at the third *Mostra Nazionale del Sindacato Fascista Belle Arti*. In the second edition of the catalogue five pages were even added where Licini's work was seen alongside that of the Aeropainters presented by Filippo Marinetti.[42] Another misunderstanding of this sort was perpetrated by the Italian-Swiss architect Alberto Sartoris, who that same year wrote an article for *Origini* significantly titled "Licini archipittore," and published the third edition of *Gli elementi dell'architettura funzionale*, which had been expanded by almost two hundred pages, with an "Introduction" by Marinetti (Le Corbusier had written it for the first). The error in this case was twofold, and it consisted not only of placing Licini under the aegis of Marinetti, but also of interpreting the works as the product of mathematical, geometric, and architectural inspiration. But above all, of believing that contemporary art—from Picasso to de Chirico, Fontana, Naum Gabo, and Licini himself—was an example of an understanding among architects (Rationalists) and painters generated by a common vision of space.[43] Siegfried Giedion's *Space, Time, Architecture*, written in the same period, has a similar, empathetic approach. Giedion was a professor at Harvard who had emigrated from Europe, but above all, as he tells us in the first pages of his book, a pupil of Wölfflin.[44]
To go back to the Quadriennale of 1939, where Morandi was awarded a prize, Licini's opinions were rather bitter, and he was prompted to write to Marchiori as follows:[45]

> You know that I was a friend of Morandi. With Morandi, when we were both young, we drank from the first Cubism, and with Morandi we fought for Futurism, at Marinetti's side, before the war .... You know that I never doubted Morandi's talent, although I saw him stoned by the opium he was offered by Soffici, Oppo, and Co., and I suffered for his walk backward, from Cézanne toward Chardin, and further back to Pompei, who commanded "Cacasenno" from "Poggio a Caiano" .... What is this veil, this

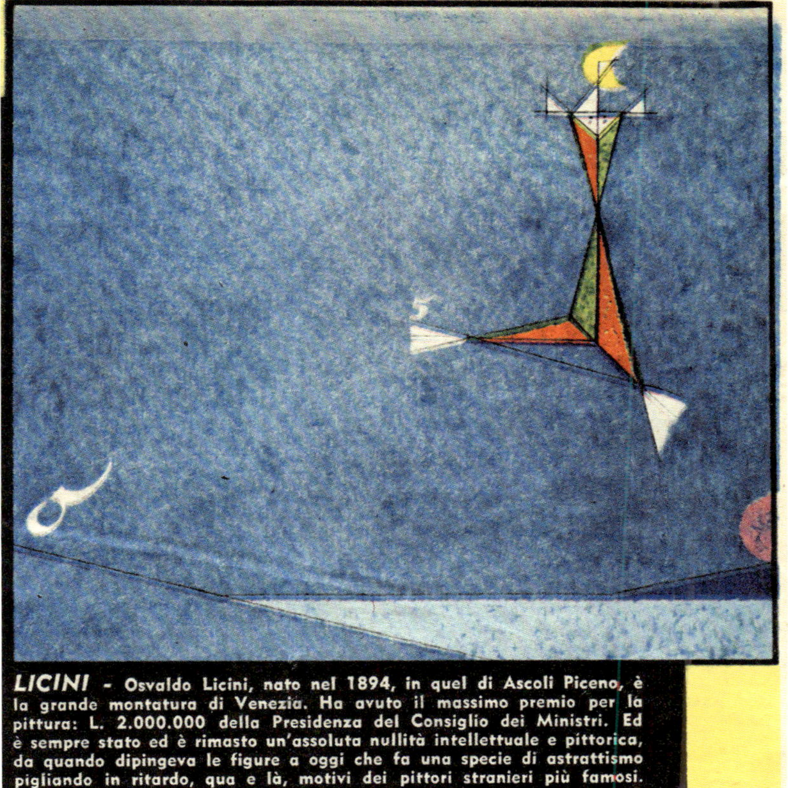

LICINI - Osvaldo Licini, nato nel 1894, in quel di Ascoli Piceno, è la grande montatura di Venezia. Ha avuto il massimo premio per la pittura: L. 2.000.000 della Presidenza del Consiglio dei Ministri. Ed è sempre stato ed è rimasto un'assoluta nullità intellettuale e pittorica, da quando dipingeva le figure a oggi che fa una specie di astrattismo pigliando in ritardo, qua e là, motivi dei pittori stranieri più famosi.

"IL 'NULLA' ALLA BIENNALE," *DOMENICA DEL CORRIERE*, JULY 6, 1958. *SAINT DOMINGO ANGEL* (*ANGELO DI SAN DOMINGO*) (1957, p. 185) IS ILLUSTRATED

> tedium that Morandi places before his paintings? Why don't these paintings made so well appeal to me, interest me, ever convince me? … There, Marchiori, that is how Morandi went down, the champion of Italian artistic and bureaucratic mediocracy; a creature of Oppo, Soffici, Cardarelli, Longanesi, Bartolini, and others like them, of all the nostalgic shrimps of traditionalism.

Licini spent the war years in the familiar refuge of Monte Vidon Corrado. When Marchiori returned adventurous from Libya, on March 24, 1943, he wrote: "And now that you have come back as a man from such muck, all you can do is purify yourself, or rather, as Nietzsche would have said, overcome yourself. But what is man? I fear that not even Nietzsche succeeded in answering the question …. Of the three people in my very holy trinity, the wanderer, the erotic one, and the heretic, the first two, during your absence, have left. All that remains in the third one, to the nth power. And that is the one speaking to you." And in another one, a month later Licini explained: "As for my work, it is best to wait …. My hour hasn't come yet. An irrevocable decision to not sell has been made: to not exhibit, to not show, to not sell for the entire duration of the war. There is pressure and flattery of all sorts coming from Milan, yet I resist. For the past two years I have been accumulating materials, materials. Soon I will be ready for my last adventure, the real, decisive one. May a total wind of madness relieve me!"

FROM THE POST–WORLD WAR II PERIOD TO THE TRIUMPHS OF THE 1950S AND BEYOND. EPILOGUE

Licini chose not to sell his paintings because he felt they were like his children, or better still, pages of a diary related to his life and therefore secret, as Marchiori had well understood. Those pages were not the bearers of dreams, but exclusively of symbols. In Bartoli's words: "How to explain the

SCANDALE A VENISE

Le Jury refuse la palme à Masson et Pevsner

La 29e Biennale établit la faillite de l'art abstrait

par Alain JOUFFROY

L'ART, cette semaine, a pour capitale Venise. Des artistes de tous les pays sont venus, comme tous les deux ans, y exposer leurs œuvres. L'amateur d'art moderne, s'il n'est pas trop chauvin, s'il ne veut pas borner son intérêt à ce qui se passe dans son pays (sinon dans sa ville), s'il veut dépasser la routine de ce provincialisme d'autruche qui a nom nationalisme, se doit de venir voir cette Biennale, quelles que soient les déceptions ou les surprises qui l'y attendent. Car ce ne sont pas seulement les critiques qui viennent la visiter. On rencontre ici, depuis deux jours, non seulement des marchands d'art et des collectionneurs du monde entier, mais des artistes, venus là pour voir où en sont les collègues et pour prendre la température de l'époque.

L'art tend de plus en plus à s'internationaliser. Ce n'est pas étonnant. Le cloisonnement spirituel du monde sera un jour considéré comme un archaïsme. La peinture, comme le théâtre et le cinéma, s'universalise au fur et à mesure que s'accroissent les facilités de contact entre les hommes. Seules, aujourd'hui, l'U. R. S. S. et la Roumanie « officielles » résistent à ce courant en perpétuant, sous l'étiquette fallacieuse de « réalisme socialiste », une peinture académique qui a sombré dans le ridicule et dans l'ennui partout ailleurs. Ainsi curieusement, le pavillon de l'U. R. S. S. est-il le plus provincial de tous. On se croirait, dans ses salles, perdu dans un petit musée d'Ukraine du début du siècle — comme si, vraiment, rien ne s'était passé dans l'esprit humain depuis ce moment, comme si ni les découvertes scientifiques, ni les révolutions, n'avaient là-bas, modifié la sensibilité de personne.

Partout ailleurs, les contradictions de l'homme moderne, ses fascinations pour la magie et pour la technique, son besoin éperdu de singularisation et de liberté, sa soif de nouveau et d'inconnu sont à ce point rendus manifestes que cela procure un malaise — mais un malaise salutaire,

La plus grande de toutes les forces, celle qui inspire le plus grand nombre d'œuvres aujourd'hui, c'est, je crois, le sentiment d'oppression que suscite la réalité extérieure, oppression que l'artiste fuit par tous les moyens, et tente de nier dans l'espace « imaginaire » du tableau, où un « jeu », gratuit ou symbolique, le distrait de toute autre préoccupation, à la manière du billard et des échecs. C'est ce sentiment d'oppression qui, à mes yeux, favorise l'éclosion de tant d'œuvres dites « abstraites », où l'artiste réussit, — c'est le but recherché inconsciemment — à s'abstraire précisément du monde où il vit, et auquel il veut que son art tourne totalement le dos. Les tableaux abstraits sont des dos tournés. Mais, bien sûr, chez les meilleurs artistes abstraits, ces « dos tournés » expriment encore quelque chose. On sait, si l'on est un peu familier des philosophies orientales, que la meilleure manière d'atteindre par l'esprit quelque chose, c'est de chasser de la conscience tout ce qui n'est pas cette chose, et d'établir une sorte de vacuum spirituel.

A cet égard, il me semble que les artistes abstraits arrivent rarement à leurs fins : ils ne savent pas ce qui est à éliminer, ni ce qui est à garder intact, car ils ignorent la plupart du temps quel est ce point de fascination qui constitue la fin dernière de leur art. Mondrian, lui, le savait. Mais ses suiveurs sont moins rigoureux et cèdent trop souvent à la tentation de la beauté extérieure, de la beauté de l'effet, ce qui rejette des œuvres à intention secrètement métaphysique dans le domaine utilitaire de la décoration. C'est le cas d'Alberto Burri, c'est celui de Fontana, c'est celui de Rothko, et c'est celui d'un très grand nombre de jeunes peintres, comme Dorazio, Dangelo, Tapiès, et des suiveurs allemands de Wols : Schumacher et Wessel.

Le mérite principal de cette Biennale est donc de mettre en évidence cette conjonction des influences de Kandinsky, de Mondrian et de Wols dans l'œuvre des jeunes peintres abstraits, qui ne parviennent pas à constituer en langage cohérent un univers de formes et de matières, qu'il faut un tempérament créateur de poète pour rendre expressives et « communicables ». Mais les tempéraments poétiques sont, aujourd'hui comme toujours, extrêmements rares et c'est dommage, car avec eux, le sentiment d'oppression fait place au sentiment de l'inconnu et de l'insaisissable. Les peintres-poètes ne refusent pas le monde, c'est le monde qui les refuse et qui les incite à en inventer un autre.

LE PALMARÈS

● Au moment où nous mettons sous presse, nous recevons de notre collaborateur le télégramme suivant :

« Scandale à Venise. Grand Prix sculpture attribué à Mastroianni au lieu de Pevsner et peinture à Licini au lieu Masson. Stop. Deuxièmes prix au sculpteur Chilida et à Mark Tobey. Stop. Manessier, prix art sacré, seul Français primé. Stop. Jury disqualifié à mes yeux ».

Alain JOUFFROY.

ALAIN JOUFFROY, "SCANDALE A VENISE," *ARTS*, JUNE 24, 1958

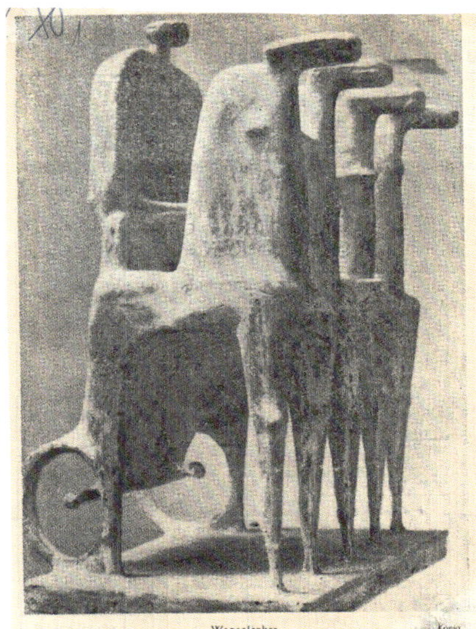

Wagenlenker

die abschaffung des künstlers

Biennale 1958 in Venedig / Von ERNST VON GLASERSFELD

Rosa Papierdrache

Osvaldo Licini

Harmonische Beziehungen

Enrico Prampolini

(Fortsetzung nächste Seite)

polemic against the dream when you don't think of it as an offshoot of the long polemic of *Cercle et Carré*, of *Abstraction-Création*, and later of *Cahiers d'Art* before the Surrealist dream?" Nonetheless, Bartoli added, "not everything matches perfectly. Other elements, the obsessive call to irrationality itself, hark back to Surrealism, or rather, to some of its motifs." My belief is that they hark back to the most provocative component of Surrealism, that of Georges Bataille, André Masson, Michel Leiris, Joan Miró, and others.[46]

Licini's Abstractionist-Rationalist inclination continued into the postwar period with his participation, in 1947, in the Milanese exhibition *Arte astratta e concreta*, thanks to Maria Cernuschi Ghiringhelli. In the winter of 1945 she had asked him to send pictures of his work to Max Bill and the architect Ernesto Nathan Rogers. In January 1946 Licini wrote this to her: "It's so easy to talk about 'popular art,' 'art that must move toward the people.' How foolish. I simply know that my duty as an artist is to go toward art (even if it means dying of hunger). Giotto, Piero della Francesca, Dante were never as popular as Cézanne, Van Gogh, Picasso, Rimbaud would be. The people do have their own so-called art: Dell'Oca Bianca, Puccini, etc. And then there are platinum postcards, artistic calendars, oleographs, dance music, popular songs." Bold assertions in light of the proud aversion of the heads of the party—and of the critics that were inspired by them—toward contemporary art, seeing that soon afterwards he was to run for mayor representing the Italian Communist

Sonntagsblatt, August 3, 1958. *Pink Kite* (*Aquilone rosa*) (1935, p. 101) is illustrated

Party. Licini was eventually reelected for a second term as well. At the Milanese exhibition in 1947, Licini showed five works made between 1931 and 1933—only one of them is captioned, *Red: Composition 1931* (*Rosso. Composizione 1931*)—alongside others by Klee, Kandinsky, Hans Arp and Sophie Taeuber-Arp, Bill, Georges Vantongerloo, Luigi Veronesi, Mario Radice, and Ettore Sottsass Jr.[47] Many times have I had the chance to observe that this exhibition revealed the two souls of Concrete Art: on the one hand, as Kandinsky originally intended, the expression *Konkrete Kunst*, a deeper level of penetration into the spirit, the effort of digging into the remoter areas of the Self; on the other, as was interpreted by an architect and painter like Bill, in the exact opposite sense. In the text he eloquently titled *From Abstract Art to Concrete Art*, Bill indicated a path that, beginning with the first avant-gardes, had gradually been freed from every natural or literary waste. Bill repudiated what he believed was included in the categories of the "irrational" and the "supernatural": not just Surrealists and Dadaists—he listed Charles Baudelaire, Apollinaire, Louis Aragon, Paul Éluard, Tristan Tzara—but also Max Ernst and Klee, for whom the catalogue reproduced a work which seemed to him to be "a symbolic-magical representation, which stands out black and menacing against a burning, incandescent background." In a letter from the same year, Licini asked Cernuschi Ghiringhelli: "what is the Altana, what are they up to that's good?" I suspect that, had he been aware of their intentions, always being so hesitant to exhibit, he might have had a few extra doubts.

In 1948, Licini showed three paintings at the Venice Biennale, as had happened before, figuring among the abstract artists: a further sign of how hard the critics found it to classify him.[48] He sent his first *Amalasunthas* to the Biennale that was held two years later. One of them was acquired by Carlo Cardazzo (*Amalasuntha No. 1* [*Amalassunta n. 1*], 1949, p. 153), and another by Lucio Fontana (*Amalasuntha No. 3* [*Amalassunta n. 3*], 1950, p. 156).[49] He explained the meaning of the word *Amalasuntha* to Marchiori—although he actually ended up concealing it even more with his subtle humor: "if I should be absent [at the opening of the Biennale] and some curious soul were to come to you, a flawless and fearless art critic, wondering about the identity of this mysterious 'Amalassunta,' about which so little has been said so far, please answer, on my behalf, without a shadow of a doubt, while smiling, that Amalassunta is our beautiful Moon, guaranteed to be of silver for eternity, personified in very few words, a friend of all rather weary hearts."

It has been said that the artist got the name from a text that Caterina, a child living with the Licinis, was reading. The text described the mythical queen of the Ostrogoths Amalasuntha, daughter of Theodoric the Great. While this may be helpful initially, the truth of the matter, as Bartoli well explains, is that it is always a question of understanding *how* in Licini's works, words, titles, bodily signifiers: in short, the complex layers of meaning "always act to enhance the image; they do not eradicate it, but rather make it grow and be elevated." The artist continues:

> The fabrication of sense or of nonsense? One might say "miraculous" senses, acrobatic images, placed at the highest points ... on the very "crest" of things or "at the South Pole," to use expressions dear to the artist .... The title, however, albeit watching figures during the act of receiving, has fantastic roots in the land of Licini's mythologies and enters into that relationship with the fantastic/concrete which we saw constituted one of the materials of the invention.... How can we overlook the fact that Bruto talks about giving the gift of a heart ("he placed his heart in the hollow of his hand")? ... How can we overlook these roots when, while observing the *Amalassunte*, we come up against a whole ritual of the exhibition of the heart, held tight between two fingers, placed in the palm of the hand or on the forehead, flying in

space? A ritual that is both Orphic and ironic, borne to the evidence of visibility, also conceived from the culture of the word.

Errante, erotico, eretico includes a plate with two sides—the caption reads "Transcription of emblematic figures from Licini originals" where we see heads of *Amalasuntha* joined with hands and eyes, written words ("MANO [HAND] + VISO [FACE] + OCCHI [EYES] + NUMERI [NUMBERS]"), numbers written out, years (1949, 1946), and the word "APOLLINAIRE," which comes back several times, also with some question marks. Not a puzzle, but rather, as Bartoli would say, "signage."

This time Licini was received with greater attention by the critics. Umbro Apollonio describes him as an artist who knew how to overcome abstraction by shedding light on a "pictorical quality" that is not at all poetic.[50] Carrieri says he is the "European of Monte Vidon Corrado" who comes closest to Kandinsky but also—one of the first times—to Joan Miró;[51] while in the São Paulo Biennale catalogue Rodolfo Pallucchini—Secretary-General of the Venice Biennale—says he is "the most genuine Italian poet of abstract form."[52] Worth noting a few years later at an international level is a book by the German critic Bernhard Degenhart, who published a full-page image of two of the artist's beautiful drawings, one with an *Amalasuntha* featuring an eye in the style of Picasso—or better still, Klee—suspended above a minuscule building (a church?) next to which two enormous breasts with a nipple rise up majestically—a rather frequent motif of the *Amalasunthas*; and an *Amalasuntha* with the numbers 2 and 5 outlined against an almost imperceptible landscape. In that period (1956) Degenhart penned one of the sharpest reflections on Licini:

> Licini's style, so unique in European art, may have been influenced by Miró and by Klee. He paints and draws using very few lines and surface compositions that are fantastic and romantic; most of them, inspired by dream, are entitled *Amalasuntha*. Among the Italians of our century, who waver between objectivity and abstraction, his paintings and drawings are those which are mostly assigned the task of lyrical poetry, where each word has a concentrated meaning and therefore also makes sense in so far as it is sound.[53]

However, it was in the following two years that Licini's success as a painter was ultimately affirmed. The first important event was the Turin exhibition *Pittori d'oggi. Francia-Italia*, curated by Luigi Carluccio.[54] Even more important was the one at the Centro Culturale Olivetti in Ivrea in 1958. That same year the artist participated in the twenty-ninth Venice Biennale, where he was awarded the Grand Prize of two million lire offered by the Prime Minister's Office. Licini was one of four artists to be given solo shows. The decision made by the board—which included Renato Birolli, Felice Casorati (president), Bruno Saetti, Pericle Fazzini, Sergio Bettini, Pietro Zampetti, and the Secretary-General Alberto Dell'Acqua—was unanimous, but not so obvious. The board had been chosen by a consulting committee—whose members were, among others, Giulio Carlo Argan, Casorati, Longhi, Giacomo Manzù, Marcello Mascherini, Morandi, Pallucchini, Giuseppe Santomaso, Marco Valsecchi, and Venturi—tasked with providing guidelines. It was precisely the election of Casorati, who was a member of both bodies, that was meant to ensure a certain amount of serenity and homogeneity of opinions. Except for the fact that, upon hearing who was on the board and who had been invited to show their work, even before the Biennale could begin its course, in a harsh letter he wrote on February 10, 1958, to President Giovanni Ponti, Longhi stepped down from the board. What was his reason for doing so? Substantially, it was due to the fact that there were too many "abstract artists" among those invited.[55] Although Saetti had been the one to suggest a solo show of Licini's works, behind the scenes Marchiori was one of the main architects of the plan.[56] Licini presented over fifty works, chosen personally by Umbro Apollonio, which ranged from the figurative ones of the 1920s to the last *Rebel Angels* (the catalogue reproduced both *Castle in the Air* and *Rebel Angel with a Red Heart* [*Angelo ribelle con cuore rosso*], 1953, p. 172).[57] Licini's words to Marchiori in 1953 concerning the strange figures, which he had conceived at the start of the 1950s immediately after the *Amalasunthas*, were as follows: "Dearest Marchiori ... we are and will always be men of dreams that surpass our strengths. All you had to do was deliver a message to me. A message on the part of the Angels of Apollinaire, those angels [that] on that day came out of our pockets to cross swords with our soul, our study, just a few steps away from the Golden Saint Mark's Basilica, at the proper and precise time: 'The hour of clarity,' dear Marchiori, the hour of our final Ecstasy, that of our Epiphany!" One month earlier he had written: "Yes, honest Marchiori, we shall say bad things about everything and everyone, clearly so ... finally, having become lighter than air, we shall rise up united in the sky, to our eternal glory, our marvelous, frenetic, scintillating, sweet 'surreal.' ... Long live the beautiful Surreal."[58]

As mentioned before, the jury overseen by Venturi chose Licini. This caused a general outcry and very few favorable voices. Venturi, in a memorable article published in *L'Espresso,* spoke of Licini as being the Italian "who has examined problems similar to those of Klee, and solved them in an original and wonderful manner." But most importantly, Venturi said that having been born in 1894, he was "an older artist who was younger than the young."[59] Palma Bucarelli praised the Biennale for having "revealed to Italians and to foreigners an artist of rare quality," and she reproduced *Dragon* (*Il drago*) (1933, p. 91).[60] Gastone Breddo instead spoke of three poets, "the Russian Pevsner, the German Wols, and the Italian Licini."[61] And Guido Ballo, by placing him alongside Kandinsky and Mark Tobey—the latter was awarded a cash prize of one and a half million lire from the City of Venice—stated that Licini "acutely reveals his lyricism in works such as *Obelisk* (*Obelisco*), and *Dragon* [where] the subtle sign is not automatic, [but rather] controlled by the mind."[62] Even some of the younger critics praised Licini, such as Enrico Crispolti, who wrote: "This year the Italian Pavilion abounded with sculptors, ones of quality, so much so that determining the winner of the prize grew complicated (while Licini's is as clear as can be)."[63] In any case it was favorable to abstract art, as "the figurative has been totally exhausted," in the words of the equally young Renato Barilli. This provoked the thunderbolts of Franco Solmi and of an even younger Gianni Celati, who instead asserted that "in abstract art there is no modernity; there is a reactionary mentality."[64]

Criticism of that Biennale far surpassed its appreciation. In the front line, much like in the 1930s, were the *Corriere della Sera* and the *Domenica del Corriere.* In numerous articles Leonardo Borgese spoke of the efforts of the "abstract artists" as "absurdly hard work to fill the void," and Licini's victory as "the great performance of Venice."[65] He was followed by de Chirico, by that time old and "meaner" than before, who spoke of the Venetian event as a "museum of national and international horrors,"[66] as well as by a plethora of other critics and journalists.[67]

There were meaningful silences as well. For instance, *Paragone*, the journal headed by Roberto Longhi that in previous years had distinguished itself with articles by Giovanni Testori and Gaetano Arcangeli against modern art,[68] said not a word, although Alessandro Parronchi did find a way to mention Licini in an essay he wrote about Ottone Rosai.[69]

The other pole against abstraction was obviously that of the most orthodox Left. While *Pravda* described the feeling of finding oneself in the "circles of a Dantesque inferno," and abstraction

GIUSEPPE MARCHIORI, "I PITTORI 'ASTRATTISTI' ALLA II QUADRIENNALE," *CORRIERE PADANO*, MARCH 20, 1935. *PRECARIOUS BALANCE (IL BILICO)* (1932, P. 75) AND *CASTLE IN THE AIR* (*CASTELLO IN ARIA*) (1933–36, P. 95) ARE ILLUSTRATED

Ufficiali italiani nell'armata napoleonica

Domenico Pino e Oliviero Peraldi

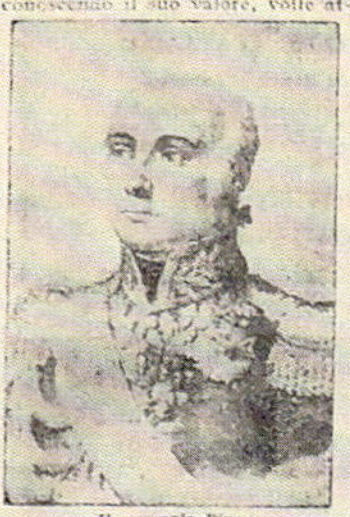

Il generale Pino

GIUSEPPE BUCCELLA

Fervore di preparativi alla Mostra nazionale dell'Agricoltura

Motoscafi per la caccia ai pirati cinesi

Visioni del Foro Mussolini

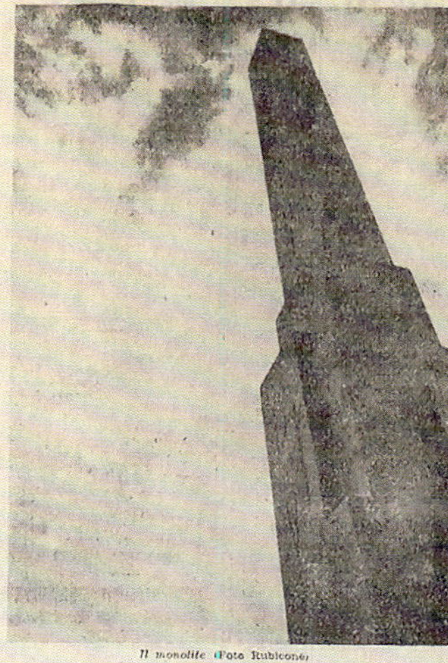

Il monolite (Foto Rubicone)

ARTE E FANTASIA

I pittori "astrattisti,, alla II Quadriennale

ROMA, marzo

«Fantasia assoluta nell'arte. Assoluta realtà nella vita». «L'arte è tutta astrazione e niente materia; la vita è tutta materia e niente astrazione. L'uomo moderno ama l'una e serve l'altra con lo stesso entusiasmo, colla stessa devozione». Questi assiomi di Carlo Belli, il teorico dell'arte astratta, sono alla base del nuovo movimento d'avanguardia, il più intransigente nello stabilire una netta distinzione tra spirito e materia, e, appartenendo l'arte soltanto allo spirito, nel negare l'*oggetto*, cioè la realtà «visiva»; per affermare in suo luogo una superiore realtà «integra e perfetta», in una zona di siderale purezza, cui la pittura dovrebbe giungere, finalmente libera del peso costituito dall'uomo-dio.

«Un'arte antropomorfica è una profanazione», dice il Belli; e alla sua incalzante dialettica non si oppongono ostacoli. Infatti, in teoria, ragionando per sillogismi, si prova quel che si vuole. Ma è possibile immaginare una arte fuori di ogni «umano senso»? Gli astrattisti che espongono alla Quadriennale realizzano (il verbo in questo caso diventa improprio) l'arte come la intuisce il Belli? Forse nemmeno il Bogliardi e il Ghiringhelli, che pur sono i più aderenti alla nuova estetica, riescono a giustificarla con le loro opere.

Prima di parlarne, conviene domandarci se materia e spirito non coincidano nell'arte — e la stessa domanda si è fatto il Bontempelli. Può esistere, nell'arte, l'assoluto in sè, l'astratto in sè? E, fino a oggi, sono state davvero *inventate* forme nuove?

Abolita ogni rappresentazione di forme «conosciute», che cosa resta della pittura? La pittura, direbbe il Belli. «Uno stato d'animo colorico» non può nascere da un freddo calcolo dell'intelletto. Il pittore non è un filosofo: potrà egli procedere per eliminazione fino a distruggere la memoria delle forme apprese, fino a negare le leggi che regolano i rapporti dei colori?

Bisognerà dunque che il pittore *ragioni*, continuamente *ragioni*, operando per contrasti di tono, fuori di quelle leggi; o in antitesi con quello stesso «stato d'animo colorico», che non dovrebbe essere turbato dalla speculazione.

Non è vero che si metta un grigio accanto a un verde, perchè la casa va accanto all'albero. Questo rapporto naturalistico non può esser presente all'artista, mentre opera sotto il dominio di quell'intuizione «colorica», che esclude ogni calcolo.

Si potranno «inventare» nuove combinazioni di forme, non «nuove» forme; e il colore, come materia espressiva, non potrà purificarsi all'infinito e superare quei limiti imposti dalla sua qualità di materia.

Esiste certamente il fatto pittorico in sè, cioè in assoluta indipendenza dal soggetto; ma nessun maestro del presente o del passato è riuscito a *realizzare* l'inconoscibile. C'è dunque nell'astrattismo una impossibilità sostanziale a concretarsi, come si vor- [illegible]

[illegible] pere di Kandinsky [illegible]

Licini Osvaldo: *Il bilico*

nel loro disperato sforzo di rinnovamento.

L'astrattismo, negando all'arte ogni contenuto umano in modo tanto assoluto e deciso, si mette all'avanguardia delle avanguardie, superandole tutte e giustificandosi come un annuncio di quella Nuova Era, che si apre all'umanità e che vorremmo, curiosi del futuro, poter vedere alle sue fatali conclusioni.

L'estetica astrattista del Belli, limitata alle arti figurative e alla musica, è dunque un tentativo d'imporre un «nuovo ordine» anche nell'arte. Ma è un tentativo serio: un segno di fede e d'intelligenza del quale conviene tener conto in un tempo di consapevoli audacie e non di romantiche avventure.

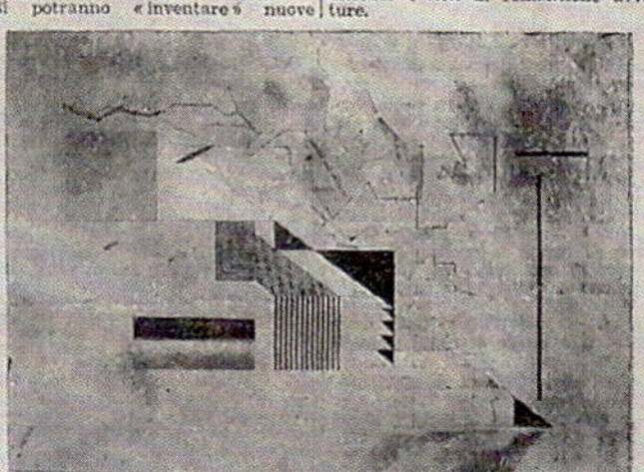

Licini Osvaldo; *Castello in aria*

Kandinsky, cui bisogna riconoscere una rigida coerenza e una dirittura morale, da porsi come esempio ai molti che cambiano «maniera» ogni stagione, è un pittore di teoremi, che spesso dalla geometria ricade nel sogno, obbedendo inconsciamente alla sua anima di slavo. Non è dunque un astrattista puro come Mondrian o Vordemberge-Gildewart.

Nondimeno gli astrattisti riconosco- [illegible]

[illegible] detto, nella geometria. In Italia il sole delimita le ombre a angolo retto e le costringe in un confine preciso»: se il cubismo fosse nato qui, nella patria della geometria, avremmo avuto, per la prima volta, «l'idea di un'arte finalmente arte». Le composizioni di Bogliardi e di Ghiringhelli sono dunque nell'ordine di quello spirito mediterraneo, che sembra guidare il mondo nel suo nuovo cammino.

In che modo si dovranno giudicare? Sarà possibile arrivare a vederle «ogni volta per la prima volta»?

Abolita anche la linea curva, Bogliardi fissa i suoi piani colorati in una staticità senza turbamento, avvicinandosi all'intuizione della forma quale la *vede* il Belli.

Ma il solito linguaggio critico è valido e proprio, in questo caso? Soltanto da un punto di vista ben diverso dal nostro si potrà stabilire il grado di «purezza» raggiunto da questi pittori. Così non ci sfuggirà qualche ricordo naturalistico nelle *Composizioni* del Ghiringhelli; ad esempio l'ombra di un rettangolo, che ridona ai vari piani un valore nello spazio, e suggerisce quindi la negata idea della profondità.

Non solo: nelle opere del Soldati sono troppi elementi caratteristici delle opere di Braque, di Picasso, di De Chirico, di Léger e di Carrà. Un vero mosaico di ricordi, che non sono superati nell'arte. Tuttavia anche il Soldati, nelle sue più recenti composizioni, sembra liberarsi delle influenze degli artisti, che pur lo tennero a battesimo, per librarsi, finalmente solo, nei cieli di quella pittura, che, con maggior ragione, avrebbe diritto al nome di metafisica.

Non parleremo di Magnelli che è da metter piuttosto vicino all'arte cosmica (è detto bene?) di Prampolini.

* * *

Tutta l'arte fino a oggi è, secondo il Belli, originata dall'assurdo proposito «di attribuire all'infinito espressione finita». Ma proprio dall'espressione finita, cioè dalla materiale combinazione di forma-colore, elevata ad *arte* dalla «virtù creativa» dell'artista, nascono quelle «integre e perfette» verità, che miracolosamente risplendono d'una luce di sovrumana [illegible]

GIUSEPPE MARCHIORI

COLONNA

ALDO CAMERINO

A Tripoli con la Lega Navale

Per il controllo in Spagna dei programmi musicali italiani

Un film su Venezia dello scrittore J. Masson girato da "L'Intransigeant"

Trasmissioni televisive nei cinema di Londra

"at the service of the most reactionary imperialist circles," complaining, among other things, about Guttuso's absence,[70] in many articles in *L'Unità* Dario Micacchi railed against abstraction, and particularly against the merchandising it represented.[71] However, a third front would soon be activated: that of the French press spurred on by Alain Jouffroy, who was outraged that the Grand Prize had not been awarded to Pevsner and Masson. Truth be told, Jouffroy did have some good things to say about Licini—and Valsecchi had a field day shedding light on the contradiction.[72]

And what about the rest of the foreign press? While the British press preferred to speak of "surprise and perplexity" about the Grand Prize being awarded to an "unknown" like Licini, in some cases even hypothesizing a loss of the prestige of the Biennale, which had in the past awarded the prize to Matisse and Georges Braque,[73] the American press substantially discussed the prize awarded to Tobey.[74] The German press showed more interest, underscoring Licini's closeness to Miró and Klee.[75]

… AND BEYOND. EPILOGUE

The following year, Licini—who died a few months after being awarded the Grand Prize—was consecrated at an international level as well. His work was shown at Documenta 2 in Kassel, for which the role of Marchiori was again significant (he received letters from Werner Haftmann ["to my dearest friend Marchiori"] and his staff).[76] In the years to come, however, Licini's work was shown in Madrid, Milan, Macerata, Bologna, Turin, Venice, and many other cities. After the aforementioned book by Paolo Fossati, the Leftist criticism, along with Antonello Trombadori, reconsidered him, placing him among the major Italian artists of his generation (there were few: Carrà, de Chirico, and Morandi).[77] Mario De Micheli did the same in 1988, also shedding light on Licini's poetic and musical passions, and favorably judging *Errante, erotico, eretico*.[78] Moreover, in the following decade, the aforementioned *Quaderni liciniani* featured an unleashing of interventions by authors of value such as Maurizio Calvesi, Mariano Apa, Giuseppe Pontiggia, the previously mentioned Torelli Landini, Maurizio Fagiolo dell'Arco, Toni Toniato, and Virginia Baradel. I believe that Torelli Landini is not cautious when, having had the chance to see a part of Licini's private library and some of his drawings, ones in which the artist began from a letter of the alphabet, modified it and turned it into *Archipaintings (Archipittura)*, the critic unexpectedly concludes: "No one could ever have guessed that Licini's famous iconography is the result of the modified relationship between the linear elements of a letter, if it hadn't been for the fact that the drawing itself unveiled the painter's trick."[79]

Rather more prudent and stimulating were Marchiori—seeking to enter the generative process of *Amalasuntha No. 3*, the fruit of the fusion of three different moments in time[80]—and Zeno Birolli in interpreting the combination of *Archangel + Brutus = Rebel Angel*. And then there was Fossati who, a decade later, starting from the threatening "long tongue" of the previously seen *Dragon*, glimpsed a sequence in the three paintings alluding to eating, *Composition—Mouth* (*Composizione – Bocca*) (p. 120) being the metaphor for the mask and a destiny. The critic referred to Apollinaire translated into Italian by Vittorio Sereni: "The mouth, the teeth, the tongue, the profile, crushed inside the stylization of a mask. The black mask, the red tongue in *Tasting* (*Assaggiare*) (p. 97), a painting alongside which we cannot but place canvases such as *Biting* (*Addentare*) (p. 99) and *Composition—Mouth*, ending up forming a triptych."[81]

Allow me to conclude with an iconographic interpretation. Marchiori underscored the intrigue that the "primitive" Sassetta held over Licini, and particularly, how during a visit to the Musée Condé in Chantilly, he had been so impressed by the *Mystic Marriage of Saint Frances* (ca. 1437–44) that he stood before the painting for several hours and had to be forced to leave by the caretakers.[82] The three angelic figures, suspended in the sky diagonally, with the tips of their toes covering the triangular summit of a black mountain, a blackness that then returns in the thin geometric striations of the terrain; the characters' clothes, partially white, partially red; the blue of the sky that is transformed into a pale blue and, then, into the gray of the underlying areas; does it not remind us from close up, as in a sort of stylization, of the figures of Licini's *Precarious Balance*?

1. I am grateful to Daniela Simoni and the Centro Studi Osvaldo Licini, Monte Vidon Corrado; Stefano Papetti and the Galleria d'Arte Contemporanea Osvaldo Licini, Ascoli Piceno; Elena Cazzaro and the Archivio Storico delle Arti Contemporanee, Venezia; Nicola Gasparetto and the Archivio Giuseppe Marchiori, Civica Biblioteca, Lendinara; Otello Sangiorgi and the Biblioteca del Museo del Risorgimento, Bologna. Thank you also to Silvia Bignami, Silvia Burini, Andrea Capriolo, Stefania Marini, Laura Safred, and the staff of the Peggy Guggenheim Collection for their support to my research.
2. Osvaldo Licini, *Errante, erotico, eretico. Gli scritti letterari e tutte le lettere*, ed. Gino Baratta, Francesco Bartoli, and Zeno Birolli (Milan: Feltrinelli, 1974). The title, as Giuseppe Marchiori explained on many occasions, refers to three succinct words that Licini had written in the guestbook at the opening of a restaurant in Burano in 1934.
3. Paolo Fossati, "Doppia lettura di Licini artista isolato e 'anomalo.' Una mostra e un libro in contemporanea," *Corriere della Sera*, November 3, 1974; also in Enrica Torelli Landini and Elena Pontiggia, eds., *Quaderni liciniani*, no. 3 (Centro Studi Osvaldo Licini, 1997), 145–47.
4. Paolo Fossati, *L'immagine sospesa* (Turin: Einaudi, 1971), 162 and passim.
5. Fossati, "Doppia lettura."
6. Vanni Scheiwiller, "I furori del 'bel Licini,'" *Il Settimanale*, December 21, 1974.
7. Pier Paolo Pasolini, "La poesia e l'antipoesia fra gli scrittori degli anni Venti," *Il Tempo*, December 20, 1974. The following quotations are from this same article, which, together with many other documents mentioned here, is in the Archivio Giuseppe Marchiori, Lendinara, box 44: *Licini Osvaldo*, folder 7-I: *Cataloghi, articoli, cartoline, inviti*.
8. Giuseppe Marchiori, "Diario di un critico. Licini scrittore," *La Voce Repubblicana*, May 17, 1975. The original four typewritten pages are in Archivio Marchiori, Lendinara, in the above cited box 44, folder 6. The text includes a note on Licini, *Errante, erotico, eretico*.
9. In *Paragone – Letteratura* II, no. 6 (1951): 56ff.
10. Enrica Torelli Landini, "Percorso biobibliografico," in Enrica Torelli Landini and Elena Pontiggia, eds., *Quaderni liciniani* 1 (1994): 201–61; hereafter *Pb*. Other information with this abbreviation is from *Errante, erotico, eretico*.
11. *Pb*, 148ff.
12. *Licini*, ed. Giuseppe Marchiori, exh. cat., Ivrea, Centro Culturale Olivetti, February 12–28, 1958 (Ivrea: Centro Culturale Olivetti, 1958), 22.
13. Giuseppe Marchiori, *I cieli segreti di Osvaldo Licini. Col catalogo generale delle opere* (Venice: Alfieri, 1968), 7; hereafter *CG*.
14. A. Forti, "La mostra dei "secessionisti" al Baglioni," *Il Resto del Carlino*, March 22, 1914; *Pb*, 203–04.
15. S. Sani, "Pittori d'avanguardia," *L'Avvenire d'Italia*, March 23, 1914; *Pb*, 203–04.
16. Part of this article, published in the Bologna *Giornale del Mattino*, March 22, 1914, is also in Marilena Pasquali, "La pittura del primo Novecento in Emilia e Romagna (1900–1945)," in Carlo Pirovano, ed., *La pittura in Italia. Il Novecento/1 1900–1945* (Milan: Electa, 1991), vol. I, no. 37, 373, where, among other things, the author has become "Mazzuccati."
17. This definition is due to an annotation by Giuseppe Raimondi, who saw similarities with the Cubist sharpness of Derain in the 1910s; see Eugenio Riccomini, *Morandi: memoria e presenza*, in *Morandi e il suo tempo*, ed. Marilena Pasquali and Silvia Evangelisti, exh. cat., Bologna, Galleria comunale d'arte moderna, November 1985–February 1986 (Milan: Mazzotta, 1985), 27–28. It is worthwhile noting that Morandi never backed this interpretation.
18. In a conversation that took place in 1984 Giuseppe Sprovieri gave Torelli Landini another explanation: "[the *Esposizione libera futurista* was] a group of artists who began their activity with avant-garde criteria.... It was Boccioni who decided to exclude a number of artists, including Licini, to valorize him later. The idea was to organize a series of organic exhibitions to define these groups, although this never came about because of the war and Boccioni's passing"; *Pb*, 204.
19. Marilena Pasquali, ed., *Catalogo generale dei dipinti di Mario Tozzi* (Milan: Mondadori, 1988); reprinted in *Pb*, 208.
20. See *Henri Matisse 1904–1917*, ed. Dominique Fourcade and Isabelle Monod-Fontaine, exh. cat., Paris, Centre Georges Pompidou, February–June 1993 (Paris: Éditions du Centre Georges Pompidou, 1993), respectively no. 118, 350–51, and no. 119, 352–53.
21. See Pierre Sanchez, *Dictionnaire du Salon d'Automne. Répertoire des Exposants et liste des œuvres présentées 1903–1945* II (Dijon: L'Echelle de Jacob, 2001). At the first Salon Licini's works were numbered 1487–89, at the second 1600–02. Licini was recorded as living at 28, Rue du Faubourg Poissonnière, Paris.
22. *Pb*, 209. Licini was not aware that his works were exhibited at the first exhibition of the Italians in Paris: Tozzi had gone to see the artist's sister Esmeralda in Paris to get his paintings. The show was held in February 1928 at the Salon de l'Escalier, and it also included Francesco Menzio, Piero Fornari, Severo Pozzati, and Arnaldo Ronchi. The slim catalogue was included in the program for the Théâtre des Champs-Élysées and was introduced by Waldemar George, who stressed the fact that these were not artists from the cosmopolitan École de Paris, but rather a group of Italian Novecento artists; see *Pb*, 213. See also *Les Italiens de Paris. De Chirico e gli altri a Parigi nel 1930*, ed. Maurizio Fagiolo dell'Arco with Claudia Gian Ferrari, exh. cat. Brescia, Palazzo Martinengo, July–November 1998 (Milan: Skira, 1998), 41–42 and passim. Another source on the matter is de Pisis; see Sandro Zanotto, *Filippo de Pisis ogni giorno. Biografia interamente costruita su documenti inediti* (Vicenza: Neri Pozza Editore 1996), 238–39 (on 1932 see p. 264).
23. *I Mostra del Novecento Italiano*, exh. cat., Milan, Palazzo della Permanente, February–March 1926 (Milan: Arti Grafiche E. Gualdoni, 1926), 30, nos. 1–3, fig. 66.
24. The review dated March 3 is in *Pb*, 215.
25. *I Mostra del Novecento Italiano*, exh. cat., Milan, Palazzo della Permanente, March–April 1929 (Milan: Arti Grafiche E. Gualdoni, 1929), 28, nos. 2-19-21, fig. 58.
26. Review in *Social—DemoKraten*, October 1, 1931; *Pb*, 218. See also *Il Novecento Italiano. Nutida Italiensk Konst*, exh. cat., Stockholm, Nationalmuseum, September–October 1931 (Helsinki, 1931). Licini exhibited *Nella* (no. 90) and two still life works (*Nature morte*). His works were displayed next to Carlo Levi of the Sei di Torino group and Umberto Lilloni from the Chiarismo movement. In the catalogue *Portrait of Nella (Nella)* (*Ritratto di Nella [Nella]*) was reproduced next to *Monterosso* by Lilloni. On these Novecento exhibitions promoted by Margherita Sarfatti see my *Il sistema delle arti in Italia 1919–1943* (Bologna: Minerva, 2000), 53–55 and 75ff.

27. In this letter Licini discussed the first Rome Quadriennale, and the seven solo shows were those of Arturo Tosi, Felice Carena, Ardengo Soffici, Carlo Carrà, Amerigo Bartoli, Ferruccio Ferrazzi, and Carlo Socrate. Cipriano Efisio Oppo was the Secretary of the Quadriennale. Licini showed two works, *Figure in Green* (*Figura in verde*) and *Landscape* (*Paesaggio*), nos. 15–16; catalogue of the *Prima Quadriennale d'Arte Nazionale* (Rome: Enzo Pinci ed., 1931). See also Vincenzo Cardarelli, *Il sole a picco* (Bologna: L'Italiano, 1929), with twenty-two drawings by Morandi. To complete the artist's northern European experience, allow me to quote from another letter, this one written to Acruto Vitali, September 18, 1931: "At the museum in Stockholm I found some magnificent Rembrandts and an excellent collection of works by Matisse, Cézanne, Van Gogh, Utrillo, Gauguin; I was also able to see a rare work by Renoir, *La Grenouillère*."
28. Giovanni Scheiwiller, *Art Italien Moderne* (Paris: Éditions Bonaparte, 1930). The *Still Life* (*Natura morta*) is no. 128, fig. 112.
29. Vincenzo Costantini, *Pittura italiana contemporanea dalla fine dell'800 ad oggi* (Milan: Hoepli, 1934), 177 and fig. on p. 175 (*Scontro*).
30. Marchiori, *Licini*, 7.
31. Unsurprisingly, in 1949 Peggy Guggenheim tasked him with curating the exhibition and the catalogue for the first exhibition that she held in her house-museum in Venice, a sculpture show; see Giuseppe Marchiori, "Sculture all'aperto," in *Mostra di scultura contemporanea presentata da Peggy Guggenheim*, exh. cat. (Venice: Tip. Carlo Ferrari, [September 1949]), unpaginated.
32. Marchiori, *Licini*, 12.
33. Fossati, *L'immagine sospesa*, 92ff.
34. Giuseppe Marchiori, "Arte e fantasia. I pittori 'astrattisti' alla II Quadriennale," *Corriere Padano*, March 20, 1935.
35. *Abstraction – Création*, no. 4 (1935): 18. The works *The Castle (Castle in the Air)* (*Il castello [Castello in aria]*) and *Precarious Balance* (*Il bilico*) were both dated 1934 in the journal, which included also works by Fontana, Ghiringhelli, Bogliardi, Kandinsky, Picasso, Moholy-Nagy, Melotti, Reggiani, Seligmann, and Vantongerloo.
36. Osvaldo Licini, "Lettera aperta al Milione," *Bollettino della Galleria del Milione* 39 (April 10–May 1, 1935), unpaginated.
37. Giuseppe Marchiori, "La mostra del pittore Licini alla Galleria del Milione," *Corriere Padano*, May 29, 1935.
38. Article dated May 16 in *Bollettino della Galleria del Milione*, no. 41 (May 25–June 10, 1935). Licini's answer to Carrà in the same issue was ironic: "When you say that in my paintings that preceded my abstract work I embraced Morandi, you misrepresent.... Would you like to know, Carrà, who my real masters were? I'll tell you now, even though you already know so perfectly well: Cézanne, Van Gogh, Matisse. Morandi's masters were: Chardin, Corot, Cézanne."
39. "Note sulla 'lettera aperta di Osvaldo Licini,'" *Bollettino della Galleria del Milione*, no. 39.
40. See "La pittura astratta," *Corriere Padano*, October 9, 1937. Carlo Belli thanked him wholeheartedly in a letter dated November 15, 1937; Archivio Giuseppe Marchiori, Lendinara, box 2, folder *Carlo Belli*, 1–13.
41. *Terza Quadriennale d'Arte Nazionale*, exh. cat., Rome, Palazzo delle Esposizioni, February–July 1939 (Milan-Rome: Editoriale Domus, 1939). Licini exhibited two works entitled *Composition* (*Composizione*), nos. 64 and 66, 154.
42. *III Mostra del Sindacato Nazionale Fascista Belle Arti*, exh. cat., Milan, Palazzo dell'Arte, May–July 1941 (Milan, 1941), room 48, *Aeropittori futuristi*, introduced by Marinetti (who also mentions Licini on p. 102). Licini showed *Precarious Balance* (*Il bilico*) and *Composition* (*Composizione*), undated, 104.
43. See A. Sartoris, "Osvaldo Licini archipittore," *Origini*, nos. 5–6 (March–April 1941): 8–11; Sartoris, *Gli elementi dell'architettura funzionale*, 2nd ed. (Milan: Hoepli, 1941), 3, 61–65.
44. See Sigfried Giedion, *Space, Time and Architecture*: *The Growth of a New Tradition* (Cambridge, MA: Harvard University Press, 2009).
45. Marchiori was also a dear friend of Morandi and did not feel up to publishing this letter until 1974, the year *Errante, erotico, eretico* was published.
46. It is no accident that in a letter written in the winter of 1930 Licini remarked to Checco as follows: "I hope you've finished with that rather foolish *Art Vivant*. So subscribe to *Documents*, an art journal that is truly alive and very well done.... I have a subscription to *Cahiers d'Art*, which I am happy about." *Art Vivant* had been created in 1924 and, among other things, the much-hated Waldemar George was one of its contributors; *Documents*, for which only a few issues were published between 1929 and 1930, had been founded by Bataille, and its contributors of both works and essays were Masson, Miró, Leiris, Desnos, and Duke Ellington. On its many articles about Surrealism and a chronology of the events that characterized it, see "Chronologie 1924–30" by Agnès de Beaumelle in *Miró 1917–34. La naissance du monde*, ed. Agnès de Beaumelle, exh. cat. (Paris: Éditions Centre Georges Pompidou, 2004), 296ff.
47. *Arte astratta e concreta*, curated by L'Altana, exh. cat., Milan, Palazzo Reale, January–February 1947, with texts by Kandinsky, Max Bill, Ettore Sottsass Jr., and Vantongerloo (Milan: Alfieri e Lacroix, 1947). It is important to note that the exhibition checklist was not included in the catalogue, but provided as two typewritten sheets, which were included in the copy I consulted at the Biblioteca della Galleria Internazionale d'Arte Moderna di Ca' Pesaro, Venice.
48. *XXIV Biennale Internazionale d'Arte*, exh. cat., Venice, May 1–September 30 (Venice, 1948), *Miracolo di San Marcc...o* and two with the same title, *Memories of Afterlife* (*Memorie d'oltretomba*), nos. 11–13, 187.
49. 9 *Amalassunta*, in *XXV Biennale Internazionale d'Arte*, exh. cat., Venice, June 8–October 15 (Venice: Alfieri Editore, 1950), nos. 17–25, 200, and *Amalassunta 5*, plate 53. The work would go to the São Paulo Biennale a year later as well; *CG*, 335. See also note 53 below.
50. Umbro Apollonio, *Pittura italiana moderna. Idea per una storia* (Venice: Neri Pozza, 1950), 143–44.
51. Raffaele Carrieri, *Pittura e scultura d'avanguardia in Italia 1890–1950* (Milan: Edizioni della Conchiglia, 1950), 259ff.
52. *Artistas Italianos de Hoje na 1° Bienal do Museo de Arte Moderna*, exh. cat., São Paulo, October–December 1951 (Venice: Officine Grafiche Carlo Ferrari, 1951), 25. *Amalassunta n. 3* (p. 156) and *Amalassunta n. 5* would later be exhibited in São Paolo.
53. Bernhard Degenhart, *Italienische Zeichner der Gegenwart*, curated by the Italian Cultural Institute of Munich (Berlin: Gebr. Mann Verlag, 1956), text p. 49, ill. p. 15 and plate 66. The "breast" is the same as the one in *Amalassunta 5*; see also note 49 above.
54. *Pittori d'oggi. Francia-Italia*, ed. Luigi Carluccio, exh. cat., Turin, Palazzo dell'Arte (Turin: Ed. La Bussola, 1957).
55. Box 83, *Arti visive. Esposizioni biennali, mostre storiche e speciali, retrospettive e personali*, folder *Sottocommissione per l'arte figurativa*, Archivio Storico delle Arti Contemporanee (Venice). On Longhi's positions on contemporary art, see my *Il sistema delle arti in Italia*, 18–19 (on Arcangeli's same aversion, 125–26). On the dispute about hosting the collection of Peggy Guggenheim at the 1948 Biennale, with Venturi (for) and Longhi (against), see Maria Cristina Bandera, *Il carteggio Longhi-Pallucchini. Le prime Biennali del dopoguerra 1948–56* (Milan: Charta, 1999), 17 and 55–56; and Bandera, "Per una cronistoria dell'esposizione della Collezione Peggy Guggenheim alla Biennale del 1948," *Paragone – Arte*, no. 37–38 (May–June 2001): 65ff.
56. Saetti was a professor of design at the Accademia di belle arti of Venice, and Marchiori had just been given an honorary academic role. Zeno Birolli, a great friend of Marchiori, wrote to him in early 1958: "[I stopped], along the way, at Porto San Giorgio, in order to say hello to Licini. I really wanted to see my old friend, one of the few free men left in Italy. He truly is a non-conformist: a real loner. All that remains for us, the final resource, is solitude"; Archivio Marchiori, Lendinara, box 13-13 bis, *Birolli Renato*.
57. *XXIX Biennale Internazionale d'Arte*, exh. cat., Venice, June 14–October 19 (Venice: Stamperia di Venezia, 1958), 32–36, ills. 11–12; Licini was introduced by Umbro Apollonio.
58. Apollinaire often wrote about "angels," in both *Alcools* and in *Calligrammes*; angels that become devils and vice versa. In *The House of the Dead* (1907), for instance, he speaks of "an angel of diamond broke all the windows / And I was approached by the dead." However, this does not provoke a gloomy, hellish sensation: the cemetery is somewhat clownish, where "The dead were cheered / To see the light pass through their bodies / They laughed to see their shadow." Or in *Heart Crown Mirror* (*Calligrammes*), through words scattered in the shape of a heart, the first-person narrator says: "In the mirror I am enclosed alive and real as one imagines the angles and not like reflections." Licini felt a close affinity with the great French poet, the

roving, sensuous, scandalous Apollinaire: three adjectives that are analogous with *Errante, erotico, eretico*; and he probably identified with some of the poet's characters. The following lines in *The Thief* remind one of Licini: "He was pale he was handsome like a leprous king / ... Thin and magical he'd have perused the heavens / Pale and magical have loved poetesses / Just and magical have spared demons / Go wander naive and red-haired with your shadow." See Guillaume Apollinaire, *Alcools*, trans. Anne Hyde Greet (Berkeley and Los Angeles: University of California Press, 1965), 111. Licini's notes on the page of the Swedish magazine *BLM* (1952) are evidence of the close affinity he felt with Apollinaire. Licini read the article with the help of his wife.

59. *L'Espresso*, June 29, 1958.

60. *La Sera*, June 18, 1958.

61. *Le Arti* (May–June 1958): 7.

62. *Avanti!*, June 14, 1958.

63. *Il taccuino delle arti*, no. 32–33 [1958]: 8.

64. See the debate initiated in Bologna's *La squilla* by Tazio Buscaroli on July 17, 1958, with the article "Dibattito sull'arte 'non oggettiva.' Astrattismo e avanguardia." The articles by Barilli, Solmi, and Celati, in answer to Buscaroli's, were published on October 16, December 29, and September 20, respectively.

65. *Corriere della Sera*, September 13, and *Domenica del Corriere*, July 6, 1958.

66. *Candido*, July 13, 1958.

67. Among them: *La Tribuna*, June 22, 1958; *Meridiano d'Italia*, July 1, 1958; *Il Travaso*, July 7, 1958; *Il globo*, July 29, 1958.

68. In 1956 Arcangeli wrote an excellent article for *Paragone – Arte*, in which he created a sort of palinode and partially took back what he had previously written against Jackson Pollock and some contemporary art. In a long letter dated May 2, 1960, he asked Marchiori to assist him with Licini's heirs for the purpose of purchasing a painting for the Galleria Comunale d'Arte Moderna di Bologna; he mentioned the "political" problems encountered with that city; see the letter, handwritten on four sides, at the Archivio Marchiori, Lendinara, box 44, folder *Eredi Licini*, November 1–8, 1958–February 16, 1988.

69. Ottone Rosai was the subject of an article by Alessandro Parronchi, who claimed that in Florence in 1913 Rosai may have experienced the same ideas "in a pre-Surrealist mode [which] could also include Licini's texts of 1913–15 on fantastic primitivism"; *Paragone – Arte* 113 (May 1959): 68. One should note that Licini was in Florence at the time too. Parronchi "legitimized" Licini as a student in the company of Rosai at the Academy in Florence, and a year later Arcangeli did the same, but with Licini as schoolmate of Morandi at the Academy in Bologna. Arcangeli later asserted that Licini's "dull color" showed "some 'fragility,' something 'not done,'" with respect to Morandi; see Francesco Arcangeli, *Giorgio Morandi* (Milano: Edizioni del Milione, 1960), 9 and passim.

70. *Pravda*, July 6, 1958.

71. *L'Unità*, June 14 and 16, 1958. Also Ugo Attardi in *Mondo operaio* (August 1958), 9.

72. Alain Jouffroy, "Scandale a Venise. Le Jury refuse la palme à Pevsner et Masson," *Les Arts*, June 24, 1958. The idea was taken up by *Le Figaro* and many other French newspapers. Jouffroy affirmed that "[Licini] is, without a doubt, a sort of Italian Klee." For Valsecchi, see *Il Giorno*, June 27, 1958.

73. See *Art News* and *Review* x, no. 14 (August 1958); *Financial Times* and *The Times*, June 24, 1958.

74. See *The New York Times*, June 22 and 29, 1958.

75. See Fritz Nemitz, "Parade der Abstrakten," *Süddeutsche Zeitung*, June 21–22, 1958. More penetrating is Ernst von Glasersfeld, "Die Abschaffung des Künstlers," *Sonntagsblatt*, August 3, 1958, who also published *Pink Kite (Aquilone rosa)* (1935, p. 101): "[Osvaldo Licini] is not seduced by large formats, the same as Klee and Mirò, from whom he unquestionably learned a great deal: Licini's charm is triggered by the unexpected and at times almost ironic contrast created by the details of his lines, which bring to life countless associations in the viewer due to the delicate and intimate scale of his compositions of colors. They would instead be lost on a large-scale canvas."

76. See Archivio Marchiori, Lendinara, box 27, folder 50, *Haftmann Werner 1955–65*. Nonetheless, as is evinced from the copious number of letters written by the Venetian critic to his heirs, Licini's definitive national and international affirmation was perhaps opposed—legally as well—between the widow Nanny Hellström and Paolo, the son he had with his first partner.

77. See *Licini*, ed. Antonello Trombadori, exh. cat., Rome, Galleria La Nuova Pesa, November 1973 (Rome, 1973). Note that Trombadori cites *L'immagine sospesa* as a book by "Luigi Fossati."

78. See *Osvaldo Licini. Dipinti e disegni*, ed. Giuseppe Malatesta, exh. cat., Ascoli Piceno, Palazzo dei Capitani del Popolo, September–October 1988 (Milan: Electa, 1988), 13–18.

79. *Pb*, 132.

80. See *CG*, 27–28. At the Archivio Marchiori (box 44, cit., folder 6) there are also one and a half typewritten pages entitled *Amalassunta n. 3*, perhaps never published in its entirety, which goes over these concepts.

81. Paolo Fossati, *Storia di figure e di immagini. Da Boccioni a Licini* (Turin: Einaudi, 1995), 277. Numerous articles and publications on Licini have been published since the mid-1990s—such as the volumes the institutions in Monte Vidon Corrado and Ascoli Piceno published to commemorate the fiftieth anniversary of his death in 2008, and the *Quaderni liciniani* published in 2013–17. However, they have not substantially changed Licini's critical assessment and therefore have not been included here. The archive of the Galleria d'arte contemporanea Osvaldo Licini in Ascoli Piceno includes the private library of the artist, with more than three hundred volumes and magazines that have yet to be properly studied.

82. See Giuseppe Marchiori, *Osvaldo Licini. Con 21 lettere inedite del pittore* (Rome: De Luca Editore, 1960), 14.

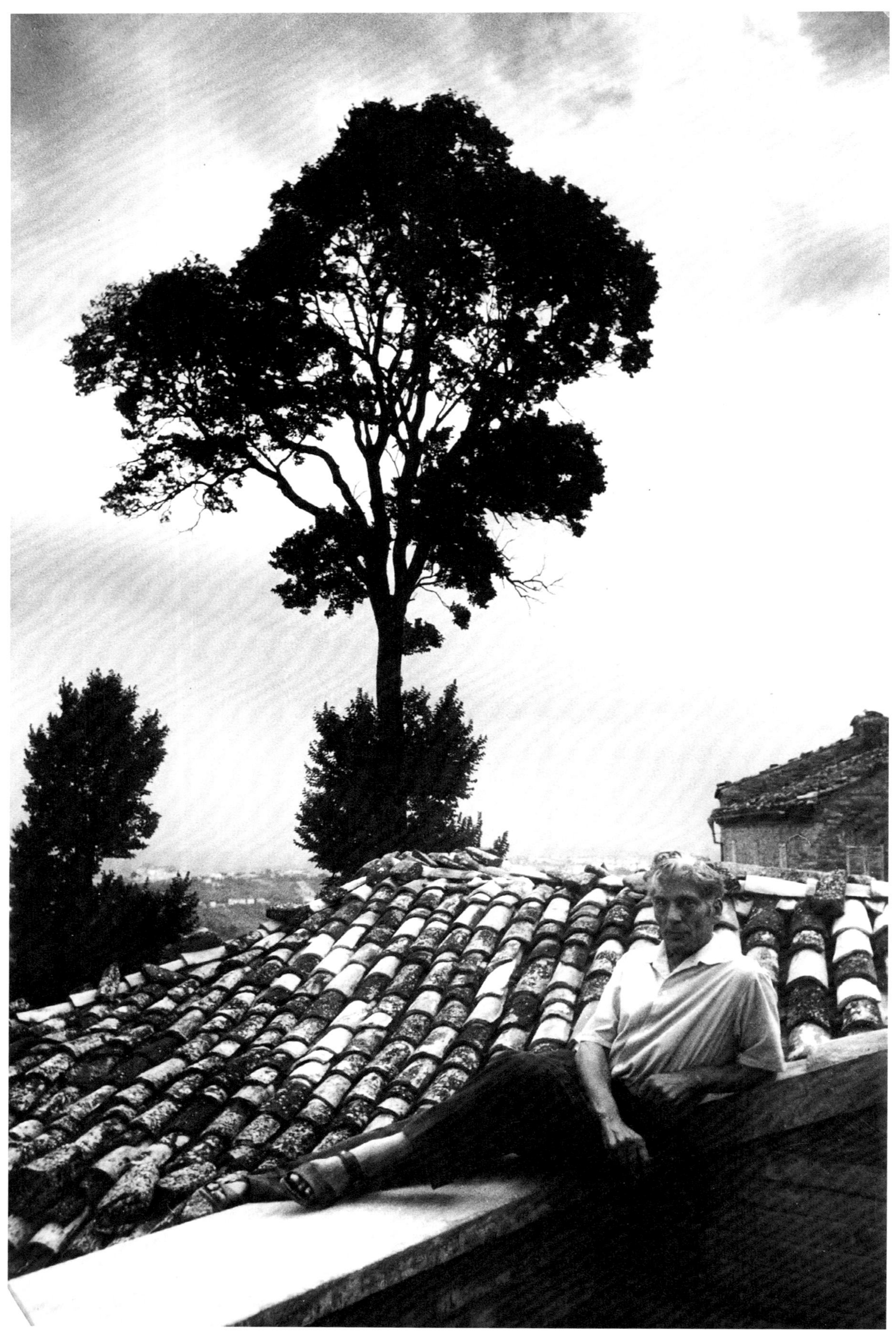

BIOGRAPHY

CHIARA MARI

OSVALDO LICINI, MONTE VIDON CORRADO, 1955

Osvaldo Licini was born on March 22, 1894, in Monte Vidon Corrado, a town in the hinterland of the Marches facing the slopes of the Sibillini Mountains. His father, Vincenzo, was a draftsman and poster designer, while his mother, Amedea Corazza, was a fashion designer. In 1902 his parents moved to Paris for work, taking along his younger sister, Esmeralda, who would become a dancer at the Opéra. The young Osvaldo remained in Italy, entrusted to the care of his paternal grandfather, Filippo. In 1908 he enrolled in the Accademia di Belle Arti in Bologna, where he took courses in drawing and painting until 1914. His fellow students were Giorgio Morandi, Mario Bacchelli (brother of the writer Riccardo), Severo Pozzati (later known as Sepo), and Giacomo Vespignani, with whom he forged strong friendships and shared a youthful enthusiasm for Futurism, which they saw as the epitome of modernity. In 1913 he met the musician Francesco Balilla Pratella, to whom he sent the first of his *Racconti di Bruto* (Tales of Brutus), written that same year, in the hope of publishing them in the literary magazine *Lacerba*. The tales recount the adventures of Licini's alter ego with a sharp, ironic and irreverent style, close to that of the Futurists. In 1914 he attended a lively university conference in Bologna by Filippo Tommaso Marinetti and an equally energetic staging of *Elettricità* at the Teatro del Corso, which ended with a clash between *passéists* and Futurists. That same year, together with Bacchelli, Morandi, Pozzati, and Vespignani, he organized a group exhibition at the Hotel Baglioni in Bologna, which critics defined as the "exhibition of the secessionists."

Late in 1914 Licini moved to Florence to study sculpture and opened a studio on Via Landino. A few months later, on May 22, 1915, he was drafted and left for the front as a soldier of the Thirty-Sixth Infantry Regiment. Seriously injured in one leg at Podgora, he returned to Florence and was admitted to a military hospital, where he met the Swiss Red Cross nurse Beatrice Müller, who would bear him his son, Paolo. Thanks to a furlough, in 1917 he moved to Paris to convalesce with his mother and sister, coming into contact with the cosmopolitan artistic milieu of the French capital. In the cafés of Montparnasse, he met Pablo Picasso, Jean Cocteau, Blaise Cendrars, Moïse Kisling, and Amedeo Modigliani's dealer, Léopold Zborowski, who showed him some paintings by the artist from Livorno, which deeply fascinated him. Licini established a genuine friendship with Modigliani, which he recalled in the 1930s in an article for the Bolognese magazine *L'Orto*. Dating from this period are the *War Episodes* (*Episodi di guerra*), as Licini defined the works made between 1915 and 1920, almost all of which have been lost. The few paintings known today feature stylized figures of soldiers, dancers, hunters, and skaters.

Until 1926 Licini alternated stays in the Marches—in 1921 he was appointed professor of drawing at the Istituto Tecnico in Fermo—and travels to Paris, where he exhibited in noteworthy shows. Between 1921 and 1925 he showed at the Salon d'Automne, the Salon de la Société Nationale des Beaux-Arts, the Société des Artistes Indépendants, in a group show held at the Closerie des Lilas, and in numer-

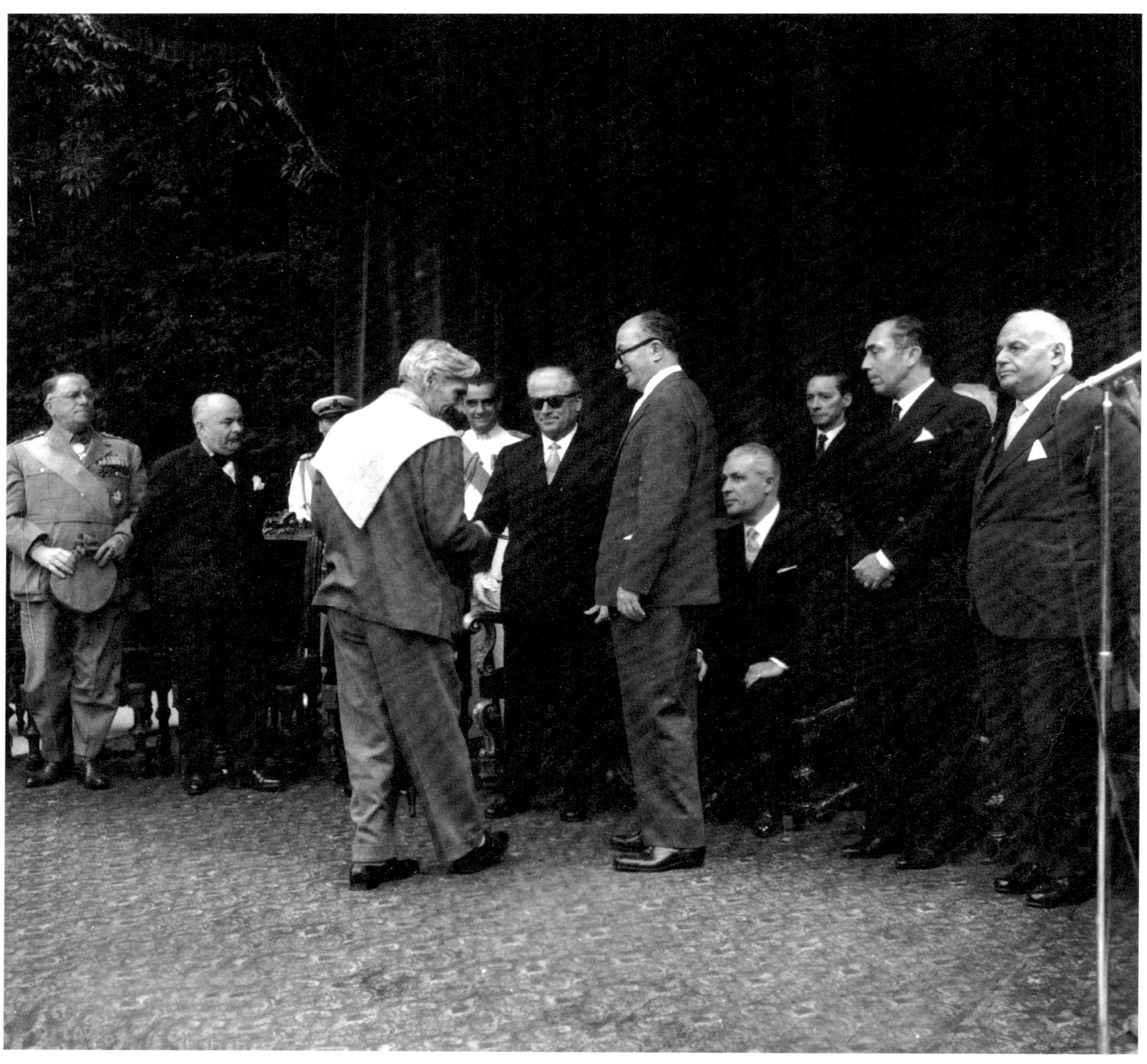

ous cafés. In 1925, during a long stay in Paris, he met Nanny Hellström, a young Swedish painter studying at the Académie Julian, who became his wife the following year. In this decade the predominant subjects of his paintings were the human figure, still life, and landscape, the latter ranging from the hills of the Marches to a series of *Seascapes* of the Saint-Tropez coast.

In 1926 Licini returned permanently to Monte Vidon Corrado. Through the mediation of Mario Tozzi, whom he had met during his studies in Bologna, he exhibited in Milan at the first *Mostra del Novecento Italiano.* Novecento was the movement led by the critic Margherita Sarfatti, who promoted the revival of a formal and thematic classicism rooted in the Italian artistic tradition. Although he also participated in the second exhibition (1929) and in other traveling shows abroad (Amsterdam, 1927; Basel and Bern, 1930; Stockholm, 1931), Licini was operating well outside the dictates of the Novecento movement, as evidenced by his paintings and writings. Invited to exhibit at the first Rome Quadriennale in 1931, he was deeply disappointed by the predominance of the tendency he described as "Neo-verismo," and commented against it in polemical statements. In the summer of that same year he traveled with his wife to Sweden and Germany. He vis-

OSVALDO LICINI IS AWARDED THE GRAND PRIZE AT THE 29TH VENICE BIENNALE, 1958. CENTER, LEFT TO RIGHT: OSVALDO LICINI, THE PRESIDENT OF THE ITALIAN REPUBLIC GIOVANNI GRONCHI, AND THE PRESIDENT OF THE BIENNALE GIOVANNI PONTI

ited museums and was particularly struck by the works of Rembrandt, whom he called "the dark Veronese." On his way back, he stopped in Paris. The sojourn was a cornerstone in the genesis of his first experiments with abstraction. With new groups such as Cercle et Carré and Abstraction-Création and their afiliated magazines, Paris was a major hub of renewed vitality in non-figurative art trends.

In 1932 Licini began to take an interest in the activities of the Galleria del Milione, Milan, managed by the brothers Peppino and Virginio (Gino) Ghiringhelli, who promoted Rationalism and abstraction. In early 1935 Licini exhibited some abstract paintings at the second Rome Quadriennale, in room nine of the Palazzo delle Esposizioni, together with Oreste Bogliardi, Cristoforo De Amicis, Gino Ghiringhelli, Alberto Magnelli, Mauro Reggiani, Atanasio Soldati, and Lucio Fontana. In March of that year he participated in the *Prima Mostra Collettiva d'Arte Astratta Italiana* in Turin and published two abstract works in the fourth issue of the magazine *Abstraction-Création: Art non-figuratif.* On April 19 he inaugurated his first solo exhibition at the Galleria del Milione, accompanied by an important declaration of his poetics that underlined how he differed from the Milanese group. He showed thirty-six paintings dating from 1923 to 1934, an academic exercise from 1909, and several drawings. Giuseppe Marchiori, with whom Licini developed a deep relationship over the years, wrote a passionate critical profile of the artist, in sharp contrast to the negative review by Carlo Carrà, to whom Licini responded in harsh tones in the pages of the *Bollettino del Milione.*

In 1936 Licini took part in the *Mostra d'arte astratta* at the Galleria Bragaglia, Rome, where his *Castle in the Air* (*Castello in aria*) was vandalized by a visitor, and in the *Mostra di pittura moderna italiana*, organized by Alberto Sartoris in Como. The following year he exhibited at the Galleria del Milione in the *Venti firme* group show and published the article "Natura di un discorso" in Marchiori's overview of abstraction for the newspaper *Corriere Padano* of October 9. The article confirmed Licini's extraneousness to the positions of Carlo Belli, the foremost theoretician of abstract art in Italy, and the architect Alberto Sartoris, reclaiming the autonomy of painting with respect to architecture.

Licini's quest for abstraction evolved in the cycle of *Archipaintings* (*Archipitture*), to which Sartoris dedicated an essay in 1941. In 1938 he met the philosopher and historian of religion Franco Ciliberti and became involved in the publication of his magazine *Valori Primordiali.* Licini grew closer to Marinetti and supported his defense of modern art against the censorial initiatives of Fascist fringes who sympathized with Hitler's proclamations against "degenerate" art. In 1939 he participated in the thirtieth anniversary of the founding of Futurism, and exhibited two abstract works at the *Mostra futurista di aeropittori e aeroscultori* in the third Rome Quadriennale, along with Mario Radice, Manlio Rho, and Soldati. He was highly critical of Morandi's solo show at the same Quadriennale.

In 1941 Licini joined the Gruppo Primordiali Futuristi, founded in Como by Ciliberti. He also began to reconsider his work—a profound reassessment resulting in the new series of *Characters* (*Personaggi*) and *Flying Dutchmen* (*Olandesi volanti*). Immediately after the war he developed the iconographic inventions of the *Amalasuntha* (*Amalassunte*) series, which depict "our beautiful moon," in his own words, and of the *Rebel Angels* (*Angeli ribelli*), which opened a new chapter in his oeuvre, described as "that last adventure, the true one, the decisive one" in a letter of 1945 to Ciliberti.

In 1946 Licini was elected mayor of Monte Vidon Corrado, running on the socialist-communist ticket, a post he held until 1956. In 1947 he exhibited at the *Arte astratta e concreta* group show organized by Max Bill in Milan, while the following year he participated for the first time in the Venice Biennale—then again in 1950 with a group of nine *Amalasunthas.* His first major recognition came in 1957, when Luigi Carluccio included a large selection of his works in the exhibition *Pittori d'oggi. Francia-Italia.* His definitive critical consecration came the following year. In early 1958 Giuseppe Marchiori curated a full retrospective of his work at the Centro Culturale Olivetti in Ivrea, which retraced his path from 1921 to 1957 and was very well received. In June Licini exhibited at the Venice Biennale in a solo show curated by Umbro Apollonio and was awarded the Grand Prize for Painting by the Prime Minister's Office.

On October 11, 1958, Licini died of pneumonia in his home in Monte Vidon Corrado, just a few months after witnessing his belated inclusion among the masters of contemporary Italian painting.

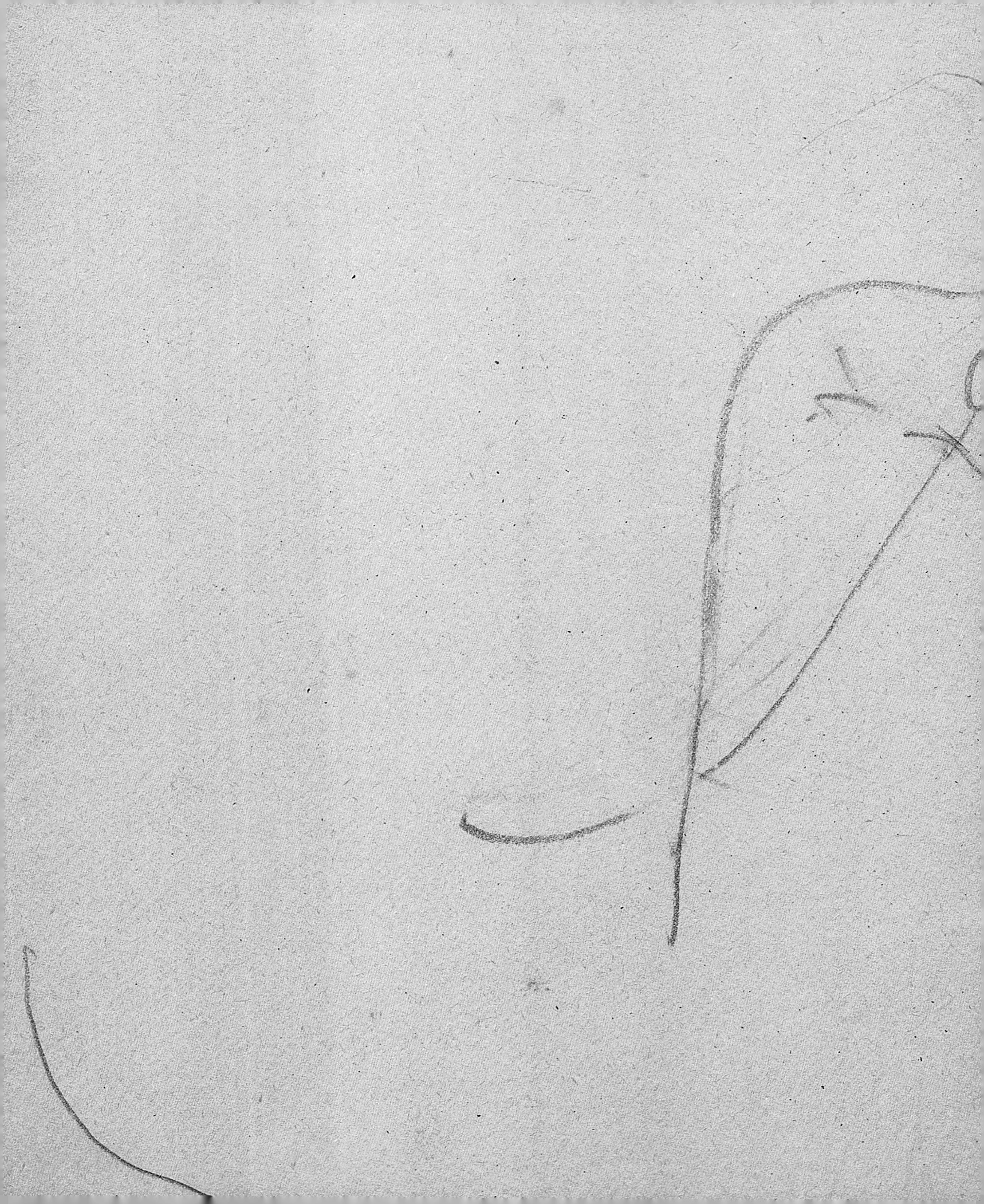

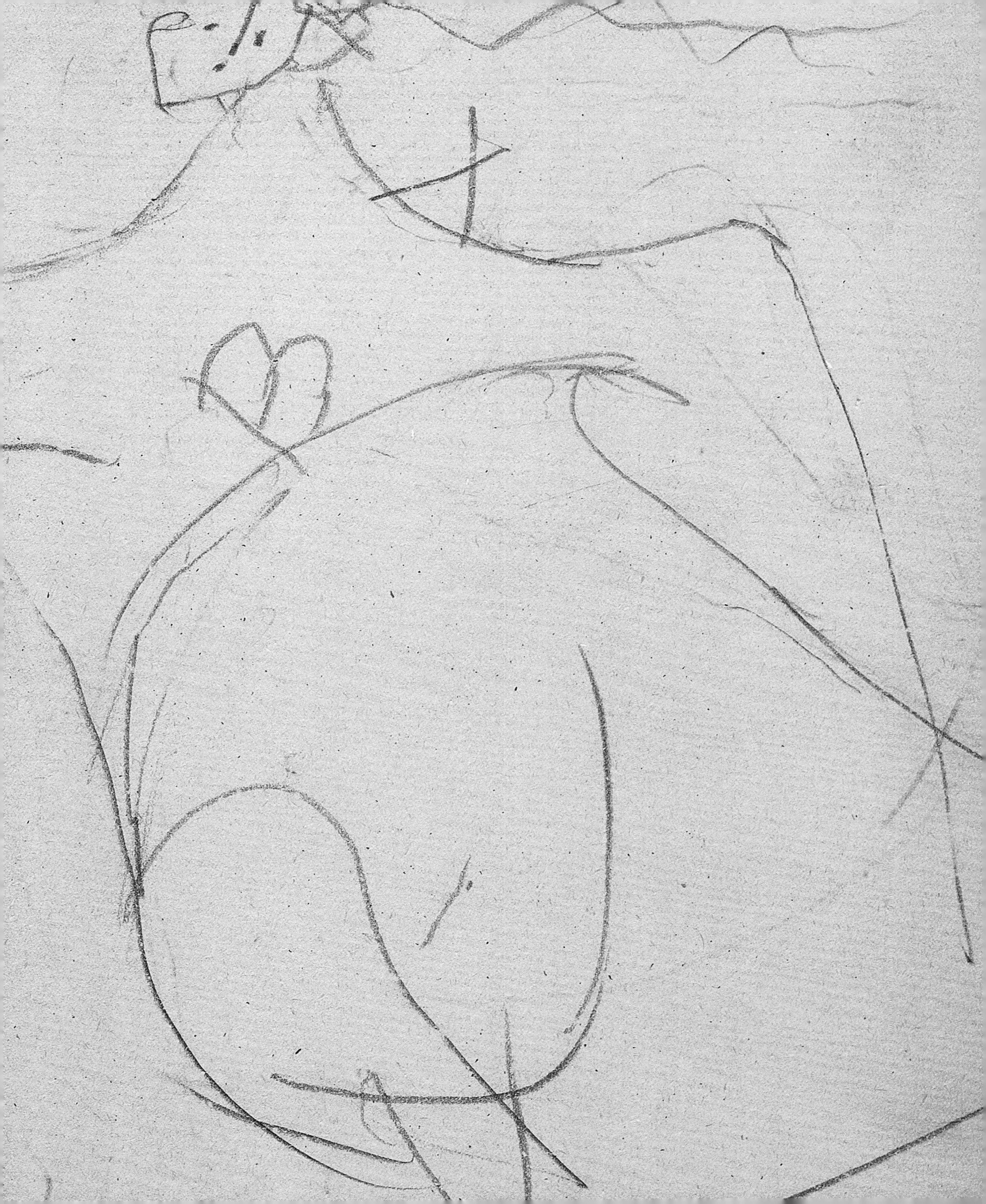

repro
Opero s.r.l., Verona

print
Color Art s.r.l., Rodengo Saiano (Brescia)

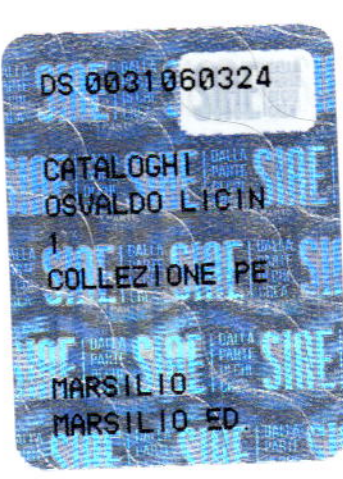